DEMOCRATIC
MARXISM

DEMOCRATIC MARXISM SERIES

Series Editor: Vishwas Satgar

The crisis of Marxism in the late twentieth century was the crisis of orthodox and van-guardist Marxism associated mainly with hierarchical communist parties, and imposed, even as state ideology, as the 'correct' Marxism. The Stalinisation of the Soviet Union and its eventual collapse exposed the inherent weaknesses and authoritarian mould of vanguardist Marxism. More fundamentally, vanguardist Marxism was rendered obsolete but for its residual existence in a few parts of the world, as well as within authoritarian national liberation movements in Africa and in China.

With the deepening crises of capitalism, a new democratic Marxism (or democratic his-torical materialism) is coming to the fore. Such a democratic Marxism is characterised in the following ways:

- Its sources span non-vanguardist grassroots movements, unions, political fronts, mass parties, radical intellectuals, transnational activist networks and parts of the progressive academy;
- It seeks to ensure that the inherent categories of Marxism are theorised within constantly changing historical conditions to find meaning;
- Marxism is understood as a body of social thought that is unfinished and hence challenged by the need to explain the dynamics of a globalising capitalism and the futures of social change;
- It is open to other forms of anti-capitalist thought and practice, including cur-rents within radical ecology, feminism, emancipatory utopianism and indigenous thought;
- It does not seek to be a monolithic and singular school of thought but engenders contending perspectives;
- Democracy, as part of the heritage of people's struggles, is understood as the basis for articulating alternatives to capitalism and as the primary means for con-stituting a transformative subject of historical change.

This series seeks to elaborate the social theorising and politics of democratic Marxism.

Published in the series and available:

Michelle Williams and Vishwas Satgar (eds). 2013. *Marxisms in the 21st Century: Crisis, Critique and Struggle.* Johannesburg: Wits University Press.

Vishwas Satgar (ed.), 2015. *Capitalism's Crises: Class Struggles in South Africa and the World.* Johannesburg: Wits University Press.

THE CLIMATE CRISIS

SOUTH AFRICAN AND GLOBAL DEMOCRATIC ECO-SOCIALIST ALTERNATIVES

Edited by Vishwas Satgar

WITS UNIVERSITY PRESS

Published in South Africa by:

Wits University Press
1 Jan Smuts Avenue
Johannesburg 2001
www.witspress.co.za

First published 2018

978-1-77614-054-1 (Print)
978-1-77614-207-1 (Web PDF)
978-1-77614-208-8 (EPUB)

The publication of this volume was made possible by funding from the Rosa Luxemburg
Stiftung and through a grant received from the National Institute for the Humanities and
Social Sciences.

ROSA
LUXEMBURG
STIFTUNG

NATIONAL INSTITUTE
FOR THE HUMANITIES
AND SOCIAL SCIENCES

Project manager: Inga Norenius
Copy editor: Lee Smith
Proofreader: Inga Norenius
Indexer: Margaret Ramsay
Cover: Hothouse, South Africa

CONTENTS

TABLES AND BOX   vii

ACKNOWLEDGEMENTS   ix

ACRONYMS AND ABBREVIATIONS   x

CHAPTER 1:   The Climate Crisis and Systemic Alternatives   1
                Vishwas Satgar

PART ONE: THE CLIMATE CRISIS AS CAPITALIST CRISIS   29

CHAPTER 2:   The Limits of Capitalist Solutions to the Climate Crisis 30
                Dorothy Grace Guerrero

CHAPTER 3:   The Anthropocene and Imperial Ecocide: Prospects for Just
                Transitions   47
                Vishwas Satgar

PART TWO: DEMOCRATIC ECO-SOCIALIST ALTERNATIVES IN THE WORLD   69

CHAPTER 4:   The Employment Crisis, Just Transition and
                the Universal Basic Income Grant   70
                Hein Marais

CHAPTER 5:   The Rights of Mother Earth   107
                Pablo Sólon

CHAPTER 6:   *Buen Vivir*: An Alternative Perspective from the Peoples
                of the Global South to the Crisis of Capitalist Modernity 131
                Alberto Acosta and Mateo Martínez Abarca

CHAPTER 7:   Challenging the Growth Paradigm: Marx, Buddha and
                the Pursuit of 'Happiness'   148
                Devan Pillay

CHAPTER 8:   Ubuntu and the Struggle for an African
Eco-Socialist Alternative   168
Christelle Terreblanche

CHAPTER 9:   The Climate Crisis and the Struggle for African
Food Sovereignty   190
Nnimmo Bassey

PART THREE: DEMOCRATIC ECO-SOCIALIST ALTERNATIVES IN
SOUTH AFRICA   209

CHAPTER 10:   The Climate Crisis and a 'Just Transition' in South Africa:
An Eco-Feminist-Socialist Perspective   210
Jacklyn Cock

CHAPTER 11:   Energy, Labour and Democracy in South Africa   231
Michelle Williams

CHAPTER 12:   Capital, Climate and the Politics of Nuclear Procurement
in South Africa   252
David Fig

CHAPTER 13:   Climate Jobs at Two Minutes to Midnight   272
Brian Ashley

CHAPTER 14:   Deepening the Just Transition through Food Sovereignty
and the Solidarity Economy   293
Andrew Bennie and Athish Satgoor

CHAPTER 15:   Eco-Capitalist Crises in the 'Blue Economy':
Operation Phakisa's Small, Slow Failures   314
Desné Masie and Patrick Bond

CONCLUSION: Vishwas Satgar   338

CONTRIBUTORS   343

INDEX   347

TABLES AND BOX

Tables

Table 12.1 Potential nuclear vendors in the South African
new build procurement   263

Table 13.1 Job estimates   281

Table 13.2 Total annual emissions in million tons of CO_2e 282

Table 13.3 Jobs in the REI4P   285

Table 13.4 Average number of new energy jobs each year   286

Table 13.5 Contribution of different modes of transport to
emissions, 2000–2010   287

Table 13.6 Commuter use of different modes of transport   288

Table 13.7 Estimated number of jobs created each year
by expanding the public transport system   289

Box

Box 5.1   Thomas Berry's Ten Principles of Earth Jurisprudence   119

ACKNOWLEDGEMENTS

This volume owes a special debt to the Rosa Luxemburg Foundation (RLF). Without the support given by the RLF it would have been impossible to hold a contributors' workshop in South Africa and to ensure the manuscript was prepared for publication. In addition, the support given by the National Institute for the Humanities and Social Sciences has enabled us to publish this volume as a digital book as well. We are also grateful for the support given by Athish Satgoor and Andrew Bennie, organisers at the Co-operative and Policy Alternative Centre (COPAC), who played a central role in organising the workshop convened with contributors and activists from various social movements and community organisations. Wits University graciously provided a venue for the contributors' workshop. Special thanks also go to Alexia Daoussis, who assisted with a language and citation edit. For translation of the chapter on *buen vivir* from Spanish to English, we appreciate the efforts of Janine Schall-Emden for the final edit and the efforts of Natalia Cabanillas and Laura Efron for the first attempt at translation. Jane Cherry has been an outstanding editorial assistant and has contributed immensely to preparing the manuscript for Wits University Press. Moreover, it is important to acknowledge the feedback given on the manuscript by Nomaswazi Mthombeni and Professor Michelle Williams. Finally, our sincerest appreciation to the team at Wits University Press, particularly Veronica Klipp, Roshan Cader and Corina van der Spoel, for supporting this volume and the Democratic Marxism Series.

ACRONYMS AND ABBREVIATIONS

ACB	African Centre for Biodiversity
AFSA	Alliance for Food Sovereignty in Africa
ANC	African National Congress
ARIPO	African Regional Intellectual Property Organisation
BRICS	Brazil, Russia, India, China, South Africa
CO_2	carbon dioxide
CO_2e	carbon dioxide equivalent
COP	Conference of the Parties
Cosatu	Congress of South African Trade Unions
EIA	Environmental Impact Assessment
FDI	foreign direct investment
GDP	gross domestic product
GEAR	Growth, Employment and Redistribution
GHG	greenhouse gas
GMO	genetically modified organism
IPCC	Intergovernmental Panel on Climate Change
MEC	minerals–energy complex
MPRDA	Mineral and Petroleum Resources Development Act
NAFN	New Alliance for Food Security and Nutrition
NDP	National Development Plan
Necsa	South African Nuclear Energy Corporation
NRWDI	National Radioactive Waste Disposal Institute
NUM	National Union of Mineworkers
Numsa	National Union of Metalworkers of South Africa
ppm	parts per million
REDD	reducing emissions from deforestation and forest degradation
REI4P	Renewable Energy Independent Power Producers Procurement Programme
SAFSC	South African Food Sovereignty Campaign
SAP	structural adjustment programme
SDCEA	South Durban Community Environmental Alliance
SEM	Solidarity Economy Movement
UBIG	universal basic income grant
UNEP	United Nations Environment Programme
UNFCCC	UN Framework Convention on Climate Change
UPOV	International Union for the Protection of New Varieties of Plants

1

THE CLIMATE CRISIS AND SYSTEMIC ALTERNATIVES

Vishwas Satgar

Climate change is the most serious challenge we face as a species. Despite numerous warnings – scientific studies, United Nations (UN) declarations, books, movies, progressive media reporting – global leadership has failed humanity. After more than twenty years of multilateral negotiations, we have not developed the solutions to solve the climate crisis decisively. Instead, we have continued emitting pollutants and intensively using fossil fuels and, as a result, have been recording the hottest years on the planet. The last two decades in the fight against the climate crisis have merely confirmed, at a common sense level, an Anthropocene-centred theory: as a geological force, we humans are heating the planet. A heating planet, induced by human action, unhinges all our certainties and places everything in jeopardy. It challenges our fixation with growth economics, 'catch-up' development and every conception of modern progress that has incited our imaginations. Most fundamentally, it prompts us to ask: has globalised capitalism lost its progressiveness? Is today's fossil fuel-driven, hi-tech, scientific, financialised and post-Fordist industrial world leading humanity down a path of ecocidal destruction? How do we survive the climate crisis?

These are the central questions of this volume, which deals with one dimension of the systemic crises of accumulation related to contemporary capitalism. This thematic focus also builds on the previous volume in the series, entitled *Capitalism's Crises: Class Struggles in South Africa and the World*. Without falling into the trap of catastrophism, end-of-times millenarianism or apolitical acquiescence, this volume treats the climate crisis as an emergency, demanding transformative politics and systemic reforms to remake how we produce, consume, finance and organise social life – it calls for civilisational transformation. It draws from and highlights the analysis, concepts and systemic alternatives emerging at the frontiers of climate justice politics and its convergence with broader anti-systemic movements. Like previous volumes in this series, there is an attempt to think with and learn from grassroots movements. Thus, many of the contributors in this volume are engaged activist scholars, grassroots activists and movement leaders.

At the same time, this volume places Marxism in dialogue with contemporary anti-capitalism in a manner that draws on its ideological and movement potentials. Marxism in the twentieth century as ruling ideology, mostly as Marxism–Leninism, has privileged Promethean growth, vanguardist authoritarianism and catch-up industrialisation, and at the same time has been ruinous to the environment. This volume articulates a Marxism that is post-productivist, resituates nature at the centre of Marxism, confronts the patriarchal and racist oppressions inherent to capitalism, challenges contemporary imperialism and appreciates the need to think and act democratically. In this journey, Marxism is shaped by its own self-reflexivity, by contemporary anti-capitalism and the challenge of confronting the climate contradiction. It is tested as an intellectual resource to be open and serve as the basis for a new future: a democratic eco-socialist world and South Africa.

THE CLIMATE CRISIS AS A SYSTEMIC CRISIS OF CAPITALIST ACCUMULATION

In 1988, National Aeronautics and Space Administration (NASA) scientist James Hansen drew attention to the heating of the Earth's temperature, otherwise known as the 'greenhouse effect' or climate change (see *Washington Post*, 3 August 2012). Yet the US refused to adopt the Kyoto Protocol, which locked in 'common but differentiated responsibilities' (Art. 3.1) for industrial countries (even this did not go far enough). Instead, the US has worked systematically to scuttle the Kyoto Protocol. Hansen, writing in the 13 July 2006 issue of the *New York Review of Books*, cautioned that the world has a decade to alter the trajectory of greenhouse gas (GHG) emissions or face irreversible changes which will bring disastrous consequences. Since this plea was made, another decade has been lost and today geologists and climate scientists are talking about a new world of unpredictable and no-analogue climatic conditions: the Anthropocene. Put simply, we are entering a world in which humans have altered planetary conditions, including our climate, breaking a 10 000-year pattern of relatively stable climate known as the Holocene.

For many, the climate crisis is a complex scientific problem. At one level it is, and it is very different from daily or seasonal variability in weather. The science of climate change has confirmed, with the measurement of GHGs and in the language of the UN Framework Convention on Climate Change (UNFCCC), that 'human induced climate change' is happening (IPCC 2014: 48). In 2015, we broke the halfway mark towards catastrophic climate change. This was confirmed by the World Meteorological Organisation, which broadcast to the world that planetary temperatures have reached a 1°C increase higher than the period prior to the Industrial Revolution.[1] We have concentrated carbon, at over 400 parts per million, taking us rapidly closer to a 2°C increase in planetary temperature.[2] With this shift, extreme weather events such as droughts, hurricanes, heatwaves, drier conditions enabling fires and floods are becoming more commonplace. Sea levels are also rising, placing many low-lying communities, populous coastal cities and island states in jeopardy. Moreover, climate change on this scale within the Earth system is not expected to unfold in a linear way. Instead, it can potentially happen abruptly or through feedback loops, further accelerating runaway climate change. For example, methane release from the Arctic ice sheet, carbon saturation in our oceans and the destruction of rain forests all feed into the climate change crisis. As we fail to address the climate crisis, it becomes more complex and more costly.

The much-vaunted UN climate negotiations, particularly the Conference of the Parties in Paris during December 2015 (COP21), promised to confirm a clear purpose and political will to ensure we overcome the climate crisis. The Paris Agreement makes a call for urgent action to prevent a 2°C increase in planetary temperature, with an emphasis on efforts to keep temperature increases below 1.5°C, at pre-industrial levels (UNFCCC 2015). Despite the promises, these targets will not be realised. As things stand, most voluntary national commitments will lead to an overshoot of 2°C. The most up-to-date analysis of national pledges suggests that these are consistent with a temperature rise of 2.6–3.1°C above pre-industrial levels (Darby 2016). Moreover, while this Agreement came into force on 4 November 2016 it will only build momentum from 2020 onwards, thus losing another four years in the context of two decades of failed action. It is also expected, given the current emission rate and trajectory, that 1.5°C will be breached sooner than expected. In a recent study it was confirmed, 'The window for limiting warming to below 1.5C with high probability and without temporarily exceeding that level already seems to have closed' (Rogelj et al. 2016: 631).

The 2°C threshold discussed in the Paris Agreement is far from being a protective barrier. Instead, it is a dangerous threshold taking the human world to the brink. Studies on tipping points (like the Arctic becoming ice free or major retreats in glaciers in the Himalayas) show that eighteen out of thirty-seven abrupt changes will happen by a 2°C change or less (Drijfhout 2015). Put more bluntly, a 2°C increase in planetary temperature is extremely dangerous. For vulnerable nations, contributing less than two per cent of current global GHG emissions, a 2°C target is nothing short of catastrophic.[3] With the current increase in global temperature, major consequences beyond their capabilities have already come to the fore for the most vulnerable twenty countries in the world, representing 700 million people and including poor, arid, landlocked, mountainous and small island states from Africa, Asia, the Caribbean, Latin America and the Pacific. These experiences provide us with a window into the future. According to the Vulnerable 20 (or V20), this is what they are already facing:[4]

- An average of more than 50 000 deaths per year since 2010, a number expected to increase exponentially by 2030;
- Escalating annual losses of at least 2.5% of their GDP potential per year, estimated at US$45 billion since 2010, a number expected to increase to close to US$400 billion in the next twenty years;
- More than half the economic impact of climate change by 2030 and over eighty per cent of its health impact for V20 and other low-emitting developing countries;
- A doubling in the number of extremely hot days and hot nights in the last fifty years as the planet has warmed appreciably;
- Countless extreme events which include typhoons with wind speeds that are around ten per cent stronger than they were in the 1970s, translating into more than a thirty per cent increase in destructiveness;
- Sea-level rise that will partially or completely submerge the island nations of Kiribati, Maldives and Tuvalu, displacing at least 500 000 people;

- The displacement of up to forty million people due to the inundation of low-elevation land resulting from climate change-driven sea-level rise;
- The threat of increasingly devastating and more frequent disasters, such as storms, flooding and drought.

This leads us to ask: what is the Paris Agreement really all about? What are its limits and contradictions? How does its political economy work against us solving the biggest problem facing the human race?

First, the Paris Agreement abandons the Kyoto Protocol commitment to 'common but differentiated responsibilities' despite formally declaring its commitments to the Protocol. The Kyoto Protocol explicitly placed a greater burden on rich industrialised countries. The Paris Agreement, by contrast, provides for voluntary and nationally determined commitments, which should not be confused with nationally binding and regulated commitments. Yet there are historical and contemporary inequalities regarding carbon emissions. Some of the rich industrialised countries of the global North have been polluting since the advent of the Industrial Revolution, in the context of uneven processes of capitalist development and imperial international relations. These countries carry a climate debt. However, climate debt and climate reparations do not feature in the Paris Agreement. Instead, there is a paltry commitment of US$100 billion from developed countries for mitigation and adaptation, which pales in comparison to the finance injected into the crisis-prone financial system. What this means is that those who have created (and continue to create) the problem, are off the hook. Without regulated commitments for reductions in GHG emissions based on historical climate debt, this inequality will not be addressed and emerging polluters, like China, will only commit to and act on what suits their interests. Moreover, the argument of industrialising countries for industrial development space cannot be addressed in the interests of the planet and all of humanity unless industrialised countries address the historic climate debt and aggressively lead the cutback in emissions through regulation. The Paris Agreement fails to do this, which means it is a 'business as usual' trajectory for globalised and fossil fuel-driven industrial development, including global shipping and airplane emissions. Transportation emissions are not even mentioned in the Paris Agreement. In short, the Agreement has turned its back on common but differentiated responsibilities. A tenuous voluntary pledge system, favoured by the US, one of the leading carbon emitters, has been entrenched despite the world running out of time.

Second, the carbon space (or budget) in the Paris Agreement for developed and developing countries is left to each country to manage, in a global political economy in which competition rules. No country in this globalised race is going to surrender any advantages to address the climate crisis unless there are reciprocal and harmonised commitments. At the same time, if the pledge and review system falters, with some countries doing more than others, this is likely to cause consternation against free riders, which could undermine the mechanism. In the context of economic stagnation, corporate capture of political systems and the entrenched power of fossil fuel interests, the Paris Agreement is already being bypassed to ensure profit rates are protected and global accumulation is maintained. The geopolitics of domestic interests will constantly threaten and push back the pledge and review mechanism. For instance, despite Barack Obama's rhetoric in praising this Agreement, the US ruling class did not support him. Instead, their approach was to keep the globalised capitalist system going on a 'business as usual' path despite the climate crisis.[5] Donald Trump, on the other hand, has given the go-ahead to expand fossil fuel pipeline development (the Dakota Access and Keystone XL), rolled back Obama's modest Clean Power Plan, weakened the Environmental Protection Agency and withdrawn the US from the Paris Agreement. Ironically, the Paris Agreement was not even a legally binding agreement and gave the US room to bring whatever it wanted into the multilateral process. With climate change denialism back on the agenda in the US, and the world's climate being pushed into greater corporate-induced chaos, the US under Trump will seek to protect 'lifeboat' America at all costs. As a result, a more securitised response is likely to come to the fore, from both the US and other wealthy countries. The only way to challenge this is if the geopolitics of international trade, finance and development is redefined. A climate-driven world cannot be held hostage by the whims of the US-led bloc. If we are to save life on Earth, neoliberalised global accumulation and the current policies of globally competitive capitalist development have to be abandoned. Given the climate emergency, a new political economy has to emerge to replace global competition. This requires 'just transitions' (discussed below) at various scales and tempos to deal with the disproportionate impacts of the climate crisis on vulnerable, poor societies, the working classes and peasantries, who are already bearing the brunt of a highly unequal world. The Paris Agreement is not up to this task and is not moving the world in this direction. With Trump, supported by fossil capital and finance, the Paris Agreement is going to be a symbolic rallying point for only some countries. In fact, the crisis of climate multilateralism has become worse and reflects a crisis of global leadership.

Third, and rather obvious, the Paris Agreement reflects a balance of forces in favour of greening capitalism. This illusion comes through the false solutions embedded in the Agreement, which include carbon trading, reforestation and preventing forest degradation and offset mechanisms (UNFCCC 2015). These solutions have been part of multilateral negotiations for the past two decades and have not worked in their implementation. Carbon trading is a clear example in this regard (Bond 2012). As we run out of time, techno-fixes become more appealing than system change. So, contrary to Anthropocene theory, which suggests that we are all responsible for the climate crisis, it is actually the capitalist system and its class champions that are responsible for the climate crisis. A system that has produced a systemic problem cannot solve the problem, given that this is a carbon-based capitalist civilisation. Nothing short of the fundamental decarbonisation of production, consumption, finance and every life world on this planet will save human and non-human nature. The Paris Agreement falls short of this imperative.

Fourth, it has become increasingly clear through numerous studies that if we extract more fossil fuels we are going to breach 2°C of planetary heating. In the most recent study done on this and cited by Bill McKibben (2016), the conclusion is simple: keeping temperature increases below 2°C requires zero extraction of fossil fuels. We have reached the limits of drilling, digging and extracting if we want to survive. More shocking is the silence of the Paris Agreement about carbon corporations and the need to restrict their activities, even as a minimum gesture to incite hope and encourage a global shift away from fossil fuels. What is patently clear is that the Agreement has not addressed the most immediate and obvious driver of climate change. Instead, by failing to spotlight carbon corporations (oil, gas, coal) it has given warrant for more deadly emissions. Fracking, tar sands, deep-water drilling and other new frontiers of complex hydrocarbons are all expanding. Trump and his class allies have given further momentum to this. This 'business as usual' approach is the face of eco-fascism and imperial ecocide. It is the biggest failing of the Paris Agreement, as it does not address the major obstacle to renewable energy systems and a transformative just transition.

The world is facing a perilous future, with a 1°C increase in temperatures since pre the Industrial Revolution already providing signs of what the 'no-analogue world' will bring. A hotter planet means the conditions to sustain human and non-human life will become ever more difficult. Global ruling classes have failed humanity and all life on the planet. We have a stark choice: end capitalism or perish. It is in this context that the rising climate justice movement is crucial, together with its potential to unite red-green forces,[6] advance deep just transitions and build systemic alternatives from below. Building this movement is our only hope for the future. The climate justice movement will not guarantee our survival but will certainly lessen the catastrophic consequences of climate change and harness the best of human solidarity to sustain life. This volume foregrounds some of the leading perspectives emerging from this movement.

CLIMATE JUSTICE, SYSTEM CHANGE AND THE JUST TRANSITION

The climate justice movement is part of a new cycle of global resistance seeking to push back neoliberal globalisation while advancing systemic alternatives. Four important conditions facilitated its emergence.[7] First was the failure of a reform agenda through the Climate Action Network inside UN climate processes. More ground was being conceded by progressive civil society until 2007, in Bali, when a breakaway was formalised through the call for Climate Action Now! (Bond 2012). Second was the increasing shift in the balance of forces within the climate negotiations favouring green neoliberal and capitalist solutions. The green-wash of UN climate summits prompted the need to develop an alternative vision, practice and politics around systemic alternatives (Angus 2010; Bassey 2012; Tokar 2010). The attempt by Bolivia in 2010, at the Cochabamba summit, highlighted the fact that only one state in the interstate system was willing to champion a more radical climate justice politics inside the UN climate negotiations. This attempt by Bolivia also came short, due to the contradictions within Bolivia, such as its own petro economy, as well as the dynamics of the power structure within UN negotiations. Increasingly, for climate justice activists UN climate summits became more about the outside, and the theatre of street politics and platforms for people's systemic alternatives. An alternative narrative of climate justice was being globalised from below.

Third, as climate shocks began emerging as part of planetary lived experience, common sense began crystallising as good sense. Hurricanes like Katrina and Sandy, California's mega drought, El Nino-induced droughts with longer duration and typhoons Haiyan and Haima battering the Philippines have all brought home the need to build from below. Fourth, the continued expansion of fossil fuel extraction, in the midst of the climate crisis, has also engendered some of the most radical activism by African women in the Niger Delta and amongst native Americans and other grassroots communities at the frontline of carbon corporations' regimes of extraction and dispossession (Bassey 2012; Klein 2014). Calls to keep 'oil in the ground, coal in the hole' have begun resonating on a global scale. Battle lines are being drawn all over the world against UN false solutions, carbon corporations and states promoting fossil economies. At the same time, systemic alternatives are coming to the fore such as food sovereignty, climate jobs, public transport, socially owned renewable energy, basic income grants, rights of nature, 'living well', ubuntu, commoning (of water, land, cyberspace), zero waste, solidarity economies and many more systemic alternatives.

The challenge of system change is key for survival. Climate justice politics foregrounds this. The most crucial idea in this regard is the notion of the 'just transition', as articulated by trade unions. Central to this notion is recognition of both the slow but immediate and long-term violence associated with the climate crisis as it impacts on the lives of the poor, the working class, the peasantry and the vulnerable. This is disproportionate and disparate, within rich countries as well. Climate shocks are induced by the capitalist system and have become internal to the dynamics of capitalism, but this does not mean the working class and poor have to bear the brunt and cost of the climate crisis. The notion of the just transition affirms the importance of transforming our societies now, but in a manner that privileges the interests of the majority as opposed to the one per cent. Moreover, as Jacklyn Cock cautions in this volume, for this to happen such transitions have to be more than shallow changes. This means that system change of everything is crucial to sustain life. It is in this context that this volume brings to the fore key systemic alternatives that would inform a transformative just transition and the building of a democratic eco-socialist South Africa, and world, from below.

At the same time, contributions in this volume realise the limits and challenges faced by climate justice politics in achieving a transformative just transition. In this regard, the chapters grapple with the following in different ways:

- Confronting the challenge of building viable and sustainable societies as part of the just transition. While the transformative politics and systemic alternatives of climate justice politics are not abstract or utopian blueprints, there is a need for a concrete vision of another world and society beyond capitalism. Drawing on the rich and emancipatory traditions of socialism together with contemporary anti-capitalism is crucial for constructing this vision.

- Connecting grassroots, frontline struggles to national, regional and global struggles. Geographical scale and critical mass is a challenge to push back fossil-fuel capitalism while creating the space for systemic alternatives. These systemic alternatives have to unleash an alternative logic, build new values-based institutions and enable momentum for democratic transformation through systemic reforms.
- Building red–green alliances is crucial and means system change and transformative politics have to enable red to become green and green more red. The working class and green movements have to converge. It is imperative to forge these alliances in practice around common analyses, campaigns and building systemic alternatives.
- Fostering and promoting transformative just transitions as a credible imperative embracing systemic change is key. This raises questions about state power and how climate justice activism should transform and re-embed the state as it builds from below.

It is with regard to these challenges that this volume orientates its contribution around systemic alternatives and transformative just transitions, particularly in relation to democratic eco-socialist alternatives.

FROM SOCIALISM TO DEMOCRATIC ECO-SOCIALISM

Marxist-inspired socialism in the twentieth century has been discredited, whether as social democracy, Marxist–Leninist–Maoist regimes, or as revolutionary nationalist projects. With the deepening crisis of contemporary capitalism, some argue that these historical failures were tainted, including by western propaganda. According to this argument, what is required is a reaffirmation and retrieval. There is a need for a better version of the same, and maybe with better leaders, outcomes will be different. Such positions lend themselves to voluntarist readings of history, of both internal and external conditions that contributed to failure, and are rather dogmatic. Moreover, such approaches fail to see problems with Marxist theory implicated in these historical experiences of socialism, the limits to forms of struggle waged, the contradictions of contemporary globalised capitalism and are closed to the new anti-systemic politics emerging amongst new anti-capitalist movements and forces. A dogmatic approach to the history of socialism will not assist the renewal of socialism.

This volume confronts this dogma by looking at the failures of twentieth-century socialism through the critique, theoretical development and practical horizons of democratic eco-socialism. In this regard, there are five crucial historical moments and approaches to the development of contemporary democratic eco-socialist analysis and struggle.[8] These moments span the latter half of the twentieth century and include the present. Such moments and approaches can be delineated as follows: (i) a Marxist ecology critique of actually existing 'socialism'; (ii) greening Marxism through ecology; (iii) refinding a complex ecology in classical Marxism; (iv) utilising a historical materialist ecology and theory of capitalist crisis to engage with current environmental problems; and (v) the rise of eco-socialist forces in the world championing systemic alternatives. Each of these is unpacked below. Moreover, this volume embraces all these approaches to eco-socialist analysis and struggle, despite tensions and unresolved positions in some instances. Each chapter in this volume can be traced back to these approaches to democratic eco-socialism.

The first moment and approach to democratic eco-socialism derives from the experience of actually existing 'socialism'.[9] These are dissident voices that have challenged the productivism of the former Soviet Bloc and contemporary China while arguing for ecological transformation. Two crucial examples stand out. Rudolf Bahro's *The Alternative in Eastern Europe*, published in 1978, provides a devastating critique of the making of 'industrial despotism' and the deep alienation central to the anatomy of party-controlled state socialism. Moreover, he argues for a remaking of the division of labour through greater worker self-determination, greater democracy and a 'cultural revolution'. Bahro wanted actually existing socialism to become a truly emancipated civilisation of 'free producers'. With the publication of his book, he was jailed and declared a spy. He was only released by the East German regime after an international outcry. In West Germany he went on to become one of the leading voices of the German Greens but was later disaffected by its narrow electoralism and convergence with the social democratic party.[10] With regard to China, one of the most incisive Marxist ecology critiques is Minqi Li's *China and the 21st Century Crisis* (2016). Li points to the class and ecological contradictions central to China's capitalism. He argues powerfully for understanding the climate crisis and oil peak as central to the unsustainability of Chinese capitalism. Ultimately, he suggests a transition is necessary which has to grapple with the challenges of reform, revolution or collapse.

The greening of Marxism, which is the second moment and approach to democratic eco-socialism, develops largely out of ecological critiques of productivist Marxism, with its emphasis on socialist modernisation and industrial accumulation. Some critiques have gone as far as suggesting that the origins of productivism lie with Marx. This is because, it is claimed, Marx did not have an adequate understanding of nature, venerated the development of the 'forces of production', was blind to ecological limits, was anthropocentric and promoted an industrial vision of a post-capitalist society based on abundance.[11] Moreover, it is argued that as a result, the Soviet Union (and now China) encapsulated the worst kind of productivist Marxism. Many of Marx's ostensible theses are considered the problem within historical Marxism and therefore Marxism is inadequate to deal with the ecological challenges of our time. Instead, Marxism has to be brought into ecology. The greening of Marxism entails taking on board the concerns of ecology, including the intrinsic value of nature, the Malthusian population challenge, the dangers of science and technology, and planetary ecological limits. Thus, Marxism has to become an ecological Marxism.[12]

The third moment and approach to developing democratic eco-socialism is by Marxists who have not accepted the critique of Marx by ecological Marxists. Instead, such Marxist ecologists have reread Marx to find the lost ecological dimension in his work. This spans various Marxist thinkers, each with a different emphasis in their reading of Marx's ecology. For instance, Paul Burkett (2014) refutes claims about Marx's thought being productivist with three arguments. First, Marx always understood human wealth as having a nature component, not just labour. Second, Marx always understood that human production, under any social system, would be constrained by natural and ecological laws. Third, Marx was very aware of the wastefulness inherent to capitalism's development of the productive forces and its destructiveness. Burkett salvages a Marxist ecology by recognising the importance of nature to Marx's historical materialism, value-form analysis of capitalism and the importance of nature in the struggle for an alternative society. John Bellamy Foster (2000) adds to this by bringing out an ecological dimension in many of the neglected aspects of Marx's thought. He draws on Marx's writing on philosophical naturalism, evolutionary theory, capitalist agriculture and soil theory. Foster's reading provides us with a conception of the metabolic rift central to Marx, which is about the separation of the human being from nature, including the divide between town and country. He demonstrates a powerful ecological sensibility in Marx.

The fourth moment and approach to democratic eco-socialism builds on Marxist ecology. It recognises that a complex historical materialist ecology, a theory of capitalism related to ecological crisis and a new democratic conception of anti-capitalist agency, has a great deal to offer in terms of an analysis of ecological contradictions. Such contradictions include: extinction of species through loss of biodiversity; acid rain; destruction of the ozone layer; desertification; pollution of oceans; contamination of lakes, rivers and streams; dispossession of people's land; overfishing; hazardous working conditions; incineration of waste; famines and breaching all planetary ecological limits, with climate change being one of the biggest challenges. David Layfield (2008) dedicates an entire text to showing how this all fits together from the standpoint of the intersection of Marxism and ecology, while activists like Nimmo Bassey (2012) and Naomi Klein (2014) demonstrate how the climate crisis is not only driven by a capitalist political economy, but is also about a new resistance that is rising at the frontlines of preventing extraction of fossil fuels and also in the context of climate justice struggles.

The fifth moment and approach to democratic eco-socialism is informed by the agency of the climate justice movement and a host of other anti-systemic forces that are rising to advance systemic alternatives.[13] The slogan 'System Change, Not Climate Change' best captures the democratic eco-socialist orientation of these movements. These movements and their organic intellectuals are fighting against carbon corporations expanding into tar sands, fracking and offshore drilling. Their systemic alternatives are informed by indigenous cultures, cosmologies and rights-based discourses. The dialogue with Marxism and how class, race, gender and ecology interact is also part of this ferment. These organic discourses are shaping the frontiers of democratic eco-socialism as well. For example, the rights of nature tribunals have been convened as part of the people's spaces alongside UN climate summits. Crucial is how the dispossession of indigenous people's rights to land, water and life has been connected to fighting corporations and capitalism.[14]

Moreover, there are movements fighting against the dispossession of the world's peasantry, mainly women, who produce almost seventy per cent of the world's food (Shiva 2015: 16), and who are taking a stand against transnational food corporations and their regimes of dispossession through food sovereignty politics. La Via Campesina, with over 200 million members and a myriad of food sovereignty alliances in different countries and regions in the world, has been crucial in advancing this systemic alternative. Food sovereignty perspectives and eco-feminists recognise that globalised industrial food systems are responsible for twenty-five per cent of the world's carbon dioxide emissions, sixty per cent of methane gas emissions and eighty per cent of nitrous oxide emissions, all deadly GHGs (Shiva 2015: 54). It is not surprising that there is a growing call for food sovereignty pathways based on the science of agroecology and the democratic building of grassroots movements.

Today, the five moments and approaches to democratic eco-socialism confirm its arrival and importance. The meaning of socialism (and to be a socialist) today is fundamentally about being democratic eco-socialist in identity and in ideological representation. Merely referring to socialism or representing one's self as socialist equates to a failed commitment to democracy as people's power, as evidenced in the twentieth century, and also equates to productivist socialism which cannot be realised on a scorched planet and, more fundamentally, will only contribute to such a disaster. Instead, a renewed democratic eco-socialism faces squarely the challenge to save human and non-human nature from capitalism's ecocidal logic through a radical practice and conception of democracy as people's power, mediated by an ethics to sustain life.

This of course does not mean that race and gender are unimportant to the identity of a democratic eco-socialist. In all the democratic eco-socialist struggles emerging today, whether through resistance on indigenous land against fracking or oil extraction, or through struggles against dispossession of women peasant farmers, or through neo-Marxist political economy analysis of ecological problems, race and gender are integral (Bond 2012; Klein 2014). A democratic eco-socialist is feminist and anti-racist and many chapters in this volume bring out these dimensions. At the same time, the conceptual remit of a renewed socialism prompts us to think more analytically and conceptually about democratic eco-socialism. To assist us we draw on Raymond Williams, a Marxist cultural theorist, particularly his book *Keywords* (1983).

In *Keywords*, Williams derives the origins of the word 'democracy' from the Greek word *demokratia* with its emphasis on *demos* (the people) and *kratos* (rule) – in other words, rule by the people. However, he is aware of its various definitions and usages and cautions us against its appropriations both by the liberal and socialist traditions. Central to the development of the term 'democracy' was the idea of class rule, or sometimes rule by the multitude. From the latter part of the nineteenth century, it was adopted in political language and used in modern party politics. Liberals tended to focus on representative democracy and qualifying the meaning of the 'people' to certain groups, such as freemen, wisemen, white men and owners of property. Socialists tended to emphasise democracy as meaning popular power and a state in which the interests of the majority were central and were exercised and controlled by the majority. However, Williams (1983: 97) cautions that in practice both liberal and twentieth-century socialist 'people's democracies' undermined people's power. Representation was manipulated and popular power was reduced to bureaucracy or oligarchy. In the twenty-first century renewal of socialism, democracy is about a radical practice, various institutional forms, conditions that protect both negative and positive freedoms and an ethics to sustain life. It is about democratic movements, direct citizen action, participatory forms, representative processes, rights and deliberated ethical choices. People's power is affirmed in all these ways to ensure that political and administrative state structures are also democratised.

Williams (1983) confirms the word 'ecology' first came into usage in the 1870s through the work of a German zoologist, Ernst Haeckel. Haeckel's conception mainly focused on the habitat of plants and animals and on their relationship with each other. Ecology in the twentieth century was briefly overshadowed by 'environmentalism', particularly in the mid-1950s, to express concern with conservation and for measures against pollution. However, ecology further extends its meaning to include human relationships with the physical world. Today, ecology situates human beings as an integral part of nature and within planetary ecosystems. It grapples with human beings' coeval relation to and co-creation of nature. In the twenty-first century, ecology has also become integral to the prefix 'eco-' within democratic eco-socialism.

The words 'socialist' and 'socialism' really get established in modern usage in the 1860s, alongside 'cooperative', 'mutualist', 'associationist' and 'collectivist' (Williams 1983: 288). Different traditions used the word 'socialism' to refer either, like Marxists, to a transitional society between capitalism and communism or, like Fabian socialists, to an understanding of socialism as the logical development of liberal society to achieve the economic side of the liberal ideal. In the twentieth century, communist parties formed out of the Russian revolution maintained a commitment to socialism but tried to distinguish their socialism from that of social democratic parties. Revolutionary nationalists also devised variants of socialism such as African socialism or Nehruvian socialism. Today socialists are championing struggles against exploitation, commodification, dispossession, oppression (racial, gender, sexual) and for greater democracy in government and the workplace. At the same time, property relations are being rethought to include various forms of the commons (land, seeds, water, knowledge) and socialised property (such as worker cooperatives, municipal ownership involving communities and workers and community trusts) while recognising the importance of democratised public ownership. Moreover, democratic planning of food systems, energy and resources (like participatory budgeting) are also being attempted in practice and are part of the just transition to sustain life. Socialism in the twenty-first century is no longer the preserve of vanguard parties but is emerging as part of anti-systemic movements, grassroots networks, progressive think tanks and democratic political instruments wanting transformative change. Conjoined to radical democracy, it is also about ethical values informing individual and collective choices to save life – both human and non-human.

Ultimately, bringing these keywords together means socialism in the twenty-first century is democratic eco-socialism. It is a living socialism in a historical process of realisation, and is informed by the five moments and approaches to democratic eco-socialist analysis and struggle mentioned above. This is explored further below, in terms of concrete democratic eco-socialist alternatives emanating from struggles in the world and in South Africa.

DEMOCRATIC ECO-SOCIALIST ALTERNATIVES

Part One of this volume focuses on a counternarrative of the climate crisis. It focuses on and deepens the analysis of the relationship between the climate crisis and capitalism.

In chapter two, Dorothy Grace Guerrero draws on her many years of advocacy and activism within UN–COP circuits and climate justice politics to provide a critical political economy analysis of global climate change negotiations. She situates her perspective in the institutional political economy of the UN climate negotiations, tracing its increasing disconnect from the imperatives of climate science, the voices of countries impacted by climate shocks and street politics. Guerrero emphasises the centrality of corporate capture within the UN system in general, including climate change negotiations. She foregrounds how corporate influence has not only obstructed serious systemic solutions from coming to the fore in the global negotiations for the past twenty years, during which carbon emissions and planetary temperatures have increased, but also how corporate interests are registered in multilateral processes. This includes the push back against regulated reductions in carbon emissions, the roll back of 'common but differentiated responsibilities', the rise of market-centred solutions, failure to address the continued use of fossil fuels and tenuous voluntary commitments by countries, which are far from adequate to prevent either a 1.5 or 2°C increase in planetary temperatures. Guerrero consistently argues that the climate crisis is more than an environmental problem – it encompasses ecological and social crises. It reflects the asymmetries of power between rich and poor countries and class hierarchies in societies. In the end, Guerrero points us in the direction of system change and transformative politics. She highlights crucial systemic alternatives emerging from climate justice forces that require transformation of political, economic, social and environmental relations.

In chapter three, Vishwas Satgar interrogates the ideological construction and function of the Anthropocene discourse, both its official version within the UN climate process but also as part of a growing popular discourse. This chapter traces the making of Anthropocene discourse, its science and its rendering as social scientific explanation. However, it is as social scientific explanation that it is critiqued. The critique highlights how Anthropocene discourse has a multivalence, which enables it to confirm technocratic practice and human triumphalism vis-à-vis nature. At the same time, the chapter engages critically with the existing Marxist engagement with this discourse. Some Marxists have shown a willingness to embrace the Anthropocene framework, mainly due to its scientific argument that humans are responsible for planetary impacts, while others embrace an anthropocentric version of the Capitalocene in which humans co-create nature. This chapter engages critically with existing Marxist ecological approaches to the Anthropocene to highlight their limits. Deriving from this is a perspective that understands Anthropocene discourse as a confirmation of the logic of imperial ecocide, having its genesis in the origins of capitalism and in its making over 500 years. It is in this process that capital is also constituted as a geological force shaping and determining the conditions of life forms and worlds. Moreover, it argues that the Anthropocene embodies power relations that affirm racialised dominance as part of imperial ecocide. Finally, the chapter concludes with a reflection on the prospects of advancing transformative just transitions.

Part Two highlights concrete democratic eco-socialist alternatives coming to the fore, mainly from the global South, but being translated in different

17

locales through transnational activist circuits that are part of climate justice activism. These alternatives seek to elaborate content for the just transition and systemic reforms, as part of the struggle for climate justice. On the ground and in struggles, these alternatives are championed as part of the lived experience of indigenous people's movements, peasant movements, worker movements, progressive think tanks, activist groups and radical intellectuals.

Chapter four, by Hein Marais, foregrounds the universal basic income grant (UBIG) as a crucial transformative response to the climate crisis and increasingly the crisis of social reproduction caused by increasing unemployment and poverty wages. Marais shows convincingly that the moment for the UBIG, is now. He highlights how wage labour is increasingly becoming an impossible way to survive. Unemployment rates are growing across the world, the conditions of work are also becoming precarious, the overproduction crises of capital accumulation are continuing in the context in which labour absorption is exhausted, labour is sharing less in the wealth created and union densities are in decline, making it near impossible to stem yawning inequalities. At the same time, the transition from 'dirty industries' and the impacts of climate shocks make it necessary to consider the UBIG as a central transformative measure in the context of the just transition. Workers need not carry the disproportionate impacts of the climate crisis with such a measure. Beyond making the case for the UBIG as a crucial alternative, Marais also navigates the deep ideological prejudices against a proposition to create a world beyond work and the appropriations of the UBIG by the neoliberal right wing wanting to roll back public goods. Most importantly, he underlines its utopian glow as expressed in its radical potential as a crucial step in liberating labour from dependence on capital, affirming citizenship but also allowing for a reclaiming of life, both human and non-human.

In chapter five, Pablo Sólon, the former ambassador of the Plurinational State of Bolivia to the UN (2009–2011) and one of the leading climate justice thinkers and campaigners for the rights of nature/Mother Earth, introduces us to this systemic alternative. Sólon places the Rights of Mother Earth alternative squarely in opposition to anthropocentrism. He makes his argument recognising that the Rights of Mother Earth is about breaking with the duality in western thought which places the human subject in opposition to other objects, living or non-living. Moreover, he brings to the fore the genealogy of this idea within Andean and more generally indigenous thought, scientific discourses on Earth system science, spiritual and religious ethical thought and juridical thinking.

Sólon furnishes us with the ideological foundations of this idea and then traces its development through Deep Ecology and Wild Law. He demonstrates how the conception of the Rights of Mother Earth is not equivalent to human rights and is not about merely extending human rights to nature. Rather, he shows how philosophically, by drawing on Thomas Berry's Earth Jurisprudence, the Rights of Mother Earth derives from the same source of life as human rights, and conceptually advocates for an Earth community in which there is no hierarchy of living or non-living forms. Humans and nature are equivalent and part of a whole. At the same time, rights are qualitatively different in this framework. Sólon further shows how these ideas have found expression in legal instruments, including the Ecuadorian constitution and the Bolivian Law of the Rights of Mother Earth. In affirming these advances, Sólon is far from reducing the Rights of Mother Earth to legal discourse. Instead, he consistently argues to recognise and struggle for its realisation through mass politics.

In chapter six, Alberto Acosta and Mateo Martínez Abarca bring to the fore the idea of *buen vivir* or *sumak kawsay* (in Kichwa) or *suma qamaña* (in Aymara), which loosely translated refers to living well. It has its roots in indigenous ancestral knowledge in Ecuador and in other countries in the region. As explicated in this chapter, this is an alternative to the conception of capitalist modernity and development transmitted to the global South. It is a critique of the productivism, materialism and dualistic relationship western thought has imposed on nature. It challenges the human separation from nature and is a discourse that gives ontological value to all living entities. It is a longstanding emancipatory perspective of indigenous peoples who have been facing 500 years of colonisation. The discourse of *buen vivir* calls forth the need to decolonise our societies and to rethink our values and social practices. It is not a blueprint or an intellectual fashion. In today's Latin America it is a deep expression of the power of rising indigenous communities that want to confront the crises of capitalist civilisation. It is about a collective journey to remake our world such that the dichotomy between humans and nature is ended. *Pacha Mama* or Mother Earth is central to how we think about society and how we refound our political economy relations. Acosta and Abarca expose the importance of this idea to the new constitutionalism in the Andes but also address how we can think through the implications of *buen vivir* for transforming the economy and its logic. In the end, they place Marxism in dialogue with a radical anti-capitalist idea emerging from indigenous communities that can assist us in constructing a solidarity economy that sustains life as part of the just transition.

In chapter seven, by Devan Pillay, there is a strong critique of the growth metric. Modern industrial and globalised economies are fixated on growth but, as Pillay argues, this is implicated in reproducing a system in which there are deepening economic, social and ecological crises. Growth, he argues, cannot be uncoupled from these crises and increasingly the 'art of paradigm maintenance' associated with growth-based economic policy making is revealing its limits and contradictions. He also demonstrates how in South Africa neoliberal economic policies, including the National Development Plan, shore up a fossil fuel-driven minerals–energy–finance complex, reproducing a pattern of systemic crisis, all in the pursuit of growth. Pillay then provides a departure from this framework by suggesting we need transformative reforms and alternatives beyond neoliberal and twentieth-century Marxist-inspired growth economies. Central to such alternatives is a retrieval of a radical humanism within Marxism (such as in Marx and Rick Turner, the latter a South African 'organic intellectual') to find common ground with materialist and atheistic philosophies like Buddhism. Pillay argues we need to refind a holistic frame of social change, central to democratic eco-socialism and the just transition, in which the existential liberation of the human being, as part of nature, is tied to larger social transformation. This means we need new concepts, emanating from counterhegemonic class and popular struggles unfolding from below, to order our relations between humans and nature, very similar to *buen vivir*, ubuntu and even the Happiness Index. A growth-centred South Africa, and world, will merely reproduce more of the same, taking us further away from a just transition and the realisation of transformative alternatives.

Chapter eight, by Christelle Terreblanche, breaks new ground in the debate about democratic eco-socialism. In her chapter, there is an attempt to reclaim ubuntu – an African understanding and ethics of humans and their interconnectedness with nature – as an ethical paradigm while placing it in dialogue with eco-socialism. This is about Africa's holistic and integrated worldview, providing ideological resources to both challenge contemporary capitalism and rise to the challenge of renewing a socialist response to the climate crisis. This is not done through abstract philosophical theorising, but rather through situating ubuntu in Africa's first wave of socialism and Marxist–Leninist regimes. Important lessons are drawn from this experience, including its failures, for finding common ground for the dialogue with eco-socialism. Moreover, the chapter reveals how ubuntu is located in contemporary African struggles, the most significant being led by women against extractivism. This has also laid the basis for a global movement to stop fossil fuel extraction and has fed into transnational activist circuits at the heart of contemporary climate justice politics. In this process, eco-socialists are brought into a dialogue with African socialist thought and its understanding of ubuntu. In this regard, the common ground between Léopold Senghor's Negritude and Joel Kovel's ecocentric ethic is interrogated. Finally, the chapter speaks to the challenge ubuntu poses to eco-socialism through its own radical conceptions of ethical praxis and decolonisation. The chapter confirms that transformative activism, confronting the climate crisis and the imperatives of the just transition, is incomplete without appreciating the central role of ubuntu.

In chapter nine, Nnimmo Bassey focuses on the devastating impacts of the climate crisis on Africa. This is occurring despite Africa's limited contribution of four per cent to global carbon emissions. This highlights the importance of a just transition which demands that those countries of the global North most responsible for the climate crisis should take the major responsibility for solving it. This is acknowledged in the logic of 'equal but differentiated responsibilities' which is built into the UNFCCC negotiations process but which is not happening. Among the negative climate impacts are increasing hunger (affecting some 240 million Africans daily) and water scarcity and stress (by 2020 up to 250 million Africans will be affected). These impacts are aggravated by false climate solutions that are not only reproducing the existing carbon pathway but, most importantly, undermining African agriculture. These false solutions are pushing back resilient, indigenous knowledge-based food sovereignty alternatives and intensifying an ecocidal logic that is destroying nature and the conditions to sustain life. Despite these consequences, powerful forces are promoting false solutions to the climate crisis, such as climate-smart agriculture, genetically modified seeds which undermine small-scale farmers, takeovers of African seed systems, land and water grabs and policies such as Reducing Emissions from Deforestation and Forest Degradation. Bassey maintains that this does not halt deforestation and is 'basically a convenient tool for market environmentalism'. At the same time, resistance to the organisations promoting these false colonialist solutions, such as the G7-led New Alliance for Food Security and Nutrition, is growing throughout the African continent. The push back of African food sovereignty is failing due to the limits and contradictions of the false solutions being imposed. Simultaneously, an increasing number of countries are adopting food sovereignty based on agro-ecology to support small-scale farmers, thus enabling the advance of a democratic eco-socialist alternative.

Part Three of this volume draws on themes in previous chapters but focuses on democratic eco-socialist alternatives for South Africa. It positions these alternatives as a challenge to shallow conceptions of the just transition and attempts to highlight climate justice systemic alternatives that are emerging in theory, in debates and from grassroots transformative struggles. Moreover, these chapters advance a post-productivist socialism which challenges twentieth-century socialism's fixation on growth, catch-up modernisation and the development of the forces of production.

Jacklyn Cock, in chapter ten, brings into focus four crucial issues for a South African engagement with the just transition. First, the chapter distinguishes the shallow variants of the just transition as envisaged by capital. Cock's argument is simple: greening capitalism through technology, market efficiencies or even modest reforms merely reproduces a class project and does not address the systemic logic of destruction driving capitalism. Second, she revisits the discrediting of feminism, environmentalism and socialism from the standpoint of exploring alternatives to capitalism. She does this to understand the tainting of these ideologies, even within grassroots common sense, while recognising the strengths, the rethinking and the possibilities these ideologies have for a renewed democratic eco-feminist socialism. Third, she locates the renewal of these ideologies in the context of actually existing struggles. This includes the emergence of eco-feminism, a renewed socialist feminism, environmental justice struggles against racism and lessons being learned by the global Left about the limits of authoritarian, productivist and statist socialisms of the twentieth century. She seeks to find a mode of intersectionality, grounded in praxis, which can bring these new thrusts in feminism, environmentalism and socialism into the struggle for a transformative and deep just transition. In this context, she grapples critically with women's oppression, racism, environmental destruction and class. Finally, Cock argues against 'blue printing' of democratic eco-feminist socialism as part of a transformative just transition, and instead stakes out the necessity for core values to inform such a renewed ideological horizon.

In chapter eleven, Michelle Williams foregrounds the energy–democracy nexus. She locates this within the overall political economy of coal and oil, which in turn resulted in the limiting of democracy to 'carbon democracy', an elite form of democracy that limits democratic claims and labour's power. Labour's power is further attenuated with the rise of market democracy in the context of global neoliberal restructuring. This analysis is further deepened in relation to South Africa's minerals–energy complex (MEC) and how it has, under apartheid and in the neoliberal context, served to also contain labour. The mechanisms of control and discipline of labour, in relation to coal, are highlighted. Moreover, such an analysis also assists with understanding why South Africa is not taking forward a deep just transition driven by renewable energy. Instead, it is locked into a coal-driven MEC that limits the introduction of renewable energy. Williams highlights that in the South African context the championing of 'socially owned renewable energy' (public, cooperative and communitarian), a proposal advocated by metalworkers, will not only enhance and deepen democracy, but also contribute to the realisation of democratic eco-socialism as part of the deep just transition that is needed.

In chapter twelve, David Fig adds another dimension to the political economy of energy and democracy. He brings into view South Africa's nuclear energy ambitions, given that nuclear has been vaunted as a crucial techno-fix to bring down carbon emissions. Like Williams, he shows how energy choices create a 'democracy deficit'. In this case, he exposes how the opaque world of nuclear power has worked in the South African policy context. Fig traces the African National Congress's initial commitment to openness around the nuclear programme inherited from the apartheid regime, to the current highly secretive, top-down and technocratic push for nuclear. Besides tracing the development of this policy commitment, he raises the corrupt state–business nexus and wider geopolitical relations that are driving South Africa's commitment to nuclear. Most commentators and analysts agree that South Africa's nuclear programme will bankrupt the state. Massive cost overruns are an in-built feature of nuclear programmes all over the world. While the stakes are high, Fig ends on a positive note, highlighting the growing climate justice resistance to nuclear.

Chapter thirteen, by Brian Ashley, foregrounds the climate jobs systemic alternative as a crucial transformative reform in the just transition. Ashley argues that climate jobs have the potential of addressing the twin challenge of the climate crisis and high mass unemployment in South Africa. He provides a crucial analytical distinction between 'green jobs' and climate jobs. In doing this, he also locates climate jobs outside of green capitalism in the South African context. Moreover, Ashley highlights how South Africa's coal-driven energy supplier and monopoly, Eskom, is in crisis together with the entire MEC in which it is located. He views this as an opportunity to introduce climate jobs into the South African economy to enable a transition to a low-carbon economy and to break our dependence on the MEC. Drawing on the research and advocacy work of the Climate Jobs Campaign, he highlights the opportunity for at least 250 000 direct and permanent jobs to be created in manufacturing and installation, maintenance and extending the electricity grid to link the renewable energy plants. This would result in at least a twenty per cent reduction in GHG emissions. He also makes the case for expanding public transport in ways that reduce our GHG emissions and which can lead to the creation of more than 500 000 climate jobs. Ultimately, if the entire economy is placed on a low-carbon transition and energy path, the Climate Jobs Campaign believes that over three million jobs can be created as we bring down carbon emissions and build the systems necessary for a sustainable society.

Chapter fourteen, by Andrew Bennie and Athish Satgoor, situates the food question at the centre of the climate crisis. While confirming that a globalised and corporate-controlled food system is failing to feed humanity, they argue that its profit-driven logic will come short even further in the context of climate shocks such as droughts. Instead, they argue for an alternative food pathway and system based on combining two complementary systemic alternatives as part of a transformative just transition: food sovereignty and the solidarity economy. Both these alternatives are being championed by powerful anti-systemic movements, such as La Via Campesina and, in the South African context, by movements of waste pickers, the unemployed, students and small-scale farmers converging within the South African Food Sovereignty Campaign (SAFSC). Deepening democracy in food relations through defending and reclaiming the commons, in land, seeds and labour, is central to their perspective on food sovereignty and the solidarity economy. They demonstrate this empirically by highlighting the transformative practice of the SAFSC in terms of a constitutive approach to power, grassroots campaigning, popular education, shifting public discourse and fostering convergence of climate and social justice movements. Bennie and Satgoor highlight the potential for a red–green alliance in South Africa through the activism of the SAFSC and for just transitions to take place from below in local spaces.

Chapter fifteen, by Desné Masie and Patrick Bond, foregrounds a new spatial fix for capitalist accumulation in South Africa: the blue or ocean economy. This site of accumulation has come to the fore as part of South Africa's National Development Plan and the resource nationalism it promotes. Operation Phakisa, the much-vaunted blue economy initiative, envisages big and fast results. Central to this scramble is a methodology that evangelises growth and foreign direct investment, with an expected leap in economic value from R54 billion to R177 billion in twenty years, plus an additional million odd jobs added to the economy. The lab methodology underpinning Phakisa expects a two to four per cent increase in GDP, at least since 2010. Central to the commodification of ecology in this framework is the extension of the MEC to include offshore extraction of gas, oil and other minerals. Moreover, the expansion in port infrastructure envisaged is meant to boost the outward movement of commodities like coal, and increase massive imports to South Africa and beyond. This drumbeat, fastened to a fast-track methodology, has undermined the efficacy of environmental impact assessments, prompted deregulatory thrusts in key legislation and failed to appreciate serious risks. Masie and Bond expose this egregious commodifying logic and its limits in relation to the collapse of global trade, the crisis of overcapacity in global shipping and the decline in commodity prices due to overproduction. The chapter brilliantly dissects how Phakisa has produced small results, and rather slowly, with a brazen neopatrimonial agenda of ecological commodification driving it. Finally, Masie and Bond show how concrete resistance from below in localised struggles is inventing an eco-socialist response as part of the just transition.

NOTES

1   See http://www.independent.co.uk/environment/climate-change/climate-change-global-average-temperatures-break-through-1c-increase-on-pre-industrial-levels-for-a6727361.html (accessed 17 August 2017).

2   See https://www.carbonbrief.org/how-scientists-predicted-co2-would-breach-400pm-2016 (accessed 17 August 2017).

3   The Vulnerable 20 (V20) Group of countries was inaugurated on 8 October 2015, in Lima, Peru.

4   See founding communiqué of V20 at http://climateandcapitalism.com/2015/10/11/most-vulnerable-nations-form-climate-action-coalition/ (accessed 17 August 2017).

5   Obama has not even been able to secure legislation in the US Congress to support his diplomacy in the UN climate negotiations process.

6   The red–green alliance or forces refers to the strategic and programmatic unity of labour-centred movements (such as trade unions, think tanks, labour networks, parties) and ecological justice forces(including climate justice, water justice, food sovereignty) to advance deep just transitions to achieve systemic transformation.

7   There is a vast literature containing documents from the climate justice movement amplifying voices from within the movement that have made the case for mobilising mass power to deal with the climate crisis. See Angus (2010), Tokar (2010), Wall (2010), Bassey (2012), Bond (2012) and Klein (2014).

8   Foster and Clark (2016) suggest there are only three moments to the development of eco-socialist analysis: greening Marxism, retrieving and defending Marx's

ecology and thinking about ecological problems through Marxist ecology. I disagree and set out a different mapping.

9   Also note Sarkar's (1999) critique of actually existing socialism and capitalism.

10   Two other of Bahro's important books which are crucial to the development of eco-socialist thought are *Socialism and Survival* (1982) and *Building the Green Movement* (1986).

11   The edited collection by Ted Benton (1996) best captures this approach. Prominent in this approach is James O'Connor's second contradiction in capitalism which suggests that capitalism undermines the natural conditions of its existence.

12   The marriage of ecology and Marxism has not been without tension. See Pepper (1993) and Kovel (2003) for critiques of the limits of Deep Ecology.

13   See Wall (2010) for a mapping of these forces. Also see Angus (2010) for a great collection of documents written by eco-socialists within the climate justice movement.

14   V. Satgar, 'The climate is ripe for social change', *Mail & Guardian*, 17 December 2014.

REFERENCES

Angus, I. (ed.). 2010. *The Global Fight for Climate Justice: Anticapitalist Responses to Global Warming and Environmental Destruction*. Nova Scotia: Fernwood Publishing.

Bahro, R. 1978. *The Alternative in Eastern Europe*. London: Verso.

Bahro, R. 1982. *Socialism and Survival*. London: Heretic Books.

Bahro, R. 1986. *Building the Green Movement*. London: GMP Publishers.

Bassey, N. 2012. *To Cook a Continent: Destructive Extraction and the Climate Crisis in Africa*. Cape Town: Pambazuka Press.

Benton, T. 1996. *The Greening of Marxism*. New York and London: Guilford Press.

Bond, P. 2012. *Politics of Climate Change: Paralysis Above, Movement Below*. Pietermaritzburg: University of KwaZulu-Natal Press.

Burkett, P. 2014. *Marx and Nature: A Red and Green Perspective*. Chicago: Haymarket Books.

Darby, M. 2016. 'Scientists: Window for avoiding 1.5C global warming "closed"'. *Climate News*, 29 June. Accessed 17 August 2017, http://www.climatechangenews.com/2016/06/29/scientists-window-for-avoiding-1-5c-global-warming-closed/.

Drijfhout, S. 2015. 'What climate "tipping points" are – and how they could suddenly change our planet'. *The Conversation*, 9 December. Accessed 17 August 2017, https://theconversation.com/what-climate-tipping-points-are-and-how-they-could-suddenly-change-our-planet-49405.

Foster, J.B. and Clark, B. 2016. 'Marx's ecology and the Left', *Monthly Review* 68(2), http://monthlyreview.org/2016/06/01/marxs-ecology-and-the-left/.

Foster, J.B. 2000. *Marx's Ecology: Materialism and Nature*. New York: Monthly Review Press.

IPCC (Intergovernmental Panel on Climate Change). 2014. *Climate Change 2014: Synthesis Report*. Contribution of Working Groups I, II and III to the Fifth Assessment Report of the Intergovernmental Panel on Climate Change. Geneva, Switzerland: IPCC.

Klein, N. 2014. *This Changes Everything*. London and New York: Penguin Books.

Kovel, J. 2003. *The Enemy of Nature: The End of Capitalism or the End of the World*. New Delhi: Tulika Books.

Layfield, D. 2008. *Marxism and Environmental Crises*. Bury St. Edmunds: Arena Books.

Li, M. 2016. *China and the 21st Century Crisis*. London: Pluto Press.

McKibben, B. 2016. 'Recalculating the Climate Math'. *New Republic*, 22 September. Accessed 17 August 2017, https://newrepublic.com/article/136987/recalculating-climate-math.

Pepper, D. 1993. *Ecosocialism: From Deep Ecology to Social Justice*. London: Routledge.

Rogelj, J., den Elzen, M., Höhne, N., Fransen, T., Fekete, H., Winkler, H., Schaeffer, R., Sha, F., Riahi, K. and Meinshausen, M. 2016. 'Paris Agreement climate proposals need a boost to keep warming well below 2°C', *Nature*, 534: 631–639.

Sarkar, S. 1999. *Eco Socialism or Eco Capitalism? A Critical Analysis of Humanity's Fundamental Choices*. New Delhi: Orient Longman.

Shiva, V. 2015. *Who Really Feeds The World?* London: Zed Books.

Tokar, B. 2010. *Toward Climate Justice: Perspectives on the Climate Crisis and Social Change*. Porsgrunn: Communalism Press.

UNFCCC (United Nations Framework Convention on Climate Change). 2015. *Adoption of the Paris Agreement – Proposal by the President* (FCCC/CP/2015/L.9/Rev.1).

Wall, D. 2010. *The Rise of the Green Left: Inside the Worldwide Ecosocialist Movement*. London and New York: Pluto Press.

Williams, R. 1983. *Keywords: A Vocabulary of Culture and Society*. New York: Oxford University Press.

THE CLIMATE CRISIS AS CAPITALIST CRISIS

2

THE LIMITS OF CAPITALIST SOLUTIONS TO THE CLIMATE CRISIS

Dorothy Grace Guerrero

There is an increasing acceptance that capitalism is directly connected with climate change and that the apocalyptic consequences of it are already causing deaths, diseases, dislocations and destruction to ecology and people's lives, which will continue as there is no decisive measure being taken to address the climate crisis. Society's relationship with nature under extractivist capitalism follows the principles of ownership and rights of access, modes of production and consumption, the need for permanent added-value, as well as class and gender relations, all of which are associated with profit maximisation and exploitation of people and nature. It is important to emphasise that the privilege to profit, overconsume and overdiscard is reserved for a small portion of society.

The extraction of fossil fuels (oil, coal, natural gas), which is the biggest cause of climate change, enables large-scale production of goods, transportation systems and efficient distribution networks of products and services. Climate change is therefore not just an environmental issue; it is both a social and an ecological crisis. Even modern wars in the last three decades, as exemplified by the invasion of Iraq, were at least partially about access to and control of the production and distribution of oil. As the impacts of climate change intensify, free-market ideology, big business and financial actors increasingly shape the strategies and priorities in addressing it. At the same time, resistance to neoliberalism, efforts to reclaim the commons (land, water and forests, knowledge, etc.), struggles against 'development aggression' by states and corporations and the promotion of alternative models of development are being globalised.

The United Nations Framework Convention on Climate Change (UNFCCC), established in 1992, is the principal and only universal intergovernmental body to tackle climate change. Its annual high-profile Conference of the Parties (COP) is attended by 196 member states. Despite the inclusion of climate change in policies after the historic 1992 Earth Summit in Rio de Janeiro that gave birth to the UNFCCC, and after more than two decades of meetings, the total global anthropogenic greenhouse gas (GHG) emissions, which cause climate change, have continued to increase.

The scientific literature is clear – an overwhelming majority of climate scientists, over ninety-seven per cent, acknowledge that humans are the primary cause of climate change (Romm 2016). However, despite the most updated and sophisticated information and analyses available to governments now, the climate negotiations are not generating appropriate solutions that match the scale of the crisis. This is because the countries that are most affected by climate change, but have contributed the least to it, have very little say to influence climate politics due to the asymmetry of political and negotiating power between the global North and the global South. At the same time, parties to the UNFCCC do not acknowledge that the capitalist economic model they espouse and rely on is based on plunder, waste and pollution. There is very little understanding of structural conditions since climate change is not seen as a class and gender issue despite the reality that the poor, especially women, who are already feeling its brunt, are left to rely on their resilience while corporations and industries are continuing their usual destructive operations and even making profits in delaying or burying real solutions.

Given this context, it is deeply problematic that Donald Trump, the president of the richest, most powerful and influential country, as well as the biggest historical and current emitter of GHG in the world, is a climate change denialist. Trump's symbolic withdrawal from the substantially weak 2015 Paris Agreement in 2017 was expected, as it was included in his main electoral campaign promises. His appointment of fellow climate change deniers to the Environmental Protection Agency and other related offices, his executive orders reversing previous policies to allow fossil fuel giants to go full-steam ahead, and his rejection of the principle that rich countries should help developing countries cope with GHG emissions by giving them subsidies are major stumbling blocks for future climate initiatives. These moves, together with his unilateralist stance on global trade and global security, show that the United States as the linchpin of the world order is breaking down the world order.

Given the present reality of global capitalism, it is indeed a huge challenge, even seemingly utopian, to call for a revolutionary strategy of 'system change, not climate change'. However, given the challenges, stopping climate change leaves the world with no other option. It is also urgent, as avoiding climate change-related disaster will be even more difficult, more costly or even impossible if the global population does not act decisively now.

A growing number of social, environmental and climate justice networks, as well as progressive researchers, now advocate systemic change as the only way to address climate change. They propose:

- A drastic emissions reduction in historically and highly polluting countries through legally binding commitments and without passing the responsibilities to poor countries through carbon trade or other offsetting mechanisms. Emerging economies should already be more responsible now as their production and wealth increases and the rest of the world will follow based on their capacities and development needs.
- Leaving eighty per cent of currently known fossil fuel reserves under the ground and developing new socially transformative and just systems of energy production and consumption.
- Starting a shift in society's relationship with nature through building low-carbon, post-capitalist and gender-fair societies. These steps require radical transformation in the access to and management of resources and relations of production and consumption.

OUR WARMING PLANET: WHERE WE ARE NOW

The last several years have seen all climate-related records being smashed. Since average global temperature record making started in 1850, the global mean temperatures reached 1°C above pre-industrial levels for the first time in 2015 (Met Office 2016). The global levels of atmospheric carbon dioxide (CO_2) breached the 400 parts per million (ppm) average in March 2015 (NOAA 2015), substantially exceeding the generally recognised safe level of 350 ppm. Two years later, scientists at the Mauna Loa Observatory reported that CO_2 passed the 410 ppm mark in April 2017 (Geiling 2017) – something never experienced before.

The Washington-based National Academies of Sciences, Engineering and Medicine report concludes that human-caused global warming is already altering patterns of some extreme weather events (NAS 2016). Global annual GHG emissions grew to an average of one gigaton (Gt) of carbon dioxide equivalent (CO_2e) per year from 2000–2010 as compared with 0.4 Gt per year from 1970–2000 (IPCC 2014: 8).

The much-celebrated COP21 in Paris, France, in December 2015 was the eleventh Meeting of the Parties since 1994. It was clear even before it started that COP21 negotiation results would not measure up to what must be done, especially in light of the lack of progress after more than two decades of high-level climate talks. Despite the aspiration stated in the preamble to the Paris Agreement to keep the increase in the world's temperature below '2°C or not more than 1.5°C', appropriate actions are still missing. James Hansen, the esteemed former National Aeronautics and Space Administration (NASA) scientist, called by many the 'father of global climate change awareness', described the Paris Agreement as a 'fraud' and a 'real fake'.[1] Since COP15 in Copenhagen, Denmark, in 2009, many climate justice and social movements have increasingly distrusted the negotiations and the resulting agreements.

Despite the protest ban in France due to the state of emergency following several terrorist attacks in the country's capital in November 2015, tens of thousands of French and global activists demonstrated in the streets before, during and immediately after COP21 to protest what could be considered an ineffective agreement. Attended by 195 country delegations and over 150 world leaders, it is to date the largest diplomatic conference on climate change. The global People's Climate March ahead of the talks on 28 and 29 November set a new record in climate-related mobilisations. More than 600 000 marched in 175 countries around the world, including Paris, to call for a strong deal. This was bigger than the New York People's Climate March in 2014, which was also organised to put pressure on leaders attending the COP20 in Peru.

COP18 and COP19 set the trend for consolidating new markets and investment opportunities for big business in the name of climate solutions. These business-oriented and market-controlled climate policies and mechanisms differ widely from the just and sustainable solutions needed by the people and the planet.[2] The intended nationally determined contributions (INDCs) submitted by countries to the UNFCCC, even if accomplished, will together produce at least a 3°C average global temperature rise. The mechanisms to review their execution and effects and the possibility of adjustments to be done every five years are simply not enough. Of even greater concern is the lack of dramatic immediate action as it only comes into force in 2020. By that point huge quantities of additional CO_2 will have been pumped into the atmosphere, making it all but impossible to limit global warming to 2°C, let alone 1.5°C.

The challenges to democracy and development in general are increasing due to the corporate capture of UN climate processes and other policy arenas. From negotiating for binding commitments, the UNFCCC capitulated to the corporate agenda of voluntary pledges and market-based initiatives that will do more harm than good to the environment and the global climate system (Climate Space 2014). Many responses have been proposed, including Clean Development Mechanisms (CDMs), reducing emissions from deforestation and forest degradation (REDD), climate-smart agriculture and various carbon market schemes. These initiatives are false solutions that will not reduce emissions or address the social crises causing climate change, but rather allow business as usual and create corporate profits in the name of combating climate change. Moreover, such measures further increase inequality by disproportionately targeting forests, territories and lands of indigenous people and small-scale farmers. The widely embraced new concept of a 'green economy' is dangerous and is being exposed and critiqued as a reconfiguration of capitalism which will reduce nature and 'nature's services' to tradable commodities.

This means that even meeting the conservative target of a 2°C average global warming – as agreed in Copenhagen's COP15 and subsequently recommended in the Fifth Assessment Report of the Intergovernmental Panel on Climate Change (IPCC 2013, 2014), as well as by the World Bank (2012), the UN Environment Programme (UNEP 2011) and many other climate studies – will be impossible.

THE CORPORATE CAPTURE OF CLIMATE POLITICS

The climate crisis must be understood as one of the many elements of the deep crisis of capitalism, and has always been both an ecological and a social problem. Scientists have known and warned about climate change for almost 200 years. In Alice Bell's (2014) account of the history of climate change, she identifies French physicist James Fourier's work as the first study on the GHG effect in 1824 and Irish physicist John Tyndall's 1861 pioneering work in identifying the gases, including CO_2, which could change the atmosphere that protects the planet from warming and determines climate. She also accredited Swedish chemist Svante Arrhenius's study of Europe's atmosphere in 1896 as the first argument for reducing CO_2 in order to lower temperatures, as he linked warming with the burning of coal and oil and the increase of CO_2 in the atmosphere. Charles Keeling started to measure atmospheric CO_2 in 1958 and scientists noted by 1963 that it went up annually (Weart 2004). Warnings about climate change's catastrophic impacts were first raised in John Sawyer's 'Man-Made Carbon Dioxide and the "Greenhouse" Effect', published in the journal *Nature* in 1972, in which he examined the anthropogenic CO_2 GHG distribution and exponential rise. He also accurately predicted the future rate of global warming from 1972 to 2000 (Bell 2014).

Studies linking CO_2 and climate change started in the 1970s, pioneered by the UN World Meteorological Organisation (WMO). In 1988, the WMO jointly established the Intergovernmental Panel on Climate Change (IPCC) with the UN Environment Programme (UNEP). Since then, the IPCC assessment reports – five in total (1990, 1995, 2001, 2007, 2014) – have consolidated global knowledge and political consensus on climate change (IPCC 1995). A limitation of most scientific studies is presenting climate change as a problem of excessive emissions produced by humans without accounting for societal conditions.

The UN Conference on the Environment and Development (UNCED), more popularly known as the Earth Summit, in 1992 produced the UNFCCC, which entered into force on 21 March 1994. Article 2 of the UNFCCC (1992) states that its main objective is to 'stabilize greenhouse gas concentrations in the atmosphere at a level that would prevent dangerous anthropogenic interference with the climate system'. Under Article 3(1), parties should act to protect the climate system on the basis of 'common but differentiated responsibilities', with developed country parties, referred to in the UNFCCC as Annex I countries,[3] taking the lead.

The Kyoto Protocol, an international agreement negotiated under the UNFCCC, set binding targets for Annex I countries' GHG emission reductions. Its pledges are made through assigned amount units of carbon space. It has two commitment periods: from 2005 to 2012 and from 2012 to 2020. In the Lima COP20 in 2014, governments agreed to submit their INDCs for GHG emission reductions in October 2015. This is a step back, as instead of binding commitments in the spirit of the Kyoto Protocol, negotiations are now reduced to voluntary pledges. Governments can simply do what they want to do. Also, instead of limiting emission reduction to 35 Gt of CO_2e by 2030 to keep average global warming to 2°C (UNEP 2013), the INDC pledges will produce 60 Gt of CO_2e emissions by 2030, proving the ineffectiveness of the UNFCCC process.

Let us recall that the Stockholm Conference on the Human Environment in 1972 and the UNCED in 1992 both emphasised equity as the framework of global environmental politics. However, the emergence of neoliberal capitalism, pushed by the Washington Consensus and deepened by the General Agreement on Tariffs and Trade (GATT) (subsequently the World Trade Organisation [WTO]), demolished this principle. The trend towards globalisation through regulatory rules for trade was consolidated and now characterises the global trade and financial regimes that govern global politics and decision making, including climate politics. In *Climate Capitalism*, Newell and Paterson (2010) explain how the character of neoliberal capitalism has fundamentally shaped global responses to climate change and highlight the need to challenge the entrenched power of many corporations, the culture of energy use and global inequalities in energy consumption.

The Bali Action Plan, adopted at COP13 in 2007, established a framework for negotiations to create a replacement agreement for the Kyoto Protocol in 2012. Initially, it was hoped that the US would return to the Kyoto Protocol negotiating process for the first time since withdrawing from it in March 2001. To encourage the US to agree to the Kyoto Protocol, the CDM became part of the agenda. However, at the end of COP13, the CDM remained but the US stayed away from the Protocol. The CDM is a carbon-trading tool that allows polluting companies, mostly from rich and polluting countries, to purchase credit through projects, mostly in developing countries, instead of reducing their emissions.

The Bali Action Plan established a two-track process (UNFCCC and Kyoto Protocol) aimed at identifying a post-2012 global climate regime from the 2009 COP15 and the Fifth Meeting of the Parties to the Kyoto Protocol in Copenhagen. COP13 did not introduce binding commitments to reduce GHG emissions. It only started the discussions on enhanced actions on adaptation, technology development and the provision on financial resources, as well as measures against deforestation that later developed into REDD. Developing country parties agreed to a '[nationally] appropriate mitigation actions context of sustainable development, supported and enabled by technology, financing and capacity-building, in a measurable, reportable and verifiable manner' (COP13 2008: 55).

Since the COP15 in Copenhagen, more than a hundred developing countries (members of the small island states, least developed countries, African group blocs in the UN process) have called for Annex I parties to increase their emission reduction targets in the second commitment period to forty-five per cent below 1990 levels by 2020. The 2007 IPCC report earlier indicated that the Annex I parties should reduce their emissions to between twenty-five and forty per cent below 1990 levels by 2020. The Copenhagen Accord was signed by 114 parties, but was not formally adopted by the COP due to the strong disagreement of some developing countries. However, many aspects of the Copenhagen Accord were brought into the formal UNFCCC process the year after in Mexico and were adopted as part of the Cancun Agreements. These agreements state that future global warming should be limited to below 2°C (3.6° Fahrenheit) relative to the pre-industrial level. Cancun's non-binding pledges totalled fifteen per cent emission reduction by 2020.

Many developing countries were unhappy about the 2°C target in the negotiations in Copenhagen. Climate justice activists argued against this threshold too as it is more of a political target, and a distinctly ideological one, forwarded by northern interests. Feminist groups assailed the inherent idea that humans can 'master' climate change, as if the climate is a machine that humans can control and that can be turned on and off. The framework of values based on power, as well as the questions of in whose agenda or interest 2°C is acceptable, and who determines what acceptable risk is, must be revealed (Seager 2009). Feminists and climate justice activists from the global South point out that considerable ecosystem and livelihood damage is already occurring and that poor countries face greater threat due to their higher vulnerabilities and lower adaptive capacities.

Real catastrophes in the global South and in pockets of communities in the global North, such as destruction of livelihoods through floods and droughts, death and starvation, are already happening. Climate change is in fact advancing at a faster rate than predicted (Archer & Rahmstorf 2010).[4] According to the 2013 Fifth Assessment Report of the IPCC, each of the last three decades was warmer than all of the preceding decades since 1850 and the first decade of the twenty-first century was the warmest thus far. The International Energy Agency also warned that failure to reduce fossil fuel consumption would result in at least 6°C of global warming (IEA 2013). All this is already occurring at the current 0.8°C rise in the average global temperature since the Industrial Revolution; a 2°C temperature increase will be even more dangerous. Hansen and colleagues (2015) predict higher sea-level rises because of indicators that were not included before.

A report by the Climate Vulnerable Forum (2012) states that five million deaths occur annually from air pollution, hunger and disease as a result of climate change and carbon-intensive economies, and that this toll will likely rise to six million annually by 2030 if current patterns of fossil fuel use continue. More than ninety per cent of those deaths will occur in developing countries. Climate change is already costing the global economy a potential 1.6 per cent of annual output or about US$1.2 trillion a year, and this could double to 3.2 per cent by 2030 if global temperatures are allowed to rise. Even developing countries may suffer GDP loss. China could see a 2.1 per cent reduction by 2030, while India could experience a more than five per cent loss of output. According to a UN Development Programme report, global warming most threatens the poor and the unborn, the 'two constituencies with little or no voice' in governance (UNDP 2007: 13).

In 2011, parties at the COP17 in Durban, South Africa, agreed to adopt the Durban Platform for Enhanced Action. This treaty was adopted in 2015 at the twenty-first COP in Paris and will be implemented in 2020. In both Durban and Doha (COP18), parties as well as observers from civil society groups expressed grave concern that current efforts to hold global warming to below 2 or 1.5°C relative to the pre-industrial level appear inadequate. Since the 2005 COP in Montreal, Annex 1 countries have found ways to avoid deep emissions cuts and have weakened this commitment. The much-needed technology and financial transfers from rich countries to developing countries are not happening, nor are those aimed at helping the latter address the increasing impacts of climate change and supporting the costs of mitigation and adaptation.

The UN's Global Compact, which encourages the role of big business in global efforts to advance UN treaties and programmes on human and socio-economic rights and environmental protection, ushered in big corporations' influence in the thinking and outcomes of climate politics. The green economy, promoted as a new and superior development concept, also follows business thinking. UNEP's (2011) green economy report argues that the environment could be saved if environmental services were given economic value.

Climate politics, even in poor and developing countries, has yet to – or refuses to – question, challenge and problematise the key role of capital in the causes and effects of climate change. The fundamental reality that climate change affects people differently and that the poor, who contribute very little to it, are the first to suffer its impacts, was acknowledged in the principle 'common but differentiated responsibilities' in the first Earth Summit in Stockholm in 1972, long before the UNFCCC's adoption of it in its basic principle in 1992.

The powers of the WTO, international financial institutions (IFIs), trans-national corporations and other agents of neoliberal capitalism must be confronted as they move to eliminate environmental policies defined as 'barriers to trade' and to prevent governments from discriminating against polluting products through bilateral and multilateral trade negotiations. New, aggressive and comprehensive trade and investment agreements (e.g. the European Union–US Trans-Atlantic Trade and Investment Partnership [TTIP] and Trans-Pacific Partnership) that are being negotiated by governments in highly secretive and exclusive processes include an extremely dangerous element, the investor–state dispute settlement (ISDS) mechanism. Once implemented, corporations can use ISDSs to sue governments for passing laws that protect the environment but diminish corporate profits, like closing or banning polluting coal mines.

Powerful corporations, through their lobbyists, have been influencing climate negotiations. A paper prepared by Corporate Europe Observatory explains how powerful European business lobbies protect business interests, especially in COP21, through promoting the global carbon market as the solution to climate change and ensuring that climate policies do not conflict with business interests (Tansey 2015). IFIs, which historically and currently still fund climate change-inducing large-scale projects like fossil fuel development, huge hydropower schemes and those that are under CDMs, play a key role in climate finance and pushing loans to victims of climate-induced natural calamities.

Climate change will not be solved through negotiations dominated by corporate interests. The governments that are supposed to lead in climate change solutions are also the ones pushing corporate trade deals like the TTIP that will benefit the fracking industry and support big agribusiness companies that undermine the ability of farmers to adapt to climate change, as well as various free trade agreements and bilateral investment treaties.

CHANGE THE SYSTEM TO STOP CLIMATE CHANGE

Climate solutions must be appropriate to the enormity of the crisis, and must also be just and sustainable. Criticising current socio-ecological problems must not be reduced to individual consumption patterns which can be solved by individual alternative lifestyles alone. Structural, political, social and economic mechanisms shape consumption. For climate change to stop, our economic, social and environmental relations must change. A crucial element of this is acceptance of the imperative for system change, climate justice and confronting capitalism. There is now a growing understanding of the need for a paradigm shift and the need to find the politics and processes for fundamental change towards more democratic and inclusive/collective ownership and control of resources and key industrial sectors along with access to their benefits. Naomi Klein describes the climate crisis in her book *This Changes Everything* as a confrontation between capitalism and the planet. The problem is neoliberal capitalism itself, which is unsustainable and needs to be transformed into a system that does not aim for a model of infinite growth but for harmony between human beings and nature and one that meets the needs of the majority (Klein 2014).

There is a need to build a politics that is strong enough to realise that process for change, ensure its course and defend it against attacks from those that want to maintain the status quo. It is not enough just to be convinced and to want this change. The actors, institutions and processes that support the status quo are powerful and will not easily give up their privileges. A growing number of groups within the climate justice movement are now organising and mobilising to promote various principles, discussed next.

Social inequalities

Climate change is linked to social inequalities between the global North and the global South, as well as to inequalities within the global North and South, as there are people living in extreme poverty in rich countries. Similarly, the elite in poor countries have access to and control over resources and use that power to exploit people and nature in their countries.

Climate debt

According to Matthew Stilwell (2012), it is important to recognise rich countries' climate debt to poor countries, for two reasons. Firstly, historically, in the course of their development, rich countries used more than their fair share of the atmosphere, which enriched their societies and disproportionately contributed to climate change. Poor countries should not follow their growth model. Rather, due to climate change, they should instead adopt more sustainable economic activities. This will, however, significantly diminish and limit their options. Stilwell refers to this as emissions debt. Secondly, what Stilwell calls adaptation debt concerns the challenges that poor countries face as escalating losses and damages and loss of development opportunities increase. The climate debt concept was submitted to the UNFCCC by over fifty countries, including Bhutan, Bolivia, Malaysia, Micronesia, Paraguay, Sri Lanka, Venezuela and the group of least developed countries in COP14 of 2008. Rich countries' failure to sufficiently reduce their emissions, passing the responsibility of emissions reductions to poor countries through CDMs and other mechanisms, while continuing to consume far more than their fair share of fossil fuels and atmospheric space, is a recolonisation of the global South.

'Just transition' from fossil fuel

This transition must start as soon as possible since the current model of production and consumption is based on fossil fuel energy, which is ecologically destructive. There needs to be a steep decrease in extractivism, with the remaining eighty per cent of known fossil fuel reserves kept in the ground. This is more than merely transitioning to renewable energy – the process must be emancipatory and transformative and address issues of ownership and access to resources, democratic control of energy and priority of use.

Food sovereignty

A major component of food production is not foreign investments, but rather a healthy ecosystem and the capacity of small-scale farmers to continue feeding the world. The close relationship between climate change, food production and vital decisions over land use made farmers' groups like La Via Campesina link their campaign for food sovereignty with climate justice. Food sovereignty is the right of people to healthy and culturally appropriate food produced through ecologically sound and sustainable methods, and their right to define their own food and agriculture systems. It is simultaneously a political project and campaign, an alternative, a social movement and an analytical framework.

Deglobalisation

More than a decade ago, the transnational policy group Focus on the Global South proposed deglobalisation as a strategy for addressing social inequality and promoting alternatives to neoliberal globalisation. Deglobalisation rests on two pillars: deconstruction of the existing order and reconstruction of an alternative development paradigm (Bello 2002; Focus on the Global South 2003). Deglobalisation argues that we must change the framework of the political economy by protecting and prioritising domestic economies and local needs. Instead of overproducing for export, we should reorient the economy and support small, local, peasant and indigenous community farming. We should promote local production and consumption of products by reducing the free trade of goods that travel long distances and use millions of tons of CO_2.

Buen vivir, or living well

Vivir bien (Bolivia) or *buen vivir* (Ecuador) is a Spanish term that emerged in the late twentieth century to refer to the practices and/or visions of indigenous peoples of the Andean region of South America. The practice of *vivir bien/buen vivir* may differ, but regardless of particularities some common elements have been identified and developed into a concept now codified in the constitutions of Ecuador and the Plurinational State of Bolivia (Focus on the Global South 2014). *Buen vivir* is a contrast to the capitalist way of life. It sees humans as an integral part of nature and not separate from it. Humans should thus not control nature but take care of it as one would take care of one's mother, the one who has given life. The goal is harmony, not growth (Solon 2014). Without growth, the current capitalist system cannot exist.

Although challenging, we must not turn away from the tasks of reconstructing or recreating processes, or the collective effort to articulate and popularise the need for alternative systems of national and global economic and political governance. Also gaining ground is the idea that the law of nature and the processes of the ecosystem, articulated as the 'Rights of Mother Earth' (World People's Conference on Climate Change and the Rights of Mother Earth 2010), must be respected as much as we respect the principles of our rights as humans.

Given what is needed and the reality on the ground, as well as the current status of the climate negotiations, there are challenges ahead for everyone. None of the 196 negotiating countries has presented a concrete plan to meet the needed emissions reductions; none has mentioned the need to keep eighty per cent of known fossil fuel reserves in the ground. The prescriptions or alternatives described above have no government or business champions to make these vital steps happen. Rather, the systemic alternatives are being promoted by social, economic and ecological justice movements and groups that are organising, doing political and development education and solidarity building aimed at putting life and the environment first in order to build an alternative world. Neoliberal capitalism's structure and institutions have perfected the art of sustaining the status quo and the leadership of hegemonic powers, not only through their control of the policy process but, more importantly, in presenting themselves as knowledge-bearers and experts on the economy, poverty, climate change and society.

CONCLUSION

A growth-driven and market-dependent system is incompatible with environmental security. Rethinking the ways that states and societies value nature and how resources are allocated and managed must be done now by those who believe in a meaningful and productive life. The climate crisis is not just an environmental issue – it is a global social and ecological crisis requiring an overhaul of the global political and economic systems. There is no time to lose.

Linking various social justice issues with the problem of climate change, coupled with radical anti-capitalist analysis and out-of-the-box solutions favouring equity and sustainability, has great potential for bottom-up social transformation. For climate justice activists, the severity of the climate crisis reaffirms the eco-socialist argument that capitalism not only generates war, poverty and insecurity but also potentially threatens human survival in vulnerable areas. The right to development and the need for alternative development also raises class issues and the divide not only between rich and developing countries, but also between the rich and poor within countries. Solving the climate crisis affects all aspects of society – the economy, technology, trade, equity, ethics, security, as well as relations within and between countries.

The only alternative is to resist the decapitating grip of exploitative capitalism and to take on the responsibility of educating oneself and being a conscious political subject, organising, mobilising, forging unities and exposing the false solutions peddled by those who created the crisis in the first place. The work of questioning reality and concepts, asking who wins and who loses in various processes and who gains from injustices, is a key component of building alternatives. It is a complex and challenging task, and not one that can be comfortably executed. It is a task where expansion and forging of new alliances and new unities beyond the usual partners is needed.

In the age of Trump, Brexit and the rise of new authoritarian/far-right politics, the phenomenon of far-right populism or extreme right-wing politics that promotes aggressive nationalism, racism, patriarchy, authoritarianism and militarism is gripping developed and developing countries alike. Various movements in the Left are already in a dangerous moment – many of our strategies as progressive organisations and movements are no longer working as effectively as we had hoped in the face of the intensified power of capital, the impunity and greed of corporations and the callousness of governments in terms of the needs of the poor majority.

Recent developments – such as the re-emergence of mass movement politics that is energising new politics in Greece, Spain and Portugal; the resistance that impeached Park Geun-hye in South Korea; the daily resistance against Trump's policies in the US; and the inspiring developments in UK politics that saw a Labour Party surge in the recent snap election – are hopeful reminders that there is always resistance and organising in the midst of seemingly chaotic political situations. Those energies should be organised sustainably to push for alternative systems of local, national and global economic governance that respect the diversity that exists in society and that ensure ecological equilibrium. More than ever, what needs to be globalised is the principle of reciprocal solidarity, the struggle for decommodification and collective action against all the bad solutions being presented as a way out of the economic and ecological crises.

NOTES

1   O. Milman, 'James Hansen, father of climate change awareness, calls Paris talks "a fraud"', *The Guardian*, 12 December 2015.

2   D.G. Guerrero, 'Time to take power away from the polluters', *The Bangkok Post*, 19 December 2014, http://www.bangkokpost.com/opinion/opinion/450770/time-to-take-the-power-away-from-the-polluters (accessed 20 August 2017).

3   These countries are Australia, all members of the European Union, Belarus, Croatia, Iceland, Kazakhstan, Norway, Switzerland and Ukraine.

4   See also A.A. Costa, 'Haiyan/Yolanda: Inside each new-born violent storm is the DNA of the fossil fuel industry and capitalism', *International Viewpoint*, 21 November 2013, http://www.internationalviewpoint.org/spip.php?article3183 (accessed 17 August 2017).

REFERENCES

Archer, D. and Rahmstorf, S. 2010. *The Climate Crisis: An Introductory Guide to Climate Change*. Cambridge: Cambridge University Press.

Bell, A. 2014. 'A very short history of climate change'. *Road to Paris: Science for Smart Policy*. Accessed 17 August 2017, http://roadtoparis.info/2014/09/05/history-climate-change-research.

Bello, W. 2002. *Deglobalisation: Ideas for a New World Economy*. London and New York: Zed Books.

Climate Space. 2014. 'Mobilise and organize to stop and prevent planet fever!' Statement of the Climate Space for the Climate March and Global Mobilisations, 19–23 September. Accessed 17 August 2017, https://climatespace2013.wordpress.com/2014/09/16/mobilize-and-organize-to-stop-and-prevent-planet-fever/.

Climate Vulnerable Forum. 2012. 'Climate vulnerability monitor, 2nd edition: A guide to the cold calculus of a hot planet'. Accessed 17 August 2017, http://daraint.org/climate-vulnerability-monitor/climate-vulnerability-monitor-2012/report/.

COP13. 2008. Report of the Conference of the Parties (COP) on its thirteenth session, held in Bali from 3 to 15 December 2007. Addendum. Part Two: Action taken by the Conference of the Parties at its thirteenth session. Geneva, Switzerland: United Nations Office. Reference: FCCC/CP/2007/6/Add.1.

Focus on the Global South. 2003. *Programme Plan 2003–2005*. Bangkok: Focus on the Global South.

Focus on the Global South. 2014. *From Latin America to Asia: Learning from our roots – a conversation on Vivir Bien*. Manila and Bangkok: Focus on the Global South.

Geiling, N. 2017. 'The Earth just reached a CO2 level not seen in 3 million years'. *Think Progress*, 21 April. Accessed 17 August 2017, https://thinkprogress.org/410-ppm-carbon-dioxide-atmosphere-71aa17fef076.

Hansen, J., Satom, M., Hearty, P., Ruedy, R., Kelley, M., Masson-Delmotte, V., Russell, G., Tselioudis, G., Cao, J., Rignot, E., Velicogna, I., Kandiano, E., von Schuckmann, K., Kharecha, P., Legrande, A.N., Bauer, M. and Lo, K-W. 2015. 'Ice melt, sea level rise and superstorms: evidence from paleoclimate data, climate modeling, and modern observations that 2 °C global warming is highly dangerous'. Atmospheric, Chemistry and Physics Discussion 15, 20059–20179. Accessed 17 August 2017, http://www.atmos-chem-phys-discuss.net/15/20059/2015/acpd-15-20059-2015.pdf.

IEA (International Energy Agency). 2013. 'How the IEA says we can avoid six degrees of warming – In three graphs'. *Carbon Brief*, 12 November. Accessed 18 August 2017, http://www.carbonbrief.org/blog/2013/11/three-graphs-showing-how-the-iea-says-we-can-avoid-six-degrees-warming/.

IPCC (Intergovernmental Panel on Climate Change). 1995. *Climate Change 1995: A Report of the Intergovernmental Panel on Climate Change*. Cambridge: Cambridge University Press.

IPCC. 2013. 'Summary for policy makers'. In *Climate Change 2013: The Physical Science Basis*. Working Group I Contribution to the Fifth Assessment Report of the Intergovernmental Panel on Climate Change. Cambridge: Cambridge University Press, pp. 3–29.

IPCC. 2014. 'Summary for policymakers'. In *Climate Change 2014: Mitigation of Climate Change*. Working Group III Contribution to the Fifth Assessment Report of the Intergovernmental Panel on Climate Change. Cambridge: Cambridge University Press, pp. 1–30.

Klein, N. 2014. *This Changes Everything: Capitalism vs the Climate*. New York: Simon & Schuster.

Met Office. 2016. 2015: 'The warmest year on record, say scientists'. Accessed 18 August 2017, http://www.metoffice.gov.uk/news/releases/2016/2015-global-temperature.

NAS (National Academies of Sciences, Engineering, and Medicine). 2016. *Attribution of Extreme Weather Events in the Context of Climate Change*. Washington, DC: The National Academic Press.

Newell, P. and Paterson, M. 2010. *Climate Capitalism: Global Warming and the Transformation of the Global Economy*. Cambridge: Cambridge University Press.
NOAA (National Oceanic and Atmospheric Administration). 2015. 'Greenhouse gas benchmark reached'. Accessed 18 August 2017, http://research.noaa.gov/News/NewsArchive/LatestNews/TabId/684/ArtMID/1768/ArticleID/11153/Greenhouse-gas-benchmark-reached-.aspx.
Romm, J. 2016. 'One fact about climate change that's worth repeating'. *Think Progress*, 6 April. Accessed 18 August 2017, https://thinkprogress.org/one-fact-about-climate-change-thats-worth-repeating-39ffa04bdf0e/.
Sawyer, J. 1972. 'Man-made carbon dioxide and the "greenhouse" effect', *Nature*, 239: 23–26, doi:10.1038/239023a0.
Seager, J. 2009. 'Death by degrees: Taking a feminist hard look at the 2°C climate policy', *Women, Gender and Research*, 34: 11–20.
Solon, P. 2014. 'Notes for the debate: Vivir Bien/Buen Vivir'. *Systemic Alternatives*. Accessed 18 August 2017, http://systemicalternatives.org/2014/07/30/1099/.
Stilwell, M. 2012. 'Climate debt: A primer'. In *Development Dialogue: Climate, Development and Equity*, edited by Niclas Hällström. Uppsala: Dag Hammarskjöld Foundation and the What Next Forum, pp. 41–46.
Tansey, R. 2015. 'Dirty hands on dirty deals: TTIP and COP21 shaped by same big business interests'. *Corporate Europe Observatory*, 21 October. Accessed 18 August 2017, http://corporateeurope.org/environment/2015/10/dirty-hands-dirty-deals.
UNDP (United Nations Development Programme). 2007. 'Human Development Report 2007/2008: Fighting climate change: Human solidarity in a divided world'. Accessed 18 August 2017, http://hdr.undp.org/sites/default/files/reports/268/hdr_20072008_en_complete.pdf.
UNEP (United Nations Environment Programme). 2011. 'Towards a green economy: Pathways to sustainable development and poverty eradication – a synthesis for policy makers'. Accessed 18 August 2017, https://sustainabledevelopment.un.org/content/documents/126GER_synthesis_en.pdf.
UNEP. 2013. 'The emissions gap report 2013: A UNEP synthesis report'. Accessed 18 August 2017, http://www.unep.org/sites/default/files/EGR2013/EmissionsGapReport_2013_high-res.pdf.
UNFCCC (United Nations Framework Convention on Climate Change). 1992. 'United Nations framework convention on climate change'. Accessed 18 August 2017, http://unfccc.int/resource/docs/convkp/conveng.pdf.
Weart, S.R. 2004. *The Discovery of Global Warming*. Cambridge, MA: Harvard University Press.
World Bank. 2012. 'Turn down the heat: Why a 4°C warmer world must be avoided'. Accessed 18 August 2017, http://documents.worldbank.org/curated/en/865571468149107611/pdf/NonAsciiFileName0.pdf.
World People's Conference on Climate Change and the Rights of Mother Earth. 2010. 'People's agreement of Cochabamba'. Accessed 17 August 2017, http://pwccc.wordpress.com/2010/04/24/peoples-agreement/.

3

THE ANTHROPOCENE AND IMPERIAL ECOCIDE: PROSPECTS FOR JUST TRANSITIONS

Vishwas Satgar

With about 200 000 years of modern human existence we are now a geological force shaping, determining and disrupting the Earth's bio-physical system. The scientific Anthropocene discourse and research agenda confirms this. This is a fundamental and profound scientific insight, which cannot be ignored. It is most stark and dangerous in relation to the Earth's carbon cycle and human-generated carbon emissions. We are now heating the planet at levels that take us beyond the limited variability and stability we have experienced over the past 11 000 years in the geological period known as the Holocene.

At the same time, an official discourse around the Anthropocene has evolved, with both scientific and popular elements, within and around United Nations (UN)-led climate negotiations. Within the multilateral negotiations on the climate crisis, not only is the ideological discourse on the crisis grounded in green neoliberalism and techno-fixes, such as geo-engineering but, as importantly, it is also conjoined to the popular rendering of the notion of the Anthropocene as the 'Human Age'. As a result, the Intergovernmental Panel on Climate Change (IPCC) in its fourth and more recent fifth report affirmed the notion of 'human-induced climate change'. This has become part of global common sense and mainstream understandings of how we should think about the worsening climate crisis. This chapter seeks to show that this politically constructed discourse is not just part of a scientific and technocratic approach to managing a deeply flawed green neoliberal consensus within the UN-led Conference of the Parties (COP) negotiation process, but is actually an ideological discourse with serious consequences for how we understand the contemporary climate crisis. Simply put, the official Anthropocene-centred approach to the climate crisis suggests that it has to be explained as a human problem for which we are all equally responsible. This chapter engages critically with the ideological discourse and theory of the Anthropocene from a Marxist ecology perspective. Through this engagement, the chapter seeks to show the limits and ideological pitfalls of the official Anthropocene-centred understanding of the climate crisis. This is not, however, about rejecting the science of climate change or the scientific discourse on the Anthropocene as it relates to Earth's systems in general.

The chapter first sets out the origins and construction of the Anthropocene-centred approach to the climate crisis, showing how it has been constructed as a scientific and popular mainstream explanation for the crisis. Second, the chapter briefly locates current Marxist approaches and engagements with the Anthropocene ideological discourse. Two broad approaches are identified. This provides for a transition into the critique offered by this chapter from a Marxist ecology perspective. Third, the chapter scrutinises the official Anthropocene ideological discourse in its assumptions and understandings of the relationship between the climate crisis and the way historical capitalism has worked. In particular, the chapter demonstrates how the Anthropocene-centred discourse lets capitalism off the hook by lacking a historical materialist understanding of the political economy of the climate crisis. An Anthropocene-centred discourse is blind to the power wielded by capitalism as a historical imperial system that has devastated and destroyed planetary ecosystems, involving human and non-human life forms, since its origins. Moreover, it does not appreciate the extent to which the structural and political power of capital has made it the main geological force on planet Earth. As a result, by failing to realise that the climate crisis is a product of, and induced by, capitalism, this discourse provides a warrant to affirm solutions that reproduce the same capitalist system and imperial logic that destroys life on the planet. Moreover, besides being functional to capitalist interests, an Anthropocene-centred approach affirms a neo-Malthusian racism in relation to the climate crisis. It blames the most

THE ANTHROPOCENE AND IMPERIAL ECOCIDE: PROSPECTS FOR JUST TRANSITIONS

populous countries and the darker nations for the climate crisis, including Africa, while failing to appreciate the disproportionate impacts on particularly black working-class and peasant women in Africa. In this sense it also reinforces white male domination.

Finally, the chapter concludes with a reflection on the imperative for a counterhegemonic politics that sustains life. It argues for 'just transitions', championed from below in different societies, based on an appreciation of necessary historical conditions to enable class and popular struggle to ensure we survive the climate crisis and, ultimately, end imperial ecocide.

THE OFFICIAL ANTHROPOCENE DISCOURSE AND THE CLIMATE CRISIS

The idea of the Anthropocene has its origins in a short essay written by Paul Crutzen, a Nobel Prize-winning chemist for his joint work on the ozone depletion challenge. In 2002, in the prestigious journal *Nature*, he published an article entitled 'Geology of Mankind'. In this article Crutzen (2002: 23) argues:

> For the past three centuries, the effects of humans on the global environment have escalated. Because of these anthropogenic emissions of carbon dioxide, global climate may depart significantly from natural behaviour for many millennia to come. It seems appropriate to assign the term 'Anthropocene' to the present, in many ways human-dominated, geological epoch, supplementing the Holocene – the warm period of the past 10–12 millennia. The Anthropocene could be said to have started in the latter part of the eighteenth century, when analyses of air trapped in polar ice showed the beginning of growing global concentrations of carbon dioxide and methane.

Moreover, in the article Crutzen also draws attention to some of the following major consequences of human activity:

- Human population explosion has contributed to increases in per capita exploitation of the Earth's resources;
- Between thirty and fifty per cent of the land surface area is exploited by humans;

49

- Tropical rain forests are being destroyed at a fast pace, increasing carbon emissions and species extinction;
- Fisheries are depleting the oceans' fish stocks;
- More nitrogen fertiliser is used in agriculture than in most terrestrial ecosystems;
- Fossil fuel burning and agriculture have caused substantial increases in the concentrations of greenhouse gases (carbon dioxide by thirty per cent and methane by more than a hundred per cent), reaching their highest levels over the past 400 millennia, with more to follow.

However, the twist is twofold in Crutzen's article. First, he argues that all of this is the result of only twenty-five per cent of the world's population. So the problem is population growth, not the capitalist system. Second, the solution to all this lies in geo-engineering. Thus, scientists and engineers are bestowed with the task of saving humanity from itself and the people have no role in all of this. For Crutzen, the enlightened elite has to rescue humanity.

Crutzen's theorising of the Anthropocene as a geological concept, and ultimately scientific explanation of the climate crisis, suggests that all humans are responsible for the destruction inflicted on nature, but more specifically on planetary ecosystems and the conditions that sustain life. We are all equally culpable. At the same time, there is a neo-Malthusian emphasis on population growth as the underlying driver. Since 2002, his idea of the Anthropocene and human-centred causality has made its way into various studies and scientific disciplines attempting to explain climate change and its impacts. For example, in a leading study on ocean acidification, the authors conclude:

> It is the rate of CO_2 [carbon dioxide] release that makes the current great experiment so geologically unusual and quite probably unprecedented in Earth history. Indeed, much of industrialisation and economic activity revolves around energy generated from fossil fuels. In other words much of humanity is, in effect, engaged in a collective and deliberate effort to transfer carbon from geological reservoirs to the atmosphere as CO_2. (Kump, Bralower & Ridgewell 2009: 105)[1]

According to this perspective, all of humanity is not part of the intensive fossil fuel use of developed economies and does not share equally in the wealth accumulated under capitalism; nonetheless, all human beings are responsible for its climate effects. Taking forward a generic human-based causality for the tragedy of the commons and the climate crisis has also spurred on a rethink in geology itself. In this regard, a leading geologist, Jan Zalasiewicz, has opened a debate in geology and has gone further to take forward the case for the Anthropocene to the International Commission on Stratigraphy, the group responsible for maintaining the Earth's history (Kolbert 2014).[2] In South Africa, on 29 August 2016, the Commission officially adopted the Anthropocene as a new geological epoch within the Earth's history, subject to scientific markers of this period being verified.

Whether the Anthropocene is officially recognised in geology or not is unimportant, as it has already gained traction within the scientific research agenda on climate change and its impacts, but also within various disciplines. This has ensured that an Anthropocene-centred discourse has found its way into the official IPCC rhetoric and technical language. In 2007, the fourth IPCC report unequivocally affirmed that 'human induced climate change' is a scientific fact; hence humans are responsible for climate change. Moreover, in the fifth report the idea of Anthropogenic effects runs throughout its framing discourse and there is an invented terminology at work that refers to 'human influence on the climate system', 'Anthropogenic greenhouse gas emissions', 'Anthropogenic forcings', 'total human induced warming' 'population growth' and so on (IPCC 2014). In effect, the main causal factor in both scientific and technocratic terms is all of humanity, including population growth.

Allied to this Anthropocene-centred ideological thrust within the IPCC is the rapid growth of a popular literature by award-winning natural science writers, naturalists and journalists. The diffusion of the official ideology of the Anthropocene and human-centred causal explanations for the climate crisis has crossed over from scientific publications into popular culture and is now an organising theme in various books and literatures. This chapter concentrates on the assumptions and perspectives emerging from three of these books in the global mainstream: the Pulitzer Prize-winning book and *New York Times* bestseller *The Sixth Extinction* (2014) by Elizabeth Kolbert; *The God Species: How the Planet Can Survive the Age of Humans* (2011) by Mark Lynas, winner of the Royal Society Prize for Science Books; and *The Human Age: The World Shaped by Us* (2014) by Diane Ackerman, one of America's acclaimed natural history writers. What follows is a critique of the Anthropocene-centred approach to the climate crisis of the IPCC and this popular literature from a Marxist ecology perspective. This critique is about unsettling official Anthropocene discourses within UN processes and their diffusion by various authoritative intellectual voices within global discourse. This does not mean the Anthropocene as discourse is rejected, but rather that it is contested and reframed as part of this encounter.

ANTHROPOCENE DISCOURSE AND MARXIST CRITIQUE

There are two dominant Marxist approaches to the Anthropocene discourse. Jason Moore's (2015, 2016) work advances a critique of the Anthropocene and supplants it with the notion of the Capitalocene. There are four parts to his engagement with the notion of the Anthropocene. First, he critiques the popular Anthropocene discourse and avoids the biophysical scientific discourse. In doing this, he places capital, power and nature at the centre of his analysis and his understanding of world ecology. From this perspective, he argues that capital has organised nature, including human beings. We are at the point where capitalism *in nature* is also about the coeval or co-creation of nature. Second, he takes periodisation of history seriously. Rather than embracing the Industrial Revolution as the critical turning point in the human–nature relationship, he argues instead for a rethink of the mercantile origins of capitalism. He maintains that the Columbian project (1492) involving the conquest of the Americas, together with European rationalist thought and a disposition to conquer nature, laid the basis for the Capitalocene. This was given further impetus with the slave trade and the development of legal and cultural conditions. His historical narrative is far from being trapped in economic reductionism. Third, he argues that historical capitalism has been about appropriating multiple natures at a low cost. This has implications for the oppression of women and races, through colonialism. He argues that women, indigenous people and Africans were expelled from humanity in this process. Ultimately, while value is created in the cash nexus of capitalism, it uses extra economic means and strategies to extract from cheap nature. This is central to the history of capitalism. There are four cheap natures: labour, food, energy and raw materials. In this process, work and energy are transformed into value and the preconditions for the Industrial Revolution are put in place. In short, the endless accumulation of capital and the commodification of the Earth's resources go together since the beginnings of mercantile capitalism. Finally, Moore argues that cheap nature has come to an end. Costs are increasing for labour, food, fossil fuels and raw materials. Neoliberalism's ecological surplus is threatened and all of this feeds into the crises of the Capitalocene rather than the Anthropocene.

The other prominent Marxist view on the Anthropocene is that of Ian Angus.[3] He draws licence for his position from Marx's and Engels's preoccupation with scientific thought in the nineteenth century. His intervention is about ensuring socialists understand the Anthropocene and Earth scientists understand ecological Marxism. There are three crucial parts to his engagement with Anthropocene discourse. First, he locates historical antecedents for the concept but affirms its emergence in contemporary scientific discourse in the early 2000s. He dismisses popular usages of the concept, particularly misappropriations, as either a marker for a particular version of 'modern times' or a modest change by humans to an ecosystem, or anthropocentric meanings which suggest humans control nature.

Second, he recognises that the category of the Anthropocene has evolved out of scientific enquiry to understand the impact of humans on the Earth's biophysical system. It is in essence an object of study today to clarify how humans have and are disrupting the Earth's biophysical system. He follows and draws on the latest Earth system science about this scale and scope of disruption engendered by human activity. Put differently, this is the crux of the concept of the scientific Anthropocene and its usage that he embraces. Third, and deriving from his understanding of the science of the Anthropocene, he argues that human disruption of the Earth system is unprecedented and with largely unpredictable consequences. The geophysical impacts of humans have inaugurated a new geological era (now acknowledged by geologists) which takes us beyond the operating range of the Earth that existed during the Holocene, after the last ice age. The Holocene began around 11 000 years ago, with limited and stable climate variability, which created conditions for human civilisations to emerge, including the neolithic agricultural revolution. Today, human-driven changes and disruptions of the Earth's systems, like the carbon cycle, have placed us in a no-analogue state. The great acceleration of carbon emissions from the mid-twentieth century inaugurated the Anthropocene. It is a global emergency. As a species that has been in existence for about 200 000 years, we have started changing Earth system conditions. This places everything in peril and requires a global emergency response. For Angus, this means building an eco-socialist society based on human solidarity, and through a powerful people's movement championing system change.

While each of these perspectives enriches a Marxist approach to the Anthropocene as a socio-political category, they are not exhaustive perspectives and neither do they provide a finished critique. What follows contributes to the deepening of the Marxist ecology critique of what is generally a scientific geophysical category and condition within official Anthropocene discourse. This is not about rejecting the scientific basis for Anthropocene discourse that affirms human disruption of the Earth's systems, but rather about further challenging the socio-political thrust of the concept as it diffuses through official Anthropocene discourse, including popular literature. Put more sharply, this chapter provides another set of challenges to official Anthropocene discourse and its popular valences as it relates to providing social explanations for the climate crisis.

DEEPENING MARXIST ECOLOGY CRITIQUE: THE ANTHROPOCENE AND THE LOGIC OF IMPERIAL ECOCIDE

US-led imperial ecocide

The first major assumption and problem shared by the growing official Anthropocene literature and viewpoint is that capitalism, as a social and historical system, is unimportant in understanding the climate crisis. Hence, it fails to bring into view the internal logic of capitalist accumulation and the imperialist tendency towards expansion, conflict and ecological destruction inherent to capitalism. As a result, the Anthropocene view is superficial and selective in its historical underpinnings and in its understanding of how capitalism has been made over time and has worked to conquer nature. The IPCC affirms merely 150 years of Anthropogenic emissions (from about 1850 to 2011), coinciding with the emergence of the Industrial Revolution (IPCC 2014). This, it is argued, is the period over which humans have been increasing carbon concentrations in the atmosphere and inducing climate change. In the ideological frame of the IPCC, this is now merely a technical and scientific fact. In *The Sixth Extinction*, Elizabeth Kolbert compares the climate crisis to five other major extinctions that wiped out various species, habitats and mega fauna within the span of deep geological time (over a period of 500 million years). However, by way of analogy, Kolbert seems to suggest the Anthropocene has to be understood as a period of catastrophism and ultimately another dramatic geological period – but induced by humans. According to Kolbert (2014: 94),

> what is sometimes labelled neocatastrophism, but is mostly nowadays just
> regarded as standard geology, holds that conditions on earth change only

very slowly, except when they don't. In this sense the reigning paradigm is neither Cuvierian nor Darwinian but combines key elements of both – 'long periods of boredom interrupted occasionally by panic.' Though rare, these moments of panic are disproportionately important. They determine the pattern of extinction, which is to say, the pattern of life.

From the standpoint of Marxist ecology, the official Anthropocene viewpoint (scientific and popular) is misleading to say the least, but is also deeply problematic in how it seeks to explain the climate crisis. For starters, not all humans are creating the catastrophe of the climate crisis. Over the past 500 years, capitalism has been through three phases of historical development: mercantile accumulation (1400s to 1800s), monopoly industrial accumulation (1750 until 1980) and transnational techno-financial accumulation (1973 until the present) (Satgar 2015). In each of these phases, it has required and ensured that imperial forms of domination facilitate the process of accumulation. Central to the logic of imperial domination has been the tendency towards ecocide, that is, the destruction of conditions that sustain life such as ecosystems, the commons, as well as the destruction of actual human and non-human life forms, to ensure capitalist expansion. Ecocide is the barbaric dimension of capitalism that has existed since the beginning and is now bringing about the sixth extinction of human and non-human species at an unprecedented rate. The idea of imperial ecocide fits into Marxist ecology in three ways.

First, it has to be located in Marx's understanding of the origins of capitalism, as a process of primitive accumulation. Marx explained and understood primitive accumulation as the necessary condition for the emergence of capitalism and the prior acquisition of capital for accumulation. In Volume 1 of *Capital*, his notion of primitive accumulation and the originary moment of capitalism affirms the existence of three dynamics: (i) the dispossession and separation of the peasantry from the commons and the means of production; (ii) the creation of pauperised pools of 'wage labourer' for factories; and (iii) an international dimension of conquest, pillage, plunder, genocide and destruction that has concentrated capital in the heartlands. In the same volume, Marx (1967: 915) says:

> The discovery of gold and silver in America, the extirpation, enslavement and entombment in mines of the indigenous population of that continent, the beginnings of the conquest and plunder of India, and

the conversion of Africa into a preserve for the commercial hunting of blackskins, are all things which characterize the dawn of the era of capitalist production. These idyllic proceedings are the chief moments of primitive accumulation.

However, as David Harvey (2003) points out, this dimension of capitalism has continued beyond the beginnings of capitalism and is even with us in the present through a process of accumulation through dispossession. This has implications for the reproduction of wage labour and the commons. Put differently, imperial ecocide prevails in the process of accumulation through dispossession; it is a historical, relational and contemporary material dimension.

Second, as John Bellamy Foster (2000) reminds us, Marx has been very conscious of the ecological contradictions of capitalism and the metabolic rift induced by capital. This started out with degradation of soils and the further alienation of land in the context of intensive industrial farming, but has also separated humans from themselves and from nature and fostered a schism between town and country. In contemporary terms, globalised food systems and fossil fuel-driven energy systems express this contradiction and logic starkly. This rift has been intensifying with the international expansion of capital. The metabolic rift is directly linked to imperial ecocide and its attempts to secure the expansion of capital at various spatial scales.

Third, imperial ecocide as a dimension of primitive accumulation and the metabolic rift has also taken on different temporal forms. Put differently, the destructive logic of capitalist expansion and imperialism has not only been about economic, military, political and geopolitical domination, but also about ecosystem destruction, the destruction of biodiversity, annihilating various human and non-human species for resources and ultimately conquering nature, during different historical phases of accumulation. Imperial ecocide has expressed itself through different historical forms. In this regard, imperial ecocide has been integral to partitioning the world into enslaved land zones during mercantile capitalism, including genocidal violence against indigenous peoples, dehumanising lives through slavery, the mass destruction of species through the fur trade, mass slaughter of North American bison and commercial whaling (Broswimmer 2002). More recently, imperial ecocide led by the US imperial state has taken on industrial characteristics as it has been tested in modern warfare. This has ranged from developing chemical weapons, like Agent Orange, and testing them in war zones like Vietnam, to the development of pesticide industries to support large-scale mechanised agriculture (Zierler 2011). Ultimately, the logic of imperial ecocide expressed through US imperial supremacy has its own historical specificity.

While grounded in the practices of imperial ecocide that are part and parcel of the logic and history of capitalism, US imperial ecocide is modern and violent in ways that are unprecedented. In this regard, the failure, for the past twenty years, by the US-led bloc to ensure a climate deal that addresses the systemic roots of the climate crisis is extremely telling, given that the climate crisis is worsening. Instead, the market-centred solutions it supports in the UN process, the Trump administration's climate denialism and growing preparedness of its military–industrial complex for abrupt climate change merely affirm that we are dealing with the destructive logic of US-led ecocide (see Guerrero in this volume). The US will sacrifice most of the human race and probably most life forms to defend an obsolete and ecocidal capitalism. In short, the US and its allies are at the vanguard of bringing about the sixth extinction, by preserving the destructive logic of globalised accumulation and expanded reproduction, centred on transnational capital. Capitalism has been destroying human and non-human life for the past 500 years of its existence, from the time of militarised mercantile accumulation, and not just for the past 150 years in which carbon has been emitted. The only difference is that this time the logic of imperial ecocide endangers every living creature and zone of life, including the imperial heartlands. In short, not all human beings are destroying the biosphere or inducing the climate crisis.

Capital as a geological force inducing the climate crisis

Despite the limits and weakness of the UN-led multilateral process on the climate crisis, it affirmed through the Kyoto Protocol the need for Annexure A countries, the industrialised countries, to lead the way in cutting carbon emissions as part of affirming the principle of 'common but differentiated responsibilities'. The anthropogenic-centred discourse in the IPCC's (2007, 2014) fourth and fifth reports is a shift away from this. Instead, the primary agential force causing the climate crisis, and responsible for it, is human beings in general. Particularly reading the fifth IPCC report through its anthropogenic discourse suggests that humans in general are also responsible for the systemic causes such as economic growth and population expansion (IPCC 2014). In short, while there is primary scientific causality between greenhouse gases and climate change, there is another level of social causality and that is the human factor, extricated from social relations. This assertion and assumption – that humans in general are responsible for climate change and are the geological force shaping the biophysical world – is flawed from a class-based perspective.

The ideological discourse that grounds this outside the IPCC is a modernising green environmentalism both concerned about human impacts on the environment but at the same time deeply romantic about the existing capitalist world, which is accepted *a priori* as progressive development, and anthropocentric about our social agency as a species. For Mark Lynas (2011), we are the 'God Species': we have conquered the Earth and all life forms on it; we can create and destroy life and so we can also determine our own fate. For Ackerman in her poetic narration of the Human Age, we are best understood when reflecting on our planet from outer space. In her reflections on the 'Blue Marble' photograph of the whole Earth floating in space, taken by the crew of Apollo 17 on 7 December 1972, Ackerman (2014: 18) has this to say:

> Released during a time of growing environmental concern, it became an emblem of global consciousness, the most widely distributed photo in human history. It gave us an image to float in the lagoon of the mind's eye. It helped us embrace something too immense to focus on as a single intricately known and intricately unknown organism. Now we could see Earth in one eye-gulp, the way we gazed on a loved one. We paste the image into our *Homo sapiens* family album. Here was a view of every friend, every loved one and acquaintance, every path ever travelled, all together in one place ... As the ultimate group portrait, it helped us understand our global kinship and cosmic address. It proclaimed our shared destiny.

In this one paragraph, Ackerman clarifies a humanism at work which seeks unity and common purpose to save the planet, yet is blind to power relations in a class-divided world. It is this kind of humanism that unintentionally reproduces the power of capital, as it is depoliticising. Kolbert, in *The Sixth Extinction*, evokes humans as a geological force to underline our destructive power. For example, she refers to the causal factor behind the high risk of extinction of Sumatran orangutans in this way:

> In this case, the threat is more peace than violence, most of the remaining orangutans live in the province of Aceh, where a recent end to decades of political unrest has led to a surge in logging, both legal and not.

> One of the many unintended consequences of the Anthropocene has
> been the pruning of our family tree. (Kolbert 2014: 254)

Again it is not about the political economy and the specificity of the social
forces destroying the habitat of the Sumatran orangutans, but us as humans in
general. The human race is to blame for every act of environmental degradation, risk to species and the climate crisis. This is a bit too overgeneralised and
exaggerated and not nuanced enough from the standpoint of political economy
and class analysis, central to Marxist ecology. In this regard, there are three
important historical materialist realities and ecological contradictions of capitalism that the official Anthropocene discourse does not take into account.

First, the assumption of endless accumulation central to the logic of capitalism has been legitimated by conferring on capital a licence of supremacy over
nature. This has ensured that since capitalism's inception, nature has been a site
of accumulation for capital (Bellamy Foster 1999). This is the metabolic rift as
ecological contradiction. Yet resources are limited and non-human nature also
has limits. Today all the major biophysical resources, from water and minerals to
fossil fuels, are commodified, owned and controlled by capital (Ridgeway 2004).
In the phase of transnational techno-financial accumulation, financialisation
has intensified the commodification of nature, including its sinks, services and
biotic resources. Extractivism, including unconventional hydrocarbons from
shale gas and oil, tar sands and deep-water drilling, are all caught in the vice
grip of this logic and its ecocidal consequences. At the same time, the Earth's
biophysical limits are showing signs of overshoot and stress. This includes biodiversity loss, climate change, the nitrogen cycle, land system change, global fresh
water use, ocean acidification and stratospheric ozone depletion (Lynas 2011).

Second, capitalist exploitation extends beyond workers and includes nature.
Martin O'Connor (1994: 8) refers to this process generically as 'capital's conditions of production', which is its mechanisms to ensure degradation of human
and non-human nature. This means long working hours together with externalising costs of production through pollution, as well as stealing 'the free gifts
of nature'.[4] At a more concrete level, with globalised accumulation, exploitation
rates have increased and so has unemployment, which also keeps wages low
(see Marais in this volume). At the same time, the degradation and destruction
of habitats, ecosystems and land has continued apace. The increase of carbon
emissions over the past three decades, with carbon concentration sitting at 410
parts per million (ppm) (way past the 350 ppm required to remain within the

safe zone of the climate boundary) and increasing rapidly, places capital at the centre of causing the climate crisis.

Third, while patterns of class formation have shown a complexity as labour markets have been restructured, it is apparent that the power of labour has diminished across the global political economy. The social contract between labour and capital has been undermined as capital has gained a foot-loose mobility and greater structural power across globalised value chains. Moreover, the financialisation of political systems has ensured that states manage risk to capital as a macro-economic priority much more than employ-ment creation. The securitisation of democracy has entrenched a class pattern of power in which transnational and monopoly capital prevail over the state, society and labour.

In short, capital is the real geologic force driving the logic of imperial eco-cide and in turn facilitated by it to ensure ongoing accumulation. Today, as Joel Kovel (2003) puts it, capital is the 'enemy of nature' – human and non-human.

Capitalism will not solve the climate crisis or save planetary life

The UN-led climate negotiations and the IPCC have resigned themselves to solutions within the logic of imperial ecocide. The embrace of carbon trading, carbon offsets, geo-engineering and using forests as carbon sinks while com-mercialising them, are all part of the agenda to deal with the climate crisis. However, these are not real systemic solutions (see Guerrero in this volume). The most glaring solution of shutting down carbon extraction, particularly oil, gas and coal, as part of a just and zero-carbon energy transition is not on the agenda (Klein 2014). Yet it is common and good sense that if we burn up cur-rent oil reserves we will breach the 2°C threshold (which in itself is not suffi-cient to prevent certain critical tipping points) and incinerate the entire planet. In the Anthropocene literature more broadly, there are three broad approaches to capital-led solutions: first, unabashed support for capitalism to save us from the anthropogenic mob. As Lynas (2011: 66–67) puts it:

> I often receive emails telling me that fixing the climate will need a world-wide change in values, a programme of mass education to reduce peo-ple's desires to consume, a more equitable distribution of global wealth, 'smashing the power' of transnational corporations or even the abolition of capitalism itself. I am now convinced that these viewpoints – which

are subscribed to by perhaps a majority of environmentalists – are wrong. Instead, we can completely deal with climate change within the prevailing economic system. In fact, any other approach is likely doomed to failure.

Second is a veneration of human science and technology. This is the thrust of Ackerman's (2014) argument in her celebration of the technological genius of human beings, from micro technologies to cyborgs and robots, suggesting that we have the power and the means to chart another evolutionary path. However, this fails to realise that either corporations or powerful states control modern technology and that technology is not neutral in these relations of production – it serves particular interests. Third is a retreat into corporate-sponsored conservation as an expression of practical and ethical hope, in the face of the encroaching sixth anthropocentric extinction (Kolbert 2014).

The assumption that capital and capitalism has the solutions to the climate crisis makes the official Anthropocene perspective not just functional to capitalist interests, but places it squarely within capitalist thought. It rejects the idea that the systemic causes of the climate crisis lie within the historical and current patterns of global capitalist production, consumption, finance and organisation of social life – the logic of imperial ecocide. It is, in the end, an affirmation of the Promethean power of capital, while rejecting the collective agency of working-class, popular and subaltern social forces. Ironically, and in its essence, it has a shallow commitment to humanity and is actually deeply anti-human in its pro-capitalist outlook. Class struggle and a mass politics engendering a counterhegemony to sustain life is the response of Marxist ecology. More precisely, the solutions to the climate crisis lie in a democratic eco-socialist alternative for society, built through transformative just transitions advanced from below and above (see other chapters in this volume).

The racism and male domination of imperial ecocide

The IPCC's (2014) fifth report is emphatic that anthropogenic population growth is a contributor to climate change. However, the argument is merely made in the aggregate, that the growth of population is a causal factor, but is not sufficiently substantiated or nuanced. It does explore per capita emissions in rich countries versus more populous rich countries, for example. It is an argument that has been made by ecologists before, such as the Club of Rome's *Limits to Growth* by Meadows et al., published in 1972. It is a neo-Malthusian argument suggesting population growth leads to resource depletion and environmental degradation and, in this case, climate change.

Neither Kolbert nor Ackerman articulates this issue explicitly, while the former is more pessimistic (and almost fatalistic) than the latter about human behaviour in the Anthropocene. Lynas, on the other hand, takes the issue head-on while trying to be cautious. He considers it as a solution, but just about stands back from its eco-fascist implications. He says:

> Certainly, fewer people by definition means lower emissions. By getting to 350 ppm by reducing the number of carbon emitters on the planet is impossible as well as undesirable: at a first approximation it would require the number of people in the world to be reduced by four-fifths down to just a billion souls or less. Short of a programme of mass forced sterilisation and/or genocide, there is no way that this would be completed within the few decades necessary. (Lynas 2011: 67)

In its evoking of human population growth as a problem without grounding it in the realities of how capitalist carbon-based overaccumulation and resource control, and the class inequalities engendered, cause the climate crisis, this is nothing short of a racist understanding of human life. This of course is not to argue against abortion and birth control, and the need for women to have control over their bodies, but instead to make the point that neo-Malthusian arguments are blind to the deeper systemic roots of the climate crisis and imperial ecocide. Moreover, in the process of the primitive accumulation marking our times, women are at the frontline of the crisis of social reproduction and bear the consequences of a male-dominated global division of labour. Not only do they earn super-exploitative wages in many parts of the peripheries, but they also struggle to survive in the age of globalised agriculture and climate impacts. African women peasant farmers epitomise this condition (see Terreblanche and Bassey, both in this volume).

This has to be understood in relation to the militarised rationality of US imperial power and the extent to which it is planning to deal with worsening climate crises. It is clear that everything will be done to maintain a globalised capitalist way of life and 'lifeboat' America, even if it means using a masculinised violence to police, pacify and destroy 'zones of instability' in the context of the climate crisis (Parenti 2011). Put differently, the failure by the US to address the systemic roots of the climate crisis both domestically and on a global scale means that the poor and the marginal, particularly black and indigenous women, will be affected the most. The 2°C goal set at the Copenhagen summit and entrenched in the Paris COP21 summit will be a death sentence for island states but also for many parts of sub-Saharan Africa (Klein 2014). The colonising of the climate commons in Africa through offset mechanisms and other market mechanisms has also not worked over the past few decades in Africa (Bachram 2009). The impacts of extreme weather patterns now are no longer correlations but directly related to climate change. These changes have and will impact disproportionately on working-class and poor families, but in particular on the black working class and the poorer darker nations of the planet. At the same time, the white males controlling the command centres of global capital will continue not taking the climate crisis seriously given their relatively secure class locations and the support, either tacit or explicit, they give to US imperial ecocide to reproduce their civilisation. Naomi Klein (2014: 46) substantiates this point in the following way:

> Overwhelmingly, climate change deniers are not only conservative but also white and male, a group with higher than average incomes. And they are more likely than other adults to be highly confident in their views, no matter how demonstrably false.

PROSPECTS FOR JUST TRANSITIONS

Klein (2014) is absolutely correct that the climate crisis changes everything and it provides an opportunity to transform the world before it is too late. It allows us to say no to financialisation, deep globalisation and neoliberalisation in order to defend and save our societies, nature and future generations. However, this reality can only lead to transformative change and a counterhegemonic strategy to sustain life provided necessary strategic conditions are realised. These conditions are necessary to shift the balance of power in the conjuncture of systemic crises and transformative resistance. This is a conjuncture, post-neoliberal hegemony in which market solutions are failing and ruling classes are facing legitimacy crises. A financialised mode of market democracy is in crisis. In responding, such necessary strategic conditions should include, first, shifting the balance of forces from below, at the level of the national, away from the failed leadership in the UN-led climate negotiations. Today there is a crisis of leadership in the multilateral system and a lack of collective will to address the systemic roots of the climate crisis and to end imperial ecocide (Gill 2012). The UN has failed humanity and the planet. Thus, the strategic initiative for transformation can only come from below through grassroots leadership committed to climate justice and systemic transformation. Most green parties have been neoliberalised and most institutional political parties are increasingly discredited. The gap between leaders and the led can only be closed through building a politics around systemic alternatives from below. This is the horizon of left politics that exists today and its historical coincidence with the climate crisis has immense potential, which did not exist two or three decades ago. This means advancing movement-based transformative systemic alternatives around food sovereignty, public transport, regulated reductions in carbon emissions, socially owned renewable energy and climate jobs, for instance.

Second is rejecting anthropocentric catastrophism and the 'ends of capitalism' perspective of the vanguardist Left. Instead, a realism about capitalism's systemic contradictions has to prevail. Capitalism is not about to collapse and neither is it about to surrender. However, it is experiencing an unprecedented set of multifaceted systemic crises: financialised chaos, climate crisis, peak oil, food system crisis and the securitisation of democracy (Satgar 2015). This is more than overproduction or financialisation crises and each of these systemic contradictions provides exit points for systemic alternatives. Capitalism today is also experiencing an unprecedented existential crisis: the crises of capitalist civilisation which gridlock, limit and even bring down parts of its accumulation processes, but not the whole system. This also places capitalism in an extremely dangerous place, with its only way out being 'business as usual' imperial ecocide. However, in this context a theory and practice of just transitions is crucial.

Third, a theory of just transitions has to emerge out of transformative practice, which also gives substance to a deep just transition. Hence, at a minimum it should work with the following elements: (i) a conception of the multiple systemic crises of capitalist civilisation, which by implication means a break with productivist understandings of development and industrialisation, including catch-ups by countries of the global South; (ii) instead, all policy needs to be guided by the principle and systemic logic of sustaining life, from below and above, in the present and for future generations. The growth principle has to be replaced by the life principle and underpinned by struggle-driven systemic reforms to sustain life; (iii) just transitions cannot be unilinear but have to be multilinear, nationally and internationally. Such transitions have to operate at different scales, locales and tempos. This means it has to be deeply democratic, allowing for all forms of democracy to shape its content and practice. This would include participatory, direct, associational, rights-based and cyber democracy having a place in constituting a just transition. This means that multiple democratic, post-capitalist logics from workplaces, communities, civil society, the internet, the public sphere and the state will shape the just transition and ensure its multilinearity. In short, wielding democracy against imperial ecocide is the best, and only, weapon we have.

Fourth, as anti-systemic movements rise and resist there are immense potentials for a new democratic eco-socialist vision to emerge (Angus 2016). Such a democratic eco-socialist vision will have to imagine and build a society in the present that can exist through ending the exploitation of nature (human and non-human) at all levels, through confronting all the oppressions of capitalism. It will have to uphold a bioethic at the level of mass consciousness so as to exist within the biophysical limits of the planet, and embrace socially owned renewable energy, democratic planning and socialisation of the commons: biophysical, knowledge and cyber. In short, a new democratic eco-socialist vision must affirm the web of life as central to an anti-ecocidal politics. This can only emerge from a radically democratic and transformative politics.

NOTES

1 Also see Caldeira and Wickett (2003) and Kolbert (2014). The latter details how this concept diffuses into soil studies and Earth system studies.
2 In this regard, see Zalasiewicz et al. (2008).
3 His work spans several articles on his blog *Climate and Capitalism* (http://climateandcapitalism.com/category/anthropocene/) dealing with the Anthropocene. However, his position is more clearly argued in his recent book (Angus 2016).
4 As mentioned, Moore (2015) develops this in his framing of cheap nature in his framework of the Capitalocene.

REFERENCES

Ackerman, D. 2014. *The Human Age: The World Shaped by Us*. London: Headline Publishing.

Angus, I. 2016. *Facing the Anthropocene: Fossil Capitalism and the Crisis of the Earth System*. New York: Monthly Review Press.

Bachram, H. 2009. 'Climate fraud and carbon colonialism'. In *Climate Change, Carbon Trading and Civil Society: Negative Returns on South African Investments*, edited by P. Bond, R. Dada and G. Erion. Pietermaritzburg: University of KwaZulu-Natal Press, pp. 99–113.

Bellamy Foster, J. 1999. *The Vulnerable Planet*. New York: Monthly Review Press.

Bellamy Foster, J. 2000. *Marx's Ecology: Materialism and Nature*. New York: Monthly Review Press.

Broswimmer, F.J. 2002. *Ecocide: A Short History of the Mass Extinction of Species*. London: Pluto Press.

Caldeira, K. and Wickett, M.E. 2003. 'Oceanography: Anthropogenic carbon and ocean pH', *Nature*, 425 (6956): 365, doi: 10.1038/425365a.

Crutzen, P.J. 2002. 'Geology of mankind', *Nature*, 415 (6867): 23, doi: 10.1038/415023a.

Gill, S. (ed.). 2012. *Global Crises and the Crisis of Global Leadership*. Cambridge: Cambridge University Press.

Harvey, D. 2003. 'The "new" imperialism: Accumulation by dispossession'. In *The New Imperial Challenge*, edited by L. Panitch and C. Leys. London: Merlin Press pp. 63–87.

IPCC (Intergovernmental Panel on Climate Change). 2007. *Climate Change 2007: Impacts, Adaptation and Vulnerability*. Contribution of Working Group II to the Fourth Assessment Report of the Intergovernmental Panel on Climate Change. Cambridge: Cambridge University Press.

IPCC. 2014. *Climate Change 2014: Synthesis Report*. Contribution of Working Groups I, II and III to the Fifth Assessment Report of the Intergovernmental Panel on Climate Change. Geneva, Switzerland: IPCC.

Klein, N. 2014. *This Changes Everything*. London: Penguin Books.

Kolbert, E. 2014. *The Sixth Extinction: An Unnatural History*. New York: Picador.

Kovel, J. 2003. *The Enemy of Nature: The End of Capitalism or the End of the World*. New Delhi: Tulika Books.

Kump, L., Bralower, T. and Ridgewell, A. 2009. 'Ocean acidification in deep time', *Oceanography*, 22 (4): 94–107.

Lynas, M. 2011. *The God Species: How the Planet Can Survive the Age of Humans*. London: Fourth Estate.

Marx, K. 1967. *Capital: A Critique of Political Economy (Vol. 1)*. London: Penguin Books.

Meadows, D.H., Meadows, D.L., Randers, J. and Behrens III, W.W. 1972. *The Limits to Growth: A Report for the Club of Rome's Project on the Predicament of Mankind*. New York: Universe Books.

Moore, J. 2015. *Capitalism in the Web of Life: Ecology and the Accumulation of Capital*. London and New York: Verso.

Moore, J. (ed.). 2016. *Anthropocene or Capitalocene? Nature, History, and the Crisis of Capitalism*. Oakland, CA: PM Press.

O'Connor, M. 1994. 'Introduction: Liberate, accumulate – and bust?' In *Is Capitalism Sustainable? Political Economy and the Politics of Ecology*, edited by M. O'Connor. New York: The Guilford Press, pp. 1–22.

Parenti, C. 2011. *Tropic of Chaos: Climate Change and the New Geography of Violence*. New York: Nation Books.

Ridgeway, J. 2004. *It's All for Sale: The Control of Global Resources*. London: Duke University Press.

Satgar, V. 2015. *Capitalism's Crises: Class Struggles in South Africa and the World.* Johannesburg: Wits University Press.

Zalasiewicz, J., Williams, M., Smith, A., Barry, T.L., Coe, A.L., Brown, P.B., Brenchley, P., Cantrill, D., Gale, A., Gibbard, P., Gregory, F.J., Hounslow, M.W., Kerr, A.C., Pearson, P., Knox, R., Powell, J., Waters, C., Marshall, J., Oates, M., Rawson, P. and Stone, P. 2008. 'Are we now living in the Anthropocene?', *GSA Today*, 18 (2): 4–8.

Zierler, D. 2011. *The Invention of Ecocide: Agent Orange, Vietnam, and the Scientists Who Changed the Way We Think about the Environment.* Athens, GA: University of Georgia Press.

DEMOCRATIC
ECO-SOCIALIST
ALTERNATIVES
IN THE WORLD

4

THE EMPLOYMENT CRISIS, JUST TRANSITION AND THE UNIVERSAL BASIC INCOME GRANT

Hein Marais

Since the nineteenth century, job creation has functioned as the primary – and in many cases the sole – strategy for improving people's well-being and life prospects. Such an approach is unsuited to current realities of tightly rationed and poorly remunerated waged work, a state of affairs that is predicted to endure. The scope and intensity of this crisis of waged work is likely to increase as digital and other job-replacing technologies are introduced more widely and as the dividend-boosting pressures of financialised capitalism persist. Given such an outlook, a universal basic income grant (UBIG) holds great appeal.

This chapter surveys the background to the current crisis before examining, in the context of a 'just transition', the advantages of a UBIG, the arguments against and its possible pitfalls. It concludes by showing that a UBIG, rare among redistributive interventions, holds great transformative potential and challenges core tenets of capitalist ideology. That potential can only be realised if a UBIG is treated not as a passive, technical intervention but as an aspect of a broader programme of societal transformation.

THE STATE OF THINGS

Chronic high unemployment, new jobs that are mostly at the low-pay end of the scale and that lack benefits and security, stagnating or declining real incomes, social protection systems that are either absent or tightly rationed, widening income inequality – those are descriptions that used to apply almost exclusively to countries on the margins of the global economy. Today, those features are increasingly generic. Jan Breman's (2013: 131) summary of trends in 'developed' economies is bracing and accurate:

> With every recession since the 1970s, prolonged episodes of high unemployment, privatisations and public-sector cutbacks have served to weaken the position of labour in North America, Europe and Japan; trade-union movements were hollowed out by the shrinkage of the industrial workforce, through factory re-location or robotisation, and the growth of the non-unionised service and retail sectors; the rise of China, the entry of hundreds of millions of low-paid workers into the world workforce and the globalisation of trade helped to depress wages and working conditions further. Part-time and short-contract work has been on the rise, along with that ambiguous category, self-employment.

Such insecurity, of course, has long typified 'developing' economies. In most of them, self-employment and family-based work still eclipse formalised waged work as the chief material basis for survival. Growth in the industrial and service sectors has seen workers' organisations proliferate in some of these economies, but their impact, while growing, has been limited. The weight of workers' organisations in 'developed' economies varies considerably (contrast the United States with France, for example), but there is a uniform trend of weakening strength and influence over the past thirty years. Overall, a situation prevails where, in Andre Gorz's (1999: 1) phrasing, 'A new system has been established which is abolishing "work" on a massive scale. It is restoring the worst forms of domination, subjugation and exploitation by forcing each to fight against all in order to obtain the "work" it is abolishing.'

Globally, labour force growth is outstripping the expansion of employment. The proportion of the working-age population that is employed[1] has shrunk in all regions since the 1990s, with the exception of the Middle East and North Africa (where female employment has risen significantly) (Van Staveren & Van der Hoeven 2012). The bulk of the increase in global unemployment has occurred in the most economically dynamic regions – East Asia and South Asia. Conservative calculations put the global unemployment rate at over six per cent in 2014, with youth unemployment (15–24-year-olds) more than double that, at thirteen per cent (ILO 2014a).[2]

In many of the countries with both the means and the desire to collect relatively accurate employment data, at least one in ten people were out of work in 2014 despite actively trying to land a job. The official unemployment rate in Colombia, Egypt, France, Ireland, Turkey and Zambia, for example, was in the eleven to thirteen per cent range, while in Portugal it was sixteen per cent, in Serbia twenty-two per cent, in South Africa and in Spain each twenty-seven per cent, and in Greece the official unemployment rate was twenty-eight per cent (IMF 2015). Those are conservative figures.

Unemployment rates, however, convey very little about the kinds, conditions and terms of work being performed, or about remuneration. Globally in 2014, vulnerable employment – either self-employment or work by contributing family workers – accounted for almost forty-eight per cent of total employment. In South Asia and sub-Saharan Africa, more than three out of four workers were working in what the International Labour Office (ILO) considers to be vulnerable employment. These workers

> are less likely than wage earners to have formal working arrangements, be covered by social protection such as pensions and health care or have regular earnings. They tend to be trapped in a vicious circle of low-productivity occupations, poor remuneration and limited ability to invest in their families' health and education. (ILO 2014a: 4)

It is worth remembering that two decades ago, the World Bank was touting the 'informal' sector as an impromptu pioneer of the kinds of flexibilisation it claimed would help kick-start economic growth and boost formal job creation. It got it wrong, and by a wide margin. In some countries in South and South-East Asia (India among them), informal employment in 2013 accounted for up to ninety per cent of total employment (ILO 2014a). And most studies on informal enterprise productivity have found that informality is associated with low economic growth and low productivity; it is not an incubator of progress (Benjamin et al. 2014).

Meanwhile, decently paid, secure work is becoming increasingly atypical in the 'advanced' economies. People entering or returning to the labour market are increasingly funnelled into informal, part-time or on-call employment. Post-recession job creation has been disproportionately of the low-skills, low-pay and low- or no-security variety. But it is in 'developing' countries that the association of work and precariousness remains strongest.

Only three per cent of people in 'vulnerable employment' reside in the 'developed' countries, according to the ILO (2013). There are data limitations, but the available data show an *increase* in the absolute number of workers employed in the informal sector in all 'developing' regions (Africa, Asia, Latin America) of the world between the early 1990s and the late 2000s, along with an increase in the relative share of informal workers in total employment in two of those three regions (Africa being the exception) (van der Hoeven 2010). Moreover, as Jan Breman (2013: 136) reminds, in much of the global South, 'labour power is squeezed not only from men and women, but from children and the elderly, since the on-and-off contribution of the whole household is required for survival. This is a huge reserve army, subjected both to over- and under-employment'.

FADING FORTUNES

The worsening predicament of workers is reflected also in the declining share of income that goes to labour. Globally, the percentage of GDP that is paid out in wages (the 'global labour share') has been falling for at least three decades. The decrease in 'developed' countries is vivid and well documented. Datasets for 'developing' countries are more challenging, but a similar pattern overall is evident in the large majority of countries (Karabarbounis & Neiman 2013). One might have expected the labour share in 'developing' countries to have risen as their economies became more integrated internationally in recent decades. That did not happen; labour's relative income in those countries declined despite rises in overall productivity (Trapp 2015).[3]

In the decades preceding the 1970s, labour's share of national income fluctuated slightly from year to year, but stayed within a stable band overall. Then the trend switched, and it did so across dozens of countries. Of the fifty-nine countries with at least fifteen years of data between 1975 and 2012, forty-two showed downward trends in their labour shares – including China, India and

Mexico. The share of labour income has been declining in countries with very different policies and economic institutions, and across all industries. The fact that the labour share has been shrinking also in major locations of outsourced production shows that the declining trend cannot be reduced simply to patterns of international trade or outsourcing (Karabarbounis & Neiman 2013). Other research shows the downward trend in the labour share in 'developing' countries has accelerated since the early 1990s, with the share dropping most sharply in low-income countries (Trapp 2015).[4]

Powerful developments are driving this trend. The relative prices of investment have been falling, making it possible to increase capital inputs while reducing labour inputs – shifts that are facilitating rising productivity while cutting labour costs overall. In 'developed' economies from 1999 to 2013, real wage growth lagged well behind labour productivity growth. The gap between real wages in 'developed' and 'developing' economies narrowed over that period, due to relatively strong but very unequal wage growth in the latter economies and declining real wages in the former (ILO 2014b).

In the US, for example, average real wages barely shifted over the past thirty years. The average hourly pay of US workers in the bottom twenty per cent of households rose by only three per cent over the entire 1979–2007 period, while productivity grew by sixty-four per cent (and education levels among workers in this quintile improved). The overall real income of these households rose slightly – mainly due to working longer hours.[5] According to the Economic Policy Institute (Mishell & Shierholz 2013), a similar trend played out among the entire bottom sixty per cent of wage earners, with wages from 2000 to 2012 either levelling or declining, while productivity grew by over twenty-five per cent. Facilitating those developments in the 'developed' economies is the waning influence of workers' organisations, most dramatically in the world's biggest economy, the US, where total union membership shrank to about eleven per cent of the workforce in 2013, the lowest in the entire post-Second World War period.[6]

The flipside of the diminishing labour share of income, of course, is the increasing share of capital. When Thomas Picketty and Gabriel Zucman analysed data from 1975 to 2010, they found the share of capital in national income in the eight biggest Organisation for Economic Cooperation and Development (OECD) economies rising with such vigour that they predicted a return to the very high capital shares seen in the nineteenth century (Picketty & Zucman 2013).

For now, capitalism seems to have solved the problem of the 'scarcity of labour' but at the cost of entrapping growing numbers of workers in a dire predicament of survival.

Even when acknowledged, these realities tend to be portrayed as temporary exceptions to the 'normal' trajectory of capitalism, which is said to be one of progressive improvement in the standards of living of ever-growing proportions of people. Yet these are not fleeting trends; they reflect profound structural changes.

Among the shifts has been the transformation from the 1970s onward of tens of millions of peasants around the world into proletarians, mostly in Asia. Coinciding with that change was the entry of vast numbers of women into labour markets. The resulting glut of labour supply dramatically depressed the 'reservation wage', the lowest wage that workers are willing to accept for any given job. It also removed the constraint of labour scarcity, which tends to boost the bargaining power of workers. Along with sustained attacks on workers' organisations over the past thirty years, those developments helped push and hold workers on the defensive.

Shifting production to zones with attractively low labour costs allied with adequate transport and other infrastructure has been a key strategy used by corporate capital to reduce aggregate labour costs. From the 1980s onward, China in particular successfully positioned itself to take advantage. However, its low-wage attractions have now faded, with labour costs (including benefits) rising by ten to fourteen per cent per year from 2002 to 2009.[7] In India, the trend has been similar since the early 2000s.[8] Other countries, mostly in South-East Asia, have sought to capitalise, but to limited overall effect due to their small labour markets and comparatively poor infrastructure.[9] At a global level, therefore, the options for cutting labour costs by reallocating production to new zones have diminished. Africa may beckon with low wages, but poor infrastructure and unreliable transport and communications systems dim its attractions.

The global economic crisis has added massive impetus to efforts to restructure the use of labour. The process has been especially stark in the US, where research by the National Employment Law Project (2012) shows that employment growth in the 2010–2012 'recovery' period was emphatically concentrated in lower-wage occupations, which grew 2.7 times as fast as mid-wage and higher-wage occupations. Trends have been similar in other industrialised economies and in semi-industrialised ones, South Africa included.

There is renewed alarm about an impending mass erasure of jobs, as new labour-replacing technologies are developed and deployed more extensively. A 2013 study by Oxford University's Martin School, for example, estimated that close to half of existing jobs in the US are at 'high risk' of being replaced by machines within the next decades (Frey & Osborne 2013).[10] Not all types of job are threatened to the same extent. Pictured visually, the job casualties of automation in manufacturing, service and distribution activities tend to plot a bell shape, with losses most severe among the middle tier of jobs. Until now, many low-skilled, low-paid jobs have survived the introduction of productivity-boosting technologies, as have high-skilled, high-paid jobs (often in the supervisory and managerial categories). The pattern could be contributing to worsening wage polarisation.

However, the Oxford study predicts that job losses will shift increasingly to low-income, low-paid jobs, forcing greater numbers of workers further onto the doleful fringes of labour markets. The workers able to sidestep that overhaul, the researchers predict, will be those who are capable of acquiring the 'creative and social skills' that are less susceptible to automation and computerisation. Activities that involve forms of emotionally alert interaction and responsiveness, or dexterous improvisation that is not easily mimicked by algorithms and machines (caregiving and various retail services, for example), will continue to require human workers. But many of those activities will be low skilled and low paid.

The number of countries with official unemployment rates higher than ten per cent has increased in recent years, and includes several in Europe (including Croatia, Greece, Ireland, Italy, Serbia and Spain), the Middle East and North Africa (IMF 2015). In South Africa, which is one of the few sub-Saharan African countries with fairly reliable employment data, the official unemployment rate exceeded twenty-seven per cent in 2017 (Stats SA 2017). Youth unemployment rates are considerably higher.

A CRISIS WITH DEEP ROOTS

Debate continues about the underlying causes of the shift away from the near-full employment that characterised the 'golden age' that lasted in 'developed' economies from the end of World War Two until the early 1970s. That period boasted high rates of growth in productivity, output and profitability, which were facilitated by the introduction of automation and more efficient transportation systems and energy generation. Real wages rose alongside burgeoning profit margins, and various work-related entitlements became the norm. Much of the political impetus for these improvements came from energised workers' movements which, in many countries, were powerful enough to act as stout stakeholders in corporatist arrangements. This, of course, occurred against the geopolitical background of the cold war, with capitalist countries anxious to prevent workers' and other social movements from radicalising to the point where they might challenge the system on fundamental terms.

The grand compromise, however, broke down in the 1970s. In Robert Brenner's (2006) analysis, the breakdown stemmed from excessive competition among what Karl Marx had termed 'the many capitals'. Intensified competition at the global level led to excess industrial capacity and overproduction, which depressed industrial profitability. In response, capital was increasingly routed away from manufacturing and towards financial speculation. The very essence of capitalist dynamism – international competition – turned out also to be the system's cardinal weakness.

Blind to that paradox, policy makers sought an exit from the downturn by intensifying competition. Reacting to falling rates of profit, corporations sought to restore profit margins by curtailing real income growth and shifting production to low-wage, union-free locations. According to Brenner (2006), the international system became increasingly entrapped in a zero-sum game in which the success of any one economy came at the expense of another economy's failure to succeed.

Moreover, 'fixes' of that sort tend to be temporary. Workers organise and wages rise, which accounts for why technological innovation that sidesteps the need for human workers remains constantly important for the accumulation of capital. And adjustments that curtail real income growth and shrink the labour share of income depress aggregate demand, which impedes economic growth.

It is in those conditions that the financial sector has become domineering. In decades past, finance capital developed and operated largely as a function of industrial growth, with its primary role being the promotion of industrial development through the merger of industrial and financial capital (Hilferding 1981). The metabolism of finance capital is now fundamentally parasitic, intent on extracting maximum returns in a minimum of time, even by dismantling industrial capacity. Spirited along obscure circuitries, financial capital now avoids rather than underwrites longer-term strategies for productive activity (Marais 2011). And it operates at a gargantuan scale: in 2010, off-exchange trading of financial derivatives alone (including the toxic assets that had caused the financial meltdown a few years earlier) was estimated at US$601 trillion, almost ten times the global GDP of US$63 trillion (CIA 2013).

There are basically two ways to tackle excess supply. One can reduce supply to bring it in line with demand (through a fearsome cull of uncompetitive companies). Or one can increase effective demand to match the supply. The latter requires that the real incomes of workers increase over time in order to generate sufficient demand for the ever-increasing volumes of goods and services that the capitalist system produces. And those increases need to be distributed relatively evenly across the wage spectrum to maximise their effect on demand.

But with excessive wages and inflexible labour standards targeted as the culprit for the long downturn, workers were driven into retreat.[11] Productivity and output was boosted, but in the biggest economies wage growth was deliberately depressed. And although the ranks of wage earners grew in many other economies (and the middle layers of income earners have swollen), this was not enough to create sufficient final demand to absorb excess supply of goods and services at the global level.

The upshot is a reality where, as Benjamin Kunkel (2014: 81) puts it, 'a proportionally shrinking body of labourers is ever more heavily exploited to ensure a rate of profit that nevertheless continually declines'. The improvised solution has been to extend credit with ever-growing enthusiasm, allowing people to borrow against income they do not have (and may *never* have). Equity and housing bubbles keep these improvisations aloft for a while, but without repairing the underlying problems.

Picketty has argued that the global growth rates of the mid-twentieth century are unlikely to be repeated. Other analysts, such as Wolfgang Streeck (2014), argue that capitalism's resilience – its ability to renew itself through crisis – is perhaps waning and that the system may have entered a phase of prolonged instability and gradual breakdown. As climate shocks accumulate and their effects rattle through societies and economies, instability will become the norm. Rates of growth will stagnate or decline, exacerbating inequality and fuelling debt, which in turn will precipitate further volatility and choke the prospects of sustained growth. Protracted instability is a very realistic prospect. Odd though it may seem, this invites a cautious optimism. As Kunkel (2014: 98) puts it, the world's exports can no longer be purchased with phantom wages. Now the project of developing internal markets in country after country will encourage the revival of true full employment as a condition of adequate overall demand. Global prosperity will come about not through further concessions from labour, or the elimination of industrial overcapacity by widespread bankruptcy, but through the development of societies in which people can afford to consume more of what they produce, and produce more with the entire labour force at work.

That cannot mean a society of paupers at work, since it would leave the problem of demand untouched. Nor should it entail a 'productivist' workhouse in which able-bodied adults spend their waking hours toiling and commuting to and from work. Instead, in Kunkel's (2014: 103) attractive reasoning, the more people work, the fewer hours each should have to work to achieve the same overall result: 'More leisure or free time, not less, would be one natural – and desirable – consequence of having more jobs.' Play out that line of thinking and, sooner or later, one arrives at the debate surrounding a UBIG.

THE APPEAL OF A UNIVERSAL BASIC INCOME

What are the core principles of a UBIG? It is paid as a cash grant on a universal basis (i.e. to everyone) and in an equal amount; it is paid to individuals, not households; and it is unconditional, so the recipient can use it in any way she or he sees fit. It is neither targeted nor means-tested. Ideally, the amount should be sufficient to cover basic needs and enable a person to participate in social life (Allegre 2014).

The grant has multiple functions and advantages. Liberals and progressives see universal, unconditional cash payments as a way to reduce extreme poverty by making sure everybody, no matter the circumstances, is able to satisfy basic needs. They also expect it to contribute to a range of other desirable social outcomes (higher school attendance in poor households, improved child health and possibly also adult health, greater financial independence for women, reduced income inequality, etc.), as well as fuel stronger basic consumer demand that can fuel economic growth and job creation.

But the grant also holds much greater potential. It can help secure the basic means for life while enabling people to avoid, even if only temporarily, being coerced into accepting dangerous, low-paying and insecure forms of employment. Relieved from desperation, people would be able to put their labour and time to other uses – studying or acquiring additional skills, achieving fairer divisions of labour in household and family life, and participating in the reciprocal networks that build and sustain resilient and vibrant communities.

A UBIG would be an important part of strategies to manage and mitigate climate shocks, and of strategies to achieve a just transition to sustainable economic models. The grant would support countries as they transition their economies from fossil fuel-dependent and greenhouse gas-intensive models toward renewables by providing a universal safety net that helps displaced workers and vulnerable communities manage that transition, rather than become mere casualties of it. This transition is not only essential, it is inevitable, as the global shift away from fossil fuels gains momentum. Countries that fail to prepare for it will be increasingly hard hit by the instabilities associated with global warming and by the reactive adjustments and strategic shifts imposed on them. Climate shocks, worsening un- and underemployment, and increasingly unstable labour market and pricing trends will go hand in hand in the years ahead. Unless deliberately and proactively prevented, the impact of those upheavals will be disproportionately concentrated in the lives of the poor.

The semantics are important. Intended or not, the term 'universal income' invites a definition in which the grant payment *replaces* other forms of welfare provision. Such an understanding slots seamlessly into neoliberal ideology. By replacing various state-managed entitlements, such a grant would pivot well-being on 'individual responsibility' and position the market as the arbiter of even the most basic means of life. Opting for the term 'basic income', on the other hand, would point to a payment that is elementary, not all-encompassing and that exists alongside other forms of institutionalised social protection. The universality of the payment is an indispensable feature, which is why the term 'universal basic income' seems most appropriate. It is 'universal' because it is available to everyone, not because it replaces other forms of provisioning.

The challenge of funding a UBIG would depend on the size of the grant and on the size and characteristics of the particular economy. Every adult would receive a monthly payment from the government, regardless of income or circumstances. For higher earners, that payment would be offset by income tax adjustments. But personal income tax payments need not be the sole or main source of funding – this is where the type of economy enters the picture. Countries with a developed financial sector could help fund it via a financial transaction tax, with reforms that tackle the offshoring of wealth, and by raising corporate and top-earner tax rates (after all, corporations net an ever-larger share of total income in most countries). Funding transfers from major polluting economies, perhaps in the form of a carbon tax, are another potential financing source. These could form part of broader initiatives aimed at ensuring that the costs of global warming and of environmental change are shared more equitably, both between and within countries.

Discussion of the merits of a UBIG is no longer confined to the fringes of national debates. When Switzerland held a national referendum in 2016 on a universal basic income, twenty-three per cent of voters (and up to thirty-five per cent in some cantons) supported the proposal to pay every Swiss national about US\$2 500 a month as a guaranteed universal income.[12] The Basic Income Initiative, a Europe-wide organisation, has campaigned for a similar plebiscite across Europe.[13] The city of Utrecht in the Netherlands is implementing a controlled trial to determine whether a universal unconditional income is feasible at scale.[14] The Canadian province of Ontario has announced plans to launch a trial run of a universal basic income, with about 4 000 participants.[15] Another pilot scheme is under way in Finland, where 2 000 unemployed people between the ages of twenty-five and fifty-eight are receiving €560 a month for two years.[16]

However, none of these campaigns and experiments seems alert yet to the radical and transformative potential of a UBIG. They tend to limit their visions to the use of cash transfers to alleviate poverty and jump-start bedraggled economies by boosting aggregate demand for basic goods and services. Those goals may be more prosaic, but they are nonetheless important – as highlighted in Mark Blyth and Eric Lonergan's (2014) reminder that occasional infusions of cash via such transfers 'could reduce dependence on the banking system for growth and reverse the trend of rising inequality. The transfers won't cause damaging inflation, and few doubt that they would work. The only real question is why no government has tried them'.

AN IDEA WHOSE TIME HAS COME?

The idea of a basic income dates to the mid-nineteenth century. Drawing on the thinking of the French socialist Charles Fourier, the philosopher John Stuart Mill argued for such an instrument in the 1849 edition of his *Principles of Political Economy*. It would require, he wrote, that 'a certain minimum is first assigned for the subsistence of every member of the community, whether capable or not of labour'.[17]

A century passed before a type of guaranteed minimum income was institutionalised in several western European countries, but these were highly conditional and typically means-tested forms of state support. Other conditional variants have included fixed payments to families for each child, irrespective of income levels. The most similar existing payment would be the old-age pension, which, although conditional on reaching a stipulated age, is usually available to all citizens (though additional criteria often decide the amount of the payment).

In the US, the idea of a basic income entered mainstream policy debate in the 1960s as economic planners struggled to deal with the re-emergence of structural unemployment: the economy was growing but job creation lagged. President JF Kennedy's economic advisers aired the idea of a guaranteed income in the form of a 'negative income tax'.[18]

The proposal languished at first, before being revived during the run-up to the 1972 US presidential election. Both the Democratic and the Republican contenders touted versions of a basic income, while more than 1 000 economists called on the federal government to adopt some kind of income guarantee.[19] Fashioned into a proposal called the Family Assistance Plan, the concept eventually made it to the floor in the US Congress, where it was voted down. The biggest criticism was not the affordability of the scheme, but concerns that it would sabotage the agricultural economies of southern states by introducing a 'disincentive' to work. That objection would become routine in later debates. At face value pragmatic, it is rooted in a deeper disquiet, as we discuss below.

WHAT HAPPENS IN PRACTICE?

A UBIG has been introduced in a few places. Canada's so-called Mincome Programme entered the annals of social policy folklore in the mid-1970s with a scheme that ran from 1974 to 1979. It entailed paying a monthly supplemental income to about 1 000 poor families in Dauphin, a small town in Manitoba province. The results? Poverty virtually disappeared, high-school completion rates rose and hospitalisation rates fell. Interestingly, the payments did not seem to discourage people from working; productivity increased. The work rate fell only among two groups of people: new mothers, who were able to spend more time with their children, and teenagers, who were able to give up their part-time jobs and focus on schooling (Forget 2011).

In the US, the Alaska Permanent Fund Dividend annually pays each resident an equal share of the returns from investments in a specially created Alaska Permanent Fund, which is financed from a small portion of the state's annual oil revenue (Cummine 2015).[20] Studies have shown that income distribution and poverty alleviation improved significantly after the dividend's introduction, though it is difficult to determine to what extent the scheme was responsible for those outcomes (Goldsmith 2012).

On a much smaller scale, a basic income grant was introduced as a pilot project in 2008/2009 in the Namibian town of Otjivero-Omitara. The grant payment of 100 Namibian dollars per month was unconditional and went to everyone younger than sixty years. Data were skewed by an influx of family members from elsewhere (which is why per capita income seemed to fall during the project). But the social benefits were substantial. The percentage of residents living in poverty fell from seventy-six to thirty-seven per cent, and among those who did not take in migrating family members it fell to seventeen per cent. School dropout rates fell sharply and child malnutrition declined by more than half (from forty-two to seventeen per cent). Recipients also became more active in income-generating activities (Haarmann et al. 2009).

With such encouraging results, why have UBIGs been introduced so rarely? The bid to introduce a UBIG in South Africa is instructive. In the late 1990s, South African trade unions, religious organisations and non-governmental organisations campaigned for a universal grant as a tool that could help alleviate poverty, support livelihood security and lay 'the foundation for more productive and skilled communities' (Cosatu 2000: para. 3.2, in Barchiesi 2006). Formally proposed in 1998, the envisaged grant was pegged at R100 per month (a little over US$12 at the time), an amount trade unionists believed was politically 'winnable'. Although the grant would be spread thinner than existing social transfers, its benefits would extend far wider, they claimed – and without the restrictive, rationing terms of existing grants. Financial simulations indicated that a grant of R100 per month for all South Africans could close the poverty gap by seventy-four per cent (Liebenberg 2002),[21] and lift about six million people above a poverty line of R400 (US$50) per month (Gumede 2005).

The South African campaign failed, largely because of the unwavering opposition of the Treasury, with the finance minister at the time, Trevor Manuel, claiming that the grant would 'bankrupt the country'.[22] Yet, after rejecting a UBIG as 'unaffordable', the South African government proceeded to massively grow its welfare system over the next decade. Fiscal objections yielded to social and, especially, political imperatives. In the context of rising inequality, stubbornly high unemployment rates and poverty levels, and a groundswell of localised protests, the prospective costs of not relieving some of the hardship outweighed the fiscal concerns. As David Everatt (2008: 303) later noted, 'the dominant voice within the ANC [African National Congress] after Mandela was one that chided the poor for remaining poor, rejected [a basic income grant] but was unable to resist pressure for major cash transfers to the poor in the form of social grants'.

Fiscal arguments alone therefore could not explain the defeat of the UBIG campaign in South Africa. The roots extended deeper, into the domains of ideology, discipline and control. It was, as former trade and industry minister Alec Erwin is said to have remarked, 'not the money but the idea' that offended (Hart 2006: 26). South Africa's former land affairs minister, Thoko Didiza, understood this: 'This discussion at the moment is about the values underpinning such a grant,' she told reporters in 2002.[23] The government's philosophical approach was straightforward: 'We would rather create work opportunities,' explained a government spokesperson. 'Only persons who were disabled or ill should get handouts' (*Sunday Times*, 28 July 2002).[24]

BEYOND WELFARE AS CONTROL

The approach taken by the South African government fitted with dominant understandings. Prevailing around the world is the insistence that waged work and entrepreneurial zest will provide a secure basis for well-being for the great majority of society. Welfare is deemed available only to those who, due to age or infirmity, cannot work (children, the elderly or disabled persons) and those who have fallen on hard times. A residual safety net, progressively shrinking to a minimum, may be suspended beneath the hapless and the luckless – 'those', as Margaret Thatcher put it, 'who had genuinely fallen into difficulties and needed some support till they could get out of them'. As for 'those who had simply lost the will or the habit for work and self-improvement', they should not look to the state for relief (Meth 2004: 25). Their only route to survival is by performing waged work.

This unforgiving sensibility is found across the spectrum of political beliefs. Marx and Friedrich Engels ([1888] 1988) listed the 'equal liability of all to work' among the ten distinguishing features of a communist society. Or as former US president Richard Nixon put it: 'The work ethic holds that labour is good in itself; that a man or woman becomes a better person by virtue of the act of working' (in Terkel 1972: i). It is an outlook which, as Franco Barchiesi (2006: 3) has written, assigns to

> wage labour powerful disciplinary and pedagogical meanings, educat-
> ing the poorest sections of the population to the idea that full citizenship
> revolves around individual responsibility, labour market activation, and
> the avoidance of 'dependency' on public spending. Conversely, the gov-
> ernment regards with suspicion policies of generalised access to social
> provisions funded via redistributive transfers.

Thatcher's remarks harked back to the English Poor Law of 1834, its infamous enforcement of 'less eligibility', and the innovation of 'deterrent poor relief' designed to enforce the work ethic and discourage dependency.[25] Those senti-ments have survived, sometimes deodorised with developmentalist prattle about 'enablement' and 'empowerment', building 'human capital', promoting individ-ual responsibility and strengthening resilience. But the disciplinary undertow has stayed unchanged. In its preferred form, social protection, particularly the payment of cash grants, is targeted, tightly rationed and short term – and it is provided on terms that 'encourage' beneficiaries to work for a wage, any wage.

Thus, as Jamie Peck (2001) shows in his book *Workfare States*, in 'developed' countries welfare entitlements and social citizenship have been steadily replaced by workfare systems. These involve a shift away from entitlement programmes, increased reliance on market-oriented social policies, and a determined push to socialise and coerce workers into low-skill, low-pay employment. In essence, social policy has been adjusted to the imperatives of neoliberal capitalism:

> In the context of a continuing trend towards short-term, unstable, 'con-
> tingent' jobs across many national economies, workfare policies exhibit
> a primitive logic: they purposefully mobilise workers for (minimum)
> waged work, holding them close to the labor market in a persistently

'job-ready' state. In a sense, they provide a forced (or 'activated') labor supply for the labor market's least desirable jobs. (Peck 2001: 77)

The prevailing outlook contains a double fiction: the idea that employment is available to those who seek it and that waged work ensures well-being. Yet, amid high un- and underemployment, poor wages and deteriorating terms of employment, very large numbers of people are unable to secure viable livelihoods through waged work. At the same time, being 'able-bodied', they are eligible for neither standard forms of social protection nor employment-based security. They fall between those stools. In a growing number of countries, cash grants are being manoeuvred into that space (Ferguson 2015).

Globally, in 2014, 130 countries (forty of them in Africa) provided unconditional cash transfers and sixty-four provided conditional cash transfers (World Bank 2015). Attracting governments to such schemes is their pacifying potential and the leverage they offer for 'engineering' certain desirable behaviours or practices in poor households (such as enrolling and keeping children in school, or having regular health check-ups), along with the perception that they are relatively inexpensive and easy to administer, and politically rewarding (Lavinas 2013). Among the best-known examples are Brazil's *Bolsa Família*[26] and Mexico's *Opportunidades* scheme.[27] These grants have been credited with a range of desirable social outcomes, including improved school enrolment (especially for girls), increased uptake of basic health services, and reduced malnutrition and stunting (Baird et al. 2014; Lagarde, Haines & Palmer 2009).

The functional importance of conditionality in such schemes has been questioned, however. Often the desired outcomes (such as school attendance) appear to be linked to the receipt of money, rather than the conditionality: more families send their children to school when they can afford to do so. The conditionality seems less a catalyst for particular desired behaviours than a lever for control.

Means-tested or targeted social grants are stigmatising, administratively expensive, complicated and relatively blunt instruments. Nevertheless, their social benefits can be significant. For example, South Africa's social grants became the single most powerful poverty-alleviating tool deployed in the post-apartheid era (Meth 2007), with the official statistical agency largely crediting them for an increase in incomes observed among the poorest thirty per cent of South Africans after 2001 (Stats SA 2008). Other effects include reduced stunting in children and improved nutrition levels (Agüero, Carter & Woolard 2006), as well as increased school enrolment of young children (Woolard & Leibbrandt 2010).

Yet the restrictions attached to cash grants also limit their potential impact. Means testing requires thresholds (usually determined by income) that are often fictive and unjust. Limiting assistance to individuals earning less than, say, US$2 a day while denying it to others earning, say, US$2.20 a day is capricious, no matter the 'clarity' of that 'poverty line'. Means testing also flounders around fluctuating incomes (of seasonal or self-employed workers, for example).

The selectivity – the lack of universality – of targeted programmes limits their impact on inequality, with research suggesting that redistribution tends to be weak in welfare systems that rely on targeted assistance to the poor. Evidence from Scandinavian countries indicates that large-scale, universal provision of decommodified services tends to be more successful in reducing inequality and poverty (Huber & Stephens 2012; Korpi & Palme 1998). In places where very large proportions of the population are poor, targeted and means-tested cash transfers defy common sense, especially if universal grants to the 'non-poor' can be taxed back, which they can (Mkandawire 2005).

HIDDEN CURRENTS

A UBIG would have a more profound impact. Due to its universality, it would avoid the drawbacks of targeted, means-tested and/or conditional cash grants – including their stigmatising effects, their burdensome administrative features, their arbitrariness and their limited ability to redistribute income on a sufficiently large scale.

The grant would disregard the normative barrier that separates the 'deserving' poor from their 'undeserving' peers, and function as a possible bridge towards a social order which is no longer hostage to the rule that, as Studs Terkel puts it, 'No matter how it dulls the senses and breaks the spirit, one must work. Or else.'[28] An arrangement that guarantees people the basic means for survival without compelling them to work for a wage would challenge a fundamental coercive tool in capitalist society. Loosening that tether weakens the allocative, arbitrating and disciplinary power of the market, and opens the door to greater fairness and justice.

Yet, many people find the lack of conditionality disturbing. It disturbs the familiar social–moral topography and unbalances the ways in which social obligations and entitlements are organised. The payment becomes more than a discreet form of assistance. It jars deeply held beliefs about what being a citizen constitutes and about the claims that citizens have on one another and on the state. And it challenges key assumptions and criteria that are used to assign worth and value to people. It is precisely for those – and other – reasons that a UBIG holds such rich promise in the imagination of the Left.

In the popular imagination, work is seen not merely as a means for achieving livelihood security and well-being; it functions as a source of dignity, status and esteem – of meaning, even. As Albert Camus is said to have famously declared, 'without work, all life goes rotten'.[29] When a claim to entitlement is not lodged in waged work, it is commonly treated as a moral offence – for a basic principle, that of social reciprocity, has been 'violated'. Since in capitalist society social citizenship is tied to one's willingness to work for a wage, there is distaste for situations where 'idleness is only rendered possible by the industry of others', as Bertrand Russell (1932) noted in his famous essay 'In Praise of Idleness'.

This feeds a deeply and widely felt affront, even when the reaction seems 'irrational', for example in societies where there is no waged work for large proportions of working-age people. The problem with the sentiment lies not so much with the principle of reciprocity, but with the way in which that principle is anchored in a very narrow and distorting understanding of work. In reality, work contains many meanings. Peter Frase (2014), for example, divides it into three categories:

> One, it can mean activity that is necessary for the continuation of human civilisation, what Engels called 'the production and reproduction of the immediate essentials of life'. Two, it can mean the activity that people undertake in exchange for money, in order to secure the means of continued existence. Three, it can mean … an activity that requires some kind of discipline and deferred gratification in pursuit of an eventual goal. These three meanings tend to get conflated all the time, even though they all appear separately in reality.

Teaching is clearly 'necessary for the continuation of human civilisation' but so is raising children. Yet the one is remunerated and called 'work' and the other is not. Some (very well-paid) work is of dubious or no social utility; Frase suggests the design of high-speed financial trading algorithms as an example. Voluntary work in the community is by definition not paid, but much of it has great social utility. Other activities require substantial time, discipline and self-denial, but are not paid – some of them relatively 'frivolous', such as train spotting or gym training, others of much greater social use, such as the emotional and other support we provide to friends and colleagues.

Consider also the work people perform in the quest for work – the drudgery of 'skills development' and 'job retraining' courses, job counselling, scanning the classifieds, preparing job applications, adjusting CVs and resumes for different occasions, travelling and queuing to drop off resumes, attending interviews, furnishing additional information. Most states demand these 'performances' as a prerequisite for receiving welfare entitlements, despite the fact that they often are purely theatrical and, in societies like South Africa or Greece today, hold scant prospect of paid work. It is the *appearance* of working or seeking to work (regardless of the meaning or utility of the work) that is valued,[30] and which – in the prevailing moral order – 'deserves' or 'earns' entitlement, even though the social or economic utility of the job seeker's exertions is minimal to nil.

These theatrics form part of a larger disciplinary system that is organised around work as the central pivot not only for physical survival and social esteem, but also for laying claim to entitlements and rights. This ideological primacy of jobs destabilises demands for social and economic justice. And so it is commonplace to see demands for a fairer distribution of the means for life channelled and filtered through demands for 'job creation' or 'decent jobs' or a 'minimum wage'. These are important struggles, but not to the extent that they encompass or encode *all* social demands.

Meanwhile, 'job creation' operates as a radiant metaphor for both a romanticised past and an idealised future in which having a job not only fulfils our needs but delivers our desires, as Barchiesi (2012) has noted. Spurious in today's world, 'full employment' historically was realised only partially, temporarily and in specific parts of the world – for a few decades in the mid-twentieth century and almost exclusively in North America and Europe. Yet, the notion's gravitational pull is strong enough to trap a great deal of progressive and leftist thought in what Barchiesi calls a 'melancholia' for a past which is in large part imagined. It locks the imagination inside the boundaries of contemporary capitalism, funnelling it towards 'solutions' that are blind to the dynamics shaping the availability and nature of waged work. So waged work continues to be idealised, even as its availability and capacity to sustain a decent life diminishes.[31]

The less attainable work becomes, the more centrally it is positioned in our imaginary. In Gorz's (1999: 1) view, it is less the abolition of work that should alarm us than the insistence that waged work should serve 'as a norm, and as the irreplaceable foundation of the rights and dignity of all'.

The perceived importance of waged work also goes beyond its promise of material security and social entitlement. It is common wisdom that not being able to work is demoralising, isolating and unhealthy. Lacking access to the social intercourse that many jobs facilitate deprives people of social solidarity, affirmation and other support. Research shows high levels of stress, unhappiness and loss of self-esteem among unemployed people (Clark & Oswald 1994). Any combination of those effects can encourage behaviours and other habits that are likely to undermine both physical and mental health (such as isolation, lack of exercise, poor diet, excessive smoking and/or alcohol use, etc.). Analysis of data from sixty-three countries over the period 2000 to 2011 also found that unemployment and job insecurity were linked to a higher risk of suicide (Carlos et al. 2015), although the association between unemployment and suicide appears to be strongest in high-income countries (Blakely, Collings & Atkinson 2003; Noh 2009).[32] Suicide is an extreme reaction to the dissatisfaction associated with unemployment, but it seems clear that the general life satisfaction of unemployed individuals diminishes significantly and is not fully restored even after having been unemployed for a long time.

But none of these effects is necessarily *inherent* in the fact of joblessness (Frase 2012). They stem largely from social discourses that equate people's worth with their work status (especially men who have been conditioned to see themselves as primary breadwinners), and from the fact that being jobless can render one indigent. Research shows that generous unemployment benefits *offset* the impact of unemployment on suicide rates, for example (Cylus, Glymour & Avendano 2014). Other research from Germany indicates that life satisfaction among the long-term unemployed increases significantly when they officially retire from the labour market and the social expectation of wage labour is lifted (Hetschko, Knabe & Schöb 2013). This suggests that the psychological damage associated with unemployment is not fully intrinsic to not having a job; much of it stems from the social stigma of being jobless. In the German study (Hetschko, Knabe & Schöb 2013), the 'long-term unemployed people benefit[ed] from the change of their social category while retiring and the associated relief from not having to meet the social norm of being employed anymore'.

The UBIG invites us to think beyond the standard notions of what constitutes work and the hierarchies of entitlement and worth that are embedded in
those assumptions. David Bolchover's (2005: 3) provocation is not as flippant
as it may seem:

> [M]any millions … go into a large office somewhere in the world every
> weekday, they go to their desk at the same time, they leave at the same
> time. And in between, they do pretty much nothing … Their home lives
> may be happy and fulfilled, but at work they are the people that time
> forgot. They contribute next to nothing. They are the Living Dead.

Yet we ennoble these years of life spent tapping at computer keyboards, standing guard in doorways, ringing up and bagging purchases, monitoring digital
displays, fielding phone calls, snipping fruit from trees, mopping other people's
floors. We invest them with magical properties, and pretend that they imbue
our lives with value, meaning and worth. Not all jobs leech the life from us, but
our glances at the clock and the dread that opens in us after a short rest has
passed merely underscore the observation that opens Terkel's magisterial book,
Working, where he informs readers that the book,

> being about work, is by its very nature about violence – to the spirit as
> well as to the body. It is about ulcers as well as accidents, about shouting
> matches as well as fistfights, about nervous breakdowns as well as kicking
> the dog around. It is, above all (or beneath all), about daily humiliations.
> To survive the day is triumph enough for the walking wounded among
> the great many of us. (1972: xiii)

RADICAL POTENTIALS

The 'prosaic' benefits of a UBIG (boosting demand and thereby possibly stimulating job creation, reducing poverty, improving health and education outcomes,
and so on) are vitally important. But it also holds other, major advantages.

In addition to providing a safety net in the context of increasingly unstable
and inhospitable labour markets, a UBIG would provide protection for workers who are displaced as economies shift and industries adapt to low-carbon

strategies. The climate change transition will unavoidably affect employment patterns and will cause significant disruption in some industries (oil, petroleum and gas most obviously). A protective mechanism such as a UBIG will be vital for helping achieve a just transition that does not unload such costs onto workers and their communities. In addition, a UBIG and particularly its lack of conditionality could counteract potential resistance to such a transition among workers in heavily affected sectors (Goodstein 1999).[33]

The grant contains radical emancipating potential. A guaranteed income opens opportunities for imagining, in Barchiesi's (2006: 5) words, 'alternative forms of social citizenship [that are] capable of liberating individuals from waged work, labour market dependence and their associated forms of social discipline'. The grant thus becomes double-edged: it is compatible with the capitalist order, but at the same time it challenges an anchoring principle of capitalism that tethers social citizenship to waged work. The UBIG would equip people with the freedom *not* to sell their labour and to withdraw, at least temporarily, from the 'race to the bottom' between low-skilled workers. It can be a profoundly emancipating intervention. Erik Olin Wright has identified three respects in which a universal income could provide such a transformative thrust: by 'strengthening the power of labour relative to capital, decommodifying labour power, and strengthening social power over economic activity' (Wright 2005).

This is a potentially radical and subversive turn that confronts the 'double separation' – from the means of production and the means of subsistence – that is customarily imposed on workers. It potentially recalibrates the distribution of power between low-skilled workers and employers. If the bare necessities of life can be secured elsewhere, demeaning and hyper-exploitative wage labour – when available – is no longer the 'only option'. This altered power relation would boost the collective strength of workers: 'Where workers individually have easier exit options, employers may have greater incentives to agree to new forms of collective cooperation with organisations of workers' (Wright 2003: 80). By tightening the labour supply, a universal income would increase the reservation wage (or the lowest wage at which a worker is likely to perform a given task), thereby boosting wages.

A grant that buffers individuals against the coercion of demeaning, low-pay and unsafe wage labour, can enhance their liberty. It would endow 'the weakest with bargaining power' (van Parijs 2003: 10) and, once linked with other interventions to strengthen well-being and expand the content of citizenship, could contribute towards a potentially significant redistribution of power, time and liberty.

The extent of such effects, though, would depend on the size of the grant. A UBIG that enables a person to live a basic, decent life (the proposal put to Swiss voters, for example, called for a US$2 500 monthly grant) would have a dramatic impact. Even a much smaller income grant could empower individuals to turn down work at least some of the time, and could subsidise some forms of decommodified work, such as caregiving, volunteering, studying and participating in community activities or production. However, it also has to be big enough to enable workers to rebuff low-wage, super-exploitative jobs, should they wish to. Otherwise the grant may end up indirectly *subsidising employers*, much as food vouchers and other welfare support in the US and the UK currently do, enabling companies to depress wages.

This liberating potential of a UBIG is disconcerting to some critics, who object that the mechanism would act as a disincentive to work. In societies with very high unemployment, the concern about a disincentive to work is odd and disingenuous when a much more impassable 'disincentive' is in place: the fact that new jobs are few in number and tend to clutter at the bottom rungs of the pay and job security ladder. In Greece, South Africa and Spain, for example, youth unemployment exceeds fifty per cent – the 'discouraging effect' of a UBIG becomes practically irrelevant in such conditions.

The evidence suggests that the effect of a UBIG on labour supply would be neither automatic nor uniform. Social experiments carried out in North America in the 1970s suggested that cash grants might encourage some recipients to give up jobs. Between 1968 and 1980, a number of US states, including Colorado, New Jersey, North Carolina and Pennsylvania, undertook randomised trials in which some households got unconditional cash transfers, while others (the 'control groups') did not. People who got the transfers worked less, as did a small percentage of secondary beneficiaries (mostly women).[34]

Other evidence suggests that, in generally impoverished settings with high unemployment rates, cash grants tend to have a negligible impact on labour market participation. Nicaragua's conditional cash transfer programme (which is linked to children's school attendance and the family's participation in maternal and child health programmes) was found to have a 'very small' impact on the labour supply of extremely poor households (Arcia 2002). In the case of Brazil's *Bolsa Escola*, people receiving the stipend tended to work more (Schwartzman 2005). The appeal of a UBIG is that it should enable people to *choose* whether or not to work for a wage, at least temporarily. Those who choose to accept work would therefore surrender their basis for complaint about others who choose not to work for a wage.

Yet there remains unease about giving money to people without the assurance that they will contribute to society. One may imagine that the *universality* of a UBIG – the fact that it would enable anyone, at least temporarily, to opt out of waged work – would weaken such opposition. It seems not to do so. There is a deep-felt sense that it is chiefly through waged work that we contribute to society and 'earn' our claims to social citizenship. It is a fiction that retains powerful coercive force.

So rather than isolating job creation as the *only* way forward, there is a strong case for 'simultaneously [demanding] policies like the Basic Income and [waging] an ideological campaign against the hegemony of the work ethic', as Frase puts it.[35] In the kinds of labour markets unfolding around the world, says Frase, 'we ought to be less obsessed with maximising job creation and more concerned with making it easier and better to not be employed'.[36] Or, to put it differently, there is a compelling case for a larger mass of labour that is less exploited and more able to choose whether and when to work for a wage (Kunkel 2014) – a stance that accommodates both the demand for better, decent work and the demand for a UBIG that enables people to say no to demeaning, insecure, poorly paid work.

A UTOPIAN SHIMMER

By liberating our notions of 'what should be' from the force field of productivism and work, the UBIG potentially creates space for what Frederic Jameson (2005) termed a 'utopian impulse'.[37] It may seem odd to assign a utopian quality to a proposal which some on the Left dismiss as 'reformist'. Yet, to the extent that the UBIG releases people from the compulsion to sell their labour at the going rate and on the going terms, it destabilises a cornerstone of capitalist ideology and breaches the limits of 'reformism'. What seems at first glance like tinkering with social policy contains radical potential, a utopian shimmer which Robert van der Veen and Philippe van Parijs (1987) teased into a tantalising thought experiment in their essay 'A Capitalist Road to Communism'.

By introducing scenarios that (temporarily) free people from involuntary, demeaning labour without losing access to the means for a decent, fulfilling life, a UBIG would support the political and normative choices of building a society that does not revolve strictly around the axis of wage labour and production: '[I]f technology really is dramatically reducing the need for human labor, then we have an opportunity to think bigger and better, getting beyond merely trying to scrape up new skills and new jobs for the displaced proletariat' (Frase 2011).

The 'post-work' vision has a rich pedigree on the Left, encompassing thinkers from Paul Lafargue to Bertrand Russell to André Gorz, all of whom invested it with slightly different meanings. At risk of oversimplification, they have pictured situations in which wage relations gradually lose their pre-eminence in securing the means for life itself, in organising social and economic life and in achieving what we may call 'fulfilment' or 'meaning' in our lives. It is not that waged work itself stops; rather, that the terms and the manner in which work is exchanged steadily change, and the social and economic 'authority' of waged work dwindles. 'Post-work', in other words, refers not to a world without work, but to one where the imbalance between waged work and what used to be called 'life' can be corrected.

The need for such an overhaul cannot be overstated. A long-standing reality in 'developing' economies, and particularly in the 'informal' sector, the dividing line between 'private' life and 'work' life is also being steadily erased in 'developed' economies as 24/7 availability, on-call labour and 'independent' contracted work become more pervasive. Employers are withdrawing the means of life (beyond unstable and tightly rationed wages or contractual fees) while commanding ever-greater parts of people's lives. Alongside this is an even more 'pervasive process of enclosure' (Barchiesi 2012: 236), evident, for example, in the 'invisible', unpaid labour we perform on social media platforms or in the enforced performance of gaiety in the service industry. We no longer sell only our time, skills and labour, but our civility, emotions and dignity. Increasingly, it is life itself that is being put to work. The challenge is not simply to find work that can finance the means to life, but to reclaim life from the demands of that work.

Gorz (1994) in particular drew a close link between reducing labour time and enhancing the autonomy people can experience in their lives, a trade-off that highlights the distinctiveness he saw in the two spheres of 'labour' and 'life'.[38] Reduced working time and the promotion of free time, in Christoph

Hermann's (2015: 32–33) phrasing, on the one hand 'restricts affluent consumption to what Gorz calls fundamental or felt needs; on the other it creates room for autonomous activities and production which is not subordinated to the goal of maximising profit'. However, there is some controversy about Gorz's stance towards a guaranteed basic income. In Hermann's recent reading, the later writings of Gorz allowed for a compatibility between using reduced work time to facilitate autonomous activities that are motivated by use values rather than exchange values, and a 'guaranteed basic income' for people who are not in paid employment. But in Finn Bowring's earlier (1996) reading, Gorz worried that a guaranteed minimum income for people who are temporarily out of work or who choose not to work at all would compensate them for their economic exclusion while leaving untouched the reality of a divided and unequal society. The central concern, he argued, was not merely material security but one's ability to live a socially rooted and socially meaningful life. A UBIG therefore would need to do more than release people from the compulsion of waged work or even separate work from income entirely; it must have a social goal: '[E]xcusing people from working by securing them an income anyway is not a way of giving them full membership of their society. You cannot become a member of any community if you have no obligation whatsoever to it ... There can be no inclusion without reciprocal obligations' (Gorz 1992: 184).

We return, in other words, to the vexing matter of *reciprocity* – except that it now has a different character, freed from the fiction that it can only be expressed through the mechanism of waged work. A UBIG would have to function as part of the reciprocal arrangement that Gorz insisted was 'essential to economic citizens and to full participation in society' (Gorz 1992: 182). That arrangement involves a positive obligation to expand 'those activities which create nothing that can be bought, sold, exchanged – and hence nothing that has value (in the economic sense) – but only non-marketable wealth with an intrinsic value of its own' (Gorz 2010: 28).

The reduction of obligatory waged work opens opportunities for what Gorz termed 'socially determined' work: activities that allow one 'to feel useful to society in a general sense, rather than in a particular way subject to particular relationships, and thus to exist as a fully social individual' (1985: 54) (see Bassey in this volume). But he saw risks as well, specifically in the ways in which a UBIG could be used to service diametrically opposed agendas: 'The guarantee of an income independent of a job will be emancipatory or repressive, from the Left or the Right, according to whether it opens up new spaces for individual and social activity or whether, on the contrary, it is only the social wage for compulsory passivity' (Gorz 1985: 40).

Gorz's concern was that the Right could use a universal income to ensure social control and passivity by paying very low 'placating' amounts to people who have effectively been reduced to supernumeraries within the capitalist order (Little 1996). The uses and functions of a UBIG are therefore fundamentally tied to the social and political processes that accompany it, and whether it forms part of broader mobilisation. If treated strictly as a technical intervention, detached from progressive social forces and programmes, it is exposed to capture and ruin. Social policy interventions do not do the bidding only of their creators.

On the Right, a basic income is eyed as a way to replace wider social protection and welfare systems with a single payment. Instead of supplementing other forms of social assistance and slotting into broader progressive social transformation, proponents on the Right see a basic income grant as a way to strip away social entitlements and extend the authority of the market even further. Indeed, arguments in favour of a UBIG sometimes merge into a blend of traditional social-democratic and more contemporary neoliberal reasoning, as James Ferguson (2007) has noticed. The grant could improve people's welfare, reduce poverty, function as a productive boost and serve as an 'investment' that lubricates individuals' deeper integration into the market system.[39]

Coursing through the debate, in other words, are profoundly different visions about the function and thrust of such a grant. Progressives and radicals see a universal income incorporated into an extensive safety net, functioning as a systemic reform that can support a just transition. The Right sees it chiefly as an opportunity to drive the state into deeper retreat and expand the domain of the market. A universal income grant that enables collectively provided public goods to be turned over to the market would be highly undesirable. Those are not insurmountable risks. But any bid for a transformative UBIG has to contend with them, and ensure that the scheme operates alongside strategies for ensuring that public services (including health, childcare, education, etc.) are free to users, for subsidised public housing, for greater job creation and for an increased minimum wage. And the best way to achieve that is for a UBIG to be won and sustained through social action. If approached as a discrete technocratic policy intervention, its transformative potential will be stillborn.

CONCLUSION

More, better-paid and socially useful jobs are vital and feasible. But waged work is only one among several routes towards the realisation of social rights, not a substitute for it. The current outlook offers no basis for an expectation that job creation will provide a sufficient basis for livelihood security and social inclusion in a great majority of countries.

The appeal and potential of a UBIG is, in one respect, quite literal and conventional, yet at the same time potentially transformative. A UBIG is a means to improve people's material, health and educational status, to reduce poverty and avert precariousness. It would function as a safety net for communities hard hit by the varied and cumulative effects of climate shocks. It would help cushion against the effects of automation and digitisation on waged work, and help protect workers who are displaced as economies transition to low-carbon models. It is a mechanism that can accompany and support forward-looking change.

Its thrust is even more radical, though. A UBIG potentially links the immediate, short-term need to secure the basic means for a dignifying life with the liberating potential of temporarily stepping free of the compulsion to sell one's labour at the going rate. By partially delinking income and basic needs provision from working for a wage, a UBIG would open new opportunities to perform socially productive activities and to rebuild circuits of social reciprocity that bypass the domain of waged work. It would support a redefinition of the meaning of citizenship and a reassertion of people's rights and entitlements.

A UBIG has a powerfully emancipatory and transformative potential. It is an opportunity to transport ourselves beyond a fate where, as Gorz (1999: 56) put it in one of his last books, we are forever 'prepared to make any and every concession, to suffer humiliation or subjugation, to face competition and betrayal to get or keep a job', since 'those who lose their jobs lose everything'.

NOTES

1 Or the 'employment to population ratio'. Working age is typically fifteen years and older.

2 Official definitions of employment generally present cosmetic pictures of reality. The definitions tend to be elastic, allowing for people in tenuous and fleeting forms

of work to be counted as 'employed'. In South Africa, for example, people who report earning an income from 'hunting', 'begging', washing cars on the street or growing their own food are tallied as 'employed'.

3   Trapp's (2015) analysis shows a decrease in the labour share of income in all regions between 1990 and 2011, except for South Asia (based on data for only Bhutan, India and Sri Lanka), where it increased slightly.

4   Using a dataset from 1960 to 1997, Anne Harrison (2002) split her sample of over a hundred countries into two groups. Her data showed that, in the group of poorer countries, labour's share in national income fell on average by 0.1 per cent per year from 1960 to 1993, with the drop accelerating after 1993, to an average decline of 0.3 per cent per year. In the richer subgroup, the labour share grew by 0.2 per cent per year prior to 1993, after which it fell by 0.4 per cent per year.

5   N. Irwin, 'Growth has been good for decades. So why hasn't poverty declined?' *New York Times*, 4 June 2014, http://www.nytimes.com/2014/06/05/upshot/growth-has-been-good-for-decades-so-why-hasnt-poverty-declined.html?ref=topics&abt=0002&abg=1 (accessed 20 August 2017).

6   M. Trottman and K. Maher, 'Organized labor loses members', *Wall Street Journal*, 23 January 2013, http://www.wsj.com/news/articles/SB10001424127887323539804578259693886663764 (accessed 20 August 2017).

7   'The end of cheap China', *The Economist*, 10 March 2012, http://www.economist.com/node/21549956 (accessed 20 August 2017).

8   T. Booth, 'Here, there and everywhere', *The Economist*, 19 January 2013, http://www.economist.com/news/special-report/21569572-after-decades-sending-work-across-world-companies-are-rethinking-their-offshoring (accessed 20 August 2017).

9   Cambodia, Indonesia, the Philippines and Vietnam have tried to capitalise on those trends, but weak supply chains, a lack of economies of scale and shortages of skilled workers have held back wholesale shifts of production in their direction.

10 Their model predicts that most workers in transportation and logistics sectors, along with most office and administrative support workers, and workers active in production, are at risk. Jobs in construction, journalism, hospitals and pharmacies are also on the 'endangered' list.

11 There are some localised exceptions to this trend, notably in parts of South America and East Asia (particularly China). But in almost all of the industrialised world, the former Soviet Union and its satellites, Africa, South Asia, the Caribbean and Central America workers at best have been fighting rearguard actions.

12 'Switzerland's voters reject basic income plan', *BBC News*, 5 June 2016, http://www.bbc.com/news/world-europe-36454060. See also www.europeanceo.com/finance/the-case-for-and-against-unconditional-basic-income-in-switzerland/ (both sites accessed 20 August 2017).

13 The website of the Basic Income Earth Network is an informative source for news, debates and academic literature about basic income proposals. See www.basicincome.org/news/category/from-web/academic-literature/ (accessed 20 August 2017). The ILO, meanwhile, seems to shun the concept, with its flagship *World of Work* reports hardly mentioning a basic or universal income. Instead, the 2014

edition claims to show, 'for the first time, that quality jobs can drive sustained growth in emerging and developing countries'. See http://www.ilo.org/global/research/global-reports/world-of-work/2014/WCMS_243961/lang--en/index.htm (accessed 20 August 2017).

14 'Dutch city of Utrecht to experiment with a universal, unconditional "basic income"', *The Independent*, 26 June 2015.

15 A. Kassam, 'Ontario plans to launch universal basic income trial run this summer', *Guardian*, 24 April 2017, https://www.theguardian.com/world/2017/apr/24/canada-basic-income-trial-ontario-summer?CMP=Share_iOSApp_Other (accessed 20 August 2017).

16 S. Sodha, 'Is Finland's basic universal income a solution to automation, fewer jobs and lower wages?' *Guardian*, 19 February 2017, https://www.theguardian.com/society/2017/feb/19/basic-income-finland-low-wages-fewer-jobs?CMP=Share_iOSApp_Other (accessed 20 August 2017).

17 See http://philosophyfaculty.ucsd.edu/faculty/rarneson/Courses/COS%20Chapter%204,%20John%20Stuart%20Mill,%20Chapters%20on%20Socialism.html (accessed 19 September 2017).

18 Milton Friedman coined the term in his 1962 book, *Capitalism and Freedom*.

19 L. Neyfakh, 'Should the government pay you to be alive?' *Boston Globe*, 9 February 2014, www.bostonglobe.com/ideas/2014/02/09/should-government-pay-you-alive/aaLVJsUAc5pKh0iYTFrXpI/story.html (accessed 20 August 2017).

20 An overview is available at https://www.opendemocracy.net/ourkingdom/karl-widerquist/alaska-model-citizens-income-in-practice (accessed 30 August 2017).

21 The poverty gap refers to the total income shortfall of households living below the poverty line. A narrower poverty gap means more households would edge closer to, or above, the poverty line.

22 The claim was moot. In the 2005/06 financial year, for example, revenue collection exceeded budget estimates by R41.2 billion (US$5.2 billion at the time), which prompted R19.1 billion (US$2.4 billion) in tax cuts in the following financial year. A R100 monthly income grant paid to each of the forty-seven million South Africans would have cost R56.4 billion in that year (see Marais 2011).

23 'Didiza cautions about basic income grant', *Business Day*, 14 August 2002.

24 Cited in Desai (2005). The spokesperson was dismissing the Taylor Committee's proposal for a basic income grant.

25 For a useful overview, see Meth (2004).

26 This means-tested scheme almost certainly has reduced female poverty, increased school enrolment and improved learning performances. Recipients decide how to use the grants, but they have to abide by several conditions.

27 This targeted and conditional scheme reaches about three million households, requires complex administration and is highly intrusive, but it has been shown to reduce poverty in beneficiary households, and improve both school enrolment and attendance as well as health status.

28 S. Terkel, 'Capitalism, for better or worse', *New York Times*, 19 March 1973.

29 Camus had the good sense to add, 'But when work is soulless, life stifles and dies.'

30 Many studies in Europe and North America show that up to one-quarter of daily work time is devoted to non-work activities that have no bearing on the job the person is

paid to perform. Some of this is 'active' or subversive 'non-work', but a fair deal of it entails performing pantomimes of work (see Bolchover 2005; Paulsen 2014).

31 In both the UK and the US, growing proportions of people receiving welfare benefits have some form of employment.

32 'Linked' or 'associated' because the causality is not clearly established. Studies in New Zealand, for example, have found that being unemployed was associated with a two- to threefold increased relative risk of death by suicide, compared with being employed. However, at least half of this association might have been attributable to confounding factors such as mental illness (see Blakely, Collings and Atkinson 2003).

33 Eban Goodstein (1999) has shown, for example, that the relative generosity and lack of conditionality of welfare regimes in western Europe tended to result in less political opposition to environmental restructuring in those countries, compared with the US.

34 Neyfakh, 'Should the government pay you to be alive?'

35 See http://www.peterfrase.com/2012/05/ (accessed 19 September 2017).

36 See http://www.peterfrase.com/2012/05/. In a few societies, full employment (meaning unemployment levels of five per cent or lower) might yet be achieved intermittently – but even there the feat is likely to arise from statistical craftiness and the use of coercive tools (legislative, material and social) to dragoon people into whatever types of work become available.

37 Thanks to Peter Frase (2013) for this insight, in his 'Curious Utopias' essay.

38 It is one of the reasons why Gorz (1994) resisted seeing reproductive and domestic labour as merely unremunerated forms of (what should be) waged work. He argued that reproductive labour is invested with qualities that make it profoundly different from most waged labour, not least because it is among the only examples of 'work for oneself' that survived industrial capitalism. The oppressive aspects of domestic labour, he argued, could not be entirely removed, but could be relieved if more time were available to do the work, and if the work were divided more equitably within households.

39 Ferguson suggests that such an amalgam of arguments that do not fit the conventional oppositions of 'progressive' social democracy and 'reactionary' neoliberalism might be creating 'new and potentially promising forms of political struggle' (2007: 84). For an edifying elaboration on these and related themes, see Ferguson (2015).

REFERENCES

Aguëro, J.M., Carter, M.R. and Woolard, I. 2006. 'The impact of unconditional cash transfers on nutrition: The South African Child Support Grant'. Accessed 18 August 2017, http://www.opensaldru.uct.ac.za/bitstream/handle/11090/46/06_08.pdf?sequence=1.

Allegre, G. 2014. *How can a basic income be defended?* OFCE Briefing Paper No. 7, February.

Arcia, G. 2002. *Macroeconomic impacts of social safety nets.* Briefing note for Consulting Assistance on Economic Reform II, Discussion Paper No. 82, Centre for International Development, Harvard University.

Baird, S., Ferreira, F., Ozler, B. and Woolcock, M. 2014. 'Conditional, unconditional and everything in between: A systematic review of the effects of cash transfer programmes on schooling outcomes', *Journal of Development Effectiveness*, 6 (1): 1–43.

Barchiesi, F. 2006. 'The debate on the basic income grant in South Africa: Social citizens, wage labour and the reconstruction of working-class politics'. Paper presented at the Harold Wolpe Memorial Trust's 10th Anniversary Colloquium, Engaging Silences and Unresolved Issues in the Political Economy of South Africa, 21–23 September, Cape Town.

Barchiesi, F. 2012. 'Liberation of, through, or from work? Postcolonial Africa and the problem with "job creation" in the global crisis', *Interface*, 4 (2): 230–253.

Benjamin, N., Beegle, K., Recanatini, F. and Santini, M. 2014. *Informal economy and the World Bank*. Policy Research Working Paper 6888. Washington, DC: World Bank. Accessed 18 August 2017, www-wds.worldbank.org/external/default/WDSContentServer/WDSP/IB/2014/05/22/000158349_20140522153248/Rendered/PDF/WPS6888.pdf.

Blakely, T.A., Collings, S.C. and Atkinson, J. 2003. 'Unemployment and suicide: Evidence for a causal association?' *Journal of Epidemiology and Community Health*, 57 (8): 594–600.

Blyth, M. and Lonergan, E. 2014. 'Print less but transfer more: Why central banks should give more money directly to the people'. *Foreign Affairs*, Sept/Oct. Accessed 18 August 2017, http://www.foreignaffairs.com/articles/141847/mark-blyth-and-eric-lonergan/print-less-but-transfer-more.

Bolchover, D. 2005. *The Living Dead: Switched off, Zoned out – the Shocking Truth about Office Life*. Chichester: Capstone Books.

Bowring, F. 1996. 'Misreading Gorz', *New Left Review*, 271: 102–122.

Breman, J. 2013. 'A bogus concept?' *New Left Review*, 84, https://newleftreview.org/II/84/jan-breman-a-bogus-concept (accessed 18 August 2017).

Brenner, R. 2006. *The Economics of Global Turbulence: The Advanced Capitalist Economies from Long Boom to Long Downturn, 1945–2005*. London: Verso Books.

Carlos, N., Warnke, I., Seifritz, E. and Kawohl, W. 2015. 'Modelling suicide and unemployment: A longitudinal analysis covering 63 countries, 2000–11', *The Lancet Psychiatry*, 2 (3): 239–245.

CIA (Central Intelligence Agency). 2013. *The World Factbook*. Washington, DC: Central Intelligence Agency, Office of Public Affairs.

Clark, A.E. and Oswald, A.J. 1994. 'Unhappiness and unemployment', *The Economic Journal*, 104: 648–659.

Cosatu (Congress of South African Trade Unions). 2000. 'Submission on comprehensive social security'. Submitted to the Taylor Task Team on Social Security, Johannesburg.

Cummine, A. 2015. 'A citizen's income and wealth fund for the UK: Lessons from Alaska'. *Opendemocracy*, 11 February. Accessed 17 August 2017, https://www.opendemocracy.net/ourkingdom/angela-cummine/citizen%e2%80%99s-income-and-wealth-fund-for-uk-lessons-from-alaska.

Cylus, J., Glymour, M.M. and Avendano, M. 2014. 'Do generous unemployment benefit programs reduce suicide rates? A state fixed-effect analysis covering 1968–2008', *American Journal of Epidemiology*, 180 (1): 45–52.

Desai, A. 2005. 'Finding the holy grail? Making poverty history in the 21st century'. Accessed 18 August 2017, http://www.sarpn.org.za/documents/d0001284/P1523-Holy-grail_Desai.pdf.

Everatt, D. 2008. 'The undeserving poor: Poverty and the politics of service delivery in the poorest nodes of South Africa', *Politikon*, 35 (3): 293–319.

Ferguson, J. 2007. 'Formalities of poverty: Thinking about social assistance in neoliberal South Africa', *African Studies Review*, 50 (2): 71–86.

Ferguson, J. 2015. *Give a Man a Fish: Reflections on the New Politics of Distribution*. Durham, NC: Duke University Press.

Forget, E. 2011. 'The town with no poverty', *Canadian Public Policy*, 37 (3): 283–305.

Frase, P. 2011. 'The machines and us'. Blog post, accessed 18 August 2017, http://www.peterfrase.com/2011/10/the-machines-and-us/.

Frase, P. 2012. 'Category errors', *Jacobin*, 22 May. Accessed 18 August 2017, https://www.jacobinmag.com/2012/05/category-errors/.

Frase, P. 2013. 'Curious utopias', *Jacobin*, 14 May. Accessed 18 August 2017, https://www.jacobinmag.com/2013/05/curious-utopias/.

Frase, P. 2014. 'Workin' it'. Blog post, accessed 18 August 2017, http://www.peterfrase.com/2014/02/workin-it/.

Frey, C.B. and Osborne, M.A. 2013. 'The future of employment: How susceptible are jobs to computerisation?' Accessed 18 August 2017, http://www.oxfordmartin.ox.ac.uk/downloads/academic/The_Future_of_Employment.pdf.

Friedman, M. 1962. *Capitalism and Freedom*. Chicago, IL: University of Chicago Press.

Goldsmith, S. 2012. 'The economic and social impacts of the permanent fund dividend on Alaska'. In *Alaska's Permanent Fund Dividend: Examining Its Suitability as a Model*, edited by Karl Widerquist and Michael W. Howard. New York: Palgrave Macmillan, pp. 49–63.

Goodstein, E. 1999. *The Trade-Off Myth: Fact and Fiction about Jobs and the Environment*. Washington, DC: Island Press.

Gorz, A. 1985. *Paths to Paradise: On the Liberation from Work*. London: Pluto Books.

Gorz, A. 1992. 'On the difference between society and community, and why basic income cannot by itself confer full membership of either'. In *Arguing for Basic Income: Ethical Foundations for a Radical Reform*, edited by Philippe van Parijs. London: Verso, pp. 178–184.

Gorz, A. 1994. *Capitalism, Socialism, Ecology*. Translated by Chris Turner. London: Verso.

Gorz, A. 1999. *Reclaiming Work: Beyond the Wage-Based Society*. Cambridge: Polity.

Gorz, A. 2010. *The Immaterial: Knowledge, Value and Capital*. London: Seagull Books.

Gumede, W. 2005. *Thabo Mbeki and the Battle for the Soul of the ANC*. Cape Town: Zebra Press.

Haarmann, C., Haarmann, D., Jauch, H., Shindondola, H., Nattrass, N., Niekerk, I. and Samson, N. 2009. *Making the difference! The BIG in Namibia*. Basic Income Grant Pilot Project Assessment Report, April. Windhoek, Namibia: Desk for Social Development.

Harrison, A. 2002. 'Has globalisation eroded labour's share? Some cross-country evidence'. Mimeo. Cambridge, MA: National Bureau of Economic Research.

Hart, G. 2006. 'Beyond neoliberalism? Post-apartheid developments in historical and comparative perspective'. In *The Development Decade? Economic and Social Change in South Africa: 1994–2004*, edited by Vishnu Padayachee. Cape Town: HSRC Press, pp. 13–32.

Hermann, C. 2015. *Capitalism and the Political Economy of Work Time*. New York: Routledge.

Hetschko, C., Knabe, A. and Schöb, R. 2013. 'Changing identity: Retiring from unemployment'. Accessed 18 August 2017, https://www.msm.uni-due.de/fileadmin/Dateien/MikroAuwi/FoSem/Knabe_20130620.pdf.

Hilferding, R. 1981. *Finance Capital: A Study of the Latest Phase of Capitalist Development*. London: Routledge and Kegan Paul.

Huber, E. and Stephens, J. 2012. *Democracy and the Left: Social Policy and Inequality in Latin America*. Chicago, IL: University of Chicago Press.

ILO (International Labour Office). 2013. *Global Employment Report 2013*. Geneva: ILO.

ILO. 2014a. *Global Employment Trends 2014*. Geneva: ILO.

ILO. 2014b. *Global Wage Report 2014/2015: Wages and Income Inequality*. Geneva: ILO.

IMF (International Monetary Fund). 2015. *World Economic Outlook: Adjusting to Lower Commodity Prices.*. Washington, DC: IMF.

Jameson, F. 2005. *Archaeologies of the Future: The Desire Called Utopia and Other Science Fictions*. New York: Verso.

Karabarbounis, L. and Neiman, B. 2013. *The global decline of the labor share*. National Bureau of Economic Research Working Paper No. 19136, June.

Korpi, W. and Palme, J. 1998. 'The paradox of redistribution and strategies of equality: Welfare state institutions inequality and poverty in the Western countries', *American Sociological Review*, 63 (5): 661–687.

Kunkel, B. 2014. *Utopia or Bust: A Guide to the Present Crisis*. London: Verso.

Lagarde, M., Haines, A. and Palmer, N. 2009. 'The impact of conditional cash transfers on health outcomes and use of health services in low and middle income countries', *Cochrane Database Systematic Review*, 4, CD008137, doi:10.1002/14651858.CD008137.

Lavinas, L. 2013. '21st century welfare', *New Left Review*, 84: 4–40.

Liebenberg, S. 2002. 'Universal access to social security rights: Can a basic income grant meet the challenge?' *ESR Review*, 3 (2): 8–10.

Little, A. 1996. *The Political Thought of Andre Gorz*. New York: Routledge.

Marais, H. 2011. *South Africa Pushed to the Limit: The Political Economy of Change*. London: Zed Books.

Marx, K. and Engels, F. (1888) 1988. *The Communist Manifesto*, edited by Frederic L. Bender. New York: Norton.

Meth, C. 2004. 'Ideology and social policy: "Handouts" and the spectre of "dependency"', *Transformation*, 56: 1–29.

Meth, C. 2007. 'What is pro-poor growth? What are some of the things that hinder its achievement in South Africa?' (research report prepared for Oxfam GB), May, Johannesburg.

Mill, J.S. 1849. *Principles of Political Economy* (second edition). New York: Augustus Kelley.

Mishell, L. and Shierholz, H. 2013. *A decade of flat wages: The key barrier to shared prosperity and a rising middle class*. EPI Briefing Paper No. 365. Washington, DC: Economic Policy Institute. Accessed 18 August 2017, http://s1.epi.org/files/2013/BP365.pdf.

Mkandawire, T. 2005. 'Targeting and universalism in poverty reduction'. Accessed 18 August 2017, http://epri.org.za/wp-content/uploads/2011/03/Mkandawire2005 TargetingUniversalism.pdf.

National Employment Law Project. 2012. 'The low-wage recovery and growing inequality'. Data brief, August. Accessed 18 August 2017, http://nelp.org/content/ uploads/2015/03/LowWageRecovery2012.pdf.

Noh, Y-H. 2009. 'Does unemployment increase suicide rates? The OECD panel evidence', *Journal of Economic Psychology*, 30 (4): 575–582.

Paulsen, R. 2014. *Empty Labour: Idleness and Workplace Resistance*. Cambridge: Cambridge University Press.

Peck, J. 2001. *Workfare States*. New York: Guilford Press.

Picketty, T. and Zucman, G. 2013. 'Rising wealth-to-income ratios, inequality and growth'. Centre for Economic Policy Research, September. Accessed 18 August 2017, http://www.voxeu.org/article/capital-back.

Russell, B. 1932. 'In praise of idleness'. Accessed 18 August 2017, http://www.zpub.com/ notes/idle.html.

Schwartzman, S. 2005. 'Education-oriented social programs in Brazil: The impact of *Bolsa Escola*'. Paper presented at Global Conference on Education Research in Developing Countries, Global Development Network, 30 March–2 April 2, Prague.

Stats SA (Statistics South Africa). 2008. *Income and Expenditure of Households 2005/2006: Analysis of Results*. Pretoria: Stats SA. Accessed 18 August 2017, http:// www.sarpn.org.za/documents/d0003023/index.php.

Stats SA. 2017. *Quarterly Labour Force Survey – QLFS Q1:2017*. Pretoria: Stats SA.

Streeck, W. 2014. 'How will capitalism end?' *New Left Review*, 87: 35–64.

Terkel, S. 1972. *Working: People Talk about What They Do All Day and What They Feel about What They Do*. New York: Ballantine Books.

Trapp, K. 2015. *Measuring the labour income share of developing countries: Learning from social accounting matrices*. WIDER Working Paper 2015/041, April. Accessed 18 August 2017, https://www.wider.unu.edu/sites/default/files/wp2015-041.pdf.

Van der Hoeven, R. 2010. *Labour markets trends, financial globalisation and the current crisis in developing countries*. UN Department of Social and Economic Affairs, DESA Working Paper No. 99, October.

Van der Veen, R. and van Parijs, P. 1987. 'A capitalist road to communism', *Theory and Society*, 15: 635–655. Accessed 18 August 2017, http://www.ssc.wisc.edu/~wright/ ERU_files/PVP-cap-road.pdf.

Van Parijs, P. 2003. 'A simple and powerful idea for the 21st century'. In *Redesigning Distribution: Basic Income and Stakeholder Grants as Alternative Cornerstones for a More Egalitarian Capitalism*, edited by E.O. Wright. London: Verso, pp. 7–38.

Van Staveren, I. and van der Hoeven, R. 2012. 'Global trends in labour market inequalities, exclusion, insecurity and civic activism'. Accessed 18 August 2017, http://www. indsocdev.org/resources/UNDP_DGR_backgroundpaper.pdf.

Woolard, I. and Leibbrandt, M. 2010. 'The evolution and impact of unconditional cash transfers in South Africa'. Southern Africa Labour and Development Research Unit, University of Cape Town. Accessed 18 August 2017, http://siteresources.

worldbank.org/DEC/Resources/84797-1251813753820/6415739-1251815804823/
Ingrid_Woolard_paper.pdf.

World Bank. 2015. *The State of Social Safety Nets 2015*. Washington, DC: World Bank.

Wright, E.O. 2003. 'Basic income, stakeholder grants, and class analysis'. In *Redesigning Distribution: Basic Income and Stakeholder Grants as Alternative Cornerstones for a More Egalitarian Capitalism*, edited by E.O. Wright. London: Verso, pp. 79–88.

Wright, E.O. 2005. 'Basic income as a socialist project'. Paper presented at the annual US-BIG Congress, 4–6 March, University of Wisconsin, Madison. Accessed 18 August 2017, https://www.ssc.wisc.edu/~wright/Basic%20Income%20as%20a%20Socialist%20Project.pdf.

5

THE RIGHTS OF MOTHER EARTH

Pablo Sólon

> The universe is a communion of subjects, not a collection of objects.
> (Berry 2006: 17)

The 'Rights of Mother Earth' is a call to leave the dominant anthropocentric paradigm and to imagine a new Earth society. The anthropocentric viewpoint is that human beings are the central and most important entity in the world; that humans are superior to non-human life because they are the only ones that have consciousness, values and moral status. Within this perspective, nature is something separate from humans; it exists for the survival and development of human societies; it is the 'environment' of humans and a set of resources that can be exploited for their benefit. Anthropocentrism is deeply embedded in modern society. The logic of capital, which tends towards commodification and the development of technology, is deeply interconnected with anthropocentrism, augmenting the gap between humans and the Earth to levels never before seen in human history.

The Rights of Mother Earth challenges this vision and argues that in order to build alternative societies, we need to overcome anthropocentrism and change our relation with nature. The language of rights gives the concept a legal tone, but, as will be seen, the Rights of Mother Earth goes beyond the need for new legal frameworks that take nature into account. The legal recognition of the rights of nature/Mother Earth is just one stage in the process of construction that is still ongoing and that cannot be limited to juridical change. The final aim of the Rights of Mother Earth proposal is to build an Earth community: a society that has humans and nature as a whole.

The constitutionalisation in Ecuador and the legal recognition of the rights of nature/Mother Earth in Ecuador and Bolivia, in 2008 and 2010, respectively, reflect significant progress towards the realisation of the Rights of Mother Earth. But it is not the case that this proposal comes from the Andean region of South America. In reality, this alternative has diverse origins and different streams (indigenous, scientific, ethical and juridical) that developed at various moments and in different parts of the world. In some ways, several streams share common ideas and voices, while in others each presents a unique perspective. Nevertheless, these disparate voices have, over the years, interacted with one another, growing and deepening one another's ideas.

Although many tend to consider the rights of nature and of Mother Earth as synonymous, there is an important difference in that Mother Earth encompasses both humans and nature, and not nature alone. Mother Earth is the whole, while nature is one part of the whole. Moreover, some might say that the concept of 'nature' is itself an anthropocentric construction to separate humans from the natural world. The word 'nature' is present in almost all of the streams that converge in the construction of this vision, while 'Mother Earth' is more present in the indigenous and the Bolivian contribution to the juridical stream.

This chapter reviews the multiple threads or streams that have converged to produce the Rights of Mother Earth. I then consider some of the attempts to institutionalise these rights, particularly in terms of efforts made by the governments of Ecuador and Bolivia in recent years. Critically examining the challenges these projects have encountered, I explore some of the deeper underlying questions linked to concepts of property and power that can help us conceptualise how to take the movement beyond the discourse of rights and towards a systemic alternative that embraces and prioritises the notion of the whole/totality mentioned in the previous chapter.

THE STREAMS

Indigenous stream
The Rights of Mother Earth reflects the vision of indigenous peoples in many parts of the world, and in particular the Andean region of South America. This

indigenous vision entails a deep respect for nature, not only at the level of livelihood but also social organisation and cosmovision/spirituality. In this vision, everything on Earth and in the cosmos has life (see Acosta and Abarca in this volume). Humans are not superior beings who are above plants, animals or mountains. Humans exist with non-human beings to form an Earth community. The division between living beings and non-living beings does not exist. In the Andean indigenous vision, everything has life, including the hills, rivers, air, rocks, glaciers and oceans. All are part of a larger living organism that is *Pacha Mama* or Mother Earth, which interacts with the sun and the cosmos. Without taking this into consideration, life cannot be explained. Humans are just one component of the Earth community. They do not own the Earth or other beings, nor are they their masters. Human existence depends on harmony with nature; a balance that is not static, but dynamic, that changes and moves in cycles, but brings misfortune when broken.

The Rights of Mother Earth is based on the indigenous premise that questions why, if we are all part of Mother Earth, some have to be higher than others. Why do some beings enjoy protection and privileges, while others are relegated to the status of things? In this vision, in order to flourish as the Earth community, we must give equal treatment and respect to all who are part of it: from glaciers to forests, animals to humans, and from plants to the wind and ultimately all beings. The Earth community speaks to the whole in terms of an equivalence or unity of all things.

The indigenous stream does not speak of 'rights' directly, as in the concept of 'rights' in the western philosophical sense, but the essence of the indigenous vision underpins the whole approach of the Rights of Mother Earth. The concept of 'rights' is a construction that comes from outside the indigenous context, and therefore the development of 'rights' for Mother Earth or 'rights' of nature in indigenous communities is not expressed in these terms, but shares the vision of an order in which all living and non-living things are in balance. The use of 'rights' language is more explicit in the other streams.

Scientific stream

Different communities of Earth scientists[1] now acknowledge that the Earth behaves as a single, self-regulating system with physical, chemical, biological and human components. The Earth system consists of the land, oceans, atmosphere and poles, and includes the planet's natural cycles – carbon, hydrogen, nitrogen, phosphorus and sulphur – as well as deep Earth processes (e.g. geodynamics and seismology). As noted in the 2001 Amsterdam

Declaration on Earth System Science, 'The interactions and feedback between the component parts [of the Earth sciences] are complex and exhibit multi-scale temporal and spatial variability.'[2] According to the National Aeronautics and Space Administration (NASA) in the United States, human life is an integral part of the Earth system. Life affects carbon, nitrogen, water, oxygen and many other cycles and processes.

Thus, from a mainstream scientific perspective, the Earth system now includes human society. Social and economic systems are embedded within the Earth system. As Will Steffen and colleagues write, the most significant finding is that in the last centuries

> human activities are significantly influencing Earth's environment in many ways in addition to greenhouse gas emissions and climate change. Anthropogenic changes to Earth's land surface, oceans, coasts and atmosphere and to biological diversity, the water cycle and biogeochemical cycles are clearly identifiable beyond natural variability. They are equal to some of the great forces of nature in their extent and impact. Many are accelerating. Global change is real and is happening now. (Steffen et al. 2004: 298)

This global change cannot be understood in terms of a simple cause and effect model. Human-driven changes cause multiple effects that cascade through the Earth system in complex ways. These effects interact with one another and with local and regional-scale changes in multidimensional patterns that are challenging to understand and even more difficult to predict.

Human activities have the potential to transform how the Earth system operates in ways that may prove irreversible and that may make this planet less hospitable to humans and other life. The probability of a human-driven abrupt change in the Earth's environment has yet to be quantified, but it is a possibility. The Earth system is affected by breaches of critical thresholds and abrupt changes in the planet's natural cycles. Human activities could inadvertently trigger such changes with severe consequences for the Earth's environment and inhabitants.

The Earth system has moved well outside the range of the natural variability exhibited over the last half-million years at least. The nature of changes now occurring simultaneously in the Earth system, their magnitudes and rates of change are unprecedented. The Earth is currently operating in a no-analogue state (IGBP 2001).

The Gaia theory James Lovelock developed in the 1970s, which states that the Earth is a living organism, is part of this scientific stream. Beyond a series of scientific arguments, some members of this stream advocate for a kind of ethical framework to address the systemic crisis that we are facing. In 2001, scientists from the International Human Dimensions Programme on Global Environmental Change, the International Geosphere-Biosphere Programme, the World Climate Research Programme and Diversitas issued the Amsterdam Declaration on Earth System Science, affirming that

> an ethical framework for global stewardship and strategies for Earth System management are urgently needed. The accelerating human transformation of the Earth's environment is not sustainable. Therefore, the business-as-usual way of dealing with the Earth System is not an option. It has to be replaced – as soon as possible – by deliberate strategies of good management that sustain the Earth's environment while meeting social and economic development objectives. (IGBP 2001)

Between 2001 and 2005, 1 360 experts from 95 countries participated in the Millennium Ecosystem Assessment, which was carried out at the request of the United Nations (UN). One of their key conclusions was that species and ecosystems have 'intrinsic value'; that 'is the value of something in and for itself, irrespective of its utility for someone else' (Millennium Ecosystem Assessment 2005: v). In this way, the scientific stream provides concrete evidence to advance the proposal of the Rights of Mother Earth to treat the planet as an Earth community.

Ethical stream

The ethical stream is very much linked to all the other threads of the Rights of Mother Earth. This set of ideas comes from numerous disparate sources – a range of voices across different epochs making an ethical case for an improved relationship with the Earth. This includes appeals to various religious ideals, philosophical positions and other moral codes developed throughout history. For example, in the twelfth and thirteenth centuries, Saint Francis of Assisi spoke for the equality of all creatures instead of the idea that humans dominate over creation. He referred to the sun, the Earth, the water and the wind as his brothers and sisters. More recently, Pope Francis expounded, 'This is our sin, exploiting the Earth and not allowing her to her [sic] give us what she has within her.'[3] From a Buddhist perspective, the fourteenth Dalai Lama both condemns environmental destruction and enjoins humanity to realise its obligations towards the planet:

> ... we are part of nature ... Among the thousands of species of mammals on earth, we humans have the greatest capacity to alter nature. As such, we have a twofold responsibility. Morally, as beings of higher intelligence, we must care for this world. The other inhabitants of the planet – insects and so on – do not have the means to save or protect this world. Our other responsibility is to undo the serious environmental degradation that is the result of incorrect human behaviour. We have recklessly polluted the world with chemicals and nuclear waste, selfishly consuming many of its resources. Humanity must take the initiative to repair and protect the world.[4]

North American conservationist Aldo Leopold (1887–1948) proposed a 'land ethic' – a body of self-imposed limitations on freedom which derived from the recognition that 'the individual is a member of a community of interdependent parts':

> The land ethic simply enlarges the boundaries of the community to include soils, waters, plants, and animals, or collectively: the land. A land ethic changes the role of Homo sapiens from conqueror of the land-community to plain member and citizen of it. It implies respect for his fellow-members, and also respect for the community as such. (Leopold 1968: 203)

Contemporary philosopher J. Baird Callicott developed this approach further and in 1970 promoted a code of 'environmental ethics' based on Leopold's (1968: 225) idea that 'a thing is right when it tends to preserve the integrity, stability, and beauty of the biotic community. It is wrong when it tends otherwise'.

Launched in 2000, the Earth Charter brought together views from forty-six countries to frame a firm ethical position on protecting the dignity of the Earth. In recognising that 'the protection of Earth's vitality, diversity, and beauty is a sacred trust', the Charter calls for 'universal responsibility' to protect the 'unique community of life', which includes all the living and non-living beings on this planet (Earth Charter 2000: 1–2). It contains a broad range of principles, from ensuring sustainable life in all its rich diversity, to promoting participatory societies with gender equality, to adopting alternative systems of production that 'safeguard Earth's regenerative capacities' (Earth Charter 2000: 2).

Juridical stream

> Legislation may not change the heart but it will restrain the heartless – Martin Luther King[5]

The juridical stream takes into account all the elements mentioned above and seeks to insert them into a legal framework, with the perspective that the scientific, ethical and indigenous principles that prescribe radical transformation in the relationship between humans and the Earth require tools for enforcing that change. This stream recognises that law and governance are social constructions which evolve over time and change with new realities. They are important mechanisms for regulating human behaviour, but need to remain flexible to account for a shift away from an anthropocentric order. In this sense, the juridical stream argues for a new jurisprudence that is Earth centred rather than human centred. According to Australian law professor Peter Burdon (2011a: 60–61):

> As Philip Allot notes ... 'law cannot be better than society's idea of itself' ... For this reason it is no surprise that many of our law's most fundamental concepts and ideas imitate an anthropocentric worldview ... Law is a significant description of the way a society perceives itself and projects its image to the world ... As an evolving social institution, law needs to adapt to reflect this understanding.

In other words, the key question is how to rethink law and governance for the necessary well-being of Earth and all of its inhabitants. If nature has intrinsic value, how do our legal frameworks reflect that for the sake of the Earth community? A legal framework which implicitly considers human beings as the final aim and end of the universe, and that holds that the universe exists to satisfy the needs and desires of human beings, is anthropocentric (Leopold 1968). We must question the values and legitimacy of any law that surpasses the ecological limits of the environment to satisfy the needs of one species.

Catholic priest and 'eco-theologian' Thomas Berry decried what he saw as a hierarchy imposed on the world through an anthropocentric conception of rights.

'All rights have been bestowed on human beings,' he wrote. 'The other than human modes of being are seen as having no rights. They have reality and value only through their use by the human. In this context the other than human becomes totally vulnerable to exploitation by the human' (Berry 1999: 4). To transform jurisprudence, then, it will be necessary to move from conceiving of the non-human world as a 'collection of objects' to seeing all – living and non-living, human and non-human – as a 'communion of subjects' (Berry 2006: 17).

The dualism between subject and object is a key aspect of western civilisation. We have assigned values to subjects and everything that is like 'us' and we deprive rights to all other aspects of the world that we tend to consider 'objects'. Subjects are able to think and create while the rest are only resources, instruments or environment.

To move away from this position, the juridical stream of the Rights of Mother Earth proposes a revolution in how we conceive of the law. As Berry (1999: 60–61) puts it:

> To the industrial-commercial world the natural world has no inherent rights to existence, habitat, or freedom to fulfill its role in the vast community of existence. Yet there can be no sustainable future, even for the modern industrial world, unless these inherent rights of the natural world are recognised as having legal status. The entire question of possession and use of the Earth, either by individuals or by establishments, needs to be considered in a more profound manner than Western society has ever done previously.

Thus, even while the law as an enforceable code of principles and ethics is a human construction to govern human behaviour, the juridical stream advocates granting the power of rights to all things that make up the Earth as a way of ensuring a healthier planet.

THE PATH OF THE RIGHTS OF MOTHER EARTH

The proposal for the 'rights of nature' was initially developed in North America and Europe in the mid-twentieth century, and was built on a platform of ideas, including those of Leopold and proponents of animal rights such as Peter Singer, Tom Regan and Jeremy Bentham. For example, in 1789, Bentham wrote,

'The day may come when the rest of the animal creation may acquire those rights which never could have been withheld from them but by the hand of tyranny ... The question is not, can they (animals) reason? Nor can they talk? But can they suffer?' (Bentham 1948: 283).

The rights of animals have developed in different ways in various countries, including codification into national legal frameworks, as in the case of Germany, where Section 90a of the Civil Code states: 'Animals are not things. They are protected by special statutes. They are governed by the provisions that apply to things, with the necessary modifications, except insofar as otherwise provided.'[6]

In the 1970s, two key sources of the juridical stream developed in Europe and North America. One is Deep Ecology, promoted by Norwegian philosopher Arne Næss, and the other is Earth Jurisprudence or Wild Law, initially developed by Berry.

Deep Ecology

Næss (1912–2009) envisioned two different forms of environmentalism: Deep Ecology, which interrogates, on the most fundamental level, the root causes of Earth's imbalance, and Shallow Ecology, which tends to focus on short-term, surface-level changes, often promoting technological fixes (e.g. recycling, increased automotive efficiency, export-driven monocultural organic agriculture) that are rooted in the same consumption-oriented values and practices of today's industrial economy. The Deep Ecology approach involves redesigning our whole system to align with values and methods that truly preserve the ecological and cultural diversity of natural systems (Drengson n.d.).

According to Michael E. Zimmerman (1989: 24),

Deep Ecology is founded on two basic principles: one is a scientific insight into the interrelatedness of all systems of life on Earth, together with the idea that anthropocentrism – human-centeredness – is a misguided way of seeing things. Deep ecologists say that an eco-centric attitude is more consistent with the truth about the nature of life on Earth. The second component of deep ecology is what Arne Næss calls the need for human self-realisation ('re-earthing'). Instead of identifying with our egos or our immediate families, we would learn to identify with trees and animals and plants, indeed the whole ecosphere. This would involve a pretty radical change of consciousness, but it would make our behaviour more consistent with what science tells us is necessary for the well-being of life on Earth. We just wouldn't do certain things that damage the planet, just as you wouldn't cut off your own finger.

Næss rejected the idea that beings can be ranked according to their relative value. For example, judgements on whether an animal has an eternal soul, whether it uses reason or whether it has consciousness (or indeed higher consciousness) have all been used to justify the ranking of the human animal as superior to other animals. Næss (1989: 166) states that from an ecological point of view, 'the right of all forms [of life] to live is a universal right which cannot be quantified. No single species of living being has more of this particular right to live and unfold than any other species'.

A primary critique of Deep Ecology focuses on the proposal of some of its advocates that 'the flourishing of human life and cultures is compatible with a substantial decrease of the human population. The flourishing of nonhuman life requires such a decrease' (Devall & Sessions 1985: 70). The main argument is that to promote birth reduction as a key solution especially targets poor countries and leads to racist attitudes. Other Deep Ecology theorists, like Warwick Fox in Australia, respond to this notion by arguing for a distinction between being *misanthropic* (hating humanity) and being *anti-anthropocentric*. In addition, many social ecologists and eco-feminists agree that Deep Ecology does not conduct sufficient analysis of the social forces at work in the destruction of the biosphere (Zimmerman 1989). Finally, others have critiqued deep ecologists who sometimes attribute human characteristics to non-human organisms, falling into anthropomorphism.

Earth Jurisprudence or Wild Law

Berry (1914–2009) inspired the movement for Earth Jurisprudence or Wild Law. Interestingly, his main point of reference was not nature or the Earth, but the universe. 'The universe is the only text without context,' he wrote (2009: 94). Everything else has to be seen in the context of the universe. 'The story of the universe is the story of each individual being in the universe' (Berry 2009: 108), and so the journey of the universe – forever evolving, continually emerging – is the personal journey of each individual' (2009: 122). 'We can read the story of the universe in the trees. Everything tells the story of the universe. The winds tell the story, literally, not just imaginatively. The story has its imprint everywhere, and that is why it is so important to know the story. If you do not know the story, in a sense you do not know yourself; you do not know anything' (Berry 1999: 83).

The term 'Earth Jurisprudence' was coined to highlight the need to overcome the anthropocentric framework of contemporary jurisprudence. Wild Law reflected the view among the movement's advocates that their work was about bringing together and balancing two different parts of the whole: civilisation and nature. Cormac Cullinan (2011: 7) explains the concept in these terms:

> I know that 'wild law' sounds like nonsense – a contradiction in terms. Law, after all, is intended to bind, constrain, regularise and civilise. Law's rules, backed up by force, are designed to clip, prune and train the wilderness of human behaviour into the manicured lawns and shrubbery of the civilised garden. 'Wild', on the other hand, is synonymous with unkempt, barbarous, unrefined, uncivilised, unrestrained, wayward, disorderly, irregular, out of control, unconventional, undisciplined, passionate, violent, uncultivated, and riotous. A wild law is a law to regulate human behaviour in order to protect the integrity of the earth and all species on it. It requires a change in the human relationship with the natural world from one of exploitation to one of democracy with other beings. If we are members of the earth's community, then our rights must be balanced against those of plants, animals, rivers and ecosystems. In a world governed by wild law, the destructive, human-centered exploitation of the natural world would be unlawful. Humans would be prohibited from deliberately destroying functioning ecosystems or driving other species to extinction.

WHY 'RIGHTS'?

Given the critique of the anthropocentric foundations of modern jurisprudence, it makes sense to question why the social movements discussed thus far have sought to make their arguments in the legalistic language of rights. Moreover, if humans constructed 'rights' to govern themselves, then why attribute rights to nature instead of discussing laws to prevent human destruction of the environment? What kind of rights does nature have? Are they similar to human rights?

The first and most comprehensive responses to these questions are in Berry's ten principles of Earth Jurisprudence (see Box 5.1). According to Berry (1999), 'rights originate where existence originates'. Beings have rights not because they have consciousness or moral status, but merely because they exist and because their existence can only be explained as interaction between the different elements of the whole. Everything is interrelated, nothing exists in isolation and all share the same source of existence: the universe.

For Berry, 'every component of the Earth community has three rights: the right to be, the right to habitat, and the right to fulfil its role in the ever-renewing processes of the Earth community'. These three rights are 'role-specific or species-specific, and limited. Rivers have river rights. Birds have bird rights. Insects have insect rights. Humans have human rights. Difference in rights is qualitative, not quantitative. The rights of an insect would be of no value to a tree or a fish'. Thus, the rights of nature are not an extension of human rights to nature. According to Christopher D. Stone (2010: 4), 'to say that the environment should have rights is not to say that it should have every right we can imagine, or even the same body of rights as human beings have. Nor is it to say that everything in the environment should have the same rights as every other thing in the environment'.

Moreover, human rights do not supersede the rights of other modes of being to exist in their natural state. According to Berry, these rights 'are based on the intrinsic relations that the various components of Earth have to each other'. No living being nourishes itself. Each component of the Earth community depends on every other member of the community for its own survival.

The concept applies only in the context of human interaction with nature and would place duties only on human beings. The 'rights of nature' concept motivates into action those people in positions to help promote or safeguard a given right (Burdon 2011b). According to Ben Price (2013: 17), it is 'a socially beneficial relationship between society and its instrument, government, and those beings entitled to obligatory respect'.

LEGAL INSTRUMENTS

In the twenty-first century, the proposals of Earth Jurisprudence began to be incorporated into legal texts. In 2006, with the help of the Community

Box 5.1: Thomas Berry's Ten Principles of Earth Jurisprudence

1. Rights originate where existence originates. That which determines existence determines rights.

2. Since it has no further context of existence in the phenomenal order, the universe is self-referent in its being and self-normative in its activities. It is also the primary referent in the being and the activities of all derivative modes of being.

3. The universe is composed of subjects to be communed with, not objects to be used. As a subject, each component of the universe is capable of having rights.

4. The natural world on the planet Earth gets its rights from the same source that humans get their rights: from the universe that brought them into being.

5. Every component of the Earth community has three rights: the right to be, the right to habitat, and the right to fulfil its role in the ever-renewing processes of the Earth community.

6. All rights are role-specific or species-specific, and limited. Rivers have river rights. Birds have bird rights. Insects have insect rights. Humans have human rights. Difference in rights is qualitative, not quantitative. The rights of an insect would be of no value to a tree or a fish.

7. Human rights do not cancel out the rights of other modes of being to exist in their natural state. Human property rights are not absolute. Property rights are simply a special relationship between a particular human 'owner' and a particular piece of 'property', so that both might fulfil their roles in the great community of existence.

8. Since species exist only in the form of individuals, rights refer to individuals, not simply in a general way to species.

9. These rights as presented here are based on the intrinsic relations that the various components of Earth have to each other. The planet Earth is a single community bound together with interdependent relationships. No living being nourishes itself. Each component of the Earth community is immediately or mediately dependent on every other member of the community for the nourishment and assistance it needs for its own survival. This mutual nourishment, which includes the predator-prey relationship, is integral with the role that each component of the Earth has within the comprehensive community of existence.

10. In a special manner, humans have not only a need for but also a right of access to the natural world to provide for the physical needs of humans and the wonder needed by human intelligence, the beauty needed by human imagination, and the intimacy needed by human emotions for personal fulfilment.7

Environment Legal Defense Fund, the town of Barnstead in the State of New Hampshire in the United States passed an ordinance that says:

> All residents of the Town of Barnstead possess a fundamental and inalienable right to access, use, consume, and preserve water drawn from the sustainable natural water cycles that provide water necessary to sustain life within the Town. Natural communities and ecosystems possess inalienable and fundamental rights to exist and flourish within the Town of Barnstead. Ecosystems shall include, but not be limited to, wetlands, streams, rivers, aquifers, and other water systems. (Margil 2011: 253)

Similar orders have been adopted in other towns in the United States. These municipal ordinances are focused on specific areas of nature, and are not of general application. They empower local communities to assume the role of guardian for nature. Authorities measure damages in terms of the actual harm caused to the ecosystem rather than to a human property owner. According to Shannon Biggs and Mari Margil (2011: 10),

> under existing environmental laws, a person needs to prove 'standing' in order to go to court to protect Nature. This means demonstrating personal harm from logging, the pollution of a river, or the extraction of water. Damages are then awarded to that person, not to the ecosystem that's been destroyed. In the wake of the BP oil spill, the only damage deemed compensable by the legal system is the financial damage caused to those who can't use the Gulf ecosystem anymore. Under a rights-based system of law, a river has the right to flow, fish and other species in a river have the right to regenerate and evolve, and the flora and fauna that depend on a river have the right to thrive. It is the natural ecological balance of that habitat that is protected. Just as the lion hunts the antelope as part of the natural cycle of life, recognising Rights of Nature does not put an end to fishing or other human activities. Rather, it places them in the context of a healthy relationship where our actions do not threaten the balance of the system upon which we depend.

THE CONSTITUTION OF ECUADOR

The most important achievement in legal text is without a doubt the 2008 constitution of Ecuador. The constitution devotes chapter seven to the rights of nature:

Article 71. Nature, or Pacha Mama, where life is reproduced and occurs, has the right to integral respect for its existence and for the maintenance and regeneration of its life cycles, structure, functions and evolutionary processes. All persons, communities, peoples and nations can call upon public authorities to enforce the rights of nature.

Article 72. Nature has the right to be restored. This restoration shall be apart from the obligation of the State and natural persons or legal entities to compensate individuals and communities that depend on affected natural systems.

Article 73. The State shall apply preventive and restrictive measures on activities that might lead to the extinction of species, the destruction of ecosystems and the permanent alteration of natural cycles. The introduction of organisms and organic and inorganic material that might definitively alter the nation's genetic assets is forbidden.

The text is clearly the result of a combination of the indigenous and juridical streams. It speaks about nature as synonymous with *Pacha Mama*, which for some is inaccurate because Mother Earth comprises nature and humans. The specific rights for nature that are recognised are the right to exist, the right to its integrity, to regenerate, to its vital cycles and the right to be restored. The constitution does not include mechanisms for enforcing these rights and gives the state the flexibility to interpret these regulations with national interests in mind. Therefore, much of the enforcement of the rights of nature depends on the will of the government and an active society.

THE CASE OF BOLIVIA

The constitution of the Plurinational State of Bolivia, adopted in 2009, does not include the concept of the 'rights of nature' and is more in line with environmental rights for the benefit of 'present and future generations' of humans

(Article 33). The most advanced development of this legal text is that 'any person, in his own right or on behalf of a collective, is authorised to take legal actions in defence of environmental rights' (Article 34),[8] a provision that is also in the Ecuadorian constitution.

In the case of Bolivia, the Rights of Mother Earth was developed after the adoption of the constitution and was directly linked to an international response to the global crisis of climate change. In 2010, in Cochabamba, Bolivia, the World's Peoples Conference on Climate Change and the Rights of Mother Earth – with 35 000 participants and delegations from more than a hundred countries – drafted the Proposal for a Universal Declaration on the Rights of Mother Earth. According to this Declaration,

> we are all part of Mother Earth, an indivisible, living community of interrelated and interdependent beings with a common destiny ... [and] in an interdependent living community, it is not possible to recognise the rights of only human beings without causing an imbalance within Mother Earth ... [T]o guarantee human rights it is necessary to recognise and defend the rights of Mother Earth and all beings in her. (Rights of Mother Earth 2010: 1)

This approach views humans and nature as part of the Earth community and therefore these rights need to be regarded as the rights of the whole and all its beings and not only of the non-human (nature) part.

The Declaration states that 'the inherent rights of Mother Earth are inalienable in that they arise from the same source as existence' and that all 'organic and inorganic beings' have rights 'that are specific to their species or kind and appropriate for their role and function within the communities within which they exist' (2010: 2).

The specific rights that are recognised for Mother Earth as a whole and for 'all beings of which she is composed' are the rights to life and to exist; to be respected; to regenerate biocapacity and to continue vital cycles and processes free from human disruptions; to maintain identity and integrity as a distinct, self-regulating and interrelated being; to water; to clean air; to integral health; to be free from contamination, pollution and toxic or radioactive waste; to not have its genetic structure modified and to full and prompt restoration.

The Declaration was presented to the UN and the climate change process of negotiations, and at the end of 2010 its text was incorporated and adopted as

Law 71 of the Plurinational State of Bolivia. The most important advancement in Bolivian law in terms of the Rights of Mother Earth is the inclusion of an Ombudsman of Mother Earth (*Defensoría de la Madre Tierra*), whose mission is to oversee the compliance and enforcement of those rights. However, the Ombudsman has not yet been put in place.

CHALLENGES AND THE WAY FORWARD

The Rights of Mother Earth concept gained momentum after the experiences in Ecuador and Bolivia, and rights of nature initiatives are spreading throughout the world. For example, in the United States there are struggles for ordinances at municipal level that recognise the rights of nature; an initiative in Europe is pushing for the European Parliament and Council to recognise that nature has rights; in New Zealand, the Crown has signed an agreement with the Iwi (the local Māori people) stating that the Whanganui River will be recognised as a person in terms of the law; in the Philippines and other countries, juridical awards have asserted that the 'health of the people and the environment ... are equally protected under our fundamental law';[9] the UN holds a 'Harmony with Nature' dialogue every year where the proposal for a Universal Declaration of the Rights of Mother Earth is discussed; also at the UN and in the International Criminal Court, a civil society initiative is pushing for recognition of the crime of ecocide; at the global level, the Rights of Nature Ethics Tribunal conducted two sessions in Ecuador and Peru in 2014 and another in France in 2015 to address the issue of climate change as a systemic violation of the Rights of Mother Earth. Many of the groups that promote these initiatives have come together in the Global Alliance for the Rights of Nature.

However, the Rights of Mother Earth movement has to address some key concerns, including compliance and implementation; payment for ecosystem services and the so-called green economy; challenging property rights; and going beyond legal texts to address key issues such as what kind of Earth democracy we want to create.

Compliance and implementation

A major challenge is ensuring the implementation and compliance of nature/Mother Earth rights where these have been recognised. In Ecuador and Bolivia, despite the legal adoption of such rights, the fact remains that they have not really been implemented. There is not a single case that can be used as a positive emblematic example. On the contrary, there have been several backlashes where government projects and decisions have been made in clear violation of these rights.

In 2011, the government of the Plurinational State of Bolivia attempted to build a road through the Isiboro Ségure Indigenous Territory and National Park (*Territorio Indigena Parque Nacional Isiboro Siboro*, or TIPNIS). TIPNIS covers 12 363 km^2 of Amazonian and Andean territory. It is among the richest reserves of biodiversity in Latin America and shelters thousands of species of flora, mammals, birds, reptiles, amphibians and fish. It is the land of the Mojeño, the Chimán and the Yuracaré, who together represent around 12 000 indigenous people.

Thanks to the resistance of these indigenous people and the mobilisation of many sectors of society, the government put the project on hold. However, this was only after acts of repression and violence from the police against the indigenous people, who marched to the city of La Paz to protest against this project. Throughout this struggle there has been no official process through which the authorities are obliged to take into account the Rights of Mother Earth that are going to be affected and violated if the road is constructed.

In the case of the Yasuni–Ishpingo-Tambocacha-Tiputini (ITT) initiative, the Ecuadorian government stated in 2007 that it would refrain from exploiting the oil reserves of the ITT oil field within the Yasuni National Park in exchange for compensatory payments from the international community. This was presented as a positive step in preserving the rights of nature in such a rich biodiversity region. However, in 2013, Rafael Correa's government announced that the oil in that area would be exploited because there was not enough economic support from the international community for the initiative. Moreover, efforts to have a national referendum on this issue have been blocked by the authorities in Ecuador. This has led to discussions around the unviability of preserving the rights of nature only when there is money and violating them when there is no money.

Besides these cases in Bolivia and Ecuador, in responses to many other mining, oil extraction, deforestation, nuclear energy, genetic modification, fracking and other projects with evident negative impacts on the rights of nature, there have been no official processes to see how the rights of nature are or will be affected and what measures should be taken. There is an evident contradiction between the discourse and the practice of these governments, and between the legal rights that are recognised and the rights that are in reality respected and guaranteed.

Nonetheless, the fact that these rights are legally recognised and well known in the affected societies has allowed various indigenous groups, social organisations and new movements, like the Yasunidos in Ecuador, to develop actions to reclaim and implement these rights.

Payment for ecosystem services

Historically, the term 'environmental services' describes the cleaning of streets and public parks. Lately, however, this term has come to refer to the functions of nature in order to measure and price them so that they can be defined as 'environmental services' or 'ecosystem services' in the market. This is what happens through the green economy, which starts from the premise that 'nature has intrinsic value' but ends up pushing in favour of the commodification of ecosystem services and the development of a new kind of 'biodiversity offset'. The latter allows a company that harms or destroys an ecosystem in one part of the world to buy 'credits' from a project in a different part of the world that is promoting biodiversity conservation. The preservation of one species cannot compensate for the destruction of another. These 'offsets' are not meant to defend ecosystems but to generate a new and speculative market based on the financialisation of nature.

According to Maude Barlow (2011), payments for ecosystem services (PES) put a price tag on ecological goods (clean air, water, soil, etc.) and the services such as water purification, crop pollination and carbon sequestration that sustain them. A market model of PES is an agreement between the 'holder' and the 'consumer' of an ecosystem service, turning that service into an environmental property right. Clearly this system privatises nature, be it a wetland, lake, forest plot or mountain, and sets the stage for private accumulation of nature by those wealthy enough to be able to buy, hoard, sell and trade it. Already, northern governments and private corporations are studying public–private partnerships to set up lucrative PES projects in the global South (Barlow 2011).

Projects like reducing emissions from deforestation and forest degradation, climate-smart agriculture, biodiversity offsetting and others are part of this new scheme that is being pushed by corporations and the UN through the Sustainable Development Goals and other instruments, with the aim of establishing targets that will allow the development of these new market mechanisms around environmental services. The implementation of these processes of financialising nature represents a new and increasing threat to the Rights of Mother Earth.

Private property

One of the main manifestations of anthropocentrism in law is the notion of property. Long before the concept of human rights was adopted, the legal concept of property rights was established and enforced: property rights over land, houses, animals, machines, tools and even other humans, such as slaves and women. Property can be sold, borrowed, gifted, split, inherited, etc. In order to have property, the object of possession has to be identified as a thing that has no rights or fewer rights than the owner of that possession. Having possession of other citizens – who have equal rights – was not acceptable even in Ancient Greece. In order to become an object of property, the other human had to be dispossessed of his or her rights through war and conquest or be born a slave.

The dominant legal relation between humans and nature has so far been through property. Laws are established to guarantee property rights over land, mineral resources, oil, animals, water, etc. Property can be private, state-owned or public, but it is always the property of certain humans who thereby have control over certain 'things' of nature. Not everything in nature is property, because in order to become property it has to be delimited, isolated, scarce and subject to being brought to the market. Property fragments nature into 'things' that in reality are never dissociated: the forest from the soil, the underground water from biodiversity, the land from the minerals. There can be different kinds of owners and property rights over all these elements of nature but it is always a relation of dominance. Eric T. Freyfogle highlights: 'When lawyers refer to the physical world, to this field and that forest and the next-door city lot, they think and talk in terms of property and ownership. To the legal mind, the physical world is something that can be owned' (in Burdon 2011a: 62).

In reality, the main contradiction is not between human rights and the Rights of Mother Earth but between rights of nature and property rights that benefit mainly a fraction of humanity. As Paul Babie says,

> in Western society, property law provides some of the most foundational ideas about the land and about our place in the environment. Many of these ideas are so ingrained that we rarely give them second thought. The common 'idea' of private property is individual or absolute entitlement over a thing (what Blackstone called 'sole and despotic

dominion'), which is protected by the will of the state. Our home is our castle, our zone of personal influence 'where we make the rules'. Our legal conception of property also tells us that the land can be divided into discrete and distinct bundles of legal relations, which individuals hold in relation to each other. (Babie 2011: 283)

In order to have a new legal framework that is not anthropocentric, it is necessary to overcome, redefine and limit the concept of property. Earth Jurisprudence can only flourish if property rights are constrained and if we have a new eco-society that is not ruled by capital. In Ecuador and Bolivia, there were important changes with the addition of new rights related to nature but there was no significant change in relation to property rights.

Beyond rights

Thomas Berry was never entirely happy with the language of 'rights', but it was the best we had to be going on with' (Cashford 2011: 8). As Martin Luther King said, 'Legislation may not change the heart but it will restrain the heartless.' The proposal of 'rights of nature' was developed to use legislation to help restore the balance in our Earth system but its main aim was never to constrain its vision to legal texts. The final aim is to build an Earth society and this requires much more than a change in legal structures. Therefore, as Burdon (2011a) notes, the implementation of Earth rights should not be restricted to the juridical model as is frequently the case. Probably in the struggle for this proposal the concept of 'rights' will be replaced by a concept that can better reflect the search for an Earth society and also 'restrain the heartless' (Burdon 2011a).

The aim of the Rights of Mother Earth movement is to create Earth governance systems at all levels – an Earth democracy that takes into account not only humans but also nature and that connects the particular to the universal, the diverse to the common, and the local to the global; a living democracy that grows like a tree, from the bottom up. According to Vandana Shiva,

> people who are grounded in a place, who know the plants and animals, seasons and signs, ecosystems and processes of that place on Earth are in the best position to speak and care for the lands, waters, and beings of that community. Earth Democracy is guided by the principle of subsidiarity, calling for decisions to be made at the lowest appropriate level of governance. (in Koons 2011: 53)

The challenge of this proposal is how to strengthen and spread these diverse experiences of local governance and to imagine the forms that Earth democracy will have at national, regional and global levels. In Berry's words, 'Loss of Imagination and loss of Nature are the same thing. If you lose one you lose the other' (in Cashford 2011: 4). In a similar vein, Cullinan (2011: 8) highlights that the main aim of the Rights of Mother Earth movement is to 'encourage creative diversity rather than to impose uniformity', and to 'open spaces within which different and unconventional approaches can spring up, perhaps to flourish, perhaps to run their course and die'. In this sense, the Rights of Mother Earth is an invitation to think and act in a non-anthropocentric world.

NOTES

1   International Human Dimensions Programme on Global Environmental Change, International Geosphere-Biosphere Programme, World Climate Research Programme, and Diversitas – an integrated programme of biodiversity science.
2   See http://www.igbp.net/about/history/2001amsterdamdeclarationonearthsystem science.4.1b8ae20512db692f2a680001312.htm (accessed 20 August 2017).
3   See Philip Pullella, 'Pope Francis calls exploitation of nature sin of our time', HuffPost, 4 September 2014, http://www.huffingtonpost.com/2014/07/05/pope-francis-nature-environment-sin-_n_5559631.html (accessed 24 September 2017).
4   See 'Politics and environment: An interview', http://www.dalailama.com/messages/environment/politics-and-environment (accessed 20 August 2017).
5   See for example http://library.law.harvard.edu/justicequotes/explore-the-room/north-3/ (accessed 1 September 2017).
6   See https://www.globalanimallaw.org/database/national/germany/ (accessed 1 September 2017).
7   http://therightsofnature.org/thomas-berrys-ten-principles-of-jurisprudence/ (accessed 1 September 2017).
8   See https://www.constituteproject.org/constitution/Bolivia_2009 (accessed 1 September 2017).
9   See 'CA upholds GM eggplant field trials ban', Rappler, 26 September 2013, https://www.rappler.com/business/industries/247-agriculture/39914-bt-talong-court-of-appeals-decision (accessed 24 September 2017).

REFERENCES

Babie, P. 2011. 'How we control the environment and others'. In Exploring Wild Law: The Philosophy of Earth Jurisprudence, edited by Peter Burdon. Kent Town: Wakefield Press, pp. 279–292.
Barlow, M. 2011. 'Building the case for the Universal Declaration of the Rights of Mother Earth'. In The Rights of Nature: The Case for a Universal Declaration of the Rights of

Mother Earth, co-produced by Global Exchange, the Council of Canadians, The Pachamama Alliance, and Fundacion Pachamama, pp. 6–11.

Bentham, J. 1948. *An Introduction to the Principles of Morals and Legislation.* New York: Hafner Publishing Company.

Berry, T. 2006. *Evening Thoughts: Reflecting on Earth as Sacred Community.* San Francisco, CA: Sierra Club Books.

Berry, T. 2009. *The Sacred Universe: Earth, Spirituality and Religion in the Twenty-first Century.* New York: Columbia University Press.

Biggs, S. and Margil, M. 2011. 'A new paradigm for nature: Turning our values into law'. In *The Rights of Nature: The Case for a Universal Declaration of the Rights of Mother Earth*, co-produced by Global Exchange, the Council of Canadians, The Pachamama Alliance, and Fundación Pachamama, pp. 60–67.

Burdon, P. 2011a. *Exploring Wild Law: The Philosophy of Earth Jurisprudence.* Kent Town: Wakefield Press.

Burdon, P. 2011b. 'Earth rights: The theory', *ICUN Academy of Environmental Law*, 1: 1–12.

Cashford, J. 2011. 'Dedication to Thomas Berry'. In *Exploring Wild Law: The Philosophy of Earth Jurisprudence*, edited by Peter Burdon. Kent Town: Wakefield Press, pp. 3–11.

Cullinan, C. 2011. *Wild Law: A Manifesto for Earth Justice* (second edition). White River Junction, VT: Chelsea Green.

Devall, B. and Sessions, G. 1985. *Deep Ecology.* Salt Lake City, UT: Gibbs Smith Books.

Drengson, A. n.d. 'Some thought on the Deep Ecology Movement'. Foundation for Deep Ecology. Accessed 18 August 2017, http://www.deepecology.org/deepecology.htm.

Earth Charter. 2000. 'The Earth Charter'. Accessed 18 August 2017, http://earthcharter.org/invent/images/uploads/echarter_english.pdf.

IGBP (International Geosphere-Biosphere Programme). 2001. '2001 Amsterdam Declaration on Earth System Science'. Challenges of a Changing Earth: Global Change Open Science Conference, Amsterdam, The Netherlands, 13 July. Accessed 18 August 2017, http://www.igbp.net/about/history/2001amsterdamdeclaration onearthsystemscience.4.1b8ae20512db692f2a680001312.html.

Koons, J.E. 2011. 'Key principles to transform law for the health of the planet'. In *Exploring Wild Law: The Philosophy of Earth Jurisprudence*, edited by Peter Burdon. Kent Town: Wakefield Press, pp. 45–58.

Leopold, A. 1968. *A Sand County Almanac.* New York: Oxford University Press.

Margil, M. 2011. 'Stories from the environmental frontier'. In *Exploring Wild Law: The Philosophy of Earth Jurisprudence*, edited by Peter Burdon. Kent Town: Wakefield Press, pp. 249–258.

Millennium Ecosystem Assessment. 2005. *Ecosystems and Human Well-Being: Synthesis.* Washington, DC: Island Press.

Næss, A. 1989. *Ecology, Community and Lifestyle: Outline of an Ecosophy.* Cambridge: Cambridge University Press.

Price, B. 2013. 'What are rights, and how can nature "have" rights?' in *Rights of Nature and the Economics of the Biosphere*, Global Exchange and Stillheart Institute. Accessed 22 September 2017, http://internationalpresentationassociation.org/wp-content/uploads/2010/09/RON-SummitReader.pdf.

Rights of Mother Earth. 2010. 'Universal Declaration of the Rights of Mother Earth'. From World People's Conference on Climate Change and the Rights of Mother Earth, 22 April, Cochabamba, Bolivia. Accessed on 19 August 2017, http://right sofmotherearth.com/images2015/declarations%20pdf/declaration-en.pdf.

Steffen, W., Sanderson, A., Tyson, P., Jäger J., Matson, P., Moore III, B., Oldfield, F., Richardson, K., Schellnhuber, J., Turner II, B.L. and Wasson, R. 2004. *Global Change and the Earth System: A Planet under Pressure – Executive Summary*. Heidelberg: Springer-Verlag.

Stone, C.D. 2010. *Should Trees Have Standing? Law, Morality and the Environment*. London: Oxford University Press.

Zimmerman. M.E. 1989. 'Introduction to deep ecology', *In Context*, 22: 24–28.

6

BUEN VIVIR: AN ALTERNATIVE PERSPECTIVE FROM THE PEOPLES OF THE GLOBAL SOUTH TO THE CRISIS OF CAPITALIST MODERNITY

Alberto Acosta and Mateo Martínez Abarca

We are currently facing a crisis that threatens not only the survival of our civilisation and humans as a species, but that of life on our planet as a whole. At the same time, the exploitation-based approach to development is facing its own limits. This is evidenced in the ever-increasing pace of natural destruction, deepening forms of oppression and the global resurgence of totalitarian and fascist approaches to social organisation. Can we continue to simply accept this trajectory as inherent to modern capitalism? Or have we drifted off too far and lost control of the juggernaut of capital accumulation and scientific development? Historically, powerful critical voices have come out of Latin America, calling for resistance against the exploitative and devastating capitalist world regime imposed over our people. Currently, these efforts have resulted in a deep reinterpretation of reality, based on the lived knowledge of ancestral indigenous nations and peoples of *Abya Yala* (Our America, as José Martí used to call it). Although these critical alternatives have been marginalised from the conventional discourse, they re-emerge in these times of crisis.

These alternative societal constructs are expressed in the constitutions of Ecuador (2008) and Bolivia (2009) through concepts such as *buen vivir*

(Spanish), *sumak kawsay* (Kichwa) and *suma qamaña* (Aymara). There are similar notions among diverse indigenous people, such as the Mapuche (Chile–Argentina), the Guarani (Paraguay, Brazil, Argentina and Bolivia) and the Kuna (Panama and Colombia). This worldview is also found in the Mayan tradition in Guatemala and among the diverse indigenous groups that inhabit Chiapas in Mexico. Beyond *Abya Yala*, there are many other inclusive philosophies across the world, which, in one way or another, are related to the search for living well, or *buen vivir*. This includes the concept of ubuntu in Africa and *svadeshi, swaraj* and *apargrama* in India.

BUEN VIVIR: AN ALTERNATIVE VISION OF CIVILISATION FROM THE WORLD'S PERIPHERY

In recent years, in the context of post-development discussions,[1] attempts to rebuild the conceptual structure, practices, institutions and discourses of development have multiplied. While some focus on criticising specific approaches to development, others propose an alternative to the concept of development. It is in this second category that we find the approaches of *buen vivir* and *sumak kawsay*.

When looking at these alternatives, it becomes clear that improving and tinkering with the current development paradigm is no longer sufficient. Rather, we need to examine the conceptual and ideological framework of current approaches to development. The concept of *buen vivir* or *sumak kawasay* provides such an alternative. While there is no clear outline of what this alternative consists of, interpretations of *buen vivir* can be seen in a number of communities in both the Andean region and the Amazon basin. These communities have embraced *buen vivir* as a form of resistance to colonialism and have, in some cases, been able to stay at the margins of modern-day capitalism.

From the outset it is important to clarify that *buen vivir* does not aim to be a blanket replacement for the current leading global paradigm, as the concept of development was in the second half of the twentieth century. *Buen vivir* is a concept that aims to dismantle the idea of a universal goal for all societies, including a 'productivist' understanding of progress and a one-dimensional understanding of development as technology driven to produce economic growth. *Buen vivir* requires a rich, dynamic and complex vision that is a path in itself, rather than a destination – it needs to be imagined in order to be built.

Buen vivir provides a unique opportunity to devise new ways of living collectively. It does not advocate a regression in history, as its critics have suggested. Furthermore, it is not a 'recipe book', as was attempted by incorporating the concept into the Ecuadorian (2008) and Bolivian (2009) constitutions. *Buen vivir* should also not be described as a fashionable idea or a novelty created by Andean countries' twenty-first-century political processes. *Buen vivir* has been integral to a long-standing search for alternative ways of living and has been shaped by the struggles of indigenous peoples over the past centuries.

This is not to say that the Andes and the Amazon basin have been the only regions to offer these kinds of alternative. Across the world, there are many diverse actions and visions that are in harmony with *buen vivir*. What is worth noting is that these alternative ideas generally emerge from marginalised groups and invite us to question mainstream development and economic-growth-driven concepts. In sum, criticising the concept of development as was done in the 1960s and 1970s is no longer enough. An overhaul of our economic system is required, and this is precisely where the idea of *buen vivir* comes in.

The concept of development does not exist in many indigenous systems of knowledge. They do not espouse a linear vision of life, such as the path leading from underdevelopment to development. This western dichotomy – as a necessary path to be followed in order to achieve welfare – is alien to many indigenous societies. Similarly, the idea of being rich or poor based on the accumulation or scarcity of material goods is anathema in this system of belief.

Buen vivir is not a fixed value proposition; rather, it is permanently evolving. That said, certain building blocks facilitate the construction of *buen vivir*, including knowledge, ethical and spiritual codes of conduct that define how to relate with the environment, and human values and visions of the future. *Buen vivir* or *sumak kawsay* is key to the philosophy of life in indigenous societies (Viteri Gualinga 2000).

From this perspective, conventional development is seen as a western cultural, colonial imposition. To evolve out of this persisting world order, distance from the concept of development is needed. The task at hand is to decolonise as well as to step away from patriarchal and racist constructions of society. As a priority, we are called upon to decolonise intellectually in order to then be able to rid politics, society and the economy of its colonial heritage.

Buen vivir, as opposed to the western school of thought, is rooted in the significance of community, and is purposefully not capitalist. It breaks the anthropocentric logic of the dominant capitalist civilisation and of the different forms of socialism that have actually been implemented. *Buen vivir* can and should be considered a socio-bio-centric vision. As Joseph Schumpeter points out, there is a need to overcome the capitalist 'civilisation of inequality' (2013: 425). This refers to a civilisation that is essentially predatory and exploitative. As a consequence, *buen vivir* proposes a change of civilisation.

Our ancestral forms of communal and social knowledge provide a starting point that helps us to imagine a different world, as well as a way to transform it. We should take into account the experiences, visions and ideas of communities – including, but not limited to, those of the Andean–Amazonian world – that are committed to living in harmony with each other as well as with Nature. It is time to recognise the value of the experiences, visions and ideas of those who have a long, deep and marginalised history. The people we are talking about are not backward or pre-modern: their values, experiences and practices are the synthesis of a living civilisation that has faced the problems associated with modern-day colonialism. These communities resisted colonialism for well over 500 years and have been imagining a different future. All of these ideas can nourish the global debate, as will be seen later.

Harmony does not mean a paradise without conflict. Human societies will always carry contradictions and tensions, yet these tensions have been exacerbated over time and have now come to a head. What *buen vivir* invites us to do is to break away from the modern-day concepts that we take for granted, starting with the ideas of progress and development.

RECONNECTING WITH NATURE

The development model inherent to western civilisation intensified the imperialist dichotomy separating the civilised from the primitive. This dichotomy was introduced violently more than five centuries ago in Latin America, during the European conquest of the American continent. The technology-driven accumulation of goods was considered progress and accelerated the destruction of Nature (Gudynas 2009).

From a global perspective, the limits of this anthropocentric vision of progress are increasingly evident. The exploitation of natural resources for economic growth is threatening Earth's resilience. At the same time, what drives us as social and human beings can only be fulfilled in community, as an integral part of Nature, as opposed to striving to dominate it.

Fear of the unpredictability of Nature has been part of human life since its beginnings. The ancestral struggle for survival gradually turned into a desperate effort to dominate Nature. Humankind evolved anthropocentric ways of organising social life and considered humans beyond the limits of Nature – that is, human beings were seen as external to Nature. This paved the way for efforts aimed at subordinating and manipulating Nature, especially under capitalist civilisation.

It is this vision of domination and exploitation that has caused society to see itself as separate from Nature and that has led to progressively worse outcomes. Red flags have been raised for a long time, reminding us that Nature is not infinite; its limits are becoming painfully evident. This crisis should lead us to question current institutions and socio-political organisations. Failing to do so, we may encourage a growth in the authoritarian tendencies that aggravate exclusion and further cement inequality as part of a capitalist vision.

While this questioning might appear to be a simple task, it is in fact extremely complex. We need to overcome the split between Nature and humans and reframe these two concepts as part of a whole. As a first step, this transformation requires us to stop seeing Nature as a commodity. Economic aims must be subordinated to the natural systems' laws while guaranteeing respect for human dignity and quality of life. We can only achieve this by engaging in a process of income and wealth redistribution. We need a consistent political endeavour to liberate Nature from its current condition of objectified property and to recognise it as an entitled subject with unalienable rights. This could be the obvious outcome of accepting that every being, albeit not identical, has the same ontological value. When we establish the rights of Nature, we will also rescue human beings' right to existence.

Indigenous people's struggles understand that protecting *Pacha Mama*, or Mother Earth, is a substantial part of their lives. There are also compelling scientific reasons to consider the Earth as a complex 'superorganism'. This organism needs to be handled carefully and strengthened. It needs to be treated as a subject entitled to dignity and rights; everything that is alive has an inner worth, whether or not it has human utility. We can even consider the Earth and life as mere elements in a vast evolutionary process of the universe. Human life is just a moment of life understood in more general terms. A central focus of indigenous belief systems is the principle of connection: all aspects of life are connected.

A concrete step towards reconnecting with Nature was taken by the Montecristi Constituent Assembly in Ecuador, which granted Nature rights under the national constitution. This step demonstrates the path to follow if we want to live in a new form of social organisation that enshrines living in communion with Nature. The Ecuadorian constitution, approved in 2008, includes Nature as a subject of the law, with the right to be restored whenever it has been destroyed. Restoration is not reparation, a concept applied to human beings whose conditions can be affected by environmental degradation provoked by other human beings. *Pacha Mama* was conceptually incorporated into the constitution as a synonym for Nature, recognising it as a cross-national and multicultural heritage. Another significant change was recognising water, and not just the access to it, as a fundamental right. As a consequence, any possible form of water privatisation is prohibited. These constitutional modifications are milestones in the history of humankind.

Granting rights to historically excluded groups is always unthinkable until it happens. The emancipation of slaves and the extension of rights to populations of African descent as well as to women and children, were historically considered absurd. It was first necessary to struggle for *the right to have rights*. Now, it is urgent to work towards a Universal Declaration of the Rights of Nature as a starting point to rebuild a harmonious relationship between human beings and Mother Earth.

ELEMENTS OF A SUSTAINABLE ECONOMY
THAT ENABLE SOLIDARITY

Enshrining the rights of Nature in international law requires another kind of economy. It presupposes an economy that shuns capitalist principles and instead upholds foundational principles such as solidarity, sustainability, reciprocity, integrality, interrelatedness, complementarity, responsibility, sufficiency (and efficiency to some extent), cultural diversity, identity, equality and more democracy. If the starting point is an economy based on solidarity and sustainability, this opens the possibility for building alternative ways of production, exchange, consumption and cooperation. Such a change would allow a different form of wealth accumulation and income distribution.

In this new economy, criteria of sufficiency need to be adopted instead of using the efficiency logic. Economic growth is fetishised when it is understood as an end in itself instead of as a means to an end. As we know, societies based on principles of competition lead towards a dystopia.

Environmental limits are not the only limits that have been reached. Voracious economic growth and capital accumulation, by speculating and endlessly producing, are structurally based on an increase in inequality. Our goal is to build an economic system based on solidarity and communitarian and reciprocal values while being subordinate to the limits of Nature. The economic process must respect ecological cycles and be sustainable over time, without the need for foreign support and without any critical scarcity of existing resources.

In order to achieve these multiple goals, we should gradually overcome the currently dominant pattern of social and environmental devastation. One of the most challenging elements in any transition[2] is to overcome the cultural patterns internalised by the majority of the population – in this case, the accumulation of material wealth. History shows that this does not guarantee well-being for every individual and community. It has been shown that a sustained increase in income per capita did not necessarily improve the Happiness Index over several decades in the United States and in other countries considered developed (Helliwell, Layard & Sachs 2012). However, orthodox economists are still worried about how to produce economic growth as a combination of the diverse factors involved. Challenging the orthodox economy means opening the space for a big transformation (in the words of Karl Marx, a revolution). It is not only about consuming better, and sometimes less, but also about getting better outcomes with fewer resources and improving the quality of life for all.

Thus, we need to consider another economic logic, one that does not require the permanent expansion of consumption in order to sustain the accumulation of capital. This economic alternative is at odds with powerful interests. It assumes a reduction in consumerism, and even 'productivism', while being based on ever-increasing self-sufficiency at the community level. It is not about minimising the state but understanding its limits and rethinking its role from the perspective of the community.[3]

This new economy requires us to stop fetishising the market. The market talks, the market protests, the market feels: capital and the markets are turned into subjects that replace the human. When the state is subordinated to the market, society gets subsumed to materialist principles and to individual selfishness. At the same time, an expansion of the state's bureaucracy does not guarantee an increase in popular participation in decision making in the democratic system.

In a solidarity economy – as part of a fully democratic society – capitalist property cannot exist, nor can public companies control the economy. There are other forms of community-based property, such as financing cooperatives as well as cooperatives for production, consumption, housing and services. The community can be positioned at the core of all kinds of associations of producers and retailers, organisations, economic associations and self-managed companies, among others. It is at this stage that many organisations from civil society need to be incorporated as centrepieces in the new economy, as they can accompany as well as provide a historical root and thus a base for such a transformation.

This economy based on principles of solidarity and sustainability will allow for multiple and diverse forms of property and production as one of its starting points. From there, it will be possible to build new relations of production and economic control, in a long-term process of multiple transitions. While fulfilling their roles using a different logic, the state and the market will still play an important role. Initially, the economy may have to be built on principles that borrow from the socialist market economy perspective, avoiding at all costs the capitalist market's hallmark of materialism. The economic goal will be to satisfy current needs without compromising the existence of coming generations, and opening pathways for increasingly harmonious relationships among human beings and between humans and Nature (as Marx anticipated in his philosophical–economic manuscripts in 1848). This is central to a society based on *buen vivir* or *sumak kawsay*.

Important as it is, this struggle is not just about fighting against the exploitation of the labour force. There is something else at stake – defending life itself. We need to dismantle organisational schemes that champion anthropocentric privileges, which cause the greatest inequality and lead to the planet's destruction through environmental exploitation and degradation. Therefore, economic goals should be subordinated to natural systems' laws, respect human dignity and aim to improve the quality of life for individuals, families and communities. Nature and its diversity cannot be sacrificed. We have to recognise that humans are part of Nature and cannot dominate, commodify, privatise and destroy it.

The key is to accept that Nature has limits that the economy should not trespass. Climate change, fuelled by voracious overconsumption, is irrefutable evidence of this. Functional economic-growth-led thinking makes 'goods' and 'environmental services' interchangeable and further fuels selfish and short-sighted behaviour that does not recognise the limits of our natural resources.

The organisation of the economy should change profoundly – something that is likely to be a significant challenge. The fetishised economic growth, to which the world's powers and large segments of the population pay homage, must be unmasked and disarmed. In addition, the extractive logic that sinks our economies into dependency needs to be dismantled. While this might sound easy enough, it will be difficult to accomplish without popular consensus and mass participation.

A new economic order that is in harmony with Nature requires a planned decrease in extractive industries. This will enhance sustainable activities that could take place in manufacturing, agriculture, tourism and knowledge production. The success of such strategies will depend on their level of popular support.

While there is no consensus, there is broad agreement on the idea of reciprocity between human beings as an integral part of *Pacha Mama*. This new economy will have to be envisioned within the framework of a holistic and systemic approach that fully integrates the concepts of human as well as Nature's rights. A variety of other viewpoints besides the philosophies of indigenous populations can be used to draw inspiration for developing a new paradigm. For example, Pierre Rabhi's (2013) 'happy sobriety' and the German reflections on sufficiency coming from the Solidarity Economy Academy[4] overlap to a great extent with *buen vivir* ideas.

The transition to a new economic model needs to focus in particular on local-level needs and recognise that the strategic approach does not have to be dictated at the national level and implemented downwards. The political and economic organisational strategy will need to be built from below, using as cornerstones the principles of community and solidarity. This approach increases the likelihood of proposals from the *barrios* or townships and rural communities influencing policy at the national level. Gradual collective political decisions, coming from below from each region, then cumulatively translate into country-level political policy, expanding outwards from each country to the global market. Such an effort needs to be supported and coordinated by each country's central government. Critical to the success of this approach is that the needs catered to are those of local-level communities. Their integration needs to be coordinated at the national level, rather than dictated by the interests of transnational capital.[5]

Developing endogenous productive capacity, including human capacities and local resources, is the main rationale behind building self-sufficiency. This should go together with a political process that promotes participation and makes space for citizen-driven political and economic counterpowers to develop. This is particularly important in places where the central government lacks the political will to implement such a vision, and where local-level pressure to change will gradually help to promote national transformations.

Transitioning to a new, self-sufficient economy will require the domestic market to be prioritised. However, that is not to say we should return to the import substitution model, which benefited local capitalists with the main intention to promote the birth of a 'national bourgeoisie'. Self-sufficiency requires the domestic market to be a collection of heterogeneous and diverse markets, as well as a general 'market for the masses'. The latter will champion the principle of 'living with our own resources and for our own people'. It is also necessary to link the countryside with the city, the rural with the urban. The product of this connection is what will determine how and where to connect with markets at the global level.

It is not possible to develop alternative economic projects without actively involving people in their design and management. At the same time, self-managed groups and associations, cooperatives or community-based units of production should be created and strengthened, from family and local micro enterprises to the regional level. This proposal urgently requires strengthening initiatives at the community level by creating an enabling environment in which they can grow and flourish – for example, indigenous farmers should associate in ways that could help them handle central issues collectively. This would include community-based processing of their products and access to markets, loans, technology and training.

We should also create the conditions necessary to promote the production of (new) goods and services, based on adapted and local technologies. Developing the capacity to adapt and change can stimulate direct learning, the spread and full use of abilities and can encourage needs-based production. This policy should benefit the collective, the family and even individual enterprises, but should also be able to self-correct if oligopolistic or monopolistic structures start forming. At a social level, such a transition invites us to re-evaluate cultural identities and place local people in charge of health, education, transport and other services, again promoted by local–regional coordination and consensus.

These processes demand that technological advances draw on and stimulate local alternatives without rejecting valuable technological contributions from abroad, particularly 'clean' and 'transitional' technologies. Local skills and knowledge in the hands of those at the community level is often marginalised, both intentionally and unintentionally, and consequently remains outside western technological development processes.

Many traditional practices are so solidly integrated in daily life that they remain almost unchanged over time. Moreover, certain productive resources, such as organic agriculture, generally have better economic outputs than those coming from conventional industrial agriculture. Building new technological forms of resilience requires drawing on age-old approaches as well as developing new ones. If the aim is to transform old approaches into 'liberating' technologies, it is important to avoid creating new models of dependency. These technologies will have to circulate freely, consume low amounts of energy, produce low levels of carbon dioxide, be less polluting and promote the creation of good job opportunities. A project of social and productive reorganisation, as an emancipatory response based on dignity and harmony, demands revisiting lifestyle expectations, especially among elites, as their lives emulate western aspirations that are unattainable for most people in the world. At the same time, it is necessary to process the reduction and redistribution of working hours in conjunction with a collective re-evaluation of needs that are in harmony with the limits set by Nature.

Sooner rather than later, the concept of 'sufficiency' rather than never-ending growth will need to be prioritised. Sufficiency can be defined as producing enough real necessities and not increasing efficiency based on uncontrolled competition and consumption that endangers social stability and environmental sustainability.

This economic transition will not be complete if it does not tackle all forms of production, particularly that of the extractive industry. Countries that mine and export raw materials provided directly by Nature and that submissively yield to the demands of the global market are the backbone of the system of global capitalist accumulation. They are, directly or indirectly, responsible for our current global environmental problems and destruction. The answer lies in strengthening representative institutions to develop a democratic culture of participation that counters current global trends and fosters local and community-driven production mechanisms.

RESCUING OR CONSTRUCTING A NEW ECONOMIC LOGIC?

In this other economy, the starting point is not capital but the human being, while always keeping in mind that humans are part of Nature. If human beings are the backbone of the economy, work becomes functional as a part of their well-being. This entails recognising every form of work, both productive and reproductive. The world of work is an essential part of the solidarity economy, also understood as 'the work economy'.

Work is a social right and duty. Thus, no form of unemployment or under-employment can be tolerated. It is not simply about producing *more* but producing to *live better*. Once we organise and prioritise correctly, work will contribute towards dignifying the person. We will have to accept work as a space of freedom and pleasure, and develop a process of work redistribution. New ways of organising the economy and society will require these processes to occur concurrently. At the same time, self-management and co-management schemes in every type of enterprise will have to be strengthened so that workers can control their own production processes.

If we want to start a wave of transformation, we have to accept that in the current capitalist economies, people- and solidarity-driven initiatives coexist and compete with the capitalist and the public economy. These solidarity-based forms of economic organisation consist of a combination of economic–social forms of organisation in which members, collectively or individually, develop processes of production, exchange, commercialisation, funding and processes for the consumption of goods and services. These organisations can be found in the productive and commercial sector, in diverse types of popular economic units, and in the financial sector in the form of savings and credit unions and banks as well as *stokvels*. Furthermore, a myriad of valuable experiences glob-ally have used alternative and local currencies. This helped to protect com-munities' purchasing power during crisis periods but has also been used to discover and maximise existing local capacities.

In most cases, these organisations promote solidarity, cooperation and rela-tionships of reciprocity in their activities. They place well-being as the aim of any economic activity rather than profit, competition and capital accumulation. The problem in the current system is that this type of producer lacks the capac-ity to accumulate capital. While competing with 'big capital', local producers do not generate enough income and are struggling to survive. Often they lack professional and technical capacity, as the state has not prioritised providing services to them that would allow them to maintain and grow a small business.

The state has an important role to play in developing these forms and alter-natives to the capitalist economic paradigm, for example by investing in infra-structure and generating proper conditions to boost small and medium-sized producers, recognising that they have vast productive potential. We should also promote business cooperation among these enterprises, generally called 'popular industrial districts'. More enterprises could share fixed costs such as machinery, buildings, equipment and technologies, and could take advantage of 'socialised' economies of scale. This would ensure greater productivity, while maintaining a balanced approach to the environment and the workforce.

To attain this balance and foster the alternative economy, the current production system requires an overhaul. Countries that produce and export raw materials need to have sovereignty over their own economy, allowing them to promote and invest in scientific and technological innovation. Needs-based innovations will in turn feed into the new production system and aim at furthering social inclusion, job training, and the creation of high levels of well-paid employment. The latter is crucial to avoid underemployment, unequal income distribution and the demographic outflow produced by migration, among other pathologies of the model of accumulation based on the export of raw materials.

This is what we mean when we say that a transition strategy must be inherently plural. We have to take concrete decisions to solve concrete problems. And in that effort, we should direct every contribution to our main goal – rescuing and enhancing ancestral praxis and knowledge, as well as all visions and experiences that are in tune with a life in harmony with Nature. We should enhance, multiply and spread different strategies. Our new economy cannot be limited to the rural world or to the urban popular and marginalised sectors. The task is to rethink cities as a whole, redesign and reorganise them, while also building a new relationship with rural areas.

CONCLUSIONS: A PATIENT CONSTRUCTION OF UTOPIA

On the basis of the above reflections, we conclude the following:

- The 'economic growth religion' needs to deconstructed. It is clear that economic growth alone cannot be the main aim of an economy. Economic growth is not the same as development for the creation of *buen vivir* or *sumac kawsay*. The pursuit of permanent economic growth in a limited world is unrealistic.
- It is crucial to decommodify Nature as part of the conscious encounter with *Pacha Mama*. Economic aims have to be subordinated to the

operating laws of our natural systems, while still respecting human dignity and seeking to ensure humans' quality of life. The economy needs to be subordinated to ecology. Decommodifying Nature will only be possible by dematerialising productive processes and orienting towards a more efficient production process that uses fewer resources.

- Decentralisation is a central aspect of the new economy. In many sectors, such as food and energy sovereignty, closer attention to the needs of people is required. In other words, the answers to problems should be produced within the communities themselves. These actions aim at placing people in control of decision-making processes. This would enhance and strengthen meaningful local participation.
- Equitable distribution of income and redistribution of wealth are basic steps for the conversion to *buen vivir*. If the economy has to be subordinated to the Earth's mandates, then capital should be subject to the demands of society, which is a part of Nature. This requires a deep-seated redistribution of wealth and power, as well as the creation of societies based on plural equities. It is not only about class struggles and a capital–work confrontation. It is also about effectively overcoming the concept of 'race' as a key element of structuring colonial and post-colonial societies.
- At the same time, it is crucial to demolish and overcome patriarchy as a capitalist form of domination. We have to value the feminist principles of a care-oriented economy based on cooperation, complementarity, reciprocity and solidarity. These concepts are relevant not only for women but for society as a whole, and should be ingrained in the process of collectively constructing a new way of organising life. New feminist approaches are furthermore needed to anchor the concepts of autonomy, sovereignty, reciprocity and equity as pillars for ending patriarchy.
- Food sovereignty is the cornerstone of a new economy. Central to this is indigenous farmers' right to control agriculture and consumers' right to control their ability to access food. Therefore, the focus should be on giving food the same human rights treatment we give to every citizen. The first aim is to eradicate hunger through an agrarian revolution that has local producers' and consumers' rights at heart. Democratic access to land – which is a public good – is a central axis of food sovereignty. This strategy requires participatory answers as opposed to bureaucratic ones. Decentralisation and a focus on the community is also critical, rather than inefficient centralised forms of food production. Lastly, we need

to value ancestral and local technologies, not marginalise them. A main actor in this process is the peasant family, especially through associations among food producers, sellers and processors.

Humankind is not composed of a community of aggressive and brutally competitive beings. Most of these negative values have been built up or even exacerbated by a capitalist civilisation, which has favoured individualism, consumption and the aggressive accumulation of goods. Science has demonstrated the natural tendency of humans to cooperate and assist each other (Fehr, Fischbacher & Gächter 2002). *Buen vivir* tends to recover and reinforce those values and institutions based on reciprocity and solidarity. Especially in the countries of the global South, sovereignty will need to flourish to allow the local economy to prosper.

These are some of the ideas that will help to imagine a post-capitalist order that builds on virtues and ancestral knowledge and can be used to form the basis of a new economic and organisational mode. To conclude, we mention as a leading principle for this transition Karl Marx's ([1875] 2009: 11) 'Critique of the Gotha Programme': 'from each according to his ability, to each according to his needs'. This should be accompanied by accepting that human beings are part of Nature.

This 'utopia' can be a sustainable and solidarity-based living project. It proposes a powerful and urgent alternative to the way of life imposed by modern capitalism. Our new economic order can and should be collectively imagined, politically conquered and created through democratic actions in every moment and circumstance.

NOTES

1   Many authors work in the critique of development. See Jürgen Schuldt (2012), Enrique Leff (1985, 2004, 2008) and Koldo Unceta (2014).

2   Nowadays many projects encourage transitions. The Permanent Working Group on Alternatives to Development of the Rosa Luxemburg Foundation is doing a remarkable job. They have published *Beyond Development* (Lang & Mokrani 2011) and *Alternatives to Capitalism/Colonialism in the Twenty-First Century* (Permanent Working Group on Alternatives to Development 2013). See also *Transitions: Postextractivism and Alternatives to Extractivism in Peru* (Alayza & Gudynas 2011).

3   In the Andean–Amazonian world, the centre of the debate is occupied by the construction of a pluri-national and intercultural state, the primary substance of which must be communities.

4 For more information, see Bender, Bernholt and Winkelmann (2012). The solidarity economy is a movement concerned with promoting concrete projects to transform the economy in many places around the world (France, Brazil, Ecuador, Italy, Spain, etc.). Also see José Luis Coraggio (2012), who is a major researcher in the field. Many concrete proposals for building a new economy have been collected in Spain. See Rusiñol et al. 2014.

5 For example, IIRSA's (*Iniciativa para la Integración de la Infraestructura Regional Suramericana*/Initiative for the Integration of South American Regional Infrastructure) multimodal axes, a project that seeks to link the region even more to the global capitalist accumulation demands.

REFERENCES

Alayza, A. and Gudynas, E. (eds). 2011. *Transitions: Postextractivism and Alternatives to Extractivism in Peru*. Lima: RedGe – CEPES.

Bender, H., Bernholt, N. and Winkelmann, B. 2012. *Kapitalismus und dann? Systemwandel und Perspektiven gesellschaftlicher Transformation*. Munchen: Oekom Verlag GmbH.

Coraggio, J.L. 2012. 'Knowledge and public policy'. In *Social and Solidarity Economy*, edited by J.L. Coraggio. Quito: Instituto de Altos Estudios Nacionales, pp. 19–44.

Fehr, E., Fischbacher, U. and Gächter, S. 2002. 'Strong reciprocity, human cooperation and the enforcement of social norms', *Human Nature* 13 (2002): 1–25.

Gudynas, E. 2009. *The Ecological Mandate: Rights of Nature and Environmental Policies in the New Constitution*. Quito: Abya-Yala.

Helliwell, J., Layard, R. and Sachs, J. (eds). 2012. 'World happiness report'. Accessed 19 August 2017, http://worldhappiness.report/wp-content/uploads/sites/2/2012/04/World_Happiness_Report_2012.pdf.

Lang, M. and Mokrani, D. (eds). 2011. *Beyond Development: Alternative Visions from Latin America*. Amsterdam: Permanent Working Group on Alternatives to Development and Transnational Institute.

Leff, E. 1985. *Ecology and Capital: Environmental Rationality, Participatory Democracy and Sustainable Development*. Mexico: Siglo XXI Editors.

Leff, E. 2004. *Environmental Rationality: The Social Re-Appropriation of Nature*. Mexico: Siglo XXI Editors.

Leff, E. 2008. 'Degrowth, or deconstruction of the economy: Towards a sustainable world'. Accessed 19 August 2017, http://www.fuhem.es/media/ecosocial/file/boletin%20ecos/ecos%20cdv/boletin_9/leff.pdf.

Marx, K. (1875) 2009. *Critique of the Gotha Programme*. Dodo Press. Ebook.

Permanent Working Group on Alternatives to Development. 2013. *Alternatives to Capitalism/Colonialism in the Twenty-first Century*. Quito: Rosa Luxemburg Foundation.

Rabhi, P. 2013. *Towards Happy Sobriety*. Madrid: Errata Naturae.

Rusiñol, P., Trillas, A., Vilnitzky, M. and Velázquez-Gaztelu, J.P. (eds). 2014. Alternativas para vivir de otra manera. *Alternativas Económicas: Edicion Especial, Extra No 1*, Febrero.

Schuldt, J. 2012. *Development on a Human and Nature Scale*. Lima, Peru: Universidad del Pacífico.

Schumpeter, J.A. 2013. *Capitalism, Socialism and Democracy*. New York: Routledge.

Unceta, K. 2014. 'Development, post growth and buen vivir'. In Constituent debate series, *Desarrollo, postcrecimiento y Buen Vivir: debates e interrogantes*, compiled by A. Acosta and M. Esperanza. Quito: Abya-Yala. Accessed 22 September, http://rosalux.org.ec/es/mediateca/mediateca-es-publicaciones/175-alternativas-al-desarrollo/830-postecrecimientokoldounceta.html

Viteri Gualinga, C. 2000. 'An indigenous vision of development', unpublished, Quito (mimeo).

7

CHALLENGING THE GROWTH PARADIGM: MARX, BUDDHA AND THE PURSUIT OF 'HAPPINESS'

Devan Pillay

I t is disappointing to many that the GDP growth paradigm, while the subject of critical debate, has reasserted itself after the 2007–2009 financial crisis. As the science of human-induced climate change becomes irrefutable, the global power elites, employing the art of paradigm maintenance, have morphed the hegemony of neoliberal economics into what is called the 'green economy' – a continuation of the post-Brundtland attempt to reduce 'sustainable development' to 'sustain development' (Wanner 2007). In this new phase, green technologies are rolled out to buttress the notion that economic growth can be 'decoupled' from resource depletion and carbon emissions. In other words, we can have our cake and eat it.

These ideas have filtered down into South Africa's National Development Plan (NDP), which maintains a commitment to the minerals–energy complex, informalised jobs growth and continued massive social inequality – but with a green twist. Indeed, there has been a concerted rollout of renewable energy in South Africa, but this is still by far subsumed under a fossil fuel-based growth economy (given this country's abundance of coal), with the threat of expanded nuclear energy.

Can South Africa, or any developing country, escape this extractivist growth paradigm? Indeed, should developing countries commit much to the global efforts towards reducing carbon emissions, given their massive social deficits (including jobs, education, health care, housing)? Or can they leapfrog dirty development pathways, using green technologies? Is the emerging 'degrowth' paradigm only applicable to 'overdeveloped' countries of the north, which need to stop growing in order for developing countries to grow – thus lowering the average growth rate for the global economy? Indeed, is the measurement of growth using the GDP metric a useful indicator of both economic growth and social welfare, or should we be considering alternatives? Should alternatives embrace a radical eco-socialist utopian vision, notwithstanding massive resistance, from above and below – given the manner in which society has become invested in the consumer economy? These are questions that are increasingly occupying centre stage as the world considers post-carbon futures.

This chapter situates the argument within the global ecological–economic–social crisis, the GDP problem and global hegemonic interests. In considering counterhegemonic alternatives, it critically engages with a Promethean Marxist (and Marxist–Leninist) perspective that still predominates within the Left in South Africa, and recalls the New Left open Marxism of the late Rick Turner, whose radical participatory-democratic vision stressed the need for a dialectical unity between inner (individual) and outer (structural) transformations. This 'utopian' vision (in the best sense of the word) has non-western ancient lineages, going back to the Axial Age[1] responses to class conflict, and provides a backdrop to the linking of an eco-Marxist approach to other eco-socialist approaches. The chapter then considers the difficult challenges of a 'just transition' from a fossil–capitalist economy to an eco-socialist economy that can both meet the developmental needs of poor countries, as well as preserve the natural environment.

THE GLOBAL CRISIS AND THE PROBLEM OF GROWTH

The GDP paradigm is based on the assumption of continuous economic growth as an end in itself. This form of economic development arose with industrial capitalism and its treadmills of production and consumption, which are essential to the system's forward momentum.[2] Because this has brought about considerable improvements in the material conditions of living of vast numbers of people on Earth, it is deeply entrenched in modern society, which marvels at its creative and innovative powers. However, it also has immense destructive powers, characterised by massive social inequality, dispossession from the land, homelessness and slummification, widespread poverty and environmental degradation on a global scale.

In other words, as Marx observed, industrial capitalism simultaneously develops and destroys. The GDP metric measures some of its economic 'goods', but omits the socio-economic and environmental 'bads'. For example, as Lorenzo Fioramonti (2013) argues, social and physical diseases caused by unfettered capitalist growth, like crime and pollution, result in increased home security or medical expenses, which is recorded as a positive GDP increase – thus grossly distorting the real well-being of a nation. More expansive indices, such as the United Nations Development Programme's Human Development Index, give a better indication of well-being but still have at their core the GDP metric. Indeed, GDP has become a talisman of the growth paradigm – mesmerising whole nations and peoples into a seductive vortex that serves the interests of *Capital*[3] as an end in itself.

In what Antonio Gramsci (1982) called a process of 'hegemony',[4] the paradigm is maintained by a variety of social mechanisms and institutions that pervade society. Capitalism has brought about a global hegemonic power bloc[5] consisting of both economic and political or state elites – what Ralph Miliband (1988), drawing on C. Wright Mills, calls 'power elites', who form the apex of the dominant class.[6] While these power elites compete with each other in various ways, often aggressively and sometimes violently (both amongst themselves at the national level and between national elites at the global level, such as in geopolitical and trade competition), they are united by their common interest in maintaining the essential features of the growth paradigm, or what Marx called the accumulation imperative of capitalism. The accumulation of profit has no intrinsic morality other than to recreate the conditions for further accumulation. As such, capital usually contradicts societal (in particular working-class) interests and nature, through various processes of dispossession, exploitation and domination. The power elite usually makes compromises (directly or through the state) only when faced with resistance of various kinds. This includes struggles for a greater share of the social surplus (higher wages and better working conditions, a social wage), resistance to dispossession of the commons (land and other public assets), resistance to environmental degradation and campaigns for greater democratic participation.

In other words, capitalism has what Samir Amin (2004) calls a growth or 'liberal virus'[7] that operates within the logic of accumulation for the sake of accumulation. This is based on its inner drive towards compound growth (Harvey 2014) that demands maximum market liberalisation, as it scans the globe (including the oceans, deeper into the Earth, as well as within our bodies, and outer space) for investment opportunities. A key dimension to this is the system's dependence on fossil fuels, what Elmar Altvatar (2007) calls 'fossil capitalism'. This generates a number of crises on a continuous basis, at social and natural levels.

Briefly, the social crises involve the increasing exploitation of workers through the informalisation of work, lower real wages, a declining social wage, rising unemployment, privatisation of the commons such as public land and services, and rising global inequality within and between countries. Almost half the world does not have enough to eat, while less than one per cent of humanity (based mainly but not exclusively in the north) possesses most of the Earth's material wealth (Oxfam 2014; Piketty 2014). This usually fuels social instability, through rising crime and political upheavals (including terrorism), which tends to further expand the security state on global and national levels, leading to a vicious cycle.

The social crisis is accompanied by ecological crises that can be grouped under three headings: the depletion of resources (in particular oil, which runs the system, but also rain forests and fresh-water sources, amongst others); pollution (including carbon emissions and their impact on climate change, as well as increasing waste and other industrial and vehicle pollutants that affect public health); and declining biodiversity (where animals and plants become extinct, with grave threats to the delicate ecosystem). This can bring human society to the precipice, where it faces extinction (Magdoff & Foster 2011).

Inevitably, when faced with extinction, society fights back, through what Karl Polanyi (1944) called the countermovement. This happened before and after World War Two, when the self-regulating market model was in severe crisis, and the welfare state took off (particularly in northern countries with strong social and labour movements). Today the poly-crisis – in particular the financial crisis which began in 2007 – has alerted citizens around the world to the failures of the neoliberal model of development, giving rise to increasing challenges to the paradigm of growth at all costs. Of course, as usual, once the dust settles, as it has temporarily, the global elite fights back with a counter-countermovement, or what Robert Wade (1996) calls 'the art of paradigm maintenance'. In order to effectively challenge the global power elite, it is necessary to first understand how it succeeds in continually making its paradigm so hegemonic.

THE ART OF PARADIGM MAINTENANCE

The system of global capitalism, even though it has been around for only about 200 years,[8] has brought about profound changes in various aspects of life. It has become associated with advances in science and technology and 'democratic' systems of various kinds, such that it has secured a high degree of legitimacy in various parts of the globe, particularly the overdeveloped[9] countries. Of course, it has been convenient to package the narrative about the freedom of human beings with the freedom of markets, rather than distinguishing them as different momentums in history.

In other words, science, technology and democratic freedoms can be decoupled from free-market capitalism – indeed, the self-regulated market undermines their essence. When scientific investigations are primarily geared towards market outcomes (i.e. the profit motive), it obscures their intrinsic value and compromises social priorities. As the state withdraws from public education, industry is increasingly engaged in funding university research, thus undermining its independence. A good example is the pharmaceutical industry, which invests heavily in cures for diseases of the rich, such as Viagra or weight loss, and much less for diseases of the poor, such as tuberculosis. There have been massive strides in private fossil fuel-based motor vehicle innovation, but much less in cost-effective public transport based on renewable energy. Investment in socially owned renewal energy innovation has not matched investments in fossil fuel energy systems, or nuclear power (although strides have been made by China and some north European countries in recent years). Democratic participation is undermined by the power of money, including the ownership and control of mass media, which ensures that the power elites control the political sphere.[10]

The failure of statism[11] in the former Soviet Union gave rise to the 'end of history' pronouncement by Francis Fukuyama (1992), where he asserted that capitalist democracy is the only system worth thinking about. If the working class has not been the 'gravedigger' of capitalism, as Marx famously predicted, and if the social crises can be contained with more security measures, can nature (i.e. the natural environment) be contained?

Indeed, as noted, nature has responded, threatening to bring down not only capitalism but the entire edifice of human civilisation. While the science on global warming and other ecological threats clearly demands a radical rethinking of the growth paradigm, the short-term thinking of the global economic elites – who prefer seeing the world in terms of GDP growth rates and profit margins – obliges them to engage in deception to maintain this system. To put it simply, the art of paradigm maintenance – perfected by global institutions like the World Bank, but used by hegemonic elites at the global, national and local levels – means agreeing that there is a problem; capturing the critical discourse and controlling it, partly by hiring or co-opting critical activist–intellectuals; using new concepts of critics (such as 'sustainable development' or 'green jobs') but emptying them of meaning; drawing non-governmental organisations (NGOs), labour and social movements into extensive 'participatory' exercises that give the illusion of participation; conceding minor reforms (such as a little renewable energy, some social grants or a temporary minimum wage); and through all of this, securing the power elite's legitimacy and maintaining the fundamental economic paradigm.

The example of South Africa's 'green economy' discourse illustrates this very clearly. After growing opposition to neoliberal policies based on the minerals–energy–financial complex – which has seen the apartheid social deficit only partially addressed, with unemployment rising to around forty per cent, growing social inequality and persistent poverty – the ruling African National Congress (ANC) ousted its leader Thabo Mbeki in 2007 and replaced him with Jacob Zuma, with the backing of the Communist Party, the ANC Youth League and trade unions, amongst others. After the 2009 national elections, Zuma became president of the country and co-opted key Communist Party and trade union leaders into government. After eight years, little has changed to meaningfully tackle the social or ecological deficit. However, government has produced new policy initiatives in the form of the New Growth Path and the NDP, drawing in respectable intellectuals and activists from academia and civil society.

The NDP, which is now government policy, is a classic example of paradigm maintenance. It contains a competent analysis of both the climate and the social crisis, and promises 'green jobs' and 'sustainable development'. However, the Economics chapter maintains the essential neoliberal economic growth paradigm, based on the minerals–energy–financial complex.[12] This effectively washes away the promises of decent green jobs based on renewable energy. It represents what Jeff Rudin (2013) calls 'symbolic policy-making' – seeming to concede with one hand, but taking away with the other – where the government talks Left, but walks Right. This strategy succeeds in winning some over to its promised development path, such as trade unions and NGOs hoping for half a loaf at least – what could be called 'reformist' reforms that may bring some cosmetic changes, only in order to maintain the paradigm.

Inevitably, as the crises deepen, the ideological discourse no longer accords with reality. This potentially opens the way to tackle the problem at its roots – what more radical social movements and trade unions have called *transformative* reforms (Bieler, Lindberg & Pillay 2008). The dominant paradigm can only be maintained if concessions can be secured for significant sections of the population, and if more radical movements fail to offer a more persuasive counternarrative. As concessions are withdrawn in the face of renewed austerity (as in Greece and other European countries), will social and labour movements be more equipped next time round to offer an alternative vision that cuts to the root of the capitalist modernisation project? Or is the South African Left still predominantly mired in the orthodoxies of the twentieth century, whether Marxist–Leninist and/or Keynesian?

DEPARTING FROM TWENTIETH-CENTURY ORTHODOXIES

As argued by ecological Marxists (see Pillay 2013), during the twentieth century the widespread belief was that Marx, as an enlightenment thinker, had a Promethean faith in the power of science and technology, in the progressive march to higher stages of historical development – from slavery to feudalism to capitalism, and then finally to socialism and communism. Capitalist economic growth, in this view, was a revolutionary advance over feudalism, despite its destructive pathways – but it had its own gravedigger in the working-class movement, which would inevitably overthrow the system. The pain of accumulation by dispossession, turning rural peasants into an urban proletariat, would eventually yield to socialist revolution, as the urban working class became the new ruling class to lead the struggle for socialism. This was the dominant *Leninist* (or twentieth-century) version of Marxism (whether Stalinist or Trotskyist) – although it was powerfully countered by the Maoist interpretation, which placed the rural peasantry at the forefront of revolution (see Neocosmos 2016).

The other controversy was whether the proletariat would automatically develop a revolutionary consciousness during the impending capitalist crisis (from a class in itself to a class for itself), or whether such a consciousness needed to be induced from the outside, by professional revolutionaries trained in working-class parties. More cautious Marxists like Rosa Luxembourg reminded the Left over a century ago that Marx did not believe that capitalist crises made socialism inevitable – barbarism was also an option (McLellan 2007).

In the past, when capitalism went through severe crises of both profitability and legitimacy, revolutions brought about dramatic changes. However, these were either of the reactionary kind, such as the rise of fascist barbarism, or socialist revolutions from below seeking (in principle if not in reality) the welfare of society in general and subordinate classes in particular. The social democratic parliamentary route also brought about more peaceful social change, the most extensive being in the Scandinavian countries after World War Two. The neoliberal counteroffensive since the late 1970s eroded, in varying degrees, the welfare structures introduced in these countries, although key aspects remain intact. After the fall of the Berlin Wall in 1989, Eastern European countries adopted neoliberal policies, along with most countries around the world. None of these 'experiments' (social democracy or state capitalism/ socialism), however, truly identified the full extent of the social and natural 'limits' (or barriers)[13] to growth which have now come to the fore. In various ways, these are all expressions of statism (see Neocosmos 2016; Olin-Wright 2010).

Whatever the differences, all these statist alternatives converged on key articles of faith: the belief in the wonders of science and technology, which itself arose out of western modernity and means–ends rationalism (with roots in ancient Greek philosophy and the Roman-Christian belief in the domination of nature); the use of fossil fuels and natural resources as free gifts of nature; rising production (increased GDP) and equitable consumption for all; and the capture of state power through a working-class party and allied organisations (such as trade unions and other social forces). Of course, the social democratic parties went on to forge a Keynesian compromise between capitalism and socialism, and honed the party form into an effective electoral machine to win elections in multiparty democracies (before losing their dominance during the post-1970s neoliberal era).

The rise of New Left politics in the 1960s (initially in Western Europe and North America) was a reaction to both the failures of corporate capitalism in the west, and state capitalism (or statism masquerading as socialism) in Eastern Europe. It arose amidst a range of social and political upheavals, including the Soviet invasion of Czechoslovakia, the Cuban revolution and subsequent missile crisis, the anti-war movement in solidarity with Vietnam, the US civil rights movement, student uprisings and a rejection of the bureaucratic, patriarchal–conservative and materialistic values of western Christian capitalism (expressed through the hippy movement and popular culture that emphasised personal freedom).

The New Left by and large embraced a more critical, open Marxism as an alternative to the sterile and authoritarian Marxism–Leninism–Stalinism practised in both Eastern Europe and China. This included the work of Gramsci, whose notions of workers' control through workers' councils resonated with the participatory-democratic ideas of Turner in South Africa. Both had a profound influence on the student activists who became part of the re-emerging trade union movement during the 1970s, as well as in community organisations that became part of the United Democratic Front and other formations in the 1980s.

Turner[14] was a highly popular and influential Political Science lecturer at the University of Natal in the late 1960s and early 1970s, before he was banned by the apartheid regime and later assassinated. He promoted 'workers' control' of both unions and industry, as a stepping stone towards maximum participatory democracy for society as a whole – a *society-focused* socialist vision, as opposed to the traditional *statist* emphasis of much of the 'socialist' world at the time. His brand of open Marxism, primarily influenced by Jean-Paul Sartre's *Critique of Dialectical Reasoning* (1991a, 1991b), was infused with a 'transcendent' (or if you like 'spiritual') essence that believed in non-violence, universal love and the unity between inner and outer transformations.

Turner's notion of workers' democracy is captured in this quote from his seminal work *Eye of the Needle: Toward Participatory Democracy in South Africa* (the title is a biblical reference to the alleged saying of Jesus that a rich person had as much chance of going to heaven as the camel had of going through the eye of the needle):

> Workers' control is not only a means whereby I can control a specific area of my life. It is an educational process in which I can learn better to control all areas of my life and can develop both psychological and interpersonal skills in a situation of co-operation with my fellows in a common task ... participation in decision-making, whether in family, in the school, in voluntary organisations, or at work, increases the ability to participate and increases the competence on the part of the individual that is vital for balanced and autonomous development. Participation through workers' control lays the basis for love as a constant rather than as a fleeting relationship between people. (Turner [1972] 1980: 39)

In many ways he embraced the concept of revolutionary love articulated by Che Guevara (1965): 'At the risk of seeming ridiculous, let me say that the true revolutionary is guided by a great feeling of love. It is impossible to think of a genuine revolutionary lacking this quality.' Indeed, if socialist 'love' means rising above ourselves as individuals and embracing the whole of humanity, as well as non-human nature, then it is no different to the 'spiritual' essence conveyed by religious philosophers, some of whom imagine an external god or gods as the embodiment of the totality of love, whilst others, like the Samkhya school and the Buddha (see later), find that capacity *within* all of us. Turner easily made connections between his Marxism and the 'spiritual' (without necessarily embracing a theism or belief in an external god).

As will be shown, eastern and other traditional beliefs, such as that of the Native American (*buen vivir* or *sumak kawsay*) and African (ubuntu), inform much of the eco-socialist perspectives that converge around the degrowth movement, and considerations of happiness, well-being and localised Buddhist economics. While ecological Marxism has some differences with these perspectives, there is no Chinese Wall between them. What follows is a brief elaboration of these linkages, in order to see the connections with Marx as a caring humanist (as opposed to the cold 'scientist' imagined by twentieth-century Leninism), whose theory of alienation had strong 'spiritual' meaning, and whose desire for social equality and human flourishing connected strongly with the yearnings of ancient philosophers seeking the end of human (and often animal) suffering.

ANCIENT LINEAGES, MODERN REAWAKENINGS

If alternatives to the hegemonic paradigm are to be considered, it is necessary to dig deeper into the roots of modernity, and fundamentally question core beliefs of the twentieth century. An ecological Marxist (or eco-socialist) perspective, which seeks to both deepen our understanding of the pitfalls of modernity as well as build bridges with other paradigms (secular and religious) that are potentially counterhegemonic, must of necessity engage with the insights of the philosophies of the Axial Age (around 800–200 BCE), which were themselves a reaction to rising class domination and inequality during their times. They departed from other more tribal, patriarchal and socially violent religious dogma and practice during their time by emphasising universal love, respect for all human beings and nature, social equality and social justice for all – with a strong emphasis on personal liberation from suffering as a vital precondition for the liberation of others. Key sayings that captured this essence, later popularised by Christianity in the west, include 'Do to others as you would have them do to you' and 'Love your neighbour as yourself' (see Armstrong 2006).

In modern terms, these are *socialist* precepts with a strong pacifist bent, summed up by the notion of 'turn the other cheek'. They arose out of the lament of prophets and philosophers who saw violent upheavals in their societies, brought about by the rise of private property, patriarchy, money, greed and the Ego as dominating principles, which overcame the previous more solidaristic modes of being based on substantial social equality (akin to what Marx recognised as 'primitive communism').[15] The Marxist scholar Debiprosad Chattopadhyaya (1970) gives a detailed account of how the Buddha learned about social equality, non-violence and democracy from classless tribal societies in India which were by then being threatened by the class-divided kingdoms, which proceeded to plunder and subjugate them.

These philosophies were absorbed into or spawned religious movements such as Hinduism, Buddhism, Jainism, Taoism, Confucianism, Judaism, Christianity and Islam – but bear little responsibility for the tribalistic, patriarchal and oppressive doctrines and practices associated with these religions through the ages (just as Marx bears little responsibility for the debased theory and practice of various shades of what was called 'Marxism' during the twentieth century).

While Marx warned against religion as the 'opium of the people', his critique was much more nuanced than that. He saw that religion was the 'sigh of the oppressed', or more accurately the 'groaning of the labouring creature' or the 'soul of a heartless world' and the 'spirit of spiritless conditions' (quoted in Duchrow & Hinkelammert 2012: 244). Marx, as an atheist, did not believe that religion should be suppressed, but felt that with the rise of a humanist atheism – where all human beings could develop to their full potential in harmony with the laws of nature (or a form of sustainable human development under communism) – it would eventually die out. In other words, the 'spirit' of religious spirituality would be replaced by the 'spirit' of atheist socialism, where alienation from the self, fellow human beings, nature, production and consumption would be overcome (Fromm 1961). The 'metabolic rift' between humans and nature, and by extension between humans and their individual and collective selves (who are part of nature), would be restored (Foster 2009).

In this sense Marx, who desired the overthrow of 'all conditions in which the human is a degraded, enslaved, neglected, contemptible being' (Duchrow & Hinkelammert 2012: 245), and who believed that labour and the land (i.e. nature) are the only sources of value (Marx [1894] 1981), could be said to be advocating the restoration of the soul or the spirit in a caring world, based on social and environmental justice. His humanist–atheistic yet 'spiritual' socialist vision – pivoted around human flourishing of all humankind – resonated strongly with that of the Buddha (approx. 400 BCE), who drew on the rationalist–atheist[16] Samkhya school of 'Hindu' philosophy (approx. 800 BCE) (Armstrong 2006; Walters n.d.). Indeed, the Dalai Lama, the spiritual leader of Tibetan Buddhism, has on a number of occasions declared that, on socio-economic matters, 'I am a Marxist' (Smithers 2014).

This transcendent thinking informs alternative pathways out of the hierarchical, patriarchal politics of the twentieth century, which focused narrowly on the state and conformed to conventional growth (production–consumption) treadmill thinking. Today, there is increasing recognition that alternatives, if they are to serve *all* the world's people and preserve the natural environment for current and future generations to enjoy, must be substantive and go beyond the interests of only the state and the market. It underlines the need for a *society*-focused development path, which means unleashing the power of ordinary citizens as agents of their own destiny, where the state and market are subordinate to societal (or the people's) general interests. The challenge is to build a participatory political and economic system for people in harmony with nature – to reinvoke the emancipatory potential inherent in the notion of 'People's Power', free from the suffocation of twentieth-century statist politics (see Neocosmos 2016).

ALTERNATIVE VISIONS AND MOVEMENTS

Alternative society-centred pathways have been attempted in the Indian state of Kerala, and in countries like Bolivia[17] as well as the small mountain country of Bhutan. While not conventionally associated with the radical alternatives, Bhutan deserves closer examination as it tries to navigate out of its feudal past into a multiparty democracy and the challenge of pursuing gross national happiness (GNH) based on balanced development. Its GNH Index offers a deep and extensive methodology to measure development in all its dimensions, and all development plans must first be subject to a GNH audit.[18] Fioramonti

(2017) prefers the term 'wellbeing economy', which avoids an association with pop 'happiness' surveys, and focuses on practical alternatives to GDP growth economics based on local economies and meaningful artisanal work. By breaking down the economies of scale, his 'artisanal revolution' means 'more mechanics, electricians, plumbers, architects, gardeners, teachers, nurses, therapists, doctors and caregivers, and fewer bankers, lawyers, CEOs and chartered accountants' (Fioramonti 2017: 220) who service big business and big government.

This vision resonates with the many and diverse range of local economic alternatives being practised in communities around the world, including cooperatives, community gardens and socially owned renewable energy projects, which can be learned from. The Bolivarian Alternative for the Americas (ALBA) offered alternative conceptions of regional trade based on cooperation, solidarity and even bartering (where, for example, Cuba trades doctors for Venezuelan oil), rather than cut-throat competition. Of course, the Venezuelan crisis has exposed the perils of path dependency (or what some call 'petrosocialism') in an era of low oil prices. While this threatens the future of ALBA, and has dented the confidence in the Latin American alternatives (known as the 'pink tide' away from US hegemony), much can be learned from attempts to build alternatives there.

Arguably, the most advanced and democratic of this wave of governments offering alternatives is Bolivia. While in recent years the ecological Left has been dismayed by what seems to be the retreat into 'neo-extractivism' (see Boron 2012), the idea of *buen vivir* and the granting of constitutional rights to the Earth remain inspirational (whatever the compromises that have had to be made in practice) (see Acosta and Abarca in this volume). Bolivia's indigenous president Evo Morales (2009: 168), who was re-elected in 2014 with a healthy majority, offers this inspiring vision of *buen vivir*:

> For us, what has failed is the model of 'living better' (than others), of unlimited development, industrialisation without frontiers, of modernity that deprecates history, of increasing accumulation of goods at the expense of others and nature. For that reason we promote the idea of Living Well, in harmony with other human beings and with our Mother Earth.

These sentiments have inspired a growing movement within the 'overdeveloped' countries around the concept of 'degrowth'. This builds on the ideas of the French Marxist Andre Gorz, who, in the 1970s and 1980s, made a forceful argument about the need for reduced working time if we are to address the problem of unemployment and reduce unnnecessary consumption. The degrowth paradigm that has emerged in recent years, mainly within the overdeveloped world, explicitly embraces the 'utopian' thinking of *buen vivir*, ubuntu and Buddhist economics, and some variants also include ecological Marxist thinking (see Acosta and Abarca, and Terreblanche in this volume). A vast literature has emerged around this new paradigm, and initial criticism that it was too focused on overdeveloped countries, with little applicability to developing countries with large unmet needs, has been addressed by conceding that there needs to be growth in the south – but balanced, ecologically sensitive growth that does not 'carbon copy' the tragedies of western development trajectories (see D'Alisa, Demaria & Kallis 2015).

Struggles against elite dominance usually bring to the fore new visionary leadership that can either break new ground or become co-opted into the dominant paradigm. To prevent the latter, as Mahatma Gandhi and later the feminist movement warned, activists must be the change they want to see. Drawing on the thinking of the ancients (discussed earlier), this involves personal transformation and continuous introspection, as well as a deep participatory politics where leaders are always held accountable to their organisations, members and communities.

In South Africa, as the dominant neoliberal paradigm fails to accord with the reality of continued deprivation, rising inequality and ecological disaster, the scales have been falling from the eyes of labour and social movement activists who have been part of the ruling Alliance. Spurred on by rising evidence of massive corruption and state failure, realignments of political forces are beginning to shake up the economic and political establishment, as fresh thinking enters the political sphere. Trade unions are beginning to consider what a just transition to green jobs or an ecologically and socially sustainable developmental path means in practice. The National Union of Metalworkers, the only union in South Africa to seriously focus on climate change and climate jobs, put forward imaginative proposals in 2012 around a carbon tax and socially owned renewable energy alternatives (Pillay 2015). These are, however, difficult challenges for unions that still find themselves trapped within a logic of the 'jobs blackmail' (Rathzel & Uzzell 2013). Nevertheless, the ground has shifted, and as the crisis deepens the potential for building broader counterhegemonic alliances is large.

In other parts of the world disillusionment with the status quo has taken on various forms, from the Arab Spring to the Occupy movements. While the former has had some success in Tunisia, in other parts of the Arab world it has faced severe setbacks. The Occupy movement may have died down in form, but as the veteran intellectual activist Angela Davis noted (*Guardian*, 15 December 2014), it gave rise to one of the largest protest movements to emerge in response to police killings in the US. She believes that there are many more anti-capitalist activists in the US today, with a clearer understanding of the nature of the system, than there were in the supposed heyday of the 1960s. Indeed, the political campaign of Bernie Sanders in 2016 drew on this energy and inserted an explict 'democratic socialist' discourse into the public domain, which endures beyond that campaign. Similarly, Jeremy Corbyn in the UK has inspired a new generation of young people with an explicit socialist message. New movements, such as Podemos in Spain, also offer the promise of something fresh and potentially transformative.

An understanding of the social and natural 'limits' to growth suggests that the art of paradigm maintenance has its own limits. It is up to activists and movements to seize these moments and work to build broad-based alliances around common struggles. The counternarrative is increasingly capturing the imagination of significant actors around the world. As the International Trade Union Confederation's Sharon Burrows told trade union members at its 2014 Berlin conference, there are no jobs on a dead planet. Capitalism and its logic of incessant growth is killing the planet. That realisation, combined with increasing anger about rising social inequality, is becoming a rallying call to action.

CONCLUSION

This chapter has argued that, given the enormous challenges of ecological destruction and social inequality in the world, a radical, utopian vision is necessary. In order to conceptualise that vision, modern thinkers such as Rick Turner have made connections between the socialist movements of today and ancient philosophies that have also grappled with their worlds in crisis, as class divisons, ecological crisis, violence and dispossession engulfed their societies. The sages of the past envisaged egalitarian social orders based on compassion and kindness towards fellow human beings and the natural world, which is the basis of democratic eco-socialist thinking.

The most advanced thinking of the ancient world was arguably that of the Buddha, who used a dialectical method to arrive at an atheist (or agnostic) humanist worldview – not unlike that of Karl Marx. This eclectic vision can form the basis of new ethically grounded social justice movements that cut across different paradigms and movements, and seek common ground. If the religious and atheist–humanist movements emphasise inner transformation and the need to change the hearts of people, Marxists emphasise structural transformation and the need to alter the balance of power in society through mass struggle. An overemphasis on the former can lead to paralysis and a retreat into individual salvation. An overemphasis on the latter has led to brutal regimes coming to power, and replicating the violence and alienation of the orders they overthrew. A combination of the two, however, is a much more radical project, one that digs deep into ourselves and into our collective powers for both inner and outer transformation.

As the Bolivian case reminds us, a utopian vision, while necessary, is different to a utopian politics that underestimates power relations and the need to navigate choppy waters that involve both struggle and negotiation, and inevitably compromises. A utopian imagination, as Atilio Boron (2012) argues, has to be one of real utopias that seek out the possible but do not fall victim to possibilism (there is no alternative); that has a utopian vision, but is not blinded by utopianism (living in a dream world). It seeks short-term tactical victories that are embedded in longer-term strategic visions that can only be guaranteed by a fundamentally democratic project, where power truly resides with the people.

NOTES

1   The Axial Age, coined by Karl Jaspers, refers to the period 800–200 BCE, when the major religions – Judaism (later followed by Christianity and Islam), Hinduism, Buddhism, Jainism, Confucianism, Zoroastrianism, Taoism and Greek philosophy – emerged as a reaction to rising social inequalities (based on money, private property and patriarchy) and human suffering (see Armstrong 2006; Duchrow & Hinkelammert 2012). This was the foundation of western modernity, and later capitalism. Armstrong, as well as Duchrow and Hinkelammert, link the emergence of class societies to the use of horse-driven chariots to invade and replace previously maternal cultures within relatively peaceful nomadic and pastoral societies in the Eurasian region. The parallel emergence of sages preaching compassion and empathy was a reaction to the rise of egotism, greed, violence and unkindness.

2   There is a growing literature on this. See, for example, Fioramonti (2013, 2014, 2017) for recent critiques of the GDP paradigm from a 'wellbeing economy' perspective,

and Foster (2009), Magdoff and Foster (2011) and Altvater (2007) from an ecological Marxist perspective (see also the freely available *Monthly Review*, which covers this perspective extensively).

3   Istvan Mészáros (1995), drawing on Marx, makes a distinction between *Capital* (meaning loosely, material wealth valued in money terms for investment purposes) as an impersonal force that has its own accumulation logic, and *capitalists* who try to ride its waves but are not always in control of its destiny (and may themselves fall victim to its destructive powers).

4   Hegemony relies primarily on ideological mechanisms to manufacture 'consent', in contrast to domination, which relies primarily on coercion.

5   In the neo-Gramscian sense of global class power, as opposed to narrow political power, a bloc is a class alliance – led by the transnational capitalist class fraction – of a range of interests necessary to secure hegemony within the global system (see Bieler, Lindberg & Pillay 2008).

6   While the power elite was analysed in relation to advanced capitalist countries, at the national level this can be extended to other countries, and to the global level, as a general convergence of political and economic interests. Miliband (1988), in an attempt to retain the two-class model of Marx and Engels in the *Communist Manifesto*, divides modern advanced capitalist societies into a highly differentiated *dominant class* (consisting of the power elite at the apex, as well as other class fractions), and the equally differentiated *dominated class* or subordinate classes, comprising various middle-class fractions, working-class fractions and the underclass. He omits the peasantry, which can be added to this framework.

7   Amin (2004) uses liberal in the economic sense, which since the 1970s has been termed 'neoliberal'.

8   The earliest humans coming out of Africa date to around 60 000 years ago, and the Bronze Age, when humans began using tools, began around 5 000 years ago.

9   This term, found in the degrowth literature, refers to what is commonly called developed countries, or advanced economies, in contrast to developing or underdeveloped countries. 'Overdeveloped' is preferred as it suggests that these countries have more than enough material resources, characterised by overconsumption and waste. Their problem is not further growth, but redistribution of what they already have.

10   This is particularly the case in countries like the US, with insufficient checks and balances against the power of money. Corporate power, however, has increased exponentially in recent decades, undermining most systems of democracy (see Palast 2002).

11   There is a debate about whether the Soviet Union and its satellites were state capitalist or state socialist – both different forms of statism (as were, to much lesser extents, the social democratic states of Europe and the ISI (import substitution industrialisation) states of the developing world during the 1950s to the 1970s). By 'statism' is meant the dominance of the state in most aspects of social life. For democratic socialists the notion of 'state socialism' is an oxymoron, as socialism has to be democratic or it is not. Similarly, for free-market capitalists, 'state capitalism' is an oxymoron (see Olin-Wright 2010).

12   N. Coleman, 'National Development Plan: The devil is in the economic detail', *Daily Maverick*, 3 April 2013.

13   See Harvey (2014) for a critique of the 'limits to capitalism' argument. Harvey argues, following a close reading of Marx, that capitalism has the ability to turn what seem like limits into barriers that can be overcome, as demanded by the accumulation imperative.

14   This short exposition is based on the 1980 edition of Turner's *Eye of the Needle*, which includes a biographical introduction by Tony Morphet, as well as a comprehensive recent MA thesis by William Hemingway Keniston (2010), who reviews his work in light of developments over the past thirty years, including various assessments of Turner's ideas and influence at various points. Only the key ideas of Turner are presented here, in relation to the purposes of this book.

15   See note 1.

16   Some prefer the term 'agnostic', which leaves open the possibility of a superior being (perhaps as an abstract energy, or nature itself), while atheists assert that there is definitely no superior being or God. This is a fine philosophical distinction, as both agnostics and atheists argue that there is no evidence of a superior being (particularly as a personal god), and live their lives as if none exist.

17   For more information, see Heller (1999), Williams (2008) and Bolivia Reborn, http://cojmc.unl.edu/bolivia/rules_toc.html (accessed 20 August 2017).

18   Details of the GNH Index can be found at the Centre for Bhutan Studies website, www.bhutanstudies.org.bt (accessed 20 August 2017).

REFERENCES

Altvatar, E. 2007. 'The social and natural environment of fossil capitalism', *Socialist Register*, 43: 37–59.

Amin, S. 2004. *The Liberal Virus: Permanent War and the Americanization of the World.* New York: Monthly Review Press.

Armstrong, K. 2006. *The Great Transformation: The World in the Time of Buddha, Socrates, Confucius and Jeremiah.* London: Atlantic Books.

Bieler, A., Lindberg, I. and Pillay, D. 2008. *Labour and the Challenges of Globalisation: What Prospects for Transnational Solidarity.* London: Pluto.

Boron, A.A. 2012. '"Buen vivir" and the dilemmas of the Latin American Left' (translated by Richard Fidler). Accessed 28 September 2015, http://climateandcapitalism.com/2015/08/31/buen-vivir-and-dilemmas-of-latin-american-left.

Chattopadhyaya, D. 1970. 'Some problems of early Buddhism'. In Rahul Sankrityayan, Debiprosad Chattopadhyaya, Y. Balaramamoorty, Ram Bilas Sharma and Mulk Raj Anand, *Buddhism: The Marxist Approach.* New Delhi: People's Publishing House, pp. 2–15.

D'Alisa, G., Demaria, F. and Kallis, G. 2015. *Degrowth: A Vocabulary for a New Era.* New York and London: Routledge.

Duchrow, U. and Hinkelammert, F.J. 2012. *Transcending Greedy Money: Interreligious Solidarity for Just Relations.* New York: Palgrave Macmillan.

Fioramonti, L. 2013. *Gross Domestic Problem: The Politics Behind the World's Most Powerful Number.* London: Zed Books.

Fioramonti, L. 2014. *How Numbers Rule the World: The Use and Abuse of Statistics in Global Politics.* London: Zed Books.

Fioramonti, L. 2017. *Wellbeing Economy: Success in a World Without Growth.* Johannesburg: Pan Macmillan.

Foster, J.B. 2009. *The Ecological Revolution: Making Peace with the Planet.* New York: Monthly Review Press.

Fromm, E. 1961. 'Alienation'. Accessed 28 September 2015, https://www.marxists.org/archive/fromm/works/1961/man/ch05.htm.

Fukuyama, F. 1992. *The End of History and the Last Man.* New York: Free Press.

Gramsci, A. 1982. *Selections from the Prison Notebooks.* London: Lawrence and Wishart.

Guevara, C. 1965. 'Man and socialism in Cuba'. Accessed 28 September 2015, https://www.marxists.org/archive/guevara/1965/03/man-socialism-alt.htm.

Harvey, D. 2014. *Seventeen Contradictions and the End of Capitalism.* New York: Oxford University Press.

Heller, P. 1999. *The Labor of Development: Workers and the Transformation of Capitalism in Kerala, India.* New York: Cornell University Press.

Keniston, W.H. 2010. 'Richard Turner's contribution to a socialist political culture, 1968–1978', unpublished MA mini-thesis, University of the Western Cape.

Magdoff, F. and Foster, J.B. 2011. *What Every Environmentalist Needs to Know about Capitalism.* New York: Monthly Review Press.

Marx, K. (1894) 1981. *Capital: A Critique of Political Economy (Vol. 3).* New York: Penguin.

McLellan, D. 2007. *Marxism after Marx.* London: Palgrave Macmillan.

Mészáros, I. 1995. *Beyond Capital: Toward a Theory of Transition.* New York: Merlin Press.

Miliband, R. 1988. 'Class analysis'. In *Social Theory Today*, edited by Anthony Giddens and Jonathan Turner. Stanford, CA: Stanford University Press, pp. 325–345.

Morales, E. 2009. 'How to save the world, life and humanity'. In *People First Economics*, edited by David Ransom and Vanessa Baird. Oxford: New Internationalist Publications, pp. 177–180.

Neocosmos, M. 2016. *Thinking Freedom in Africa: Toward a Theory of Emancipatory Politics.* Johannesburg: Wits University Press.

Olin-Wright, E. 2010. *Envisioning Real Utopias.* London: Verso.

Oxfam. 2014. 'The cost of inequality: How wealth and income extremes hurt us all'. Oxfam Media Briefing. Accessed 18 January 2013, https://www.oxfam.org/sites/www.oxfam.org/files/cost-of-inequality-oxfam-mb180113.pdf.

Palast, G. 2002. *The Best Democracy Money Can Buy: An Investigative Reporter Exposes the Truth about Globalization, Corporate Cons and High Finance Fraudsters.* London: Pluto Press.

Piketty, T. 2014. *Capital in the Twenty-first Century.* Cambridge, MA: The Belknap Press of Harvard University Press.

Pillay, D. 2013. 'Marx and the eco-logic of fossil capitalism'. In *Marxisms in the 21st Century: Crisis, Critique and Struggle*, edited by Michelle Williams and Vishwas Satgar. Johannesburg: Wits University Press, pp. 143–165.

Pillay, D. 2015. 'Half full or half empty? The Numsa moments and the prospects of left revitalisation'. In *New South African Review 5: Beyond Marikana*, edited by G.M. Khadiagala, P. Naidoo, D. Pillay and R. Southall. Johannesburg: Wits University Press, pp. 48–60.

Polanyi, K. 1944. *The Great Transformation: The Political and Economic Origins of Our Time*. Boston: Beacon Press.

Rathzel, N. and Uzzell, D. (eds). 2013. *Trade Unions in the Green Economy*. London: Palgrave.

Rudin, J. 2013. 'NDP: The deadly road from GEAR to climate change'. In *The National Development Plan: 7 Critical Appraisals*, edited by Progressive Economics Network. Cape Town: AIDC, pp. 18–30.

Sartre, J-P. 1991a. *Critique of Dialectical Reason Volume 1: Theory of Practical Ensembles*. London: Verso.

Sartre, J-P. 1991b. *Critique of Dialectical Reason Volume 2: The Intelligibility of History*. London: Verso.

Smithers, S. 2014. 'Occupy Buddhism: Or why the Dalai Lama is a Marxist'. Accessed 30 May 2014, https://tricycle.org/trikedaily/occupy-buddhism/.

Turner, R. (1972) 1980. *Eye of the Needle: Toward Participatory Democracy in South Africa*. New York: Orbis Books.

Walters, T.A. n.d. 'Humanist compatibilities between Marxism and Buddhism'. Accessed 20 September 2014, https://xhyra.wordpress.com/page/42/.

Wade, R. 1996. 'Japan, the World Bank and the art of paradigm maintenance: The East Asian miracle in political perspective', *New Left Review*, 217: 3–37.

Wanner, T. 2007. 'The bank's "greenspeak": The power of knowledge and "sustaindevelopment"'. In *The World Bank: Development, Poverty, Hegemony*, edited by David Moore. Scottsville: UKZN Press, pp. 145–170.

Williams, M. 2008. *The Roots of Participatory Democracy: Democratic Communists in South Africa and Kerala, India*. New York: Palgrave.

8

UBUNTU AND THE STRUGGLE FOR AN AFRICAN ECO-SOCIALIST ALTERNATIVE

Christelle Terreblanche

I am not a prisoner of history. I should not seek there for the meaning of my destiny. I should constantly remind myself that the real leap consists in introducing invention into existence. In the world through which I travel, I am endlessly creating myself. I am a part of Being to the degree that I go beyond it. (Fanon 1967: 179)

Nowhere is the quest for an ecologically just existence more urgent than in Africa, a continent hovering on the brink of ecocide after centuries of subjugation of its people and looting of its riches. This chapter argues that Africa's worldview and philosophy, known as ubuntu in southern Africa,[1] embodies an ecological ethics that could inspire green socialist imaginaries in the battle against climate change. As a living ethics, ubuntu demands an activism of solidarity and decolonisation in the face of what Vishwas Satgar terms an 'imperial ecocide' (see Satgar in this volume).

Ecological socialism (eco-socialism hereafter) and ubuntu are both held as unfinished, evolving and aspirational projects (Cornell & Van Marle 2015; Kovel 2011). Both strive for more inclusive, egalitarian and ecocentric solutions to contemporary crises. It is argued that despite the failure of historic attempts to fuse ubuntu and socialism into endogenous post-capitalist projects, compelling reasons remain for reopening a conversation about their comple-mentarity. As this chapter aims to illustrate, an ubuntu ethics has already played midwife to the radical notion of post-extractivism, that is, leaving behind for future generations the fossil fuels and minerals that drive destructive capitalist accumulation and its crises, notably climate change.

Ubuntu is understood as an Africa-wide ethical paradigm that, notwith-standing regional versions, is practised widely across sub-Saharan Africa (Chuwa 2014).[2] As an ethics of interrelationships, situated in a communitar-ian social fabric of caring and sharing, ubuntu may equal, and even exceed, socialist notions of a 'radical egalitarianism' (Cornell 2009; Cornell & Van Marle 2015). An emerging consensus holds that ubuntu cannot be compat-ible with capitalist relations, the commodification of nature or inequality.[3] The first endogenous attempts at systemising a political economy of African philosophy – the work of scholar-leaders Amilcar Cabral, Leopoldt Senghor, Frantz Fanon and Julius Nyerere, among others – still hold potential (Chuwa 2014; Metz 2014a) for a more communitarian ecological paradigm. This archive of endogenous ideas allows us to reread previous attempts at decolonisation and social justice from the perspective of a transition to a more just ecological future.

Historically, ubuntu has been misappropriated and co-opted for sense-less, and even violent, nation-building projects and shallow corporate social responsibility ventures. Ubuntu also tends to be dismissed as hierarchical and outdated. Evidence to the contrary suggests, however, that it is thriving – as practice and philosophy – from rural commonages to urban townships (see Cornell 2002). Contemporary reviews point to its potential as a counterhegem-onic alternative: a 'revolutionary ubuntu' that informs life and death struggles against capitalist enclosure and fossil fuel imperialism. This chapter cannot claim to provide a full exposition of ubuntu as a worldview that values inter-relationships between humans and nature. The aim is rather to tease out those tenets of ubuntu that could catalyse a project of radical transformation to a more ecologically just future.

It is important to highlight the significant complementarity between Latin America's *buen vivir*[4] indigenous ethics and ubuntu. Both reject modernity's nature–society duality and regard restorative justice as the principle mecha-nism to achieve harmony with the cosmos (Shutte 2009a). Harmonious rela-tionships with nature are central to the community's and the individual's emergence and reproduction – premised on communitarian, decentralised forms of self-governance (see Benedetta & Margherita 2013; Walsh 2011). Both could be seen as guides to challenge the limits of liberal democracy, liberal rights and unlimited growth for post-colonial and post-capitalist futures (see Collard, Dempsey & Sundberg 2015; Praeg & Magadla 2014).

This chapter also assesses the compatibility of ubuntu values with eco-socialist ideals. Attempts to fuse ubuntu with socialism during the post-colonial years did not realise the radical egalitarianism of either philosophy and, therefore, require critical review. An ubuntu perspective demands a thorough decolonisation of nature as exploitable resource (Bassey 2013). It requires ecologically just modes of transition to go beyond 'shallow, technocratic progressivism' (Kovel 2011) that obscures the consequences of technology-led 'just transitions' for workers in advanced countries and that often happens at the expense of the global South (Goodman & Salleh 2013; Salleh 2014). Such techno-paradigms or defensive transitions, as Jacklyn Cock (2014) argues, would at best result in a shallow transformation.

DRAWING LESSONS FROM AFRICA'S FIRST-WAVE SOCIALISM AND MARXISM

Post-colonial statehood projects founded on socialism and ubuntu ethics did not outlive their founders. The mostly disastrous repertoire of nearly all Marxist–Leninist and socialist nation-building experiments bequeathed us with few inspiring and authentically African lessons. John Saul (2013) and Daryl Glaser (2013) suggest[5] that exceptions include the socialist and ubuntu principles of Nyerere's *ujamaa* ('family socialism') in Tanzania and Senghor's Negritude in Senegal.[6] This section argues that these early socialist visions, as historic decolonial alternatives to western instrumental rationality, may yet inspire endogenous eco-socialist imaginaries (Chuwa 2014; Glaser 2013; Kanu 2014).

While attempts to foster an African endogenous socialism failed, it needs to be stressed that both African governance generally and Marxism globally foundered historically (Glaser 2013). All African liberation movements, regardless of ideology, adopted modernisation and industrial development models once in power, attempting to make up for purported historical backwardness. Instead of actual development, dependency and marginalisation ensued. These structural inequalities deepened Africa's mal-integration into the global economy, thus leaving fledgling states with 'sub-optimal choices' (Amin 2014: 32).

African socialist parties differed historically from orthodox (scientific socialist) Marxism–Leninism equivalents in Angola, Ethiopia and Benin, among others. These orthodox projects were characterised by violent state-centred imposition of rapid industrialisation and large-scale mechanised farming. Repression of language and cultural rights (Glaser 2013) was widespread, notably also of indigenous practices and philosophies such as ubuntu. By contrast, the earlier socialist post-colonial leaders – including Kwame Nkrumah, Nyerere, Senghor and Guinea's Sékou Touré – are credited with envisioning a more authentic anti-imperialism, based on critiques of Eurocentric modernity, communitarian democratic norms and solidarity economies (Glaser 2013; McCulloch 1981).[7] African ideals of a deeper participatory democracy, as expressed in ubuntu (Shutte 2009a), were discarded once in power, thus denying citizens the right to challenge ideological orientations (Glaser 2013). Statist and totalitarian tendencies emerged (Glaser 2013) and the peasantry was pushed out of feudalism towards modernity. This patently violated the respect for diversity that lies at the root of ubuntu practice (Chuwa 2014). Neglect of rural populations and even violent imposition of development blueprints marked nearly all African post-colonial projects, including some promising endogenous experiments, such as Nyerere's *ujamaa* programme.

Ujamaa was a conscious, albeit overambitious, attempt at fusing ubuntu with socialism (Chuwa 2014; Ibhawoh & Dibua 2003; Saul 2013). The plan anticipated an African socialism at national scale based on collective ownership *and* decision making. A centrepiece was the *ujamaa vijijini* ('villagisation') scheme for rural transformation based on autonomous communal peasant modes of production reorganised around village cooperatives. In an idea not so different to today's ambitions for sustainable production through metabolic circles, the villages were to be part of a virtuous circle of 'ever increasing exchanges between city and country, between industry and agriculture' (Saul 2013: 205). Saul argues this scheme was meant to lay the tracks for a Tanzanian 'alliance of workers, peasants and others – on a democratic road to revolutionary socialism' (2013: 204–206).

Ujamaa's environmental philosophy was never fully defined, but Nyerere pronounced the proposal anti-capitalist given that Africans were already concerned about one another's welfare through care and reciprocity (Chuwa 2014). These ethics are cornerstones of ubuntu, but were undermined by coerced enforcement of rural 'villagisation', which ultimately led to *ujamaa* being discredited (Saul 2013).[8] The degeneration of ubuntu ethics into a rigid non-interactive 'political ideology' is regarded a core reason for *ujamaa*'s failure (Chuwa 2014). A critical lesson for the renewal of Marxism through ecological values is that imposed development 'negated the time tested ecological practice of the peasant farmers' (Ibhawoh & Dibua 2003: 70).

Contemporary scholars regard *ujamaa* and Senghor's Negritude as genuine attempts at delinking from capitalist circuits, aimed at national self-reliance and the achievement of social equity and distributive justice (Chuwa 2014; Ibhawoh & Dibua 2003; Legum 1999). Nyerere's political philosophy is being reread as a radical revision of liberal justice that questions the concept of equal rights superimposed upon capitalism's socio-economic structural inequalities. Equality, for Nyerere, was a demand for dignity and, therefore, equality should supersede liberal individual rights (Issa Shivji, in Praeg & Magadla 2014).

It is the originality of some intellectual contributions, notably Fanon's and Senghor's humanism, that has outlasted the national experiments and continues to inspire contemporary left politics (Glaser 2013; Wallerstein 2009). This is especially pertinent to the ecological crisis, given Fanon's emphasis on the relational character of collectives in opposition to western individualism and its dualities, such as the separation between society and nature. The historic repression of rural populations also runs counter to the instincts of both Fanon and Cabral that the peasantry's agency was a significant factor in true liberation as a negation of colonialism's modes of exclusion (McCulloch 1981; Naicker 2011). Today, peasant agency remains crucial to quests for ecological justice among Africa's social movements, for example food sovereignty and anti-extractive networks (see Bassey, and Bennie and Satgoor in this volume).

Significantly, what all post-colonial thinkers had in common was a rejection of private property and self-enrichment. Nyerere and Senghor, however, both had doubts about the forced distribution of welfare that socialism demanded, given their conviction that the community was already a distributive agent through caring and sharing (Chuwa 2014). African philosophy is critically dismissive of private property relations – as a violation of all other relations – and this is where a conversation with eco-socialism could start (Caromba 2014; Chuwa 2014; Kanu 2014). A growing consensus holds that ubuntu's political economy is not compatible with capitalist relations (Caromba 2014), private property (Van Norren 2014) and, especially, pervasive inequality (Cornell & Van Marle 2015). One argument is that African humanism 'demands a sustained attack on mass poverty by means of a Venezuelan- or Bolivian-style welfare state' (Biney 2014, cited in Caromba 2014: 210).

This is where the argument for a red–green alliance based on indigenous values becomes tenuous. Latin America's recent attempts to merge indigenous worldviews with socialism – known as the 'pink tide' revolutions – may have made progress on mass poverty, but failed to implement the ecological trans-formation agreed to with indigenous populations. In Bolivia and Ecuador, the (green) indigenous (*buen vivir*) principles that promised to decolonise society–nature relations were violated as progressive labour movements fell into elite traps (see Acosta and Abarca, and Sólon in this volume). Constitutional guarantees of alternatives to development and harmony with nature were abandoned as state–corporate elites succumbed to a dependency on environ-mentally destructive extractive exports during the commodity boom of the 2000s to expediently facilitate social distribution agendas (Svampa 2013).

Similar contradictions undermined Africa's post-colonial socialist states. Many maintained close relationships with western corporations (Praeg 2014, in Metz 2014a) and development took precedence over sustainability concerns. Africa's mineral wealth and increasing post-colonial dependency on raw mate-rial exports remains a significant challenge to environmental and social justice. The continent's resources are still plundered at an unprecedented scale in a new scramble for Africa, with the complicity of its own governing elites (Bassey 2012; Bond 2015). Ubuntu scholars argue that given the corporate capture of nation-states, 'only a continent-wide socialism is viable' (Sjivji 2014, cited in Metz 2014a: 450). Critics of Latin America's failed 'pink tide' revolutions, too, contend that neoliberal state facilitation of capital means that ecological justice (for example, post-extractive transitions) might have more potential beyond the state, at local, regional and interregional levels (Gudynas 2013; Sólon 2016).

Given that crucial mistakes were made in the post-colonial era, Glaser (2013) argues that Marxism today is only one among many democracy-respecting discourses in Africa's struggles to overcome capitalism's hidden abode of (re)production in the global South. In such a quest, however, there is room for conversation with, among others, ecologists, about reframing social justice and democracy. We may therefore dismiss the possibility of an African ubuntu eco-socialism. Alternatively, as Saul (2013) maintains, more could be lost in deciding not to dare – the *fait accompli* of neocolonialism.

For a renewal of Marxism in Africa, therefore, it is important to tease out convergences through which we could bring ubuntu and eco-socialism into conversation. In the following section, this potential is examined first through the window of current struggles in their everyday validation of Africa's ethics, and then through a comparison between contemporary eco-socialist principles and earlier ubuntu-inspired socialist templates.

GRASSROOTS STRUGGLES RECLAIMING AN AFRICAN ECO-ETHICS AND SOCIALISM

The revival of ubuntu – as an activist eco-ethics – could be located at the concurrence of struggles against neoliberalism and climate change in the early 1990s. Neocolonial state–corporate alliances have continued to undermine autonomous community agency and the environmental commons in resource-rich regions of the south. Environmental destruction from oil extraction had already been destabilising Niger Delta communities for decades when the Nigerian state executed Ken Saro-Wiwa and eight fellow environmental activists for peaceful resistance against petro-imperialism (Bassey 2012; Klein 2014). Before his execution, Saro-Wiwa ([1995] 1996) predicted all of us would be on trial for jeopardising future generations.

His last message catalysed a global quest to leave fossil fuels in the soil. A 1995 meeting of minds between prominent climate activist Nnimmo Bassey's Nigeria-based Environmental Rights Action movement and Ecuador's Amazon basin eco-watch group *Acción Ecológica* resulted in the formation of the global Oilwatch network. Their rallying cry became to 'leave it in the ground' (Bassey 2012; Klein 2014). These struggles raised the profile of ecological justice globally, along with the indigenous cosmovisions of those so often at the coalface of extractivism, such as Latin America's indigenous communities and their worldview, *buen vivir* (see Acosta and Abarca, and Sólon in this volume). As an ethical guide for ecological justice, the prominence of *buen vivir* spurred renewed interest in ubuntu as a companion counterhegemonic eco-alternative.

In the years that followed, ubuntu re-emerged on several fronts, in ways that accentuated its restorative justice and intergenerational ethics in relation to the environment. Just weeks after Saro-Wiwa's death, South Africa's Truth and Reconciliation Commission popularised the idea of ubuntu as forgiveness for apartheid's sins. In the context of the African National Congress government's betrayal of social justice, the metaphor of forgiveness was nothing but controversial.[9] It nevertheless provoked expansive reflection about ubuntu ethics and its critique of capitalism – a compelling point of departure for a dialogue with eco-socialism.

In her book *This Changes Everything*, climate activist Naomi Klein (2014: 12) argues that although we have the means to make a just transition to a post-carbon and post-capitalist society, we lack the 'mindset'. She contends that we need a new communal ethos to take the leap, critically one outside the dualist mindset and crisis-prone logic of western capitalism. Overcoming the deadly separation between humans and nature on which capitalism relies would require a battle of worldviews: '… a process of rebuilding and reinventing the very idea of the collective, the communal, the commons, the civil, and the civic after so many decades of attack and neglect' (Klein 2014: 404).

Africa's ubuntu worldview already embodies such a communal mindset, as evidenced in struggles at the cusp of fossil fuel destruction, from the Niger Delta to the mines of South Africa's minerals–energy complex at Marikana; the coalfields of KwaZulu-Natal, Mpumalanga[10] and Limpopo; and new oilfields and coal mines in Kenya,[11] nearly all threatening age-old ecological and cultural sites and sustainable peasant agriculture. South Africa's continued coal addiction has seen the livelihoods, as well as ubuntu enactments, centred on 'sacred sites' sacrificed at the altar of mega-coal – from vhaVenda women's battles against the aggressive encroachment of coal mines on 'sacred' water sites (Sibaud 2012), to similar struggles by the largely women-organised Fuleni communities against the impacts of coal intrusion on their livelihoods and on the Umfolozi River basin which feeds into the iSimangaliso Wetland Park, a World Heritage Site.[12]

Niger Delta communities continue to wage some of the most sustained counterstruggles on the continent, demonstrating Africa's radical restorative activism. These struggles are based on local understandings that crude oil impoverishes the community, but also the Earth. Klein (2014: 265–266) describes this as 'another kind of climate change': an attempt 'by a group of people whose lands had been poisoned and whose future was imperiled to change their political climate, their security climate, their economic climate, and even their spiritual climate'.

Petrochemical company Shell was successfully evicted from Delta territories through peaceful resistance by the 1990s (Klein 2014), but Nigeria's heavy reliance on oil export revenue means petro-elites are never fully deterred. Niger Delta women often take the lead in counterstruggles to protect the commons, because as small-scale farmers and fishers, they are disproportionately impacted by the poisoning of water, air and land from reckless extraction practices. In 2002, they occupied oil facilities, stripping naked to embarrass men for making deals that undermined their livelihoods (Turner & Brownhill 2004).

A 'pan-Delta defence' against Nigerian and US military repression was orchestrated to close down about forty per cent of Nigerian crude oil facilities. Significantly, the women's stand inspired activism far beyond the Niger Delta: global movements took up their case to oppose the impending US invasion of Iraq to protect its oil supplies, culminating in a fifty-million-strong global protest in 2003. Women's peasant agency represents what has been described as a far-reaching challenge to fossil fuel power, anywhere, by *evicting them at source* (Turner & Brownhill 2004).

The radical agency at work cannot be divorced from regional Niger Delta ubuntu eco-ethics, such as the Ibibio worldview *eti uwem*, which expresses 'restorative justice' succinctly as meaning that no monetary price can be placed on life. Hence, they demand restoration, rather than compensation, for fossil fuel harms. *Eti uwem*, like ubuntu, means living in harmony with nature and all peoples by communally caring for the environment. As an ethic, it rejects the speculation, exploitation, expropriation and environmental destruction wrought by fossil extraction. Struggles to bring into being such ethics are citizen-driven participatory processes aimed at moving 'from ecologically disruptive living to one where energy and other production and consumption modes are respectful of nature' (Bassey 2013).

Post-extractivism[13] was further mobilised by the radical Durban Declaration (2004), endorsed by over 300 climate justice lobbies, mostly from the global South. The Declaration insists that carbon trading, notably the 1997 Kyoto Protocol schemes, deepens the financialisation of nature while 'causing more and more military conflicts' globally. The aim to 'leave it in the ground' has since become an important point of convergence between eco-socialism and ubuntu ethics because many eco-socialists endorse capping fossil fuel consumption. Respected eco-socialist Joel Kovel (2007) is among those who support 'leave it in the ground' because it imposes limits on capitalist expansion and prevents the continuous disruption of the global South.

Saro-Wiwa's legacy continues to spread through new alliances and networks of activism, among others through Bassey's 'Yes to life, no to mining' campaign[14] to stop a rapid increase in mining across the continent. The campaign aims to protect *the conditions upon which life depends*, including healthy ecosystems, which in turn make possible food sovereignty for current and future generations. The birth of the global movement to 'leave it in the ground' could thus be attributed in part to Africa and its ubuntu ethics. Struggles against extractivism show that ubuntu both calls forth and provides a template for activism and decolonisation of the capitalist reproduction of nature. As an ethical, political and ideological concept, ubuntu always arises in struggle, most pertinently, in historical terms, as an anti-colonial, anti-racist and anti-imperial injunction against western modernity, which founded itself on the 'spectral other' of blackness (Cornell & Van Marle 2015; Garuba 2013; Praeg & Magadla 2014).

These struggles are emblematic of ubuntu's restorative ethics as they imply non-extraction, in contrast to mainstream western notions of compensation for heinous environmental crimes (Metz 2014b) or the perverse practice of counting production of non-renewable resource exports as GDP growth when, instead, it inflicts an ecological debt on future generations. As Bassey (2012: 151–152) argues, the mass poisoning of extractivism is the greatest violence communities can endure: 'Revenue derived from crude oil exploitation, for example, can hardly finance restoration efforts that may be needed following years of impacts on the environment.' This finds equivalence with Latin America's *buen vivir*, which rejects monetary reparations for environmental impairment in favour of restoration of ecosystems (see Acosta and Abarca, and Sólon in this volume).

The question remains how ubuntu-inspired struggles may enable us to conceive of a broader political project in conversation with eco-socialism. And do African socialist templates offer us authentic threads to tie eco-socialism with ideological visions based on ubuntu ethics? To find answers, the following section compares the ecological principles spelled out through Senghor's Negritude with those of contemporary eco-socialist slates.

TOWARDS AN ECOLOGICAL REFRAMING OF UBUNTU AND ECO-SOCIALISM

Senegal's philosophy of Negritude was perhaps most explicit among its post-colonial counterparts about the interdependence between the ecosphere and the social. Negritude asserts that Africans view the world 'beyond the diversity of its forms, as a fundamentally mobile, yet unique, reality that seeks synthesis' (Chuwa 2014: 58). This emphasises responsibility to counter the immorality of *violence to nature* that is held as tantamount to *violent acts against human-ity*. As a cultural perspective, it invokes an ethical consideration for healing dysfunctional biospheres (Chuwa 2014) that motivates struggles against extractivism.

It should be noted that not all scholars regard Senghor's legacy as progres-sive, despite the Marxist roots of Negritude among Africa's diaspora intel-lectuals. Some see Senghor as having drifted towards French culture and conservatism and criticise his dismissal of the need for opposition parties in African democracies (Legum 1999). Cabral regarded Negritude as an essen-tialisation of a bygone African culture that could obstruct the road to modern universalism.[15] Nevertheless, Negritude (as a fusion of Marxism and ubuntu) allows us to juxtapose contemporary notions of eco-socialism with an endoge-nous African political economy, promoted as four negritudes during Senghor's term as Senegal's president (between 1960 and 1980):

- Political negritude based on decentralisation of power and federalism (power sharing) – based on traditional African polities;
- Economic negritude spelled out African society's prohibition against pri-vate property and wealth. Labour is defined as 'collective and free';
- Social negritude centred on the family (community) as the sum of all persons living and dead, who acknowledge a common ancestor. It is an inclusive concept, but not fully compatible with Marxism's secularism;
- Cultural negritude extends relationships to the more-than-human, because 'the reinforcement of man is at once the reinforcement of other created things' (Senghor 1975, cited in Kanu 2014: 525).

In order to find touchstones between this African socialist vision and eco-so-cialism, I turn to Kovel, whose influential *The Enemy of Nature* (2007) provides two definitions of eco-socialism. Both definitions emphasise freely associated labour reunited with the means of production. This would be 'ecocentric' pro-duction because markets would be curtailed and the limits to growth respected. While rejecting a 'shallow, technocratic progressivism', Kovel's emphasis on production units as pivots for a just transition to eco-socialism does not fully break with teleological industrial modernisation and its dependence on the commons of the global South. Nor does it overcome the dualist human–nature tendencies of Eurocentric thought, something inherently rejected by indige-nous cosmovisions such as ubuntu and *buen vivir*.

Setting out four criteria for eco-socialism as prefigurative *struggles* necessary for a just transition, a 2011 template by Kovel nevertheless provides a base-
line for comparison with Senghor's vision. These struggles would inherently
resist centralisation and hierarchy; gender distinctions that permeate patriarchal society; the logic of endless growth; and would '*spontaneously adopt an
ethic of ecocentrism, that is, of caring for nature*' (Kovel 2011, emphasis added).

Correspondences between Kovel's template for eco-socialism and Senghor's
formulation of an African proto-eco-socialism are unmistakable in their
emphases on decentralised autonomy in the reproduction of just social relations and caring for the environment. Neither template is compatible with
imposed doctrinal Marxism. Although expressed differently, both stress the
need to move beyond private property relations, which trumps other forms
of social relations in its pursuit of capitalist expansion. Absent from Senghor,
however, is the more explicit objective of gender equality, although the latter is
implicit in Negritude critiques of the western creation of black and gendered
'others' as inferior and exploitable. In ubuntu, gender is often understood as a
pronounced category of difference among humans, but women are not a lesser
'other self' (Shutte 2009a), although it cannot be denied that unjust gender
power relations continue to pervade African society.

Kovel (2007) moots the concept of sufficiency as a substitute for jaded sustainability talk, by linking basic needs to a social justice approach – much like
the 'pink tide' revolutions in Latin America. While eco-sufficiency is central
to eco-feminist and indigenous proposals for a just transition, it is important to understand sufficiency in a broader ecological justice framework (see
Salleh 2009; Sólon in this volume). Like many eco-socialist and eco-Marxist
templates, Kovel's lacks an explicit acknowledgement of the counterhegemonic potential of alternative worldviews and the agency of more-than-human
nature. Considering ecocentric alternatives, it is important to recognise alternative rationalities about *what it is we value and want to reproduce for future
generations*.

Most eco-socialists, however, endorse a concept commensurate with ubuntu
and other peasant and indigenous practices that could help us conceive of a
deeper conversation: 'commoning' – acts of solidarity, mutual aid and struggles
to defend the commons. Kovel (2011) argues that such non-capitalist modes of
sharing could help construct eco-socialism through his four struggles (above)
as they are 'internally related and each implies the other'. All are regarded as
functions of the free association of labour grounded in forms of commoning.[16]

The commons also bring together the interests of productive and reproductive workers in a just transition. Ashley Dawson (2010: 17) stresses the importance of reframing 'pre- and post-industrial social formations' in contesting ensuing enclosure of the commons – in line with Antonio Gramsci's 'vision of uniting workers and peasants across geographical and cultural divides'. Social movements, such as anti-fossil fuel networks and global food sovereignty campaigns, notably La Via Campesina, are emblematic of commoning across race, class and gender divides. They show its potential for bridging the human–nature divide through ecocentric struggles to care for nature, the commons and future generations (see Bassey, and Bennie and Satgoor in this volume).

Ubuntu ethics are evident in these ready-existing commoning practices found among the world's 'meta-industrial' reproductive workers. These are the women, men, peasants and indigenous people whose agency embodies precaution, eco-sufficiency and autonomy in pursuing ecological justice through everyday regenerative labour at the cusp of nature (Goodman & Salleh 2013; Salleh 2009). The potential of indigenous ethics such as ubuntu and *buen vivir* as prefigurative counterhegemonic alternatives (McAfee 2016) contrasts starkly with just transitions conceived via techno-decoupling modalities based on sustaining industrial production at the expense of ecological well-being.

Senghor's and Kovel's visions provide us with a theoretical platform from which to explore a dialogue between contemporary ubuntu and eco-socialism. The last section seeks a deeper evaluation of ubuntu's evolving principles to highlight its inherent eco-ethics as a *site of critique*. The purpose is to locate contemporary interpretations of ubuntu ethics that allow for convergence with eco-socialism in shaping the emancipatory potential of an endogenous African alternative.

UBUNTU'S CHALLENGE TO ECO-SOCIALISM

Current debates about ubuntu largely affirm the archive of post-colonial articulations. While ubuntu has been defined as anything from indigenous knowledge to tribal belief and ethics or post-colonial ideology, it will remain a controversial concept (Graness 2015b). Yet, as a form of critique of such liberal prejudices, ubuntu is also 'staging a dissensus': 'By way of everyday practices and ordinary lives, traditional liberal assumptions of the self, but also of law, justice and power are thwarted' (Cornell & Van Marle 2015: 4). The point is that recognition of its radical praxis could help us open a space for reflection, critique and processes of restoration at large.

Recent scholarship explores ubuntu ethics from several ecological angles that broadly affirm Senghor's and Nyerere's political economy as well as the ethos behind grassroots activists' resource resistance. Central to both is the community as the pivot of interrelationships, eco-sufficiency and care, requiring an ethics of doing no harm. Being and becoming in ubuntu entails building improved communities inclusive of non-human nature.

Breaking out of the idea that ubuntu is an archaic and patriarchal relic, contemporary debates recognise ubuntu's *activist ethos*, which inherently challenges oppression and harmful development (Chuwa 2014; Cornell 2009). Ubuntu is affirmed as an 'ethical demand to bring about a shared world' that actively 'promotes the actual experience of building, enhancing and, at times, repairing the moral fabric of an aspirational community' (Cornell 2009: 48). Ubuntu compels solidarity in the face of injustice and requires 'reparation of broken relationships' (Metz 2014b: 153). Its mode of reproduction is a continuous process – often denoting struggle – centred on the *moral agency* residing in interrelationships between human community members, but critically also with and through non-human life (Chuwa 2014; Le Grange 2012; Shutte 2009a). As eco-ethics it therefore poses a counterhegemonic challenge to the anti-politics of capitalist development (McAfee 2016).

Ubuntu is regarded as a deeply bio- or ecocentric ethic.[17] African 'concern' about the environment goes beyond Eurocentric 'fascination' with nature. It demands capacity to 'empathize with nature' (Mazrui 1977, cited in Murove 2009: 325) and holds potential for a global alternative to western environmentalism, which has not been able to halt gross environmental abuse (Bujo 2009; Naicker 2011). Ubuntu scholar Munyaradzi Murove (2009: 315) asserts that 'Africa yet possesses in its own traditional culture the roots of an ethical paradigm to solve the current environmental crisis. This is an ethic of an interdependence of individuals within the larger society to which they belong and to the environment on which they all depend'.

Restorative justice is premised on strong self-governance of both communities and resources, intended to maintain harmonious relationships across generations with humans and the environment. The original practice is based on clan meetings such as *indaba*, which are (in theory) radically inclusive and open consensus-seeking processes (Naicker 2011; Shutte 2009a). Critically, this implies a preference for regional and local governance (Shutte 2009b), in line with Senghor's and Kovel's emphasis on decentralised autonomy. Thus 'care' – and its relation to restoration – derives from both community and solidarity in 'sharing a way of life'. Although alternatives such as 'sharing' are often shunned by eco-socialists as not sufficiently counterhegemonic (see Kovel 2011), ubuntu's care ethic make an important contribution to the debate as it emphasises solidarity and dialogue in determining *that which ought to be restored* (Metz 2013). Its ethic of care and restoration speaks to the autonomy of human–nature relationships in the environmental commons (Metz 2013). This points towards convergence for a just transition between eco-socialists, eco-feminists, indigenous peoples, social movements, non-capitalist social experiments and other peripheral groups, especially in the global South.

Another element in ubuntu's restorative justice is the intergenerational building of just communities inclusive of non-human life and ecosystems. Intergenerational ethics, like restorative justice, is not uncommon among indigenous worldviews, with a pronounced seventh-generation principle in Indochina and across the Americas (Gibson 2012; Goodwin [1994] 2001).[18] Its significance for a just transition is nevertheless that in most indigenous communities 'one almost always finds institutions with rules that serve to limit short-term self-interest and promote long-term group interest' (Berkes 2008, cited in Sullivan 2014: 227). In this context it is important to recall Karl Marx's view that we are responsible for the Earth, which cannot be just 'property' as we have to hand it down in 'an improved condition': 'From the standpoint of a higher economic form of society, private ownership of the globe by single individuals will appear quite absurd ... Even a whole society, a nation, or even all simultaneously existing societies taken together, are not the owners of the globe' (Marx, cited in Kovel 2007: 268).

Africa's worldview speaks to Marx's stance that humanity has a duty to hand down the Earth 'to succeeding generations in an improved condition'. Its activism and ethics thus already embodies '*an ethic of ecocentrism ... of caring for nature*' (Kovel 2011, emphasis added). An ubuntu dialogue with eco-socialism could not be conceived of without this inherent intergenerational activism and its underlying care and restorative ethics – critically enabled by a critique of the Eurocentric othering of nature, women and Africans.

A deeper notion of an African eco-socialism would also recognise ubuntu as an African well-being alternative with political and legal importance and communitarian moral responsibility to south–south solidarity (Van Norren 2014). Far from a shallow proposition, it proposes a 'fundamental reshaping of our thinking ... where acting out of "self-interest" is balanced by the notion of "not existing without the other"' (2014: 261). Ubuntu as 'site of critique' of Euro-modernity is therefore a radical challenge that cannot be taken lightly: 'Ubuntu *will never accept final restoration* because it "resides in a perpetual remarking of default"'. This is because ubuntu 'continually marks and re-marks a loss of humanity, and of human dignity' – processes of restoration that can never be finite (Cornell & Van Marle 2015: 4, citing Sanders 2007, emphasis added).

Ubuntu's restorative justice ethics could therefore also be seen as a form of insurgency because its political economy exposes power imbalances and the evasion of responsibility when decisions are made about *that which ought to be restored*. It challenges those state–corporate alliances that subvert the fulfilment of needs (Sullivan & Tifft 2006). As such, ubuntu is also emerging as a 'broader project of subaltern legality' because it challenges the limits of legality of western law and policy through, among others, mass mobilisation (Cornell 2014, cited in Graness 2015a: 146–147), as exemplified by the Niger Delta activists. Racism, too, is contested at all levels – in law, philosophy and politics. It is argued that ubuntu thereby articulates a radical conception of democracy that ought to be taken seriously in any project that aims to renew what Drucilla Cornell calls 'the philosophical and political project of human solidarity ... This it can only do if we take seriously the emancipatory potential for radical transformation embodied by "revolutionary Ubuntu"' (Cornell 2014, cited in Praeg & Magadla 2014: 11).

The South African shack-dwellers' movement Abahlali baseMjondolo coined the term 'revolutionary ubuntu' to explain that ubuntu cannot be compatible with capitalism. A range of ubuntu scholars agree, although not all see its ethics well matched to socialism either (Metz 2014a). Ubuntu's denunciation of private property rights and wealth, however, provides a bridge to eco-socialism (Chuwa 2014; Ramose 2014, in Caromba 2014) as it inherently rejects what David Harvey (2008: 23) slates as the primacy of 'property rights over process, things and social relations' in capitalism, which trumps all other rights. Ubuntu justice infers that there are always rights that are morally more important than property in relationships between people and the Earth, given that the Earth is a 'commonwealth to all humanity' (Odera Oruka, cited in Graness 2015b: 129–130). Such a radical quest for social justice steeped in a relational eco-ethic represents a constructive avenue for dialogue and solidarity with eco-socialism.

Potential for a dialogue, however, requires acknowledgement of the radical inequalities wrought on Africans and the absence of private property ownership and its material relations in debates on justice (including ecological justice). The reality of humans as relational beings and the basic needs required for them to act as moral beings are not always appreciated (Graness 2015b). Equally important for a discussion about the compatibility of ubuntu and eco-socialism is to take heed that ubuntu cannot be separated from its decolonial aspirations and is therefore irrevocably shackled to its resistance to modernity, a context into which socialism was also born (Praeg 2013). As site of critique and dissensus, ubuntu helps us to conceive of a discourse with socialism's own critique against capitalist relations. But it demands an unsettling of categories of race, gender, class and all 'others' – notably 'nature' itself – as created by Euro-modernity. In contrast to Eurocentric rational modes of continuous 'dis-enchantment' with the world, the practice of ubuntu implies a 'continual re-enchantment' which rejects 'boundaries, binaries and demarcations and the linearity of modernity' (Garuba 2013: 50).

Decolonisation will remain central to counterstruggles and radical alternatives in the face of imperial ecocide. Ubuntu could serve as a *decolonising spirit* (Carroll 2013), catapulting ubuntu discourses to an international level to show how the 'burning issues of the global South are the burning issues of nation states everywhere in the world' (Graness 2015a: 147). Ubuntu as critique therefore represents a challenge to the north to rethink its assumptions about democracy and justice. Yet, as Fanon warned fifty years ago, decolonisation is a 'profoundly unsettling process' because it 'sets out to change the order of the world' (1963: 36, cited in Collard, Dempsey & Sundberg 2013: 329).

NOTES

1   Ubuntu (isiZulu, isiXhosa) and *botho* (Sesotho and Setswana) mean 'humanness', while Zimbabwe's *ukama* (Shona) stresses 'relatedness' (Murove 2009).
2   Regional counterparts include *bomoto* (Bobangi), *gimuntu* (Kikongo), *umundu* (Kikuyu), *Vumunhi* (Xitsonga), *Uhuthu* (Tshivenda), *Umuntu* (Uganda), *Umunthu* (Malawi) (Benedetta & Margherita 2013; Murove 2009).
3   The values and ideas underpinning ubuntu are central to all African cultures (Shutte 2009a). As ubuntu, it is most prominently practised in southern Africa, also known as *ukama* in the Zimbabwe region (Naicker 2011), and in Nigeria as *eti uwem* (Bassey 2013).

4   *Buen vivir* or *vivir bien* is the Spanish approximation of regional ethics denoting 'living well' (see Acosta and Abarca, and Sólon in this volume).

5   See Volume 1 of this series.

6   *Ujamaa* was founded on Tanzania's post-independent Arusha Declaration, which extrapolated from 'the traditional way of life' a *set of rights*, including human equality; human right to life, dignity and respect; equal rights as citizens; right to just reward for human labour; equal right of access to national natural resources and major means of production (Chuwa 2014). Negritude emphasises African cultural values, humanism and solidarity (Chuwa 2014; Kanu 2014).

7   See also F. Manji, 'Amilcar Cabral's revolutionary anti-colonialist ideas', *ROAR Magazine*, 5 February 2017, https://roarmag.org/essays/amilcar-cabral-revolutionary-anticolonialism (accessed 12 April 2017).

8   Some scholars give a more qualified view, suggesting the village scheme failed, but *ujamaa* nevertheless delivered the only successful agrarian revolution in Africa, with improved communal health, education and sanitation projects (Legum 1999).

9   See Christoph Marx (2002) for an incisive critique of ubuntu as cynical manipulation for nation building without equity.

10   See, for example, S. Bega, 'Eco-warriors at the coal face in Mpumalanga', *IOL News*, 27 May 2017, http://www.iol.co.za/saturday-star/news/eco-warriors-at-the-coal-face-in-mpumalanga-9380336 (accessed 28 May 2017).

11   See Jonathan W. Rosen, 'As the world cuts back on coal, a growing appetite in Africa', *National Geographic*, 10 May 2017, http://news.nationalgeographic.com/2017/05/lamu-island-coal-plant-kenya-africa-climate/ (accessed 14 May 2017).

12   See for example S. Harris, 'iMfolozi coal mines raise concerns', *Business Day*, 25 August 2014, https://www.businesslive.co.za/bd/national/2014-08-25-imfolozi-coal-mines-raise-concerns/, and 'iMfolozi wilderness faces shock new coal mining threat', 9 March 2017, http://saveourwilderness.org/2017/03/09/imfolozi-wilderness-faces-shock-new-coal-mining-threat/ (both accessed 2 June 2017).

13   Theoretically, 'extractivism' refers to more than fossil fuels, including a proliferation of mineral and gem quarrying, factory farms, biofuels, wood and water – mostly for export.

14   The Africa-wide 'Yes to life, no to mining' network contends that mining does not benefit communities but puts pressure on their commons and sacred spaces, where diversity is treasured. In line with ubuntu ethics, the campaign aims to build communities and to support them to say no to mining, to revive their customary laws and to restore ecosystems (AFSA 2015).

15   In Manji, 'Amilcar Cabral's revolutionary anti-colonialist ideas'.

16   Commoning is widely practised in Africa and Latin America as well as among the urban poor (see Bennie and Satgoor in this volume).

17   The lack of explicit environmental content found in South African expressions of ubuntu could be blamed on the magnitude of loss of land (Green 2013), regarded as the seat of ubuntu-being (Mbiti 1969). The land-centred interdependence of ubuntu is better understood from the broader ontological concept of *ukama* (as practised in Zimbabwe) – denoting 'relatedness' with the entire cosmos (Le Grange 2012; Murove 2009).

18   Communities in Pakistan/India, for example, studied new maize seed for seven generations before using it among their crops (Goodwin [1994] 2001), thus yielding systems far more resilient than imposed developmental practices.

REFERENCES

AFSA (Alliance for Food Sovereignty in Africa). 2015. 'African civil society says no to mining – yes to life!' Accessed 16 July 2015, http://afsafrica.org/african-civil-society-says-no-to-mining-yes-to-life/.

Amin, A. 2014. 'Understanding the political economy of contemporary Africa', *Africa Development*, 39 (1): 15–36.

Bassey, N. 2012. *To Cook a Continent: Destructive Extraction and the Climate Crisis in Africa*. Dakar and Oxford: Pambazuka Press.

Bassey, N. 2013. 'Between Eti Uwem and capitalism (green democracy)'. Accessed 2 March 2014, http://www.africavenir.org/fr/newsdetails/archive/2013/february/article/nnimmo-bassey-between-eti-uwem-and-green-capitalism-green-democracy.html?t.

Benedetta, C. and Margherita, G. 2013. 'Indigenous voices: Enriching contaminations between buen vivir, ubuntu and the western world'. Study paper in the Department of Economics, Roma Tre University, Rome.

Bond, P. 2015. *Climate's value, prices and crises: Geopolitical limits to financialization's ecological fix*. Leverhulme Centre for the Study of Value Working Paper Series No. 9, University of Manchester. Accessed 19 August 2017, http://thestudyofvalue.org/wp-content/uploads/2015/01/WP9-Bond-Climates-value-prices-crises.pdf.

Bujo, B. 2009. 'Ecology and ethical responsibility from an African perspective'. In *African Ethics: An Anthology of Comparative and Applied Ethics*, edited by Munyaradzi F. Murove. Pietermaritzburg: University of KwaZulu-Natal Press, pp. 281–297.

Caromba, L. 2014. 'Review of *Ubuntu: Curating the Archive*', *Strategic Review for Southern Africa*, 37 (1): 208–211.

Carroll, W.K. 2013. 'Alternative policy groups and global civil society: A report from the field'. Department of Sociology, University of Victoria. Accessed 27 April 2014, http://www.web.uvic.ca/~wcarroll/TAPGsReport31Dec2013.pdf.

Chuwa, L.T. 2014. *African Indigenous Ethics in Global Bioethics: Interpreting* Ubuntu (*Vol. 1*). New York: Springer.

Cock, J. 2014. 'The "green economy": A just and sustainable development path or a "wolf in sheep's clothing"?' *Global Labour Journal*, 5 (1): 23–44.

Collard, R., Dempsey, J. and Sundberg, J. 2015. 'A manifesto for abundant futures', *Annals of the Association of American Geographers*, 105 (2): 322–330.

Cornell, D. 2002. 'Exploring ubuntu: Tentative reflections'. Accessed 4 May 2015, http://www.fehe.org/index.php?id=281.

Cornell, D. 2009. 'Ubuntu, pluralism and the responsibility of legal academics to the new South Africa', *Law Critique*, 20: 43–58.

Cornell, D. and Van Marle, K. 2015. 'Ubuntu feminism: Tentative reflections', *Verbum et Ecclesia*, 36 (2): Art. #1444: 1–8.

Dawson, A. 2010. 'Introduction: New enclosures', *New Formations*, 69 (1): 8–22.

Durban Declaration. 2004. 'Climate justice now! The Durban Declaration on Carbon Trading'. Accessed 19 August 2017, http://www.durbanclimatejustice.org/dur-ban-declaration/english.html.

Fanon, F. 1967. *Black Skin, White Masks*. London: Pluto Press.

Garuba, H. 2013. 'On animism, modernity/colonialism, and the African order of knowledge: Provisional reflections'. In *Contested Ecologies: Dialogues in the South on Nature and Knowledge*, edited by L. Green. Cape Town: HSRC Press, pp. 42–51.

Gibson, K. 2012. 'Take back the economy, any time, any place: Pedagogies for securing community economies'. Antipode Lecture Series, Royal Geographical Society. Accessed 8 May 2014, http://www.onlinelibrary.wiley.com/journal/10.1111/%28ISSN%291467-8330/homepage/lecture_series.htm.

Glaser, D. 2013. 'Retrospect: Seven theses about Africa's Marxist regimes'. In *Marxisms in the 21st Century: Crisis, Critique and Struggle*, edited by Michelle Williams and Vishwas Satgar. Johannesburg: Wits University Press, pp. 168–195.

Goodman, J. and Salleh, A. 2013. 'The "green economy": Class hegemony and coun-ter-hegemony', *Globalizations*, 10 (3): 411–424.

Goodwin, B. (1994) 2001. *How the Leopard Changed Its Spots: The Evolution of Complexity*. Princeton, NJ: Princeton University Press.

Graness, A. 2015a. 'Ubuntu: Curating the archive', *South African Journal of Philosophy*, 34 (1): 143–147.

Graness, A. 2015b. 'Is the debate on "global justice" a global one? Some considerations in view of modern philosophy in Africa', *Journal of Global Ethics*, 11 (1): 126–140.

Green, L. 2013. 'Contested ecologies: Nature and knowledge'. In *Contested Ecologies: Dialogues in the* South *on Nature and Knowledge*, edited by L. Green. Cape Town: HSRC Press, pp. 1–12.

Gudynas, E. 2013. 'Transitions to post-extractivism: Directions, options, areas of action'. In *Beyond Development: Alternative Visions from Latin America*, edited by M Lang and D. Mokrani. Amsterdam: Transnational Institute. Accessed 19 August 2017, https://www.tni.org/files/download/beyonddevelopment_complete.pdf.

Harvey, D. 2008. 'The right to the city', *New Left Review*, 53: 23–40.

Ibhawoh, B. and Dibua, J.I. 2003. 'Deconstructing ujamaa: The legacy of Julius Nyerere in the quest for social and economic development in Africa', *African Journal of Political Science*, 8 (1): 59–83.

Kanu, I.A. 2014. 'Negritude and the quest for an African identity', *Indian Journal of Applied Research*, 4 (8): 523–525.

Klein, N. 2014. *This Changes Everything: Capitalism vs. the Climate*. Canada: Alfred A. Knopf.

Kovel, J. 2007. *The Enemy of Nature: The End of Capitalism or the End of the World?* London: Zed Books.

Kovel, J. 2011. 'Five theses on eco-socialism'. *Ecosocialist Horizons*, 25 November. Accessed 26 August 2011, http://ecosocialisthorizons.com/2011/11/five-theses-on-ecosocialism/.

Le Grange, L. 2012. 'Ubuntu, ukama and the healing of nature, self and society', *Educational Philosophy and Theory*, 44 (2): 56–67.

Legum, C. 1999. *Africa since Independence*. Bloomington, IN: Indiana University Press.

Marx, C. 2002. 'Ubu and ubuntu: On the dialectics of apartheid and nation building', *Politikon: South African Journal of Political Studies*, 29 (1): 49–69.

Mbiti, J.S. (1969) 1977. *African Religions and Philosophy*. London: Heinemann.

McAfee, K. 2016. 'Green economy and carbon markets for conservation and development: A critical view', *International Environmental Agreements: Politics, Law and Economics*, 16 (3): 333–353.

McCulloch, J. 1981. 'Amilcar Cabral: A theory of imperialism', *The Journal of Modern African Studies*, 19 (3): 503–511.

Metz, T. 2013. 'The western ethic of care or an Afro-communitarian ethic? Specifying the right relational morality', *Journal of Global Ethics*, 9 (1): 77–92.

Metz, T. 2014a. 'Ubuntu: Curating the archive', *Philosophical Papers*, 43 (3): 447–453.

Metz, T. 2014b. 'Harmonizing global ethics in the future: A proposal to add south and east to west', *Journal of Global Ethics*, 10 (2): 146–155.

Murove, M.F. 2009. 'An African environmental ethic based on the concepts of ukama and ubuntu'. In *African Ethics: An Anthology of Comparative and Applied Ethics*, edited by Munyaradzi F. Murove. Pietermaritzburg: University of KwaZulu-Natal Press, pp. 315–331.

Naicker, I. 2011. 'The search for universal responsibility: The cosmovision of ubuntu and the humanism of Fanon', *Development*, 54 (4): 455–460.

Praeg, L. 2013. 'An answer to the question: What is [ubuntu]?' *South African Journal of Philosophy*, 27 (4): 367–385.

Praeg, L. and Magadla, S. 2014. 'Introduction'. In *Ubuntu: Curating the Archive*, edited by L. Praeg and S. Magadla. Pietermaritzburg: University of KwaZulu-Natal Press, pp. 1–9.

Salleh, A. 2009. *Eco-Sufficiency and Global Justice: Women Write Political Ecology*. London: Pluto Press.

Salleh, A. 2014. 'Ecosocialism, gendered imaginaries, and the informatic–securitization complex', *Capitalism Nature Socialism*, 25 (1): 24–39.

Saro-Wiwa, K.B. (1995) 1996. 'Statement before execution'. Accessed 19 August 2017, http://www.colorado.edu/journals/standards/V5N2/ESSAYS/wiwa.html.

Saul, J.S. 2013. 'Socialism and southern Africa'. In *Marxisms in the 21st Century: Crisis, Critique and Struggle*, edited by Michelle Williams and Vishwas Satgar. Johannesburg: Wits University Press, pp. 196–219.

Shutte, A. 2009a. 'Ubuntu as the African ethical vision'. In *African Ethics: An Anthology of Comparative and Applied Ethics*, edited by Munyaradzi F. Murove. Pietermaritzburg: University of KwaZulu-Natal Press, pp. 85–99.

Shutte, A. 2009b. 'Politics and the ethics of ubuntu'. In *African Ethics: An Anthology of Comparative and Applied Ethics*, edited by Munyaradzi F. Murove. Pietermaritzburg: University of KwaZulu-Natal Press, pp. 375–390.

Sibaud, P. 2012. *Opening Pandora's Box: The New Wave of Land Grabbing by the Extractive Industries and the Devastating Impact on Earth*. London: The Gaia Foundation.

Sólon, P. 2016. 'Some thoughts, self-criticisms and proposals concerning the process of change in Bolivia'. *Systemic Alternatives*, 25 February. Accessed 27 March 2017, https://systemicalternatives.org/2017/03/26/some-thoughts-self-criticisms-and-proposals-concerning-the-process-of-change-in-bolivia/.

Sullivan, D. and Tifft, L. 2006. 'Introduction: The healing dimension of restorative justice'. In *Handbook of Restorative Justice: A Global Perspective*, edited by D. Sullivan and L. Tifft. London: Routledge, pp. 1–16.

Sullivan, S. 2014. 'Nature on the move III: (Re) countenancing an animate nature'. In *Nature™ Inc.: Environmental Conservation in the Neoliberal Age*, edited by B. Büscher, W. Dressler and R. Fletcher. Tucson, AZ: University of Arizona Press, pp. 222–245.

Svampa, M. 2013. 'Resource extractivism and alternatives: Latin American perspectives on development'. In *Beyond Development: Alternative Visions from Latin America*, edited by M. Lang and D. Mokrani. Amsterdam: Transnational Institute. Accessed 19 August 2017, https://www.tni.org/files/download/beyonddevelopment_complete.pdf.

Turner, T.E. and Brownhill, L.S. 2004. '"Why women are at war with Chevron": Nigerian subsistence struggles against the international oil industry'. Accessed 11 December 2014, http://www.lbrownhill.com/docs/JAAS-Nigeria-6sept.rtf.

Van Norren, D.E. 2014. 'The nexus between ubuntu and global public goods: Its relevance for the post 2015 development agenda', *Development Studies Research: An Open Access Journal*, 1 (1): 255–266.

Wallerstein, I. 2009. 'Reading Fanon in the 21st century', *New Left Review*, 57: 117–125.

Walsh, C. 2011. 'Afro and indigenous life-visions in/and politics: (De)colonial perspectives in Bolivia and Ecuador', *Bolivian Studies Journal/Revista de Estudios Bolivianos*, 18: 49–69.

9

THE CLIMATE CRISIS AND THE STRUGGLE
FOR AFRICAN FOOD SOVEREIGNTY

Nnimmo Bassey

Despite over twenty years of international negotiations, there is no agreement on the reduction of carbon emissions. In fact, emissions have risen sixty-one per cent over this period and are having devastating impacts, particularly on the African continent. This is occurring despite Africa's limited contribution of four per cent to global carbon emissions, pointing to the importance of securing a 'just transition' to a post-carbon world. Justice demands that those countries of the industrial north that are most responsible for the climate crisis should take responsibility for solving it. This is acknowledged in the logic and principle of 'common but differentiated responsibilities'[1] built into the climate negotiations process. However, climate negotiations are increasingly shifting away from measurable mandatory emissions reduction by industrialised nations, while African nations are pushed relentlessly to buy into an agribusiness agenda through initiatives such as the New Alliance for a Green Revolution in Africa and the New Alliance for Food Security and Nutrition (NAFN). These top-down initiatives are ultimately aimed at undercutting, displacing and impoverishing smallholder farmers, who produce between sixty and seventy per cent[2] of the continent's food. These initiatives undermine the realisation of food sovereignty, a genuine people's alternative to control the food system in Africa. It is the final offensive in a calculated drive by capital to conquer the African agricultural market and impose the largely discredited industrial agricultural model, an agenda that has been relentlessly pressed on the continent in one guise or the other over the past forty years. This model 'has created a complex system of interlocking oligopolies that span seeds, agrochemicals, biotechnology, trading, retailing and consumer goods companies' (Hilary 2013: 120). John Hilary points out that 'just three transnational corporations – Monsanto, DuPont and Syngenta control between them over half the world's entire commercial seed market' (2013: 120). The impact of this model on the African continent is devastating and aggravated by the process of accelerating climate change.

THE IMPACT OF CLIMATE CHANGE ON AFRICA

Africa is set to suffer severe impacts from global warming if nothing is done to drastically cut carbon emissions. The Intergovernmental Panel on Climate Change (IPCC) stresses that

> continued emission of greenhouse gases will cause further warming and long-lasting changes in all components of the climate system, increasing the likelihood of severe, pervasive and irreversible impacts for people and ecosystems. Limiting climate change would require substantial and sustained reductions in greenhouse gas emissions which, together with adaptation, can limit climate change risks. (IPCC 2014: 55)

In its fifth assessment report, the IPCC states that

> each of the last three decades has been successively warmer at the Earth's surface than any preceding decade since 1850. The period from 1983 to 2012 was *likely* the warmest 30-year period of the last 1400 years in the Northern Hemisphere, where such assessment is possible. (IPPC 2014: 2, emphasis in original)

The report affirms that human influence on the climate system is very clear and rates recent anthropogenic emissions of greenhouse gases as the highest in history. Without drastic emissions reduction, and if current polluting patterns continue, it is expected that by 2100 global temperature will have risen by an average 2.5 to 7.8°C.

That quantum of temperature rise will mean a cooking Africa. According to the IPCC, temperatures in the African continent are projected to rise more rapidly than in other land areas during this century, particularly in the more arid regions. The projections also suggest that, under a high-emissions scenario, by the middle of the century average temperatures in most of the African continent will experience a temperature rise above the 2°C threshold set in current international agreements (Niang et al. 2014).

As the most vulnerable region to climate change (Kotir 2010), tales of climate woes for Africa are unending and the continent will be hit by droughts and intensified desertification. Under a range of climate change scenarios, it is estimated that by the 2080s, there will be an increase of sixty to ninety million hectares or five to eight per cent of arid and semi-arid land in Africa (Niang et al. 2014). Other estimates indicate that in the semi-arid scenario, up to twenty per cent of sub-Saharan Africa's arable land will be less suitable for farming by 2080. It has also been estimated that production from rain-fed agriculture will be reduced by fifty per cent in some African countries by 2020.[3] A 2°C temperature rise may result in permanent reductions in per capita food consumption of four to five per cent (WFP 2010).

These temperature increases will also have dramatic impacts on nutrition on the continent. Already it is claimed that some 240 million Africans are affected by hunger daily (Bremner 2012). It has been estimated, for example, that by 2050 a change of 1.2 to 1.9°C may increase the number of the continent's undernourished by twenty-five per cent, to ninety-five per cent. Central Africa will experience a twenty-five per cent increase, East Africa fifty per cent, southern Africa eighty-five per cent and West Africa ninety-five per cent. Moreover, the Economic Commission for Africa estimates that countries in Africa could lose between two and sixteen per cent of their GDP due to stunting of children as a result of malnutrition.[4] Decreasing crop yields and increasing population will put additional pressure on an already fragile food production system. Experts warn that if the current situation persists, Africa will be meeting only thirteen per cent of its food needs by 2050.[5]

Climate change is set to deepen the perception of Africa as the poster image for hunger and the subject of philanthropic capitalism. The projected crop failures and population rise, as climate impacts intensify, provide new impetus for demands to find new approaches to solving the hunger question. However, as will be shown, the so-called new approaches are not really 'new'. Instead, they are more of the same prescriptions dressed in new clothing.

By 2020, between seventy-five and 250 million Africans will face water stress. Indeed, by 2025 only a handful of African countries will not be suffering from water scarcity or stress. This will have dire implications not only for crop farmers but also for pastoralists. Furthermore, such scarcity can lead to tensions between different nations. Water-sharing arrangements between nations are contentious, as has been seen between Egypt, Sudan and Ethiopia, for instance. Egypt's decision to proceed with a major diversion of water from the Nile has implications for water use in Sudan and Ethiopia, both of which may want to secure water from the Nile for their own purposes. Similarly, the Niger River, with its source in Guinea and extending for 4 200 kilometres across Mali, Niger and Nigeria before emptying into the Gulf of Guinea at the oil-rich Niger Delta, is the site of tensions between these nations. It has been estimated that climate change-related temperature increases and rainfall variability may bring about a fifty-four per cent increase in civil wars, insurgencies and violent conflicts on the continent by 2030 (Levy & Sidel 2014). This will increase the number of climate refugees.

It is expected that climate impacts will seriously affect Africa's 'arid-semiarid rangeland and the drier mixed systems across broad swathes of the continent, particularly in southern Africa and the Sahel, and coastal systems in eastern Africa' (Thornton et al. 2006: 3). The impacts of climate change include land degradation caused by flooding, droughts or related erosion. This in turn leads to situations where the land loses soil cover or its ability to retain nutrients and to filter or absorb water.

Lake Chad, at the intersection of Cameroon, Chad, Niger and Nigeria, used to be one of Africa's largest lakes. It has diminished in size to less than ten per cent of what it was in 1960, shrinking from 22 772 to 15 400 square kilometres between 1966 and 1973. Satellite images show the lake's size to be 2 276 square kilometres by 1982 and a mere 1 756 square kilometres by 1994. The problem is compounded by the presence of invasive species, which constitute about fifty per cent of those left at the lake.[6] This has led to the displacement of fisherfolk and pastoralists who depended on the lake for their activities. Although the management of the river systems that recharge the lake may be a contributory factor in its shrinkage, it is estimated that climate change contributes at least fifty per cent to the current situation.

Paradoxically, while drought and water scarcity are real threats in Africa, floods often ravage the continent. Floods have already had severe impacts on Africa. These will intensify as weather events become more unpredictable and intense as climate change accelerates. In 2012, floods led to the displacement of 530 000 people in Niger Republic between July and September, while in Nigeria six million people were displaced, with over 300 deaths. Thousands more were displaced in Mali, Kenya, Uganda, Chad, South Africa, Mozambique, Cameroon, Burkina Faso, Ethiopia and Mauritania. Heavy rainfall in December 2014 and January 2015 led to flooding that affected thousands in Mozambique, Madagascar, Malawi and Zimbabwe. Floods have seriously impacted crops, livestock and infrastructure. In Mozambique alone, about 160 000 people were affected by the 2015 floods and 65 000 hectares of crops were washed away. The death toll stood at 158.[7]

In addition to flooding from rains, inundation from sea-level rise and coastal erosion has serious implications for agriculture. These include loss of farmlands as well as impacts on fisheries, including the increased salinisation of fresh-water systems.

MARKETING FALSE SOLUTIONS TO CLIMATE CHANGE IN AFRICA

A number of the solutions promoted globally help to lock in polluting activities and thus exacerbate the climate crisis. Some of these false solutions include reducing emissions from deforestation and forest degradation (REDD), carbon trading, climate-smart agriculture and genetically modified or engineered crops. They are generally solutions that depend on the current business infrastructure, including that of the fossil fuels industry. Of concern in this chapter are those so-called solutions that have direct implications for agriculture in Africa. These include promoting biofuels as an alternative or supplement to fossil fuels, synthetic biology, geo-engineering[8] and other market mechanisms. Synthetic biology, for example, is used to produce artificial vanilla as well as cocoa butter. Replacing natural vanilla with the synthetic version is already threatening farmers in Madagascar, Kenya, Uganda, Tanzania and Malawi. The replacement of cocoa butter will threaten farmers in Cote d'Ivoire, Ghana and Nigeria. Further, if synthetic coconut and palm kernel oils enter the market, farmers in Cote d'Ivoire, Cameroon, Nigeria, Madagascar and elsewhere will be hit.[9] These false solutions perpetuate the climate crisis but also undermine the realisation of food sovereignty. The analysis that follows shows how this is happening.

REDD HERRING

REDD is one of the tools being proposed as a way to capture carbon and, through the offset, to allow polluting industries and nations to continue polluting. It works on the basic principle that since trees and soils store carbon, the carbon stocks in designated forests can be computed and used as a means of exchange for cash and for a clear conscience to continue polluting. It is heralded as a means of halting deforestation, but is actually a way of avoiding emissions reduction at source and helps industrialised nations to balance their carbon accounting books without taking real actions. REDD and its variants are just carbon trading mechanisms and are fundamentally not about forest regeneration or protection.

Indigenous groups and opposing networks such as the No REDD in Africa Network insist that this is nothing but carbon colonialism. REDD, at best, displaces deforestation to other locations. It does not halt deforestation and is basically a convenient tool for market environmentalism. It promotes land and forest grab and, for Africa, may well be heralding a continent grab.

REDD-related land grabs have led to the displacement of people in Kenya, some conflicts in Uganda and simmering discontent elsewhere (Hall 2013). For REDD, as is the case with other UN programmes or projects, a plantation is recognised as a forest. This means that if a REDD forest is converted into a monoculture (where only one crop is cultivated) plantation, it would nevertheless still be regarded as a forest and provide needed carbon stocks to the carbon investor. The implications for food and hunger are inescapable. The impact of monocultures erodes and captures overall cultures and livelihoods.

GENETICALLY MODIFIED FOODS' UNSUCCESSFUL PUSH

The food shortage crisis in Zambia in 2000 brought the debate over genetically modified organisms (GMOs) and genetically modified foods in Africa forcefully into the public domain. By 2002, the debate had become intense. The US offered Zambia food aid in the form of whole-grain GMO corn. The country refused the whole grains and insisted on non-GMO food aid or, if it had to be GMO, for the grains to be milled before shipment from the US. It became a huge political issue. Why would hungry people choose what sort of food was on offer? The *Zambia Daily Mail* (5 November 2002) raised a pertinent point when it stated:

> It is very interesting to note that for the first time Zambia was being forced to accept a gift. Doesn't this worry us as recipients that the giver is insisting that we take the GM foods? Are the Americans just concerned about our stomachs or is there something behind the gift?

Zambia's resistance to accepting GMO food aid was based on caution around not wanting some of the whole grains planted or accidentally dropped on farmlands where they would contaminate the fields with genetically engineered traits. The country was also following the working principles of the World Food Programme (WFP), which recognises the right of any country to accept or reject GMOs in food aid. Some countries in southern Africa were already refusing GMO food aid as early as 2000. The two key agencies providing food aid, the WFP and the US Agency for International Development, were not quick to provide alternatives and the problems did not go away. And then on 15 May 2003, the US Senate passed a bill tying foreign aid to the acceptance of GMOs (Friends of the Earth International 2003).

Ironically, while some regions in Zambia were experiencing food scarcity that required aid, other regions had bumper harvests. A simple solution would have been to move food from the areas that had surpluses to those with a food deficit rather than waiting for food aid from across the seas and deserts. However, finance, infrastructure and logistics made this untenable. This underscores the fact that hunger is not necessarily the result of a lack of food, but may instead be due to lack of physical and financial access.

The politics of GMOs in food aid can assume almost comic dimensions. In 2004, Sudan was pressured to accept whole-grain GMOs as food aid after strenuously resisting it. The same happened in Angola. In 2007, Sudan was again faced with a food crisis as a result of a combination of factors, including climate change and the violent conflict in the Darfur area. With 2.4 per cent of people that had fled the conflict in Darfur depending on food aid, it took a great deal of courage to insist on aid that did not include genetically modified seeds.

With food aid not managing to deliver the GMO 'magic' to Africa, the next attempt was with non-edible cotton. Bt cotton was presented as a sure route to wealth for cotton-growing countries. The effort to show that small-scale farmers could flourish on Bt cotton was first tried at the Makhathini Flats in

South Africa. The magic worked for a few seasons as the farmers were heavily supported with inputs, subsidies and a strong dose of propaganda. However, the success story did not last for long and the farmers soon looked for better ways of ensuring that they had food on their tables (Pschorn-Strauss 2005).

Burkina Faso presented the next poster opportunity for Bt cotton. Again, after a couple of seasons and despite countries like Nigeria and Ghana regularly citing Burkina Faso as a transgenic cotton success story to be emulated, the false promise was soon exposed for what it was. The African Centre for Biodiversity (ACB) maintains that

> Burkina Faso began cultivating pest resistant cotton (known as 'Bt' cotton) in 2008 and the media has since been awash with reports of miraculous performance and increased yields ... After only two seasons of cultivation farmers were up in arms because their cotton harvest was downgraded due to short fibres, causing them to lose out on decent prices while having paid for the more expensive GM technology. (Swanby 2015: 4)

Cotton companies in Burkina Faso have since denounced their contracts with Monsanto and intend to phase out GM cotton altogether over a three-year period. In addition, stakeholders are discussing compensation for losses due to the low yields and low-quality fibre. This occurred just after some African governments, such as Nigeria, Ghana and Malawi, started seriously attempting to introduce GM crops, while others, such as South Africa and Sudan, had already commercialised GM cotton (Swanby 2015).

The ACB notes that GM cotton has impoverished smallholder farmers due to the expense of the technology, lower yields than promised and other inevitable technological failures associated with GM cotton crops. The group warns that with African producers already disadvantaged in the current global cotton sector, African governments risk placing more burdens on smallholder farmers, including through bigger debts, onerous crop management techniques and the ever-present risk of crop failures in a trading environment where prices are declining and smallholders are merely price-takers.

The push to have Africa adopt GM technology has been painfully slow for the biotech industry and the forces behind it, but for good reason, as evidenced by the experiences of small-scale farmers. Today, the arguments are that Africa needs climate-smart agriculture and that modern biotechnology is the most assured way of solving malnutrition on the continent. GMOs are presented as the convenient malnutrition-busting silver bullet.

However, a 'one solution fits all' silver bullet that solves every problem is manifestly anti-culture because culture thrives in diversity. Industrial agriculture, especially when based on genetic modification, is not just about monocultures but about agricultural systems that are essentially expressions of monoculture because they are based on the principle of narrowing down species to certain types that dominate the market.

The argument now is not how hungry Africans are, but how stunted and malnourished the majority are. The industrialised purveyors of GMOs have shifted the narrative to how Africans, who allegedly do not eat balanced diets, can be made to do so by genetically engineering crops to enhance the nutritional content. The reality is that nutrition is not something you manufacture in the laboratory (Bassey 2013b). Nutrition comes from eating wholesome food.

Many experiments have aimed at enhancing the nutritional value of crops through genetic engineering. A famous case was the hastily acclaimed golden rice,[10] which was genetically engineered to have heightened levels of vitamin A. The experiment was not that successful, however, because independent scientists revealed that one would need to eat many kilogrammes of the cooked rice every day to obtain the same amount of vitamin A that could be had from eating two carrots. Today the targets are staple crops on the continent: cassava, bananas and cowpeas.

On the need to introduce biotechnology into cassava farming in Nigeria for export purposes, experts at the Umudike Institute compiled a compendium titled *Root and Tuber Crops Research for Food Security and Empowerment* (Amadi et al. 2011) and explained that

> biotechnology provides a means of designing crops for specific environments which is a major departure from traditional agriculture. There is therefore a need for genetic engineering to be applied to improve cassava production as well as the enhancement of nutrient availability, pest and disease control. (in Charles 2013)

There has been no public information as to what the results of the field trial of the GM cassava have been in Nigeria. There is also no information as to whether Nigerians are eating genetically modified cassava.

The love of the G8 (now G7)[11] for Africa was underlined at their meeting in May 2012 when the group declared, among other things, that they would 'seek to maintain strong support to address current and future global food security challenges, including through bilateral and multilateral assistance, and agree to take new steps to accelerate progress towards food security and nutrition in Africa and globally, on a complementary basis' (The White House 2012). The main target of this thrust was clearly Africa, with the global possibility added to blunt the edge of the plan.

When the NAFN emerged from that G8 meeting, it was received as a Eureka moment and celebrated at a 'Nutrition for Growth' summit hosted by the UK government in June 2013. It was an event that saw countries like Nigeria, Ethiopia, Burkina Faso, Côte d'Ivoire, Ghana, Mozambique, Senegal, Tanzania, Benin and Malawi scrambling to become members of the Alliance. NAFN has been unmasked as a wedge to pry open the African door to corporate control.

A fact sheet on the NAFN issued by the White House (2013) states that, in 2012, the US leveraged its presidency of the G8 to deepen the global commitment to food security through establishing the Alliance, which will work 'with the African Union and Grow Africa, lift 50 million people out of poverty in sub-Saharan Africa by 2022'.

The fact sheet further states that the heavily business-oriented plan seeks the commitment of development partners, African governments, and international and local private companies 'to specific policy reforms and investments that will accelerate the implementation of country food security strategies under the Comprehensive Africa Agriculture Development Program, and sustain inclusive agriculture-led economic growth'. Working with the private sector, the Alliance was able to 'leverage' more than US$3.7 billion in private investment into African agriculture within its first year. Membership also grew within that period to include Benin, Malawi and Nigeria, in addition to the old team made up of Burkina Faso, Cote d'Ivoire, Ethiopia, Ghana, Mozambique and Tanzania. According to the fact sheet, these nations crossed the hurdles of rigorously negotiated 'Country Cooperation Frameworks for accelerating investment that include[s] policy reforms, private investment intentions, and donor commitments'.

Critics of the G8 initiative saw their major pull as being

> the $3 billion of private sector investment, across the entire agricultural chain of production. In total, 45 multinational companies plan to invest, most of which are based outside Africa, including agribusiness giants Monsanto, Cargill and DuPont. Swiss agrochemical company Syngenta

is to invest over $500 million to develop seeds for local farmers. (Global Agriculture 2012)

In an article in the *Guardian*,[12] the Alliance was presented as a flawed project that wrongly 'prioritises unprecedented access for multinational companies to resources in Africa. To access cash under the initiative, African governments have to make far-reaching changes to their land, seed and farming policies'.

Kicking small-scale farmers (who are actually the biggest aggregate investors in agriculture) aside in favour of agribusiness will mean more land grabs on the continent, more displacement of smallholder farmers, deeper poverty and more hunger. It is clear that if nutrition depends on the purchasing power of citizens, it will remain a fleeting illusion, to be pursued but never attained.

Diversity predisposes us to survive the crises we have yet to encounter. Large-scale industrial agriculture consolidating under the control of a small number of mega-corporations is a monoculture, not just a force creating monocultures (Heinemann 2009). Enhanced and supported traditional knowledge and local food production are key to securing a nutritious food future. It is time to stop flying the false nutrition kite powered solely by profit and the colonising control motive.

CLIMATE-SMART AGRICULTURE

Climate change provides a good opportunity for institutional protection of African agriculture. On the other hand, it could also build a sense of helplessness that leads to a colonisation of the entire agricultural system. The latter could occur if the tales of crop failures, hunger and malnutrition are not questioned. In such a scenario, almost any proposal to tackle these challenges captures attention and appears acceptable, especially if it comes from public institutions, well-resourced corporations or philanthropists[13] with solid political backing. In this context, the need to ensure agricultural resilience cannot be overstressed. Farmers have experimented with plant varieties and selected the ones most adapted to their environments for centuries, and supporting them should be a top priority for policy makers and institutions.

In northern Burkina Faso, the local farmers use local knowledge and technology to combat the harsh threats of global warming. Farmers using the traditional zai system are able to cultivate crops on virtually any sort of soil. The zai method of soil reclamation is hinged on trapping scarce water, nutrients and seeds in the soil. This is achieved through stone ridges and zai holes in which they place organic matter. Keeping animals and attracting birds to their farms ensures that droppings from these animals both enrich the soil and carry seeds. With low financial costs and intense commitment to working with nature, these farmers reap good harvests, and soils that would otherwise have gone barren are now teeming with life. In fact, some of their forests, like that of Yacouba Sawadogo, provide an ecosystem in the Sahel.[14]

Small-scale farmers illustrate how ecological agricultural practices restore soils, fight climate change and do not depend on the technological manipulation of seeds or on chemical and artificial additives. These local-knowledge techniques keep the culture alive in *agriculture.* They illustrate the truth that nature's biodiversity is inherently climate-smart. In other words, there are local varieties, including those developed by farmers and breeders through practical knowledge, that are already climate responsive and resilient. We should not be hoodwinked by concepts such as 'climate-smart agriculture' that appear smart but in reality are not helpful except to those who use them for market control.

SEED COLONIALISM

So-called climate-smart seeds are being presented as genetically modified or engineered varieties whereas local varieties exist that are smart in the true sense. The fact that GM crops are not a silver bullet to fight hunger in Africa or globally has been noted in various reports.[15] Seed saving and exchange are key to African agricultural practices. In such settings, farmers always have access to seed and this provides a strong safety net for those who may not have a large seed bank. Hunger in this context is literally the preserve of the lazy. However, this practice may soon be eclipsed by the strong external push to introduce regulatory mechanisms to make seed control, certification and trading mandatory. It is already a given that GM seeds must be purchased at every planting season. Since the GM machine is not spreading fast enough, an alternative route appears to be through the so-called African Regional Intellectual Property Organisation (ARIPO).[16] At the time of writing, a draft ARIPO protocol was about to be discussed by African states. ARIPO is based primarily on the International Union for the Protection of New Varieties of Plants (UPOV) convention.

The convention covering the UPOV was initially adopted in Paris in 1961 and went on to be reviewed and modified in 1972, 1978 and 1991. The 1991 revision is regarded as the one that really solidified the interests of the seed industry. The milestones en route to what appears to be the great seed grab took two big leaps when the 1978 Act came into force in 1981, and when the 1991 Act came into force in 1998.

Of significance in the entire seed 'protection' effort is that African governments did not take part in the negotiations. With this in mind, the ACB states:

> Unsurprisingly, UPOV 1991 especially, does not reflect the concerns of Africa, and imposes a 'one-size-fits-all' inflexible legal framework that limits the ability of countries to design their national laws to suit the particular needs and take into account the interests of small farmers. (ACB 2012: 13)

Although no ARIPO member country is a member of UPOV, African countries have been pressurised to ratify the UPOV 1991 convention by organisations with vested interests, such as the African Seed Trade Association and the Alliance for Commodity Trade in Eastern and Southern Africa. This is happening without regard to an independent seed protection trajectory that African countries have championed over the years. These African initiatives were drawn up with the understanding that in this region up to eighty per cent of the seeds are produced by local farmer-breeders. Cognisance was also taken of the fact that African food production is mostly through small-scale or family farms.

The UPOV and its uniform laws in Africa would remove the life supports on which African agriculture has hung since the lethal doses of structural adjustment programmes (SAPs). It would lead to a severe restriction of the farmer-managed seed systems as well as erosion or disappearance of local varieties developed over centuries of experimentation and selection (Bassey 2013a).

Shortly before the ARIPO meeting, the Alliance for Food Sovereignty in Africa (AFSA) argued that the proposed legal framework is unsuitable for ARIPO members. In particular, AFSA stressed that ARIPO 'erodes farmers rights and the right to seed and food' because it 'outlaws centuries-old practices of farmers freely using, exchanging and selling seeds/propagating material' (AFSA 2014: 1). The body also stated that such practices, often referred to as the informal seed sector, are of crucial importance for seed security in Africa and supply more than eighty per cent of the total food crop seed used by farmers (Shashikant 2015).

LAND AND WATER GRABS

Climate change is not the only problem faced by the African continent. The massive scramble for land in Africa is set to have huge impacts on water quality and accessibility, as well as on food security on the continent, as the grabbed lands are used mostly to cultivate crops for export. Another dimension of the continent grab relates to industrial, mining and oil companies and the related devastating impacts on land and water as a result of extractivism. Harvests from grabbed lands feed other continents while profits from mined lands feed corporate pockets.

The impunity with which resources are appropriated and with which polluting actions are carried out can best be described as sheer ecocide – actions that so harm nature that its natural cycles are irreparably hampered. For societies deeply dependent on smallholder agriculture and on the natural environment, ecocide spells disaster on a heightened scale. Ecocide is the twenty-first-century variant of colonisation – 'it is no longer confined to the enslavement of people but enslavement of the planet' (Higgins 2010: 66).

A key question is why a previously largely self-sufficient continent would end up with a beggar's bowl. The SAPs of the International Monetary Fund and the World Bank brought about a grand adjustment of African agriculture. Those programmes constricted governments' roles in society and declared that the private sector would take the driving seat in providing public/social services and supporting public enterprises. As noted by Walden Bello (2009: 79),

> reality refused to conform to the doctrinal expectation that the withdrawal of the state would pave the way for the market and private sector to dynamise agriculture. Instead, the private sector saw reduced state expenditures as creating more risk and failed to step into the breach. In country after country, the opposite of neoliberal predictions occurred: the departure of the state 'crowded out' rather than 'crowded in' private investment.

In 1986, the USA's agriculture secretary made a point at the start of the Uruguay round of trade negotiations that it was unreasonable for African countries to think of feeding themselves: 'The idea that developing countries should feed themselves is an anachronism from a bygone era. They could better ensure their food security by relying on US agricultural products, which are available, in most cases at lower cost' (Bello 2008).

The SAPs were carefully calibrated mechanisms to further such outlooks and to paralyse African agriculture by eliminating support structures under the guise of minimising the role of the government. The SAPs opened the floodgates for cheap agricultural produce that suffocated local production and perhaps even altered dietary preferences. For instance, parts of chickens and pigs – like the legs, feet and some of the innards – that are not usually found on European dining tables are shipped to the African market. While the SAPs opened up African markets for dumping imported produce, subtle political narratives that further lock in dependency continue unchecked.

CONCLUSION

As powerful as the forces pushing false climate solutions are, the people at the receiving end have been organising and mobilising arguments and actions to show what the real solutions are. People power can overturn those false arguments and autonomous actions can illustrate the foolery in the propositions that Africans can only be assured of food and nutrition through the products of laboratories, such as GMOs, or that climate-smart means modern biotechnology.

Climate change undermines planetary life-support systems. It attacks resilient systems and cultures developed over millennia. Unfortunately, rather than seeing the climate crisis as requiring urgent systemic changes, policy makers and others with vested interests work to entrench the systems that caused the problems in the first place. But there is hope in the activities of smallholder farmers, whose practices work in sync with nature and do not depend on artificial inputs that degrade soil and biodiversity.

The present wrong-headed and false solutions are not a result of lack of knowledge. Rather, they are due to selective knowledge driven by the neoliberal ideology. We have centuries-old knowledge, new knowledge and evolving knowledge that needs to be transformed into practical tools for actions that align with nature's cycles. This calls for a clear rejection of false technologies and the building of solidarity economies. The real solution is a low-hanging ripe fruit clearly within our grasp. Peasant farmers led by La Via Campesina and other social movements are vigorously promoting this low-hanging fruit – food sovereignty.

Food sovereignty stresses the human right to food and prioritises local food systems and local markets. It is against food dumping and promotes culturally appropriate and wholesome foods. Food sovereignty goes beyond the provision of wholesome food, however, and fundamentally fights hunger by ensuring that local farmers maintain control of their farming and food systems. This approach reduces the use of artificial and chemical inputs and has direct implications for food pricing. Moreover, through food sovereignty, farmers and other defenders of local food systems, such as the continental AFSA and the South African Food Sovereignty Campaign, directly resist the neocolonial narrative and systems that suggest that Africa cannot feed itself and must depend on food aid and genetically engineered crops as the only means of combating hunger and malnutrition (see Bennie and Satgoor in this volume). The false solutions package should remind us of the survival diets that were forced on slaves a few centuries ago, to keep them supplying needed plantation labour.

This is a critical moment to intensify the struggle for the decolonisation of African agriculture and food systems, as corporations and imperialist systems fight with gloves off to shove mercantilist products in our faces. Among the countries that have made food sovereignty part of their national food policy are Mali and Senegal. Other countries in the world to have done so are Ecuador, Bolivia and Venezuela (Wittman, Desmarais & Wiebe 2011). The African Union should take a leaf from the book of these nations and take this up as a key tool to regain total independence and set the continent on such a path. We can only secure food sovereignty by supporting the majority of our farmers in their small-scale agro-ecological farming. With sufficient support, including through extension services, agro-ecological farming can produce more than industrial agriculture, reduce the gender gap, increase employment, increase income, protect agricultural biodiversity, promote health and nutrition and mitigate global warming.

NOTES

1   See https://sustainabledevelopment.un.org/getWSDoc.php?id=4086 (accessed 4 September 2017).
2   See Graeub et al. (2016) for some of the latest statistics.
3   See https://www.ipcc.ch/publications_and_data/ar4/wg2/en/ch9s9-4-4.html (accessed 14 September 2017).
4   R. Munang and J. Andrews, 'Despite climate change, Africa can feed Africa', *Africa Renewal*, 2014, http://www.un.org/africarenewal/magazine/special-edition-agri-culture-2014/despite-climate-change-africa-can-feed-africa#sthash.rr9STZGQ. dpuf (accessed 20 August 2017).
5   Munang and Andrews, 'Despite climate change, Africa can feed Africa'.

6   Grid Arendal, 'Lake Chad: Almost gone', http://www.grida.no/search?query=lake+chad+almost+gone (accessed 20 August 2017).

7   'Southern Africa: Floods – Jan 2015', Reliefweb, www.reliefweb.int/disaster/fl-2015-000006-mwi (accessed 20 August 2017).

8   Geo-engineering is a quick-fix technology by which humans engage in large-scale intentional manipulation of Earth systems. Manipulation of rainfall through geo-engineering could intensify the unreliability of rainfall and rain-fed agriculture in the African Sahel. The implication of such an impact will be severe because up to seventy per cent of citizens in the Sahel region depend on agriculture for subsistence.

9   J. Mbaria, 'Africa's farm products could be pushed out of global market by synthetic biology', *The East African*, 14 April 2015, http://www.theeastafrican.co.ke/news/Why-Africa-is-worried-about-synthetic-biology/2558-2685452-y2cj7y/index.html (accessed 20 August 2017).

10   The rice was enhanced with the organic compound beta-carotene.

11   Canada, France, Germany, Italy, Japan, the UK and the US.

12   K. Chandrasekaran and N. Bassey, 2013. 'G8's new alliance for food security and nutrition is a flawed project', *The Guardian*, 7 June 2013, http://www.theguardian.com/global-development/poverty-matters/2013/jun/07/g8-new-alliance-flawed-project (accessed 20 August 2017).

13   For example, the Alliance for a Green Revolution for Africa, presented by the Rockefeller Foundation and the Bill and Melinda Gates Foundation.

14   See Bassey (2015) on a visit to the Sahel region of Burkina Faso.

15   Reports include those by the International Assessment of Agricultural Knowledge, Science and Technology for Development (IAASTD 2009), Friends of the Earth International (2015), Health of Mother Earth Foundation (2017), AFSA (2017) and ACB (2017).

16   ARIPO is a regional entity that administers various intellectual property instruments on behalf of its nineteen mostly Anglophone sub-Saharan African countries: Democratic Republic of São Tomé and Príncipe, Botswana, The Gambia, Ghana, Kenya, Lesotho, Liberia, Malawi, Mozambique, Namibia, Rwanda, Somalia, Sierra Leone, Sudan, Swaziland, United Republic of Tanzania, Uganda, Zambia and Zimbabwe.

REFERENCES

ACB (African Centre for Biodiversity). 2012. *Harmonisation of Africa's Seed Laws : A Recipe for Disaster: Players, Motives and Dynamics*. Johannesburg: ACB.

ACB. 2017. 'The GM maize onslaught in Mozambique: Undermining biosafety and smallholder farmers'. Accessed 14 September 2017, https://acbio.org.za/wp-content/uploads/2017/06/GMO-in-Mozambique-Report-Web.pdf.

AFSA (Alliance for Food Sovereignty in Africa). 2014. 'AFSA submission for urgent intervention in respect to draft ARIPO Plant Variety Protection Protocol (PVP) and subsequent regulations'. Accessed 19 August 2017, http://acbio.org.za/wp-content/uploads/2015/02/AFSA-Susbmission-ARIPO-PVP-Protocol.pdf.

AFSA. 2017. 'Agroecology: The bold future of farming in Africa'. Accessed 14 September 2017, http://afsafrica.org/wp-content/uploads/2017/02/Agroecology-the-bold-future-of-farming-in-Africa-ebook-2-page-spreads.pdf.

Amadi, C.O., Ekwe, K.C., Chukwu, G.O., Olojede, A.O. and Egesi C.N. (eds). 2011. *Root and Tuber Crops Research for Food Security and Empowerment*. Umudike, Nigeria: National Root Crops Research Institute.

Bassey, N. 2013a. 'Stopping the false nutritional kite'. Blog post, accessed 19 August 2017, http://nnimmo.blogspot.com/2013/10/stopping-false-nutritional-kite.html.

Bassey, N. 2013b. 'African policymakers must reject seed colonialism'. *Africa Report*, 15 July. Accessed 19 August 2017, http://www.theafricareport.com/North-Africa/opinion-african-policymakers-must-reject-seed-colonialism.html.

Bassey, N. 2015. 'Fighting climate change in the Burkina Faso Sahel'. Blog post, accessed 14 August 2017, http://nnimmo.blogspot.com/2015/05/fighting-climate-change-in-burkina-faso.html.

Bello, W. 2008. 'How to manufacture a global food crisis: Lessons from the World Bank, IMF, and WTO'. Transnational Institute. Accessed 11 September 2017, https://www.tni.org/es/node/10827.

Bello, W. 2009. *The Food Wars*. London: Verso.

Bremner, J. 2012. 'Population and food security: Africa's challenge'. Policy Brief. Accessed 15 September 2017, http://www.prb.org/Publications/Reports/2012/population-food-security-africa-part1.aspx.

Charles, E. 2013. 'Why Nigeria cannot export cassava now – experts'. *AllAfrica*, 29 August. Accessed 19 August 2017, http://allafrica.com/stories/201308290704.html.

Friends of the Earth International. 2003. *Playing with Hunger: The Reality behind the Shipment of GMOs as Food Aid*. Amsterdam: Friends of the Earth International.

Friends of the Earth International. 2015. 'Who benefits from GM crops? The expansion of agribusiness interests in Africa through biosafety policy'. Accessed 14 September 2017, http://www.foei.org/wp-content/uploads/2015/02/Who-benefits-report-2015.pdf.

Global Agriculture. 2012. 'Concern as G8 relies on agribusiness to fight hunger'. Accessed 19 August 2017, http://www.globalagriculture.org/whats-new/news/en/25747.html.

Graeub, B.E., Chappel, M.J., Wittman, H., Ledermann, S., Bezner Kerr, R. and Gemill-Herren, B. 2016. 'The state of family farms in the world', *World Development*, 87: 1–15.

Hall, R. (ed.). 2013. 'REDD+ and the underlying causes of deforestation and forest degradation'. Global Forest Coalition. Accessed 19 August 2017, http://globalforestcoalition.org/wp-content/uploads/2013/11/REDD-and-UC-report-final.pdf.

Health of Mother Earth Foundation. 2017. 'Not on our plates! Nigeria does not need GM food'. Accessed 14 September 2017, https://nnimmo.files.wordpress.com/2017/03/not-on-our-plates1.pdf.

Heinemann, J.A. 2009. *Hope Not Hype: The Future of Agriculture Guided by the International Assessment of Agricultural Knowledge, Science and Technology for Development*. Penang: Third World Network.

Higgins, P. 2010. *Eradicating Ecocide: Laws and Governance to Prevent the Destruction of our Planet*. London: Shepheard Walwyn.

Hilary, J. 2013. *The Poverty of Capitalism: Economic Meltdown and the Struggle for What Comes Next*. London: Pluto Press.

IAASTD (International Assessment of Agricultural Knowledge, Science and Technology for Development). 2009. 'Agriculture at a crossroads: Global report'. Accessed 4 September 2017, http://www.fao.org/fileadmin/templates/est/Investment/Agriculture_at_a_Crossroads_Global_Report_IAASTD.pdf.

IPCC (Intergovernmental Panel on Climate Change). 2014. *Climate Change 2014: Synthesis Report*. Contribution of Working Groups I, II and III to the Fifth Assessment Report of the Intergovernmental Panel on Climate Change. Geneva, Switzerland: IPCC.

Kotir, J.H. 2010. 'Climate change and variability in sub-Saharan Africa: A review of current trends and impacts on agriculture and food security', *Environment, Development and Sustainability*, 13: 587–605.

Levy, B.S. and Sidel, V.W. 2014. 'Collective violence caused by climate change and how it threatens health and human rights', *Health and Human Rights Journal*, 16 (1), http://www.hhrjournal.org/2014/07/01/collective-violence-caused-by-climate-change-and-how-it-threatens-health-and-human-rights/ (accessed 19 August 2017).

Niang, I., Ruppel, O.C., Abdrabo, M.A., Essel, A., Lennard, C., Padgham J. and Urquhart, P. 2014. 'Africa'. In *Climate Change 2014: Impacts, Adaptation, and Vulnerability. Part B: Regional Aspects*. Contribution of Working Group II to the Fifth Assessment Report of the Intergovernmental Panel on Climate Change. Cambridge: Cambridge University Press, pp. 1199–1265.

Pschorn-Strauss, E. 2005. 'Bt cotton in South Africa: The case of the Makhathini farmers'. *Seedling*, April. Accessed 19 August 2017, http://www.grain.org/system/old/seedling_files/seed-05-04-3.pdf.

Shashikant, S. 2015. 'Draft ARIPO Plant Variety Protocol undermines farmers' right to save, exchange and sell seeds'. Accessed 19 August 2017, http://afsafrica.org/draft-aripo-plant-variety-protocol-undermines-farmers-right-to-save-exchange-sell-seeds/.

Swanby, H. 2015. 'Cottoning onto the lie: The introduction of genetically modified cotton in Africa will harm, not help, smallholder farmers'. African Centre for Biodiversity. Accessed 19 August 2017, http://acbio.org.za/wp-content/uploads/2015/06/GM-Cotton-report-2015-06.pdf.

The White House. 2012. 'Camp David declaration'. Accessed 20 August 2017, https://obamawhitehouse.archives.gov/the-press-office/2012/05/19/camp-david-declaration.

The White House. 2013. 'The new alliance for food security and nutrition'. Accessed 20 August 2017, https://obamawhitehouse.archives.gov/the-press-office/2013/06/18/fact-sheet-new-alliance-food-security-and-nutrition.

Thornton, P.K., Jones, P.G., Owiyo, T., Kruska, R.L., Herrero, M., Kristjanson, P., Notenbaert, A., Bekele, N. and Omolo, A. 2006. *Mapping Climate Vulnerability and Poverty in Africa*. Nairobi: International Livestock Research Institute. Accessed 14 September 2017, https://cgspace.cgiar.org/bitstream/handle/10568/2307/Mapping_Vuln_Africa.pdf?sequence=1&isAllowed=y.

WFP (World Food Programme). 2010. 'Climate change and its impact on development. Prepared for the Joint Meeting of the Executive Boards of UNDP/UNFPA, UNICEF and WFP'. Accessed 11 August 2017, http://home.wfp.org/stellent/groups/public/documents/resources/wfp213809.pdf.

Wittman, H., Desmarais, A.A. and Wiebe, N. (eds). 2011. *Food Sovereignty: Reconnecting Food, Nature and Community*, edited by H. Wittman. Oxford: Pambazuka Press.

DEMOCRATIC ECO-SOCIALIST ALTERNATIVES IN SOUTH AFRICA

10

THE CLIMATE CRISIS AND A 'JUST TRANSITION' IN SOUTH AFRICA: AN ECO-FEMINIST-SOCIALIST PERSPECTIVE

Jacklyn Cock

The climate crisis presents us with a historic opportunity because to solve it we need radical transformative change in how we produce, consume and organise our lives. It is in this sense that a 'just transition' from the current fossil fuel regime in South Africa could both address the climate crisis and contain the embryo of a new, democratic, eco-feminist-socialist order.

This chapter suggests that reclaiming the hybridised and travelling discourses of feminism, environmentalism and socialism could give strength and coherence to a just transition to a post-carbon future. While there is no blueprint, all three discourses contain flashes of a vision of a post-capitalist society driven by a different energy regime and promote the solidarities necessary to drive transformative change. A major difficulty is that in contemporary South Africa all three discourses are, to some extent, contaminated. Feminism is widely viewed as elitist and individualist; environmentalism as focused on the conservation of threatened plants, animals and wilderness areas to the neglect of social needs; and socialism as productivist, authoritarian and repressive, as evidenced in the historical experience of the Soviet Union and – with more immediacy – the practices of the South African Communist Party (SACP). The chapter argues that the concept of social reproduction is especially relevant to this process of reclaiming.

THE MARXIST–FEMINIST APPROACH TO SOCIAL REPRODUCTION

Grounded in a Marxist–feminist analysis, this concept is important for six reasons. Firstly, it points to the possibility of unifying different struggles in the name of a reclaimed and reinvigorated feminism, environmentalism and socialism. It does so through building on the powerful Marxist capacity to *explain* different forms of domination through reinserting the special relevance of class into conceptions of intersectionality. It also does so through relating these struggles to material conditions of life. As Meg Luxton writes:

> Politically, a social reproduction perspective validates a wide range of struggles that directly relate to standards of living. These include wages and working conditions, a living income for all, access to housing, healthy food, and communities and households free of violence. *Issues such as climate change and other environmental concerns are clearly connected, inviting alliances.* (2015: 7, emphasis added)

Secondly, it directs us to the class-based, material realities of the everyday. As David Harvey writes, 'the politics of everyday life is the crucible where revolutionary energies might develop' (2014: 34). Thirdly, it focuses us on one of the most serious of the many dimensions of the climate crisis, which we face in contemporary South Africa – the impact of droughts and floods on food production and food prices. The food crisis is defined by the coexistence of hunger, extravagant overconsumption on the part of the elite, and waste. This is one of the most serious dimensions because twenty-five per cent of children under the age of six are showing signs of stunted growth, both physical and mental, due to malnourishment. These are poor, black children and much of the daily experience of the crisis takes place in the privatised sphere of the black, working-class household.

Fourthly, the Marxist–feminist approach to social reproduction provides us with an exposé of how capitalism operates, including the expansionist logic which is driving climate change. Fifth, it validates other anti-capitalist struggles and, lastly, it points us to alternative social forms.

The core of social reproduction is the insight from Karl Marx that 'the most indispensable means of production' is the worker and the 'maintenance and reproduction of the working class remains a necessary condition for the reproduction of capital' (Marx 1976: 718). What Marx neglected was that this 'maintenance' and 'reproduction' involves a great deal of work done by women.

Marx was not gender blind. He argued that women were an important element in the resistance to capitalism and was especially impressed by the role of women in the 1871 Paris Commune (Brown 2013). But Marx lacked the feminist analysis necessary to reveal the systematic character of unequal gender relations. So while he looked behind the sphere of exchange into what he called the 'hidden abode of production' in order to understand capitalism, Marxist–feminism takes this further to explore the 'hidden abode of social reproduction'.

The core of the integration of Marxism and feminism lies in this concept of social reproduction. It refers to the complex tasks and processes that ensure the production and reproduction of the population on a daily and on a generational basis. It means meeting caring and provisioning needs, including child rearing, producing and preparing food. In much of this work, a reliance on fossil fuels means additional expense and health hazards.

While women's work is often naturalised, obscured or trivialised as non-work, Marxist–feminist analysis has shown how women's unpaid care work that reproduces the working class acts as a subsidy for capital. It does so by externalising the costs of social reproduction. The wage labour on which capitalism depends could not exist in the absence of domestic work. As Nancy Fraser writes, 'Social reproduction is an indispensable condition for the possibility of capitalist production' (2014: 61).

Asking who does this work of social reproduction, who benefits and who bears the cost, exposes how power operates and how it is experienced in people's lives. For example, in South Africa this work of social reproduction is mostly performed by black, working-class women, either in their own homes or in a commodified form in the households of the dominant classes as domestic workers. Much of the highly racialised privilege of apartheid remains intact and means that women of the dominant classes continue to have the power to displace a great deal of this domestic labour onto women of the subordinate classes. Furthermore, it is black, working-class women who are the shock absorbers of the current climate crisis, experiencing most intensely the health hazards of exposure to carbon emissions and the devastating impacts of rising food prices, water pollution and energy poverty (Jacobs 2012; Munien & Ahmed 2012). These factors all mean that women have to work harder to stretch inadequate wages and social grants further. It was poor, black, working-class women who were most affected by the forty per cent increase in the price of maize in 2016. Their interests should be at the centre of the process of reclaiming feminism in South Africa.

RECLAIMING FEMINISM

It is a broad generalisation, but feminism is widely seen as problematic and sectarian. In various encounters in the research for this chapter, feminism was described as 'contaminated', as 'divisive' by depicting 'men as the enemy', as linked to lesbianism and as elitist. As one informant said, 'there is a distrust throughout the southern African region about feminism' (Interview, key informant, Johannesburg, 8 August 2014). For many women, feminism means 'gender equality', which some viewed as a thin notion that is inadequate to the task of transformation. An informant said, 'Gender equality is a very bourgeois concept – we can do it under capitalism – it is not transformative' (Interview, key informant, Johannesburg, 9 August 2014).

Other comments were that feminism has been reduced to issues of representation. The first democratic parliament included the highest number of women in any parliament in the world, and many women have been appointed to parliamentary committees, government departments and parastatals. But informants frequently expressed the concern that these women have not furthered the interests of working-class women. A feminist analysis of the centrality of the gendered division of labour to women's oppression is largely absent. It is not questioned but simply asserted and thus affirmed.

The reasons for this 'contamination' are multiple and complex. They include the deep historical roots of patriarchal understandings and practices in which a gendered division of labour is deeply ingrained and normalised. As Shireen Hassim writes, 'Zuma has shifted the public debate to the right on issues of gender and crude patriarchalism is far more evident under his presidency' (2015: 16). During apartheid the struggle against racial oppression was prioritised and the African family was generally seen as a space to be defended against the depredations of capital and the state, rather than as the site of women's oppression in the vein of 1970s radical feminism, exemplified by the notion of the family as an 'anti-social institution' (Barrett & McIntosch 1982). The African National Congress Women's League is socially conservative, has smothered radical demands for redistribution and is best described as 'womanist', meaning promoting values of 'family centeredness, community building, mothering and nurturing ...' (Mabawonku 2010: 4).

A reclaimed feminism could give strength and coherence to current scattered and ephemeral struggles. The multiple, extreme and racialised forms of inequality in South Africa demolish any conception of feminism as limited to challenging patriarchal power. As bell hooks (2015: 22) writes:

> Feminism, as liberation struggle must exist apart from, and as a part of the larger struggle to eradicate domination in all its forms. We must understand that patriarchal domination shares an ideological foundation with racism and other forms of group oppression, and that there is no hope that it can be eradicated while these systems remain intact.

This is at the core of the black feminist critique of white 1970s feminism which emanated from the US – a feminism concerned with individual advancement rather than collective struggle, in which white feminists tended to project their experiences of female oppression as universal. This is the crucial insight in 'intersectional analysis' which takes account of the multiple, interconnected sources of oppression to which different women are differently subjected (Crenshaw 1988). It stresses that we must understand how relations of domination reinforce each other but also how they are experienced differently, for example how black women experience racism differently from black men. An intersectional lens exposes 'how power actually works and can promote struggles against power's multiple and differentiated effects' (Chun, Lipsitz & Shin 2013: 920). In the South African context its significance lies in how it forces white feminists to acknowledge race and class privilege and the benefits deriving from living in what Yvette Abrahams has named as a 'white supremacist heteropatriarchal capitalism' (2010: 2).

But intersectional analysis asserts that all forms of oppression are equally oppressive as they have an equivalent value, whereas Marxist–feminism gives a special relevance to class in capitalist society. According to Marxists, class is more than an identity category; it is a relational category, part of a system of power relations, a constituent of capitalist accumulation. Martha Gimenez (2001) points out that 'the flattening of oppressions and their lack of anchor shed no light whatsoever on their possible causes or why they persist' (cited in Aguilar 2015: 213). Class analysis has an explanatory primacy – it enables us to comprehend race and gender oppression and how these identity categories are activated to promote accumulation. Oppression is multiple and intersecting but its causes are not.

'A feminism that speaks of women's oppression and its injustice but fails to address capitalism will be of little help in ending women's oppression' (Holmstrom 2002: 8). Reclaiming feminism and achieving gender justice means challenging capital's dependence on women's unpaid labour in social reproduction and experimenting with alternative social forms, institutions and practices outside of capitalism, such as collective arrangements for child-care; cooperatives; bulk buying; decentralised, community-controlled forms of renewable energy; the development of 'people's restaurants'; community food centres and seed sharing, to mention a few examples. It means promoting solidarities with working-class women's struggles against oppression in the workplace and beyond.

Current organisational initiatives with specifically feminist perspectives include WoMin (Women in Mining), a regional alliance of organisations formed in 2013 which emphasises the theme of solidarity among African women against extractivism (Interview, WoMin organiser, Johannesburg, 3 June 2014). In 2015, WoMin began convening gatherings of activists of different organisations in the region, calling for building 'popular alliances against Big Coal' and a new form of development 'that recognises and supports the work of care and reproduction' (WoMin 2015: 2). It pointed out that women's cheap and often unpaid labour subsidises the profits of polluting coal corporations.

WAMUA, the Women's Wing of Mining Affected Communities United in Action (MACUA), focuses on the impact of mining on livelihoods in Mpumalanga, which contains the most fertile land in the country and, as of 2017, is threatened by forty new coal mines. A WAMUA organiser explained:

> It was decided to form a separate organisation because when men and women are together men tend to dominate ... there are very limited numbers of such separate and autonomous women's organisations in which women organise independently of the influence of men ... but we include many strong, energetic, young women. (Interview, Johannesburg, 8 June 2014)

The Rural Women's Assembly, formed in 2009, brings together some 500 community-based organisations working on food, energy and land issues. It describes itself as 'a self-organised network or alliance of national rural women's movements, assemblies, grassroots organisations and chapters of mixed peasant unions, federations and movements across eight countries in the SADC

[Southern African Development Community] region'.[1] It emphasises women's unpaid care work and has established a number of 'feminist schools'. In 2016 it brought together 160 women from nine countries, representing 100 000 small farmers.

These organisations are building solidarities, organising exchange visits across Africa, directing protest actions and promoting alternatives to fossil fuel capitalism, such as 'food banks' which operate as redistribution mechanisms, biogas digesters, solar heating, seed saving and agro-ecology. They are developing an understanding of how black, working-class women are subject to multiple forms of oppression and that what are often experienced as individual problems have social or structural causes and solutions. This approach could change the focus on singular issues such as gender-based violence in isolation from their social context. Contextualising would involve connecting domestic violence to frustrations relating to the high rate of unemployment which limits black men's ability to conform to hegemonic notions of providing for their families, or to the specific tensions involved in prolonged strike violence by employed workers. This illustrates how a social reproduction approach can potentially validate and link separate struggles.

RECLAIMING ENVIRONMENTALISM

Analogous to ways in which feminism has been somewhat 'contaminated' by its associations with elitism and many activists are reluctant to call themselves 'feminists', 'environmentalism' and the label of 'environmental activist' also carry negative connotations from the past. However, working-class black women are active and often drive environmental and social justice initiatives confronting climate change, sometimes in survivalist, defensive and ameliorative ways, but also in challenging neoliberal capitalism, building solidarity and promoting alternatives.

Women are active in many of these struggles because their role in social reproduction means they deal most directly with the damaging effects of toxic pollution of the air and water on health and life. Women are leading resistance to the threat to their land and livelihoods from extractivism: for example, the women of Xolobeni, who are opposing titanium mining on their land,[2] and the women of Somkhele's struggle against anthracite mining.[3] Many of these women's organisational initiatives are building 'transformative power' (Wainwright

2014). For example, Earthlife Africa, which focuses on climate change, the impact of coal mining (especially on food security), the cost of electricity and the dangers of nuclear power, is empowering grassroots women. According to an Earthlife Africa official who founded a Women, Energy and Climate Change Forum,

> people were having problems with pre-paid meters. The majority of people in the protest marches and memos to the authorities were women. We focused on education, on the impacts of climate change. We connected electricity with women's everyday issues … In the Forum we had to demystify policy, especially climate change and energy policy which is often written in scientific, technical language. We had workshops, we went to people's homes, we met with parliament, Eskom and government. We insisted on using our own language. So people became confident. Young women are beginning to stand up and feel confident about talking about energy issues. Women are putting a human face on the issue. (Interview, Johannesburg, 12 July 2014)

Another initiative which is empowering grassroots women involves concretising the food–water–energy nexus through Earthlife's Sustainable Energy and Livelihoods Project. On seven sites throughout the country, the project is establishing renewable energy technologies such as solar panels and biogas digesters, as well as tanks for rainwater harvesting and food gardens. The focus of this project is on building resilience to climate change but it also demonstrates a post-carbon future (Interview, Earthlife Africa official, Johannesburg, 15 August 2014).[4]

These are examples of how the Marxist–feminist stress on social reproduction validates other struggles, particularly the struggle for environmental justice. The explanation of women's preponderance in these environmental struggles is not essentialist; it is not based on any natural affinity which women have with nature. The explanation lies in the gendered division of labour which allocates women to caring work. Women's experience in the production and provision of food could mean that they are more positioned to promote a new narrative about our relationship with nature – a revaluing of nature as something more than a store of natural resources for economic activity to be utilised for short-term gain without concern for long-term survival. The notion of environmental justice represents an important shift away from the traditional authoritarian concept of environmentalism to include urban, health, labour and development issues (Cock & Koch 1991).

Many of the new initiatives confronting the climate crisis are drawing from this travelling discourse of environmental justice, which is broad and inclusive. It originated in the US in opposition to practices termed 'environmental racism', meaning the disproportionate effects of environmental pollution on racial minorities (Bullard 1993). The discourse was radicalised in the process of translation in South Africa. Fusing equity with ecological sustainability, it is foundational to many current struggles. These target the persistence of environmental racism in the form of exposure to toxic pollution and a severe lack of environmental services in many black communities.

This pattern continues despite the democratic constitution proclaiming the right of all 'to live in an environment that is not harmful to health or well-being' (Section 24 of the Bill of Rights). Millions of poor, black South Africans are exposed to what Rob Nixon (2011) has called 'the slow violence' of toxic pollution in a process which is insidious and largely invisible. Many black South Africans continue to live on the most damaged land, in the most polluted neighbourhoods, often adjoining working or abandoned mines, coal-fired power stations, steel mills, incinerators and waste sites or polluting industries, without adequate services of refuse removal, water, electricity and sanitation. In Gauteng province alone, over 1.6 million people live either on or adjacent to mine dumps in conditions contaminated with uranium and toxic heavy metals, including arsenic, aluminium, manganese and mercury.

Recently, the notion of 'environmental inequality' has emerged 'to encompass additional factors associated with disproportionate environmental impacts such as class and gender ...' (Sze & London 2008: 1333). The discourse is a powerful challenge to the anodyne concept of sustainable development, and the increasing commodification and financialisation of nature, packaged as 'the green economy'. In this sense, it is a potential carrier of transformation that is not class, gender or race blind. Addressing climate change involves addressing racism, both globally and locally. It has been suggested that racism is one reason for the failure of twenty-one years of international negotiations to achieve any binding global agreement on the reduction of carbon emissions: '... racism is what has made it possible to systematically look away from the climate threat for more than two decades'.[5] In the US, it has allowed the worst health impacts of fossil fuels 'to be systematically dumped on indigenous communities and on the neighbourhoods where people of colour live work and play' (Klein 2014: 3).

Furthermore, racism also makes it possible to look away from Africa, which contributes only four per cent of global carbon emissions but is the worst affected by climate change (see Terreblanche and Bassey, both in this volume).

Paradoxically 'there is no clearly identifiable, relatively unified and broadly popular environmental movement in South Africa' (Death 2014: 1216). Instead, environmentalism is fractured and diverse and much popular mobilisation is related to access to services, such as water and energy, and is localised, episodic, discontinuous and not framed as 'environmental struggles'. However, a new, embryonic environmental justice 'movement' could be emerging. Older organisations such as Earthlife Africa, Groundwork, the Vaal Environmental Justice Alliance and the South Durban Community Environmental Alliance (SDCEA) are consolidating. Newer anti-extractivist organisations that bridge ecological and social justice issues include the Mining and Environmental Justice Community Network of South Africa, which formed in 2012 and has seventy organisational members; MACUA, which brings together over a hundred different organisations; the Highveld Environmental Justice Alliance, made up of some twenty-five grassroots organisations; and WoMin. Furthermore, there is growing collaboration among environmental justice organisations.

All over the world, environmental justice struggles are challenging neoliberal capitalism. The particularistic and ameliorative nature of many of these struggles means that the challenge is not immediately evident. 'Contesting a waste dump here or rescuing an endangered species or a valued habitat there is in no way fatal to capital's reproduction' (Harvey 2014: 252). But, as an understanding of the ecologically destructive impacts of capital's logic of expansion spreads, particularly in relation to carbon emissions, this could change. 'The environment movement could, in alliance with others pose a serious threat to the reproduction of capital' (Harvey 2014: 252). The 'others' could include feminists and socialists with a clear vision of an alternative post-capitalist social order.

RECLAIMING SOCIALISM

A diverse socialist tradition has historically made strong claims regarding human emancipation, justice, democracy, freedom and equality. Marx conceived of socialism as 'an association of free human beings which works with common means of production' (cited in Löwy 2006: 307). For Marx, 'socialism is the point where we begin collectively to determine our own destinies. It is democracy taken with full seriousness rather than democracy as (for the most part) a political charade' (Eagleton 2011: 75).

But for many people socialism is discredited because its claims have been marred by a history of authoritarianism, productivism, human rights abuses and environmental destruction. In the Soviet Union especially, 'productivist methods, both in industry and agriculture, were imposed by totalitarian means while ecologists were marginalised or eliminated' (Löwy 2006: 296). For many, this contamination is irreversible. Dennis Wrong (2000: 177), for example, writes, 'Despite the authentically democratic and egalitarian credentials of most western socialists, the economic failures of the communist states … are likely to prove permanently devastating to the future of socialism as an ideal.'

Furthermore, twentieth-century socialism denied many freedoms and rights, especially the right to disagree. The vanguardist, anti-democratic practices of the SACP illustrate this, in addition to an emphasis on industrialisation and economic growth that ignores environmental issues and promotes a 'statist' approach to social change. The party failed to mount a challenge to the government policy document, the New Growth Path released in 2010, which promised a move away from the stranglehold of the carbonintense minerals–energy complex which continues to dominate the economy. Increasing dissent and tension within the SACP has led to a dramatic decline in membership from the 75 000 claimed by Martin Legassick in 1995 (Legassick 2007: 522).

Both globally and locally many activists now talk only of 'anti-capitalism' because socialism has been stripped of its earlier positive meanings. The outcome is that today, much of the global opposition to capitalism is reduced to protest rather than the formulation of alternative visions. Hence, the 'reclaiming' has to involve building a 'new' form of socialism that is democratic, ecological, ethical and feminist, as well as building public ownership and democratic control of productive resources.

There are many inspirational accounts of an alternative socialist vision, demonstrating how it is necessary for survival. For example, Michael Löwy writes of 'a new eco-socialist civilisation, beyond the reach of money, beyond consumption habits artificially produced by advertising, and beyond the unlimited production of commodities that are useless and/or harmful to the environment' (2006: 302). Justice means that eco-socialism is necessary because the present mode of production and consumption of advanced capitalist countries, which is based on the logic of boundless accumulation (of capital, profits and commodities), waste of resources, ostentatious consumption, and the accelerated destruction of the environment, cannot in any way be extended to the whole planet. (Kelly & Malone 2006: 62)

Furthermore, 'Capitalist expansion threatens human survival. The protection of the environment is thus a humanist imperative' (2006: 62). This means we have to 'reclaim planning from the failed practices of authoritarian communism' because democratic planning is indispensable 'for an ecologically viable socialist society' (Panitch & Leyes 2006: xiii). While in disarray at present, the labour movement could be the carrier of a new socialism that is ethical, democratic and ecological.

THE LABOUR MOVEMENT AS THE DRIVER OF A JUST TRANSITION

In South Africa, there are different groupings within the labour movement that claim a strong socialist identity and understand a just transition to mean the possibility of revolutionary change. Zwelinzima Vavi, former general secretary of the Congress of South African Trade Unions (Cosatu), claims that recent struggles within Cosatu reflect 'contradictions between those leaders who have been won over to the side of the defenders of a neoliberalist South African capitalism' and 'those who are determined to continue the struggle for socialism' (cited in Satgar & Southall 2015: 4). Certainly many trade unionists emphasise the links between the climate crisis and neoliberal capitalism. This found organisational expression in two Cosatu committees established in 2010 consisting of representatives from all affiliates and from key environmental organisations. These structures conducted educational workshops with many affiliates, promoted shared research into coal mining, chemicals and poultry farming with the National Union of Mineworkers (NUM) and the Food and Allied Workers Union, as well as collaboration with key environmental justice organisations such as Groundwork and the SDCEA. This collaboration also produced a Climate Change Policy Framework, which stressed that capitalist accumulation has been the underlying cause of excessive greenhouse gas emissions, leading to global warming and climate change (Cosatu 2012). This was an important organisational step towards strengthening the linkages between labour and environmental activists, and could continue in a new labour federation that is closer to civil society.

However, there is little consensus within the labour movement as a whole. Two broad approaches to the notion of a just transition exist within the global labour movement: the minimalist position of the International Trade Union Confederation and the International Labour Organisation, which emphasises shallow, reformist change with green jobs, social protection, retraining and consultation. The emphasis is defensive and shows a preoccupation with protecting the interests of vulnerable workers. An alternative notion views the climate crisis as a catalysing force for massive transformative change (Cock 2012), with totally different forms of producing and consuming, perhaps even moving towards socialism, but a new kind of socialism which is democratic, ethical and ecological.

However, this could be a false binary, a distinction which fails to distinguish between the long- and short-term interests of labour. As Naomi Klein (2014) powerfully demonstrates, addressing the climate crisis 'changes everything' and is in the long-term interests of labour, but the short-term, immediate needs of vulnerable workers in extractive industries have to be met. This is particularly true in relation to increasing unemployment and poverty in South Africa, what Irvin Jim of the National Union of Metalworkers of South Africa (Numsa) has called a 'bloodbath'.[6] It implies that more attention needs to be paid to strategic rather than principled positions, in other words, to the modalities of a just transition led by labour. Clearly, the needs of workers in extractive industries must be addressed. They will be crucial to solving the climate crisis through meaningful, decent and productive work in alternatives such as renewable energy, public transport, home insulation, energy efficiency and mine rehabilitation. Meticulous research by the collaborative, cross-sector Climate Jobs Campaign has demonstrated that three million such jobs are possible in South Africa (see Ashley in this volume).

There are elements of both the defensive and the transformative approaches to a just transition in the Cosatu policy on climate change, which affirms that 'a just transition towards a low carbon and climate-resilient society is required' (Cosatu 2012: 56). While this policy statement was endorsed by all affiliates at the time, strong differences have emerged between the NUM and Numsa, for example. The NUM is increasingly defensive of the interests of some 90 000 coal miners in the face of the threats of job losses from mine closures, falling coal prices (sixty per cent since 2012), mechanisation, demands from environmental activists to 'keep the coal in the hole' and the divestment movement. Differences over models of economic growth also need to be addressed because while many environmental activists advocate 'deindustrialisation' and 'zero growth', labour prioritises economic growth for job creation. Furthermore, efforts to restore the 6 000 abandoned or ownerless mines in the country have been largely unsuccessful. The NUM favours 'clean coal' from expensive and untested technological innovations such as carbon capture and storage. One source claimed that 'the just transition' is 'a thin notion which has not been sufficiently debated within the labour movement' (Interview, Cosatu social policy coordinator, Johannesburg, 12 November 2014). Numsa has argued that the shift to a low-carbon economy, and particularly that the development of the privatised renewable energy programme, is being dominated by green capitalism. Numsa's vision was of a socially owned renewable energy sector and other forms of community energy enterprises where full rights for workers are respected. Social ownership means energy being claimed as a common good that can take a mix of different forms such as public utilities, cooperatives or municipal-owned entities. It means 'energy democracy' which 'offers perhaps the only feasible route to a new energy system that can protect workers' rights and generate decent and stable jobs, make just transition real and be responsive to the needs of communities' (Sweeney 2012: 3). In the South African context, this notion is spreading and is understood to involve resisting the agenda of the fossil fuels corporations and reclaiming the energy sector as part of 'the commons', meaning part of public resources that are outside the market and democratically controlled. But as one informant commented,

> there is a conflict of interests within the labour movement which needs to be balanced. For example, the case of workers in the car industry, versus the call for more public transport . . . we need to manage competing interests. Numsa is focusing on manufacturing and energy efficiency, neglecting the issue of mass based public transport and the manufacturing of buses and rail . . . leaving that up to Satawu [South African Transport and Allied Workers Union]. (Interview, Cosatu official, Johannesburg, 4 September 2015)

Furthermore, until the current heteronormative model of gender relations is truly challenged, women's oppression will continue within the labour movement. A social reproduction perspective also directs attention to women's position within the labour force, to their low-paid work as nurses, cleaners and teachers as well as their unpaid work in the household. This could counter a powerful masculinist interpretation of socialism that subordinates the struggle against women's oppression to a narrow view of class struggle or a distraction.

This masculinism takes a variety of forms, from the trivialisation of 'women's issues', demeaning treatment, sexual harassment and marginalisation to violence. It is a further instance of where the Marxist–feminist emphasis on social reproduction could forge new alliances. The issue of access to healthy and affordable food connects the workplace and the community. The relation between rising food prices and climate change requires more attention from trade unionists. Food inflation, at 9.5 per cent at the time of writing compared to the usual figure of seven per cent, should feature in wage negotiations. Placing the food crisis on the agenda of the labour movement could strengthen campaigns for food sovereignty.

A DEMOCRATIC ECO-FEMINIST-SOCIALIST TRANSITION

There is no blueprint for a democratic eco-feminist-socialism. Such an alternative has to be built from the bottom up in a process of extensive, democratic participation. However, several core values which contrast with the values of neoliberalism, such as materialism and an intense individualism, could provide a kind of compass for a vision of an alternative social order.

The aim of the struggle for socialism is, in the first instance, to replace a society based on profit with one based on satisfying the needs of people. This would involve access to decent work, quality and affordable education, health care, public transport, housing and energy.

At the core of a democratic eco-socialism is the link between the principles of sustainability and justice. To illustrate: the key question in terms of ecological sustainability is not only to protect limited resources but to ensure that they are used for the benefit of all, not only the privileged few. For example, in South Africa twenty-two per cent of households lack access to energy, either due to the lack of infrastructure or to unaffordable pre-paid meters. Justice demands the provision of affordable energy for all. Linking justice and sustainability demands that energy not only be affordable but also clean and safe, which means renewable energy that is socially owned and democratically controlled.

A democratic eco-socialism implies that the socialist emphasis on collective ownership and democratic control of productive resources must be connected to several other imperatives, especially gender justice, participatory democracy and a new narrative of the relation between nature and society. New social forms involving relations of reciprocity, solidarity and cooperation are emerging around these ideas and they embody fragments of a vision of an alternative post-capitalist future. The foundational concepts of food sovereignty, transformative feminism, energy democracy and environmental justice are among the building blocks for eco-socialism. The localisation of food production in the shift from carbon-intensive industrial agriculture to agro-ecology as part of food sovereignty could promote not only cooperatives and more communal living, but also a more direct sense of connection to nature. The mass rollout of renewable energy in the name of energy democracy could mean decentralised, socially owned energy with much greater potential for democratic control. As Harvey writes, it is these 'struggles of the everyday that contain the possibility of revolutionary energy' (2014: 3).

A just transition implies a new, more participatory form of democracy. In a parallel recognition that growth (now in the form of 'green growth') is intrinsic to capitalism, there is a growing understanding that western-style democracy legitimates capitalist inequalities. As Walden Bello writes, 'Even more than dictatorships, Western-style democracies are ... the natural system of governance of neoliberal capitalism, for they promote rather than restrain the savage forces of capital accumulation that lead to ever greater levels of inequality and poverty' (2014: 5).

It also implies a new narrative of relations with nature, grounded in the acknowledgement that humans exist as part of an ecological community. This involves rethinking economic growth and development (particularly extractivism). The recognition is growing that further economic growth could mean ecological catastrophe. As Maude Barlow expresses it:

> Let us be clear no amount of talk of green futures, green technology, green jobs and a green economy can undo the fact that most businesses and nation state leaders, as well as UN and World Bank officials, continue to promote growth as the only economic and development model for the world. Until the growth model is truly challenged, great damage to the earth's ecosystems will continue. (Barlow & Clarke 2012: 250)

Finally, an eco-feminist-socialist society could be based on relations of trust, cooperation and reciprocity, rooted in a confidence in human beings – in the capacity of both men and women to reason, to share, to learn from mistakes, to cooperate, to care for each other – and, most importantly, in our capacity to work together to create a more just and equal world. This confidence implies social relationships that are marked by solidarity, meaning a commitment to collective empowerment rather than individual advancement. It is diametrically opposed to 'Capitalism as a system (which) thrives on the cultivation and celebration of the worst aspects of human behaviour – selfishness and self interest, greed and competition. Socialism celebrates sharing and solidarity' (Angus 2009: 197).

One of the main constraints to achieving such a vision is an understanding of a just transition limited to the goal of a low-carbon economy. This could contain the embryo of a very different order. But it could also mean a nuclear energy programme in which electricity becomes totally unaffordable for the mass of South Africans. The expansion of the present privatised renewable energy programme is problematic. Kolya Abramsky has pointed out that 'Renewable energy at the service of capital accumulation could result in even harsher patterns of displacement and appropriation of land than those brought about by other forms of energy' (2012: 349). Without the social ownership and democratic control of production, exploitation will continue. Environmentalists' call for a reduction of consumption could mean the simplification of middle-class lifestyles, with reduced waste, extravagance and ostentation, but deep-seated inequality would remain. Without a shift in the gendered division of labour, working-class women will remain the shock absorbers of climate change, working harder to stretch the wage or social grant further as food prices rise. In other words, we need total transformative change and not the minimalist change envisaged in the green economy with its emphasis on expanding markets and new technology.

CONCLUSION

There are several immediate political tasks involved in promoting a transformative just transition from fossil fuel capitalism. For many people socialism is discredited because of its history of authoritarianism, human rights abuses, intolerance of dissent and environmental destruction. Reclaiming involves stress on a new kind of socialism that is ethical, democratic and ecological. It means building a strong, unified labour movement as an important driver of a just transition. Reclaiming feminism means women acting in solidarity to challenge corporate and patriarchal power as part of a larger struggle to end all forms of oppression. It involves supporting the black, working-class women who are confronting the climate crisis and challenging extractivism. Reclaiming environmentalism means a new relationship with nature based on the notion of an ecological community. This means changing the instrumental approach to nature as simply a store of resources for economic activity, or a sink for our waste products. But most important is supporting the diverse cooperative social forms involving relations of mutual sharing, support, reciprocity and cooperation. These are the building blocks for a just transition. They demonstrate an alternative paradigm, a different relationship between human beings and between human beings and nature – what Hilary Wainwright (2014: 38) calls 'power as transformative capacity'. And these social forms are important because capitalism systematically obliterates any notion of alternatives.

But to achieve an eco-feminist-socialist order as an alternative to a fossil fuel capitalism which threatens human survival, we need a new political imaginary, an imaginary which links these diverse forms. We have to move beyond 'denunciatory analyses' to ask 'what do we want?' (Ferguson 2009: 167). This chapter is intended to provoke debate on this question. As Donna Haraway once admitted, 'If I had to be honest with myself, I have lost the ability to think of what a world beyond capitalism would look like' (1991: 23). This inability is being further eroded by commentaries on the deepening ecological crisis that promote 'catastrophism', an apocalyptic vision of a future in which human existence is uncertain. The outcome is what Harvey calls a 'double blockage': 'the lack of an alternative vision prevents the formation of an oppositional movement, while the absence of such a movement precludes the articulation of an alternative' (2010: 227).

Exploring alternatives and strengthening analytical and strategic capacities for a more unified collective action from below is where a revolutionary potential lies. This is the potential within the notion of a just transition. Change is inevitable. As Jason Moore writes, 'Capitalism will give way to another model – or models – over the next century' (2015: 292). Our challenge is to draw from reclaimed notions of feminism, environmentalism and socialism to ensure that the change means a shift from fossil fuel capitalism to ensure both justice and sustainability.

NOTES

1   See https://ruralwomensassembly.wordpress.com/about/ (accessed 7 September 2017).
2   See for example http://www.news24.com/SouthAfrica/News/xolobeni-villagers-are-tired-of-being-abused-20170415 (accessed 7 September 2017).
3   See http://aidc.org.za/women-defending-water-land-life-northern-kwazulu-natal/ (accessed 7 September 2017).
4   Earthlife Africa, Report at the Annual General Meeting, Johannesburg 2014, unpublished.
5   Naomi Klein, 'Why #BlackLivesMatter should transform the climate debate', *The Nation*, 12 December 2014, https://www.thenation.com/article/what-does-black-livesmatter-have-do-climate-change/ (accessed 7 September 2017).
6   'Numsa demands a socially owned energy renewables programme', *Daily Maverick*, 5 May 2017, https://www.dailymaverick.co.za/opinionista/2017-05-05-numsa-demands-a-socially-owned-energy-renewables-programme/#.WbEMtLhGTng (accessed 7 September 2017).

REFERENCES

Abrahams, Y. 2010. '"Stop complaining about the price of bread! Start a bakery!": Colonial patriarchy as the cause of the current high food prices'. Feminist Consultative Conference on Women and Socially Excluded Groups Bearing the Social Costs of the Economic and Social Crisis, 30/31 October 2008, Athlone, Cape Town. Accessed 19 August 2017, https://khoelife.com/the-politics-of-food/.
Abramsky, K. 2012. 'Energy and social reproduction', *The Commoner*, 15: 337–354.
Aguilar, D. 2015. 'Intersectionality'. In *Marxism and Feminism*, edited by Shahrzad Mojab. London: Zed Books, pp. 203–220.
Angus, I. (ed.). 2009. *The Global Fight for Climate Justice*. London: Resistance Books.
Barlow, M. and Clarke, T. 2012. *Blue Gold: The Fight to Stop the Corporate Theft of the World's Water*. New York: The Free Press.
Barrett, M. and McIntosch, M. 1982. *The Anti-Social Family*. London: Verso.
Bello, W. 2014. 'How liberal democracy promotes inequality'. *Foreign Policy in Focus*, 5 December. Accessed 19 August 2017, http://fpif.org/liberal-democracy-promotes-inequality/.
Brown, W. 2013. *Marx on Gender and the Family: A Critical Study*. Chicago, IL: Haymarket Books.
Bullard, R. (ed.). 1993. *Confronting Environmental Racism: Voices from the Grassroots*. Cambridge, MA: South End Press.
Chun, J., Lipsitz, G. and Shin, Y. 2013. 'Intersectionality as a social movement strategy: Asian immigrant women advocates', *Signs*, 38 (4): 917–940.
Cock, J. and Koch, E. (eds). 1991. *Going Green: People, Politics and the Environment*. Cape Town: Oxford University Press.
Cock, J. 2012. 'South African labour's response to climate change: The threat of green neoliberal capitalism'. In *Labour in the Global South: Challenges and Alternatives for Workers*, edited by Sarah Mosoetsa and Michelle Williams. Geneva: ILO, pp. 37–57.
Cosatu (Congress of South African Trade Unions). 2012. *A Just Transition to a Low-Carbon and Climate Resilient Economy*. Johannesburg: Cosatu.

Crenshaw, K. 1988. 'Race, reform and retrenchment: Transformation and legitimation in anti-discrimination law', *Harvard Law Review*, 101 (7): 1331–1342.

Death, C. 2014. 'Environmental movements, climate change and consumption in South Africa', *Journal of Southern African Studies*, 40 (6): 1215–1234.

Eagleton, T. 2011. *Why Marx Was Right*. New Haven, CT: Yale University Press.

Ferguson, J. 2009. 'The uses of neoliberalism', *Antipode*, 41 (1): 167–185.

Fraser, N. 2014. 'Behind Marx's hidden abode', *New Left Review*, 86: 55–72.

Gimenez, M. 2001. 'Marxism and class, gender and race: Rethinking the trilogy', *Race, Gender and Class*, 8 (2): 23–33.

Haraway, D. 1991. *Simians, Cyborgs and Women: The Reinvention of Nature*. New York: Routledge.

Harvey, D. 2010. *The Enigma of Capital and the Crises of Capitalism*. London: Profile Books.

Harvey, D. 2014. *Seventeen Contradictions and the End of Capitalism*. Oxford: Oxford University Press.

Hassim, S. 2015. 'Who's afraid of feminism: Gender in South African politics', *Africa Files*, 17: 13–39.

Holmstrom, N. (ed.). 2002. *The Socialist Feminist Project: A Contemporary Reader in Theory and Politics*. New York: Monthly Review Press.

hooks, b. 2015. *Talking Back: Thinking Feminist, Thinking Black*. New York: Routledge.

Jacobs, P. 2012. 'Household food insecurity, rapid food price inflation and the economic downturn in South Africa', *Agenda*, 24 (86): 38–51.

Kelly, J. and Malone, S. (eds). 2006. *Ecosocialism or Barbarism*. London: Socialist Register Books.

Klein, N. 2014. *This Changes Everything: Capitalism vs the Climate*. New York: Alfred A. Knopf.

Legassick, M. 2007. *Towards Socialist Democracy*. Pietermaritzburg: UKZN Press.

Löwy, M. 2006. 'Ecosocialism and democratic planning'. In *Coming to Terms with Nature*, edited by Leo Panitch and Colin Leys. New York: Monthly Review Press, pp. 294–309.

Luxton, M. 2015. 'Marxist feminism and anticapitalism: Reclaiming our history, reanimating our politics', *Studies in Political Economy*, 95: 1–10.

Mabawonku, O. 2010. 'Womanism'. Blog post, accessed 19 August 2017, https://afeministtheorydictionary.wordpress.com/2007/07/17/womanism/.

Marx, K. 1976. *Capital Vol. 1*. Harmondsworth: Penguin.

Moore, J. 2015. *Capitalism in the Web of Life: Ecology and the Accumulation of Capital*. New York: Verso.

Munien, S. and Ahmed, F. 2012. 'A gendered perspective on energy poverty and livelihoods', *Agenda*, 26 (1): 112–123.

Nixon, R. 2011. *Slow Violence and the Environmentalism of the Poor*. Cambridge, MA: Harvard University Press.

Panitch, L. and Leyes, C. (eds). 2006. *Coming to Terms with Nature: Socialist Register 2007*. Toronto: Palgrave.

Satgar, V. and Southall, R. (eds). 2015. *Cosatu in Crisis: The Fragmentation of an African Trade Union Federation*. Johannesburg: KMMR Books.

Sweeney, S. 2012. *Resist, reclaim, restructure: Unions and the struggle for energy democracy*. Cornell University, Global Labor Institute Discussion Paper. Accessed 19 August 2017, http://unionsforenergydemocracy.org/wp-content/uploads/2013/12/Resist-Reclaim-Restructure.pdf.

Sze, J. and London, J. 2008. 'Environmental justice at the crossroads', *Sociology Compass*, 2 (4): 1331–1354.

Wainwright, H. 2014. *The State of Power*. Amsterdam: Transnational Institute.

WoMin (Women in Mining). 2015. 'Declaration: Women stand their ground against big coal'. Accessed 19 August 2017, https://womin.org.za/images/docs/women-stand-their-ground.pdf.

Wrong, D. 2000. 'Reflections on the death of socialism: Changing perceptions of the state/society line', *Theory and Society*, 29 (2): 175–218.

INTERVIEWS

Cosatu social policy coordinator, Johannesburg, 12 November 2014.

Cosatu official, Johannesburg, 4 September 2015.

Earthlife Africa official, Johannesburg, 12 July 2014.

Earthlife Africa official, Johannesburg, 15 August 2014.

Key informant, Johannesburg, 8 August 2014.

Key informant, Johannesburg, 9 August 2014.

WAMUA organiser, Johannesburg, 8 June 2014.

WoMin organiser, Johannesburg, 3 June 2014.

11

ENERGY, LABOUR AND DEMOCRACY
IN SOUTH AFRICA

Michelle Williams

The issue of climate change 'changes everything', to use Naomi Klein's (2014) pithy meme, and requires a fundamental shift in the way in which we extract, produce, subsidise, distribute and consume – in short, the way in which we live. The devastating role that the extraction and use of fossil fuel energy has played on the natural and social world – whether through climate change, habitat destruction, environmental racism or the environmentalism of the poor – has received considerable and important attention (e.g. Bond 2004; Hargreaves 2014; Klein 2014; Kovel 2003; Mitchell 2011; Nixon 2012; Sachs 1999). In this chapter, I take a different angle and look at the link between energy, labour and democracy.

One of the hidden stories behind the organisation of the global economy is the way in which powerful economic forces have shaped democracy for the past 150 years. In this chapter, I argue that the issue of energy is integrally linked to democracy. The link between nature and democracy occurs through the way in which mega corporations, most importantly in the energy sector, shaped (and continue to shape) politics and economics in the twentieth century. The sourcing, processing, distributing, subsidising and consuming of energy governs the way in which we live, the way in which we are governed and the way in which we organise our economy, including the way we produce and consume. After reviewing the global shift from coal to oil and the implications for democracy,

I look at the South African experience of coal energy and democracy. I conclude by looking at the potential role of renewable energy for democratising democracy.

ENERGY AND DEMOCRACY

The connection between energy production and democracy cannot be understated. The social relations surrounding energy have changed over time from an early period in which waterwheel energy allowed labour a degree of power (Malm 2013) to the transition to coal, in which its labour demands further opened space for democratic claims to a context in which labour's power eroded as corporates centralised power with the shift to oil and technological developments in the coal sector (Mitchell 2011). While the waterwheel provided better and cheaper energy to the British cotton industry, its major weakness was logistical as people had to be brought to the energy source (i.e. the waterwheels), rather than bringing energy to already-existing populated areas. Andreas Malm (2013: 33) explains that the coal-fired steam engine 'did not open new stores of badly needed energy so much as it gave access to exploitable labour' in towns. Coal freed capital to move to where workers were located. While this move provided capital certain advantages, the concentration of workers also brought opportunities for labour.

The extraction, production, subsidisation, distribution and consumption of fossil fuels have shaped the political organisation of societies since the nineteenth century. The discovery of massive reservoirs of coal together with technological advances in the development of the steam engine and steel and iron for railways required immense labour demands along all points of production, distribution and consumption processes. Workers were needed to mine and process the coal, to put it on trains and to drive the trains, to construct the railways, to offload the coal and to manage the coal-powered energy stations (Kernot 2000). As a result of the large numbers of workers at every node in the process, labour unions formed and spread throughout the industry. Thus, the late nineteenth century to the mid-twentieth century in Europe and the United States was marked by powerful labour movements that were able to make democratic claims on their polities. In this process, workers' movements pushed for more democracy in the political and economic realms, more egalitarian distribution of profits, collective control over natural resources, and improvements in and regulation of the conditions of work, such as limiting working hours and introducing pensions and medical aid.

Thus, the concentration of energy supply flowing through very specific channels created opportunities for new forms of political power and democratic claims. New repertoires of collective action, most notably the strike, became effective 'because of the flows of carbon that connected chambers beneath the ground to every factory, office, home or means of transportation that depended on steam or electric power' (Mitchell 2011: 21). Between the 1880s and 1940s in the US and Europe, mineworkers, dock workers and railway workers found new strategic convergences that allowed them to coordinate their efforts into larger democratic demands such as the right to vote, the right to form labour unions and political organisations, and the right to take collective action (Mitchell 2011: 24–26). It was not just that coal connected workers underground to those in industries above ground, but it also connected the industrial urban centres with agricultural developments in the countryside through the mass production and transportation of food (McMichael 2008). As industrialisation increased, the demand for food to feed the growing urban populations created a further need for energy. Food now had to be grown in mass quantities and transported from rural areas to the burgeoning urban areas to feed the teeming numbers of industrial workers. Agricultural production was now an epiphenomenon of industrialisation, both of which were heavily reliant on fossil fuel energy and large numbers of workers.

After a number of high-profile moments of sabotage – such as strikes, go-slows, work-to-rule – the strategic location of energy workers was not lost on the energy corporations and their respective states. If the first part of the twentieth century was marked by new forms of workers' power and the expansion of democracy, the second half of the century brought increasing challenges to the gains made for more inclusive economic development. As energy corporations and their respective states sought to restrict the power of labour, they also sought to ring-fence democracy and concentrate power in the hands of corporations. While expanding democracy was the means through which workers were pushing for more redistributive demands and increased egalitarianism, democracy also posed a latent threat in that it could also become a means through which the economic and political elite regulated the population by limiting their demands.

There are two dominant forms of democracy: a mechanism of governance to generate consent and limit popular dissent, and a popular form of governing in which ordinary citizens actively participate in decision making and governing. The first form of democracy is narrow and places power in the hands of the political and economic elite, while the second is expansive and vests power in the hands of citizens. The twentieth century was dominated by the former, though there were repeated and regular attempts by popular forces to push through a more expansive and deepened democracy. The amalgamation of corporate power and state power, especially in the US, unleashed a particular type of corporate democracy that represented 'the *political* coming of age of corporate power and the *political* demobilization of the citizenry' (Wolin 2008: xviii, emphasis in original). While the narrow form of democracy was immensely strengthened through neoliberal state policies and practices, the more expansive form of democracy continues to find its mooring in local communities, social movements (including labour movements) and popular struggles for a more egalitarian world. Crucial to which form of democracy prevails is the way in which issues are framed, including what gets defined as common interests and who has power to control the commons.

The expansive form of democracy is thus about controlling the dispensation of public and private goods, protecting human beings and the environment, ensuring redistribution and pursuing socio-economic justice. The argument made by some on the Left that democracy is a liberal invention is patently untrue. Liberal political classes that espouse tolerance and 'civic culture' have very often opposed democratisation, preventing the extension of the political rights of the working class and the poor, of colonial subjects and of women. Struggles for democratisation have been pushed and led by working and popular classes. Indeed, it was out of the modern urban life, mines and factories that forces emerged to struggle for democracy. Students and young people around the world have again demonstrated this point in the recent period – Occupy Wall Street, Arab Spring and student protests in various countries all pushed for a more expansive and people-led democracy.

Karl Polanyi captured this in his seminal work *The Great Transformation* (1944) as the self-regulating market versus society, with the two in constant tension with each other. What Polanyi's analysis does not capture is that this struggle between the self-regulating market and society is also a struggle between two types of democracy – one limited and the other expansive. The state's role in both forms of democracy is central. In the one, the state restricts popular forces, narrowly defines public issues and the commons, ensures power is concentrated in the hands of the elite, and is accountable to the elite through party funding, control of markets and the global economy, and direct personal benefits. In the other, the state protects society from the market and facilitates democratic deepening by creating spaces for popular control over the commons, including public goods. Thus, the two moments in Polanyi also suggest two types of power with two corresponding types of democracy. What I argue in this chapter is that the power (who controls it and the source of it) and democracy that predominates is directly linked to the political economy of energy. The way in which energy is subsidised, sourced, processed, shipped and consumed governs political spaces and creates particular subjects.

GLOBAL SHIFT FROM COAL TO OIL: IMPLICATIONS FOR DEMOCRACY

The shift to oil in the early to mid-twentieth century as the main source of energy was also a shift towards the narrower form of democracy as well as the consolidation of US hegemony. The common story talks about how oil affects the producer states (e.g. Middle East, Africa, South America) from building pipelines, locating refineries, negotiating royalties and ensuring sympathetic and pliable governments (Mitchell 2011: 5). The end result of these relations is often undemocratic oligarchies which, together with the mega oil companies, ensure the majority of people do not benefit from the natural resources of their countries. Thus, the geopolitics of oil produced anti-democratic tendencies in the oil-producing states from the Middle East and Africa to Venezuela (e.g. Southall & Melber 2009). While this story might be true, there is also another side to the story. The use of oil in the industrial north also represented a shift to an energy source that limited the points at which large labour movements could evolve and make democratic demands on the political system and corporations. In other words, oil also engendered anti-democratic tendencies in the industrial north. In contrast, the earlier rise of coal in the late nineteenth century opened space for democratic claims by workers throughout the extraction, production and distribution processes.[1] Coal's massive labour needs provided unprecedented opportunities for labour to organise and collectively act to push for greater egalitarian distribution and increased democracy. The shift to oil curtailed these openings for democratic claims. In other words, for the global North, oil as the main source of energy limits the democratic claims of citizens within those states just as it curtails democratic processes in many of the producing states (Mitchell 2011).

The production, processing, distribution and consumption of oil did not require the same concentrated labour demands as coal in relation to the quantity of energy produced, and therefore limited the power of workers. In contrast to coal, which relies on enormous amounts of human labour at all points in the process, oil is relatively labour scarce as the extraction is done by pumps deep beneath the earth, is managed on the surface by a relatively small number of workers under the surveillance of managers (as opposed to the multitude of coal miners working below ground), and is piped across vast distances (as opposed to railways with railway workers) (Mitchell 2011). There are no teams of people loading and unloading at multiple junctions, accompanying the oil on its journey, and continuously operating engines and railway stations. One of the major benefits of pipelines is that they limit people's ability to stop the flow of energy (Mitchell 2011: 36) although they are not immune to sabotage, as demonstrated in the twenty-first century in the Middle East.

In addition, oil is lighter and more easily transported than coal and therefore can be easily shipped in large quantities. The role of shipping further weakened labour's power as shipping companies could avoid labour regulation and taxation by registering their ships in countries with 'convenient' regulatory environments. Thus, the way oil is organised and the reliance on technology for transporting oil systematically weaken the power of labour or other organised forces such as environmental movements to control the sites of energy production. Timothy Mitchell (2011: 38) captures the difference between coal and oil:

> Whereas the movement of coal tended to follow dendritic networks, with branches at each end but a single main channel, creating potential choked points at several junctures, oil flowed along networks that often had the properties of a grid, like an electricity network, where there is more than one possible path and the flow of energy can switch to avoid blockages or overcome breakdowns.

Oil has other advantages that allow oil companies to maintain the control of energy. While coal was directly linked to industrial centres – inadvertently connecting workers across sectors – oil regions were located in remote areas. In addition to the relatively labour-scarce production process, the oil companies also learned from earlier experiences in the coal sector of the dangers of strong labour movements and, together with their governments in the industrialised north, came down hard on strikes and other attempts by labour to wield their power to fight for socio-economic gains. To be sure, there were attempts by labour to push for more inclusive and democratic planning and public ownership of the oil industry (Quam-Wickham 1994), but companies successfully limited these demands. While labour won certain economic concessions, the more far-reaching post-World War Two proposals 'for industrial democracy, in which workers would play a role in managing an enterprise and earn shares in its profits', were defeated (Mitchell 2011: 28).

The extraction and control of oil engendered a geopolitics of domination in which the US figured prominently (Satgar 2015b; van der Pijl 2006). Having consolidated its own oil industry in the first half of the twentieth century with five of the seven major oil companies – Exxon, Mobil, Socal, Gulf and Texaco, Royal Dutch Shell, British Petroleum and CFP – US owned (Bromley 2005: 232), the US was instrumental in this shift by tying the US-funded European reconstruction programme – the Marshall Plan – to US-style industrial management, the integration of Europe's coal industry, and the shift from coal to oil as Europe's main energy source (Mitchell 2011: 29; Painter 1984). All three of these components helped to weaken democratic claims made by labour and increase the power of oil corporations. Mitchell explains that oil companies were the big winners of the Marshall Plan:

> Over ten per cent of ERP [European Recovery Program] funds were used to procure oil, representing the largest single use of Marshall Plan money. The ERP financed more than half the oil supplied to Marshall Plan countries by US companies during the period of the Plan (April 1948 to December 1951), making the oil companies among the largest beneficiaries of Marshall Plan aid. (2011: 30)

Through the rest of the century large oil companies with the support of their governments (especially the US) controlled the oil market. These varying social relations of coal and oil have had enormous implications for democratic claims making by workers and other organised forces.

In order to ensure continued profits, oil companies had to control the supply of oil as well as create reliable and growing markets for their product (Bridge 2008). To ensure growing markets, the oil companies pushed for converting oil as a form of lighting into a source of mechanical power through the internal combustion engine (Mitchell 2011: 32–33). To manage the supply of oil, the oil companies helped create the continued importance of oil under their control by fabricating the frame of 'peacetime security' which intertwined oil interests with the state through 'imperial interests' and later 'national security interests'. Through this frame, oil became a state interest and oil companies became integrally intertwined with their states in the global North. This ensured state involvement in maintaining a limited supply – in the context of abundance, the companies needed to control and limit the supply – by framing the production and control of oil in the Middle East as integral to the security interests of Europe and the US and thus also in the public interest. With the oil industry controlled by seven mega corporations, the oil companies were able to collude in order to maintain limited supplies, prices and profits. Thus, together with their states acting in their interests, oil companies shape the supply and use of oil.

In addition, carbon-energy-intensive lifestyles were pushed on the American public and eventually globalised to other countries in Europe and the newly emerging economies of China, India, Russia, South Korea, South Africa and Brazil. Within a very short period of time, US consumers (and eventually global consumers in wealthy and middle-income countries) were using extraordinary quantities of energy. American consumers became the pioneers of 'mass consumption as well as the consumption of mass cultur, both of which were based in mass production' (Bromley 2005: 229) relying on enormous amounts of oil-dependent energy. One of the most important areas of development was mass transport in the private sector. For example, while Europe was developing energy-efficient, compact cars, the US automobile industry was encouraged to build large V-8 engines that consumed vast amounts of petroleum. The US public was turned into oil-dependent, wasteful energy consumers that became vital to maintaining the oil system. The intensive energy consumer became the aspirational norm for consumers around the world, which deepened the dependence on carbon energy and further entrenched the power of the oil corporations. These developments were made possible by oil's central role, but are not shared equally across the globe. Consumption patterns are concentrated in three regions of the world – North America, Europe/Eurasia and the Asia Pacific – which, by the first decade of the new millennium, accounted for '85 per cent of the world's total consumption' (Bromley 2005: 233). The consumption of oil overlaps with the concentration of economic and political power in the US, Europe, Russia, India and China.

Over the latter part of the twentieth century, the growth rate of oil production slowed significantly. Oil production grew between 6.5 and 7.5 per cent annually from 1913 to 1973, but for the rest of the 1970s and the 1980s the growth rate slowed significantly and, since 1992, has grown at a meagre two per cent per annum (and one per cent during recessions) (Bromley 2005: 234). Studies by oil corporations confirm that global oil production reached its zenith by the early 2000s (Satgar 2015b: 35). A 2007 study by the International Energy Agency confirmed that global oil production is declining more than expected and that the rate of decline grows yearly (Klare 2012). This decline has led to new forms of extractivism as oil companies turn to unconventional hydrocarbons such as tar sands, shale gas and oil, and deep-water drilling (Yergin 2012).

One of the consequences of this system is that over the course of the twentieth century, democracy was increasingly curtailed by private international capital and the growth of speculative financial systems. Democracy has thus been hollowed out from its more radical form of popular governance to a narrow mechanism for limiting popular dissent. Thus, the relationship between the growing importance and role of oil and the nature of democracy in the twenty-first century was not accidental or contingent, but was systematically constructed over the course of the twentieth century. The end result is that energy production was less vulnerable to political claims by those who produced it, and ultimately reinforced the power of oil companies and the anti-democratic tendencies within states. The political machinery that developed out of this system is facing challenges with the diminishing hegemony of the US, Europe's internal challenges, the mass migration of people from war-torn, oil-rich regions, and popular demands for democratisation (e.g. Occupy Wall Street, Arab Spring, Venezuela's constitutional reforms, student protests).

SOUTH AFRICA'S ENERGY–DEMOCRACY NEXUS

With its heavy reliance on coal, South Africa's experience of energy production, distribution and use bears many similarities with other parts of the world. Since the early twentieth century, mineworkers have played a vital role in making claims from the 1922 strike, the strikes in the 1940s and, most recently, the 2012 Marikana mineworkers' strike. The community–union linkages pioneered in the liberation movement connected workers across sectors such as mining, transport and manufacturing, as well as connected workers with communities, making South Africa's labour movement one of the most powerful labour movements in the world. The role of labour in pushing democratic demands in the liberation movement and in the nation-building project of the early 1990s cannot be understated. Organised labour in South Africa played a defining role in expanding and consolidating democracy.

There are, however, significant differences between South Africa and the rest of the world in terms of the link between energy and democracy. One important difference is that South Africa's abundance of coal (it is the seventh largest coal producer in the world) (Stats SA 2012) meant that it never shifted to oil to the same degree as the industrialised north. From its very early years, South Africa developed a carbon-intensive economy heavily dependent on cheap coal (Satgar 2014: 139), in part because the discovery of coal happened at almost the same time as that of diamonds, gold and other essential minerals. Coal was discovered in South Africa in 1878 in the Vaal River coalfield and quickly became a vital source of energy for the booming diamond- and gold-mining industries sprouting up in various parts of the country. The growth and development of mining and coal energy reinforced each other to such a degree that together they became the central features of the minerals–energy complex (MEC) which defines the South African economy (Fine & Rustomjee 1996). The growth of coal and mining were mutually constituting: mining grew through its reliance on coal energy and the coal industry grew through mining's ever-growing demands for more energy.

By the early twentieth century, coal was being used for power generation on mines across the region, with one company, Vereeniging Estates, controlling the industry. After World War Two, Anglo American bought the controlling share of Vereeniging Estates and by the 1950s the South African energy parastatal Eskom was buying sixty per cent of the group's output (Kernot 2000: chap. 2, p. 14). Having sewn up the local market, they turned to international markets, which had a number of important implications for the industry. First, expanding to international markets required a two-stage beneficiation process that produced a low-ash coal which would increase the energy content by reducing the amount of waste that would be transported (Kernot 2000: chap. 2, p. 15). Second, because all the collieries are located inland, a rail and port network system had to be developed and became an integral part of the South African coal industry. Coal had to be moved easily and efficiently across the country and transported to the specially designed Richards Bay Coal Terminal, which expanded over the years from its original twelve million tons per annum in the 1970s to seventy million tons per annum by 2000 and ninety-one million tons per annum by 2010 (Richards Bay Coal Terminal 2015). By 2011, South Africa was producing 255 million tons (South African Coal Roadmap 2011) of coal – up from 178 million tons in 1989 (Gwatidzo & Benhura 2013) – eighty-five per cent of which was produced by five major coal companies: Anglo American Coal (twenty-three per cent), BHP Billiton (fifteen per cent), Sasol Mining (seventeen per cent), Glencore Xstrata (ten per cent) and Exxaro (seventeen per cent) (South African Coal Roadmap 2011: 33). By 2013, South Africa was exporting twenty-eight per cent of its coal, making it the fifth largest coal exporter in the world.

Ben Fine and Zavareh Rustomjee (1996) demonstrate that South Africa's extraordinary deposits of minerals, gold, diamonds and coal have defined the economy for the past 140 years. In this minerals–energy mix, coal figures prominently and has decidedly shaped the contours of the economy and polity. By 2013 coal was the most important mineral in the South African economy, outperforming platinum (ranked second) and gold (ranked third) in terms of value added to overall mining. Coal's value added rose to 22.5 per cent in 2013 from 17.4 per cent in 1993, while platinum's value added came in at 21 per cent and gold at 18.5 per cent in 2013 (from 51.1 per cent in 1993). Coal's contribution to the economy rose from R37 billion in 1993 to R51 billion in 2013, whereas gold dropped from R115 billion to R31 billion in the same period (Stats SA 2015) and is the third largest export earner. Thus, coal's importance both as an energy source and as a contribution to the economy has deepened over the past twenty years.

The fact that coal remains the primary energy source and has a vital role in the economy begs questions around the power of labour, the nature of the democracy, and the possibilities for an alternative energy mix that promotes socially owned renewable energy. With the massive increase in production, coal continues to require vast numbers of workers along various points in the production and distribution processes. In 2012, coal was the third largest employer in mining, employing 91 605 people (of whom approximately 30 000 are unionised) accounting for seventeen per cent of the total mining workforce (platinum employed thirty-eight per cent and gold twenty-seven per cent). Interestingly, the growth in output coincided with a seventy-five per cent employment growth between 2002 and 2012, while gold shed twenty-nine per cent of its employees (Stats SA 2015). When we include workers in downstream jobs connected to coal, the numbers are much higher. In 2010, Eskom employed 36 547 direct employees and Sasol 28 978 workers, bringing the total number of workers employed in coal-related sectors to over 150 000 (South African Coal Roadmap 2011: iv).

Worker remuneration remained relatively consistent at about twenty-two per cent of total cost since 2000 (Gwatidzo & Benhura 2013: 17). Yet, inequality within the sector is extremely high: 'The average CEO remuneration of R20.2 million (in 2011) is 420 times that of the South African minimum wage and 355 times that of the mining sector median minimum wage' (Gwatidzo & Benhura 2013: 18). Despite this glaring inequality, wages in the mining sector for elementary, plant and machine operators, and craft and related trades, are higher than their counterparts in other industries (Gwatidzo & Benhura 2013: 18), suggesting that mineworkers have been able to secure some wage benefits. One of the advantages for labour is that coal in South Africa comes from nineteen separate coalfields with the sixteen main sites 'contained in six basins covering an area of 500 km east-west and 700 km north-south. The main coal producing area of Gauteng has thick seams whereas anthracite is produced in Kwa Zulu Natal from thin seams' (Kernot 2000: chap. 2, p. 18). The concentration of coalfields into a relatively small region of Gauteng, Mpumalanga and KwaZulu-Natal facilitated labour organising, as linkages across coalfields, beneficiation refineries and transport networks were easily made. Thus, the way in which coal was mined, refined and transported required vast numbers of workers at every point in the production process and the particular conditions in South Africa allowed for dense networks of workers and their organisations across sectors to emerge.

Not surprisingly, among the largest and most powerful unions to emerge over the course of the second half of the twentieth century were the National Union of Mineworkers (NUM), the National Union of Metal Workers of South Africa (Numsa), and the South African Transport and Allied Workers Union, all of which have moorings in the coal industry. One indication of the centrality of mining in movement history is the number of struggle heroes and powerful post-apartheid political leaders that come from the NUM. For example, Cyril Ramaphosa (one of the richest South Africans and the deputy president under Jacob Zuma), Kgalema Motlanthe (former deputy president under Thabo Mbeki and interim president) and Gwede Mantashe (African National Congress general secretary) are all former NUM general secretaries. The fact that the NUM has served as a pathway into political leadership – and powerful sectors of the state and economy – for a number of union leaders indicates the importance of the mining sector (and perhaps the power of the NUM) in the economy and polity.

While coal remains the primary energy source and the sector continues to boast strong worker organisations, suggesting possibilities for democracy, the MEC together with the state has also consistently sought to curtail democratic claims by workers. Historically, the state managed the power of labour in the mining sector through a racialised labour regime, which proved extraordinarily effective not only in engineering racialised division in the economy, but also in underpinning apartheid's racialised 'democracy' in which whites had a monopoly of power. In other words, apartheid engendered a narrow and racialised democracy that excluded the black majority, including energy workers, from power in both the economy and polity. In the post-apartheid period, however, this was no longer an avenue of control that the state and mining companies could use. The post-apartheid democracy diverged from this history of racialised control to incorporate the African majority into the polity through a narrow market democracy. As a result, the neoliberal economic conditions – including increasing precarity, frequent retrenchments and the dismantling of industrial policy – continue to undermine the power of workers by dismantling the social contract on which the post-apartheid consensus was premised. Thus, workers, including energy workers, are structurally weakened even if their numbers and wages have increased in the coal sector and despite unions continuing to fight for working-class agency.

Another important way in which capital has minimised the democratic claims and power of workers is through the mechanisation of mining.[2] Mechanisation not only limits the reliance on labour, but also increases production: energy production has doubled since 1980, but employment has halved in the energy sector as a whole (Worthington 2009: 132).[3] In addition, mining companies have tried to minimise the power of labour by locating coal refineries near the mines in order to reduce transport needs in an effort to minimise vulnerability to labour sabotage. Moreover, the (re)organisation of the energy sector in South Africa continues to locate decision making, wealth creation and power in the hands of an elite few made up of experts and the politically and economically powerful, leaving the vast majority far from any forms of power or decision making. Nevertheless, coal workers still maintain a degree of power in negotiating their wage agreements. This was demonstrated in the coal workers' strike in October 2015, which was resolved within one week. While such victories highlight the relative power of coal workers, the way in which the sector is organised does not promote democracy but rather ensures the concentration of power and resources in energy corporations and the state. In terms of democracy, the post-apartheid period witnessed the construction of a narrow form of elite-led democracy in which mining, and the energy sector in particular, has figured prominently and has curtailed an expansive form of democracy that vests power in the hands of communities, workers and ordinary citizens.

THE 'JUST TRANSITION' AND ENERGY DEMOCRACY

One area that organised labour has given insufficient attention to is the eco-logical impacts of fossil fuels, especially coal. As in other parts of the world, extraction of fossil fuels comes with great social and environmental costs. By the first decade of the new millennium, eighty-five to ninety per cent of South African electricity generation came from coal, the mining and pro-cessing of which is extremely polluting; dangerous for workers, who still die in mining; and which leaves polluting waste that leaches into vital water resources (Worthington 2009). Roughly half of the coal mined in South Africa is through open-pit mining, which is especially dirty and polluting; subsurface mining accounts for the other half. Approximately eighty-five per cent 'of South Africa's fossil-fuel CO_2 [carbon dioxide] emissions of 119 million metric tons of carbon [2008 estimate] were from coal' (Boden, Marland & Andres 2011). With 3.5 per cent of the world's coal resources (Chamber of Mines of South Africa n.d.) and approximately fifty years of coal production left at the current rate of production,[4] the environmental impacts will be devastating.

Given South Africa's abundance of possible renewable energy sources such as sun (South Africa has 2 500 hours of sunshine a year, placing it among the world's top three countries for solar power potential),[5] wind, hydro, biogas and tidal, it would make sense to see more renewable energy developments over the coming years. Renewables have the additional benefit that they lend them-selves to democratic processes and decision making. However, South Africa's post-apartheid 'carbon democracy' has used planning to reproduce the MEC paradigm and its overwhelming reliance on fossil fuels such as coal, gas and oil (McDonald 2009). For example, the National Development Plan (NDP) (South African Government n.d.) envisions a mix of energy sources, but the overwhelming dominance within the mix is forms of energy – such as highly mechanised coal, nuclear, oil and fracking of natural gas – that limit democracy rather than extend it. Similarly, the Department of Economic Development's New Growth Path (South African Government 2010a) espouses ostensibly green principles and promotes green industries and renewable energy sources, but also explicitly states that 'mining is a crucial growth sector, particularly the promotion of coal and platinum exports, and calls for the creation of a state mining company' (cited in Satgar 2014: 138). In the long-term vision, the state only sees itself reducing energy reliance on coal to sixty-five per cent by 2030, which will be complemented by twenty per cent from nuclear, five per cent from hydro and only nine per cent from other renewable sources (Satgar 2014: 138).

While renewables lend themselves to democratic processes, the National Development Plan and the New Growth Path continue along market-driven principles that underpin the MEC by adding new players such as nuclear, gas and oil, with a very minimal role for renewable energy. For example, the Development Plan's support of fracking and cap-and-trade deepens the old paradigm of a market-driven energy industry that benefits capital and is integrally interconnected to the political elite. The National Development Plan undermines workers and the environment by promoting fossil fuel extraction and the expansion of highly mechanised coal-fired power stations. It sees the investment in coal as 'reducing the carbon footprint of existing and planned coal-powered power stations through retrofitting, clean coal technologies and investigating the financial and environmental feasibility of carbon capture and storage technologies' (South African Government n.d.: 202). This emphasis on techno-fixes for the destructive nature of fossil fuel energy also has implications for labour and communities, as the mechanisation it entails weakens labour's power to make democratic claims and assert its interests. In other words, these highly mechanised forms of energy production minimise democratic space. Thus, the NDP's promotion of elite-run energy sources – i.e. coal, oil, nuclear and natural gas – continues the MEC dynamic, reinforces an energy complex that deepens anti-democratic processes and continues to rely on dirty fossil fuels. But, like many states, the South African state is also extremely contradictory. While a number of government documents give a limited role to renewables, the 2010–2030 Integrated Resource Plan (South African Government 2010b) envisions the renewable energy sector contributing an unbelievable 17 800 gigawatts to the national energy mix (equivalent to forty-two per cent of total power generation capacity).[6] Sadly, there is no evidence to suggest that the government is serious about this target, and the Department of Energy has only committed to a very modest 13 225 megawatts from renewables by 2025.[7] Moreover, in December 2015 the state quietly set the foundations for a multi-trillion-rand deal in Russian-made nuclear energy plants.

Nevertheless, there has been investment in renewables, but the government's approach to renewable energy prioritises private sector interests. Since 2011, the renewable energy sector has exploded in South Africa through the much-celebrated private–public partnerships that have driven its development and promoted large private corporations that have been able to benefit from the complicated state incentive programmes. For example, renewables attracted R192.6 billion in investment, of which twenty-eight per cent (R53.2 billion) was foreign investment (which equalled 85.8 per cent of all foreign investment in 2014). According to Kevin Nassiep, the investment frenzy created over 25 000 jobs and 'cut the equivalent of 4.4 million tonnes of carbon dioxide'.[8] Despite these achievements, developing the renewable energy industry through the private sector has undermined a potential arena in which workers and communities could play a vital role in expanding democracy through democratising energy production. Renewable energy sources potentially provide a great deal of democratic space if decentralised to communities, but the current approach promotes a 'competitive bid process' which favours well-resourced private corporations (Satgar 2014: 144). South Africa's recent experience goes against the grain of some exciting experiments that are happening elsewhere in the world.

'Energy democracy' provides an important avenue for communities, including workers in the energy sector, to a just transition, expansive democracy and the promotion of renewables. The US-based Trade Unions for Energy Democracy explains that

> an energy transition can only occur if there is a decisive shift in power towards workers, communities and the public – energy democracy. A transfer of resources, capital and infrastructure from private hands to a democratically controlled public sector will need to occur in order to ensure that a truly sustainable energy system is developed in the decades ahead. (Sweeney 2012: ii)

The idea of energy democracy challenges the fossil fuel frenzy and private sector-led renewables that the state and corporations continue to pursue in South Africa.[9] While national states and corporations fail to provide space for an energy democracy to emerge, cities across the world are leading the way through municipal ordinances; the transition town movement, which seeks to wean communities off fossil fuels and which now exists in 460 communities in forty-three countries; and local food movements that reduce the use of carbon energy for food production and consumption (Klein 2014: 364).

Perhaps the best example of this shift to energy democracy is Germany's *Energiewende* – the shift to green, renewable energy that has swept the country – which propelled the renewable energy contribution, mostly wind and solar but also biogas and hydro, to electricity from six per cent in 2000 to twenty-five per cent in 2013 (Klein 2014: 97). What is particularly noteworthy is the way in which the German approach has been led by local communities reclaiming their power and control over energy production. Klein (2014: 97) explains: 'one key factor that has made possible the world's most rapid shift to wind and solar power: the fact that in hundreds of cities and towns across the country, citizens have voted to take their energy grids back from the private corporations that purchased them'. As a result, more than seventy new municipal utilities have formed and public operators have taken over from private companies more than 200 concessions (Klein 2014: 98) and created over 400 000 jobs (as opposed to the 60 000 workers in fossil fuel industries). Citizens across Germany are demonstrating their renewed interest in the way in which their energy is sourced, produced, distributed and consumed and in the process are renewing local democracy in their communities. Uruguay also provides important lessons as it shifted to renewables in less than ten years: 'Uruguay had proved that renewables can reduce generation costs, can meet well over 90% of electricity demand without the back-up of coal or nuclear power plants, and the public and private sectors can work together effectively in this field.'[10] While Germany's shift has been largely led by local communities, Uruguay's has been led by a democratic government at the national level pursuing a renewable planning agenda. Both cases deepen democracy through energy production and supply.

As these experiences demonstrate, renewable energy is an area in which energy production and democratisation can converge. In South Africa the idea has emerged through Numsa's proposal for a socially owned renewable energy sector (Satgar 2015a). In two separate, well-researched documents, Numsa (2012a, 2012b) put forward concrete proposals for the way in which its own carbon-intensive sector can be restructured toward renewable energy production in a way that creates jobs and deepens a broad democratisation process. Numsa's vision of a socially owned renewable energy sector concretises energy democracy and a just transition in the South African context. For example, a transition to a more just energy democracy in South Africa would entail localised production of renewables to ensure workers are involved and can shift from fossil fuel industries; energy sovereignty and socially owned renewables – allowing for energy pooling in generation, storage and supply through, for example, community-owned wind farms, solar parks and hydroelectric plants; household feedback tariffs and embedded generation; a government-owned

247

renewable energy parastatal; and government planning and subsidies (shifting subsidies from fossil fuels and redirecting them to renewables).

There are a number of environmental, social and political benefits to renewable energy (Worthington 2009: 132). Environmentally, renewable energy technologies provide system stability, reduce transmission losses and are cleaner energy sources. Socially, there is also widespread agreement that investment in renewable energy technologies would create far more jobs than in other sectors of energy generation such as coal, oil and nuclear. Indeed, the One Million Climate Jobs campaign has modelled the numbers and estimates that over one million jobs could be created in South Africa through a shift to renewable energy (see Ashley in this volume). Politically, renewables lend themselves to social ownership, public planning and democratic decentralisation. This would require shifting from elite-led carbon democracy to a just transition and energy democracy – that is, democratic eco-socialism.

CONCLUSION

Given the dominance of anti-democratic forces in the MEC, we must ask where the possibilities are for democratisation within the energy sector. While coal may have given space to democratic claims making, these gains are being undermined with the restructuring of the industry and mechanisation. Indeed, the post-apartheid transition shifted from apartheid's narrow democracy based on the MEC to another equally – albeit differently – narrow form of market-driven carbon democracy. The energy mix has had devastating effects on the environment and climate change. So what are the possibilities for socially, economically and environmentally just relations between democracy and energy?

Alternatives are available that are not only better for the environment (e.g. renewables) but are also more democratic (e.g. collective ownership and democratic planning). When we speak of alternatives today, we are looking beyond the twentieth-century experiments in socialism, one-party dictatorships and narrow liberal democracy. Democracy and democratic planning are central to any vision of an alternative rooted in local conditions, the aspirational values of ordinary people and the ecological limits of our times. Michael Löwy argues that ecological socialism entails '(a) collective ownership of the means of production ("collective" here meaning public, cooperative or communitarian property); (b) democratic planning, which makes it possible for society to define the goals of investment and production; and (c) a new technological structure of the productive forces' (2006: 294; Klein 2014). Socially owned renewable energy will be central to any such vision.

The relation between energy and democracy is complex, with the nature of the energy source (e.g. coal versus oil versus renewables), the organisation of its extraction and production (e.g. labour requirements versus mechanisation), and the linkages across sectors (e.g. mining, manufacturing, transport) and between production and consumption shaping the possibilities for democratic claims making. Renewable energy not only operates on a totally different paradigm, it also provides immense possibilities for democratic claims in the political and economic spheres. A socially owned renewable energy sector could deepen the just transition towards democratic eco-socialism.

NOTES

1   The story of coal is complex as its origin was directly linked to easy access to more exploitable labour (see Malm 2013).
2   The highly mechanised Richards Bay Coal Terminal is a harbinger of the changing nature of the sector. Mechanisation is increasing production and distribution, while decreasing the number of workers needed along all points in the production and distribution processes.
3   This is interesting to note as employment in the coal sector increased during this period.
4   See http://www.energy.gov.za/files/coal_overview.html (accessed 20 August 2017).
5   K. Nassiep, 'South Africa's renewable energy plan a global success story', *Business Day*, 7 October 2015, p. 15.
6   Nassiep, 'South Africa's renewable energy plan a global success story'.
7   Nassiep, 'South Africa's renewable energy plan a global success story'.
8   Nassiep, 'South Africa's renewable energy plan a global success story'.
9   In this way, South Africa resembles the global dynamic. According to the United Nations Environmental Programme (UNEP 2011), coal accounts for more than fifty per cent of new energy demand and fossil fuels are still to meet two-thirds of energy demand by 2035.
10 J. Watts, 'Uruguay makes dramatic shift to nearly 95% electricity from clean energy', *The Guardian*, 3 December 2015, http://www.theguardian.com/environment/2015/dec/03/uruguay-makes-dramatic-shift-to-nearly-95-clean-energy (accessed 27 December 2015).

REFERENCES

Boden, T.A., Marland, G. and Andres, R.J. 2011. 'Global, regional, and national fossil-fuel CO_2 emissions'. Carbon Dioxide Information Analysis Center, Oak Ridge National Laboratory, U.S. Department of Energy, Oak Ridge, Tenn., USA. Accessed 9 June 2017, http://cdiac.ornl.gov/trends/emis/tre_saf.html.

Bond, P. 2004. *Unsustainable South Africa: Environment, Development and Social Protest.* Pietermaritzburg: UKZN Press.

Bridge, G. 2008. 'Global production networks and the extractive sector: Governing resource-based development', *Journal of Economic Geography* 8: 389–419.

Bromley, S. 2005. 'The United States and the control of world oil', *Government and Opposition*, 40 (2): 225–255.

Chamber of Mines of South Africa. n.d. 'Coal: Key facts and figures'. Accessed 9 June 2017, http://www.chamberofmines.org.za/sa-mining/coal.

Fine, B. and Rustomjee, Z. 1996. *The Political Economy of South Africa: From Minerals–Energy Complex to Industrialisation.* London: Hurst and Company.

Gwatidzo, T. and Benhura, M. 2013. *Mining sector wages in South Africa.* LMIP Working Paper 1. Accessed 12 December 2015, http://repository.hsrc.ac.za/handle/20.500.11910/9581.

Hargreaves, S. 2014. 'Extractivism, its deadly impacts and struggles towards a post-extractivist future', unpublished paper.

Kernot, C. 2000. *The Coal Industry.* Cambridge: Woodhead Publishing.

Klare, M. 2012. *The Race for What's Left: The Global Scramble for the World's Last Resources.* New York: Metropolitan Books.

Klein, N. 2014. *This Changes Everything: Capitalism vs the Climate.* New York: Alfred A. Knopf.

Kovel, J. 2003. *The Enemy of Nature: The End of Capitalism or the End of the World?* London: Zed Books.

Löwy, M. 2006. 'Eco-socialism and democratic planning'. In *Coming to Terms with Nature: Socialist Register 2007*, edited by Leo Panitch and Colin Leys. New Delhi: Leftword Books, pp. 294–309.

Malm, A. 2013. 'The origins of fossil capitalism: From water to steam in the British cotton industry', *Historical Materialism*, 21 (1): 15–68.

McDonald, D.A. 2009. 'Introduction: The importance of being electric'. In *Electric Capitalism: Recolonising Africa on the Power Grid*, edited by David A. McDonald. Cape Town: HSRC Press, pp. xv–xxiii.

McMichael, P. 2008. *Development and Social Change: A Global Perspective.* Thousand Oaks, CA: Pine Forge Press.

Mitchell, T. 2011. *Carbon Democracy: Political Power in the Age of Oil.* London and New York: Verso.

Nixon, R. 2012. *Slow Violence and the Environmentalism of the Poor.* Cambridge, MA: Harvard University Press.

Numsa (National Union of Metalworkers of South Africa). 2012a. 'Building a socially-owned renewable energy sector in SA'. Numsa 9th National Congress, June.

Numsa. 2012b. 'Towards a socially-owned renewable energy sector in SA'. National Executive Committee (NEC) Position Paper, February.

Painter, D. 1984. 'Oil and the Marshall Plan', *Business History Review*, 58 (3): 359–383.

Polanyi, K. 1944. *The Great Transformation: The Political and Economic Origins of Our Time.* Boston, MA: Beacon Press.

Quam-Wickham, N. 1994. 'Petroleocrats and proletarians: work, class, and politics in the California oil industry 1917–1925', PhD dissertation, Department of History, University of California, Berkeley.

Richards Bay Coal Terminal. 2015. 'Our history'. Accessed 10 December 2015, http://www.rbct.co.za/about-rbct-4/our-history/.

Sachs, W. 1999. 'Sustainable development: On the political anatomy of an oxymoron'. In W. Sachs, *Planet Dialectics: Explorations in Environment and Development.* London: Zed Books, pp. 71–90.

Satgar, V. 2014. 'South Africa's emergent "green developmental state"?' In *The End of the Developmental State?* edited by Michelle Williams. London: Routledge, pp. 126–153.

Satgar, V. 2015a. 'A trade union approach to climate justice: The campaign strategy of the National Union of Metalworkers of South Africa', *Global Labour Journal,* 6 (3): 267–282.

Satgar, V. 2015b. 'From Marx to the systemic crises of capitalist civilisation'. In *Capitalism's Crises: Class Struggles in South Africa and Beyond,* edited by Vishwas Satgar. Johannesburg: Wits University Press, pp. 20–49.

South African Coal Roadmap. 2011. 'Overview of the South African coal value chain'. Accessed 10 December 2015, http://www.coaltech.co.za/Roadmap/SACRM-Value-Chain-Overview.pdf.

South African Government. 2010a. *New Growth Path.* Department of Economic Development. Accessed 19 August 2017, http://www.economic.gov.za/communications/publications/new-growth-path-series.

South African Government. 2010b. *Integrated Resource Plan for Electricity 2010–2030.* Department of Energy.

South African Government. n.d. *The National Development Plan 2030: Our Future – Make It Work.* Johannesburg: Sherino Printers.

Southall, R. and Melber, H. (eds). 2009. *A New Scramble for Africa? Imperialism, Investment and Development.* Pietermaritzburg: University of KwaZulu-Natal Press.

Stats SA (Statistics South Africa). 2012. 'National accounts: Mineral accounts for South Africa: 1980–2009'. Accessed 13 December 2015, http://www.statssa.gov.za/publications/D04052/D040522009.pdf.

Stats SA. 2015. 'The importance of coal'. Accessed 10 December 2015, http://www.statssa.gov.za/?p=4820.

Sweeney, S. 2012. *Resist, reclaim, restructure: Unions and the struggle for energy democracy.* Cornell University, Global Labor Institute Discussion Paper. Accessed 19 August 2017, http://unionsforenergydemocracy.org/wp-content/uploads/2013/12/Resist-Reclaim-Restructure.pdf.

UNEP (United Nations Environmental Programme). 2011. 'Keeping track of our changing environment: From Rio to Rio +20 (1992–2012)'. Accessed 19 August 2017, http://www.grid.unep.ch/products/3_Reports/GEAS_KeepingTrack.pdf.

Van der Pijl, K. 2006. *Global Rivalries: From the Cold War to Iraq.* London: Pluto Press.

Wolin, S. 2008. *Democracy Inc.: Managed Democracy and the Spectre of Inverted Totalitarianism.* Princeton, NJ: Princeton University Press.

Worthington, R. 2009. 'Cheap at half the cost: Coal and electricity in South Africa'. In *Electric Capitalism: Recolonising Africa on the Power Grid,* edited by David A. McDonald. Pretoria: HSRC Press, pp. 109–148.

Yergin, D. 2012. *The Quest: Energy, Security, and the Remaking of the Modern World.* London: Penguin.

12

CAPITAL, CLIMATE AND THE POLITICS OF NUCLEAR PROCUREMENT IN SOUTH AFRICA

David Fig

The imperative of moving away from fossil fuels begs a number of strategic questions in a largely coal-based electricity economy like South Africa. What would a 'just transition' look like? How do we debate this notion, what are its contents, how do we develop confidence in the concept, and who will act as a fair arbiter of its implementation?

In general, the South African government has strategically promoted further investment in coal. It is building two large-scale coal-fired power stations (of a capacity of 4 800 megawatt electric each), and encouraging rent seeking by black capitalists from new coal mines established in water-scarce areas on the country's finest arable land. At the same time, it seeks to invest in a number of alternative energy options, including renewables, carbon capture and storage, and additional nuclear energy, with gas (shale and imported liquefied natural gas) seen as a 'transitional' option.

In this chapter, I focus on the country's nuclear plans and argue that nuclear development is a false solution to climate change. Those who claim it is carbon-neutral look only at the low generation of greenhouse gases in the reactor, while failing to take into account the entire nuclear fuel chain, in some stages of which carbon intensity is considerable.

Nuclear technology also compromises building future job opportunities in the energy sector. It is punitive in terms of costs and would add massively to the debt crisis facing South Africa. Finally, the adoption of further nuclear power is likely to add to energy dependency rather than building popular energy sovereignty, and will curtail energy democracy. It will feed into the extension of patrimonial politics and curb the building of democracy.

I look first at the relationship between crisis and nuclear procurement, and then examine some of the dilemmas raised by the procurement process itself. These extend from the formal policy-making process to the shadowy, less visible patrimonial politics that have characterised the Jacob Zuma presidency. Finally, I visit the relationship between democracy and nuclear energy.

THE CONTEXT OF CRISIS

South Africa is facing a multiplicity of interconnected crises. Its economy is failing its citizens: over twenty-seven per cent of the population is formally unemployed. Inequality has never been so pronounced, with South Africa edging out Brazil as the industrial country with the biggest gap between rich and poor.

Drought and unsustainable agricultural practices have exacerbated food insecurity and driven up food prices; staples like maize now have to be imported. Massive hunger exists in a country that could once feed itself. Whole sectors of industry are contracting. With the global commodities boom over, mining is shedding labour (Anglo American is letting 85 000 miners go), assets are being written down and big corporations' share values are plummeting. Manufacturing is heavily hit, with fifty per cent of factory owners planning to downsize their operations. The value of the rand has taken a severe knock and continues to slide. Ratings agencies downgraded the country to junk status in April 2017 (which had already befallen the energy utility Eskom, downgraded by S&P in March 2015).[1] Communities are vulnerable to the effects of climate change and the ecological crisis, as water rights and arable land disappear into the hands of coal entrepreneurs. Despite pledges to reduce its carbon production, the country is building some of the largest coal power stations in the world, with World Bank finance and corrupt subcontracting deals.

Simultaneously, many state-owned enterprises, often the infrastructural backbone of the country, are in grave disarray due to financial, governance and management crises and conflicts. Since 2008, Eskom has failed to deliver sufficient electricity to consumers. Planned and unplanned power cuts have dogged industry and individual households. The major reason for this is the significant underinvestment in new energy over recent decades. A renewable energy production programme has been launched and has achieved early success, although little of it is socially owned. Prices of renewable electricity sources have dropped and are beginning to compete successfully with coal. South Africa's Executive has also been punting a major additional nuclear fleet. Many consumers are so fed up with power cuts that they are prepared to overlook the negative consequences of coal and nuclear to ensure their expansion. This takes the form of an imposed 'moral panic', herding people into welcoming measures that are ultimately in their worst interests.

The electricity crisis therefore also has an impact on a country bent on moving away from poverty and inequality and towards building a strong democratic culture, and so combating the legacy of apartheid. However, the nuclear option is fraught with secrecy, mendacity and the shrinking of popular power. In the public policy arena, public debate, participation and the exercise of agency have all been curtailed with respect to taking important decisions on energy futures. The democratic deficit has expanded as patrimonial politics – centred around the office of the president – takes a greater hold over public life. Can popular agency be retrieved in time to prevent the disastrous procurement of major new nuclear power? I argue that although the presidency is isolated, public opposition is crucial and will need to be articulated in a more organised form. This is one element of the crisis that can be rolled back.

TOWARDS NUCLEAR PROCUREMENT: THE TWISTED ROAD OF FORMAL POLICY MAKING

The proposals to add additional nuclear energy to our electricity mix have been in the pipeline for some time. This flies in the face of the initial response by the African National Congress (ANC) on taking power.

In the run-up to the first democratic elections in February 1994, a conference was held in Cape Town under the joint auspices of the Environmental Monitoring Group – a non-governmental organisation (NGO) – and the Science and Technology Desk of the Western Cape ANC. At that time, energy policy within the ANC rested within its economics department, headed by

Trevor Manuel. Manuel's keynote address promised that 'we shall not tolerate circumstances in which policy on issues as critical as a nuclear programme be confined to experts in dark, smoke-filled rooms. The debate must be public and the actions transparent' (EMG & Western Cape ANC Science and Technology Desk 1994: 5).

The ANC did not commit immediately to dismantling South Africa's nuclear industry. In practice, however, the commitment to non-proliferation of nuclear weapons entailed the closure of uneconomic units of the fuel chain, such as conversion, enrichment and fuel fabrication. The staff component of the Atomic Energy Corporation (AEC), which in 1999 became the South African Nuclear Energy Corporation (Necsa), was substantially reduced. The government also embarked on a review process of all state-owned scientific corporations, of which the AEC was one.

It therefore seemed that the ANC was ready to wind down the parts of the industry that had not proven economically viable, and even considered reviewing the utility of the Koeberg nuclear power station. An energy summit was convened in 1996. This was a moment for government engagement with energy stakeholders, including representatives of urban and rural communities, NGOs, provincial governments, labour and the private sector. In the deliberations at the summit, it was clear that civil society organisations were expressing an anti-nuclear stance.

However, in the document that emerged from the summit, the Energy White Paper (1998), the Department of Minerals and Energy (DME) proposed that there would be a review of Koeberg and any further investment would only be considered within a context of broader energy planning (DME 1998). Meanwhile, however, the nuclear lobby was not asleep. The White Paper allowed for the following fudge: 'Whilst it is unlikely that additional nuclear capacity will be required for a number of years, it would not be prudent to exclude nuclear power as a supply option' (DME 1998: 60). It also alluded to the feasibility studies being undertaken for a new high-temperature reactor, the Pebble Bed Modular Reactor (DME 1998). A coach and horses had been driven through the policy: the government was not going to abandon the nuclear lobby.

Indeed, when the DME finally produced a nuclear policy document in 2008, it deferred to the Energy White Paper as 'approved by Government at the end of 1998, where [nuclear energy] was retained as one of the policy options for electricity generation' (DME 2008: 10). In fact, from 1998, Eskom oversaw the development of the pebble bed project. Initially, it was presented as largely for export, with the emphasis on constructing a demonstration plant by 2003 as a prelude to commercial production. At the time it was budgeted as a R847 million project, including the fuel fabrication. By 2009, and after five significant design changes, the completion of the demonstration plant was set for around 2020 and commercialisation for around 2025; the budget for its construction had escalated to R31 billion (Fig 2010: 32). The state had already advanced just short of R9 billion by 2010 and it seemed that there was no finalised design, no partner, no export orders, and Eskom itself was reluctant to purchase any of these reactors. By 2010, Barbara Hogan, minister of public enterprises, called an end to the project.

Earlier, the Environmental Impact Assessment (EIA) for the pebble bed reactor had run into administrative difficulties when it became clear that objections from Earthlife Africa had not been taken into consideration during the process. Litigation resulted in the judge setting aside the procedure, as well as prevailing upon government to produce a national policy document on nuclear waste. Despite having had a nuclear establishment since 1948, the government had never developed such a policy document.

Eskom was more interested in adding a fleet of conventional reactors to its existing two plants at Koeberg. Foresight had led to the strategic purchase of land in the mid-1980s at Thyspunt (west of Port Elizabeth) and Bantamsklip (on the boundary of what later became the Agulhas National Park). Other land was earmarked for purchase on the farms Brazil and Schulpfontein on the coast of Namaqualand.

In the attempt to set up a procurement process, government realised it needed to have completed a 'nuclear policy and strategy' document endorsing the acquisition of further large-scale reactors. This resulted in the policy being published in 2008, after minimal public consultation. The statutory requirement for public comment on the proposals – poorly advertised and lasting through the Christmas break (South Africa's summer holiday season) – elicited twenty-seven responses, mainly from members of the nuclear lobby. There was no attempt by government to host a public debate and the decision by cabinet to adopt it was therefore peremptory. The government has since used the adoption of this policy document as the principal justification for new nuclear build.

However, the haste to see the policy adopted did not help much. The procurement process went ahead during 2008. Two vendors made applications: Areva, the French state-owned reactor builder and successor to Framatome, which led the consortium that built Koeberg; and Westinghouse, whose blueprint had been used by Framatome for Koeberg, and which had been purchased by the Japanese corporation Toshiba. Both companies' proposals proved to be far more expensive than Eskom had imagined. Budgetary problems related to the global financial meltdown of 2008 caused a rethink by Eskom, and the procurement process was shelved for the time being.

Cautious about the need to fulfil the Energy White Paper's promise of integrated energy planning, the government realised that it had to convene such a process prior to resuming any further nuclear procurement, despite a hiatus of eleven years. An initial attempt to develop an Integrated Resource Plan (IRP1) had enjoyed minimal consultation and legitimacy. A second version – IRP 2010 – was initiated, using a committee comprising the large-scale users of electricity and a few pliant academics to draft a new plan. The committee favoured the continued use of coal and nuclear to meet South Africa's energy needs, but also argued for the ramping up of renewable energy in the mix. Nuclear was to increase its existing capacity by 9 600 megawatts (MW), reflected in the final policy-adjusted scenario. Proposals for a non-nuclear scenario to be considered were rejected. The many public objections to the IRP were set aside. It looked like government was determined to use this outcome as backing to procure a large nuclear fleet by 2023.

Government still uses the IRP 2010 as justification for 9 600 MW of nuclear power, despite changing circumstances. The IRP is supposed to be reviewed biennially, and the 2013 revision document claims that there should be reconsideration of the procurement process for the present. It argues that the scientific underpinning for the IRP 2010 has changed significantly, and that the economic recession and electricity cuts have led to a drastic downturn in demand. The 2013 IRP revision document has not been recognised by the Department of Energy for planning purposes.

In an attempt to speed up the procurement process, the EIA for 'Nuclear-1', the nominal first reactor of the fleet, has to be in place before any orders are taken. This has resulted in consultants being given instructions to finalise the process, despite the blatant anomaly of not having any idea of which type of reactor will be chosen or how the specifics of its design will contribute to its impact. Somehow, the Department of Environmental Affairs, which has authority to issue a legal record of decision for each EIA, has accepted that you can measure the impacts of an as yet unchosen design. The process of consultation with interested and affected parties ended in December 2015, the deadline for receiving public comment.

Another piece of the policy woodwork was the signing of memoranda of understanding with the vendor states. Undertaken by the Department of Energy in relation to its counterparts in the vendor countries, these documents lay down the framework for collaboration on nuclear matters. Generally, this is not the place for details of any contractual nature to be included. South Africa has crafted such agreements with the potential vendor nations (South Korea, USA, Japan, France and China) but it was particularly in its agreement with Russia that the document strayed from the usual conventions (discussed later).

In his Medium Term Budget Policy Statement on 21 October 2015, former minister of finance Nhlanhla Nene granted the Department of Energy R200 million with which to research the procurement process. Cabinet finally approved the procurement initiative in late December 2015, two years after the documentation had been submitted by former energy minister Ben Martins. As with the earlier nuclear policy document, the decision was notable for being taken during the Christmas holiday season, when most South Africans are on their summer break. The document states that the process has to be 'fair, equitable, transparent, competitive, and cost-effective' (in line with section 217.1 of the constitution) and will be managed by the Department of Energy.[2]

The gazetted document was, however, one that was prepared some years previously, and using it masks the failure of the Department of Energy to observe the updated 2013 version of the IRP. This is one factor amongst numerous others used by Earthlife Africa and the Southern African Faith Communities' Environmental Institute in their legal challenge to the nuclear procurement procedure.[3]

ZUMA AND THE PARALLEL NARRATIVE OF PATRIMONIAL POLITICS

The preceding discussion looked particularly at the implementation of legal and administrative processes in setting out the justification for new nuclear energy. As noted, the process is highly flawed and eminently contestable. Instead of observing the spirit of post-apartheid legislation, the policy has served special interests and displayed many elements of a democratic deficit.

This narrative does not give the whole picture, though. It bypasses the more opaque layers of politics which have come to characterise Zuma's presidency (2009 until the present). Zuma came to power after a brief period in the political wilderness. Former president Thabo Mbeki had appointed Zuma as his deputy. In a trial of Zuma's financial advisor, Schabir Shaik, it went on court record that Zuma had received bribes from French arms dealers. Mbeki used this information to dismiss Zuma. Instead of disappearing politically, Zuma used the opportunity to mobilise. Support from trade unions, the South African Communist Party and sections of the ANC helped Zuma take power as party president at a congress of the ANC, and the subsequent ousting of Mbeki as party leader led to his dismissal from the state presidency. Zuma was able to quash charges of corruption in the run-up to the elections, which he won in 2009.

Parts of the Left were bedazzled by Zuma, and assumed that his term in office would lead to a revision of the neoliberal economic direction assumed by the state under Mbeki. The reality was that Zuma was no left ideologue or reformist. Large corporations remained untouched and were allowed to continue their privileged position in the economy. Economic inequality has widened. Zuma's power base included substantial sections of the new black middle class, which benefited from its ties with the state and, in particular, with the 'tenderpreneurs' who were making money out of preferential procurement policies.

To smooth the way for beneficiaries in the public sector, Zuma ensured that those most loyal to him would gain positions of power in government administration, parastatal institutions and the state-owned corporations (transport, broadcasting, post office, national airline, electricity, oil and gas, etc.). Pressures have been placed on more independent institutions to bring them into line with party fiat.

During Zuma's term of office, the turnover of government office-bearers has been substantial, and each of the state-owned enterprises has fallen into severe crisis or dysfunction. The Department of Energy has seen four ministers take office, and the Department of Public Enterprises has seen five changes of minister during Zuma's watch. Eskom has had four board chairs, six CEOs and five chief financial officers during the same period (Styan 2015: 54).

To coordinate the complex moves towards nuclear procurement, the cabinet created a National Nuclear Energy Executive Coordinating Committee on 9 November 2011, led by former deputy president Kgalema Motlanthe. By April 2013, control over the committee was reassigned to the president himself.

In July 2014, the committee was given a wider brief and converted to a cabinet subcommittee, the Energy Security Subcommittee, once again under the president's leadership. The subcommittee has membership of nine government departments.

The size of the nuclear deal has been contested – the lowest estimates are R400 billion and the most elevated are R1.2 trillion. With the recent slump in the exchange value of the rand, these estimates are somewhat obsolete. It is always extremely difficult to make accurate estimates because the nuclear industry is notorious for major cost overruns, and the estimates are based on notional 'overnight' costs which cover only the cost of construction. Whatever the exact costs, if it goes ahead the nuclear deal will be by far the largest infrastructural spend ever undertaken by the South African state. Opportunities for subcontractors will no doubt abound.

During the last years of the Mbeki presidency, former environment minister Valli Moosa served simultaneously on the ANC finance committee and as chair of the Eskom board. During this double tenure, Moosa signed off on a deal whereby Toshiba Power Africa would gain a R38.5 billion contract for the provision of boilers during the construction of the Medupi power station. In addition, twenty-five per cent of Toshiba Power Africa shares were owned by Chancellor House Holdings, an investment company owned by the ANC. As a result, the party gained a R50 million windfall due to the relationship. In due course the conflict of interest was recognised by the ANC, but it took four years before Hitachi bought back the shares owned by Chancellor House. During this time it was revealed that Hitachi was responsible for over 7 000 flawed welds in the boilers. This delayed the Medupi project by a further two years and resulted in penalty costs, which remain to be paid.

Other conflicts of interest in the energy sphere relate to the exclusive award of 90 000 km^2 of the semi-arid Karoo region to Royal Dutch Shell to conduct shale gas operations. Shell has a long history of giving support to the ANC, including the donation of its original national headquarters in Johannesburg, known as Shell House. Shell has separate operations for upstream (exploration) and downstream (distribution) functions in South Africa. Around twenty-five per cent of its downstream operation is owned by Thebe Investments, part of which belongs to Batho Batho, another ANC investment company.

Another cause of some national concern is the close relationship between Zuma and the Gupta family, formerly of Uttar Pradesh in India. The Guptas made their fortune in information technology and related industries, and moved to South Africa in the early 1990s. They have employed two of Zuma's children and one of his wives. They have established a foothold in local media (a daily newspaper and a TV news channel supportive of the government) and bought into large-scale minerals investments, including coal, gold and uranium. Their subsidiary Oakbay owns the country's only dedicated uranium mine (currently out of production due to technical problems and the low uranium price). Traditionally, uranium has been a by-product of the gold-mining industry. Media accusations against Oakbay include its operation of coal mines without the necessary water licence at a time of drought and water shortages. The Gupta's interests are also said to have been behind the recent reshuffle of the minister of mines, whose replacement, a backbencher with no track record in the sector, is close to the family.[4]

As noted, the major state-owned corporations are in disarray, mostly due to management, governance and/or financial problems. This condition has not bypassed two of the state-owned nuclear corporations, namely Necsa and the National Radioactive Waste Disposal Institute (NRWDI). Necsa is based at Pelindaba outside Pretoria and is responsible for South Africa's nuclear research and commercialisation of its products. Formerly it also managed the disposal site of South Africa's low and intermediate-level nuclear waste at Vaalputs in Namaqualand. NRWDI was set up to take over the management of nuclear waste from Necsa, and to develop solutions to the disposal of high-level nuclear waste.

Thirteen months after the launch of NRWDI in April 2014, the minister of energy announced that she was setting up a task team to investigate 'serious mismanagement in relation to corporate governance and management issues' at NRWDI and Necsa.[5] The task team consists of representatives of the departments of energy, mineral resources, international relations and cooperation, as well as the National Energy Regulator of South Africa (Nersa).

Concerns of the task team were said to include the fact that Necsa was in the red to the extent of R147.8 million. Although it was supposed to report back by 31 March 2015, no report had entered the public domain by 10 May 2017. Conflicts within the board continue to dog Necsa.[6] 'If left unattended,' the minister stated, '(the concerns) may adversely impact on the effectiveness of the board in overseeing and guiding NECSA and NRWDI operations.'[7]

In view of the procurement of six to eight new nuclear reactors, the minister cannot afford to have such a serious governance crisis in key nuclear institutions, particularly in the practical management of large new volumes of nuclear waste. In addition, the National Nuclear Regulator has long been underfunded and short of necessary skills. It is partly funded by the state and partly by licensing fees from nuclear facilities. It therefore has an innate interest in seeing the expansion of these facilities.

The constitution calls for fairness and transparency in any procurement process. Fairness would imply even-handedness towards competing vendors. However, what should have been a framework memorandum of understanding between South Africa and Russian nuclear establishments provoked an enormous controversy. Negotiations in which Zuma took control were initiated at the time of the BRICS[8] summit at Fortaleza, Brazil, in July 2013. The agreement was said to have been finalised when Zuma met Vladimir Putin on a medical holiday in Russia in August 2014. It was signed jointly by South Africa's energy minister, Tina Joemat-Pettersson, and Rosatom's Sergey Kiriyenko. This happened in Vienna while both were attending the fifty-eighth International Atomic Energy Agency's General Assembly on 22 September 2014 (The Presidency 2014).[9]

The contents of the agreement were not revealed by either signatory. Both Russian and South African authorities were thrown off balance by the media frenzy resulting from the agreement. Research by Vladimir Slivyak, head of Ecodefence, a Moscow-based NGO, found it lodged on the website of the Russian foreign ministry and he conveyed it to Earthlife Africa in Johannesburg.

Unlike similar documents that had been signed with other vendors, such as the US (2009), South Korea (2011) and later with China and France (2014), the agreement with Russia contained legally binding contractual details. Its underlying assumption was that Rosatom would obtain the tender for the new nuclear build. Specific clauses held that South Africa would lose full control of its domestic nuclear industry, and would have to get Russian permission for any exports of nuclear materials developed during the course of the agreement. Russian activities would be tax exempt and enjoy other unreciprocated privileges. Furthermore, Russia would be indemnified against any liabilities for nuclear damage or accident.

Prior input on the agreement during draft stages by state law and nuclear advisors who were critical of these clauses had not been taken into account, and it seemed that the original Russian draft was uncontested and unmodified. Zuma was ostensibly acting in Putin's and Rosatom's best interests, without specifying any *quid pro quo* in exchange for blatantly ceding sovereignty on domestic nuclear matters.

Table 12.1 Potential nuclear vendors in the South African new build procurement

Areva	France
China Guangdong Nuclear Power Co.	China
Korea Electric Power Corporation	South Korea
Rosatom	Russia
Westinghouse/Toshiba	US/Japan

Given Zuma's track record on corruption, how susceptible is he to the pressures of the vendors? Vendor parades have been conducted for Department of Energy officials from each of the prospective applicants (Table 12.1).

Space prevents a detailed analysis of their respective offerings and the terms on which their offers will be based. However, like the arms industry, it is well known that the nuclear vendors are likely to lace their offers with sweeteners aimed at decision makers. Rent-seeking behaviour is fairly standard in the industry and built into the economics of the deal. Zuma also must realise that the magnitude of the procurement increases the extent to which he could garner political support (and directly fill the coffers of the ANC) from subcontracts.

There are also geopolitical gains to be made, especially teaming up with Russia or China. As a fellow member of the BRICS group of nations, albeit a minor one, cementing a deal with, say, Russia, would create practical ties between the two nations, to the advantage of the vendor. Trade between South Africa and Russia, currently limited, would be given an important boost. South Africa would be drawn more and more into the political ambit of Russia in global affairs. This might complicate relations with its other key trading partners, especially the European Union. Russia's less than exemplary human rights record would go unchallenged and further compromise the legacy of Nelson Mandela and the erstwhile moral content of South Africa's foreign policy.

A key example of Zuma succumbing to patrimonial instincts is to be seen in the dismissal of the first black African finance minister in South African history, Nhlanhla Nene, in December 2015. Nene had a strong orthodox economic training and was a keen upholder of fiscal integrity and balanced books. He came into conflict with Dudu Myeni, chair of both the board of South African Airways (SAA) and the Jacob D Zuma Foundation. It is thought that Myeni had complained directly to Zuma, demanding the ousting of Nene. According to the Public Affairs Research Institute report on state capture, Nene was dismissed on the day that his position against the nuclear procurement was placed before cabinet and rejected (Bhorat et al. 2017).

Acting with impunity, Zuma's first instinct was to appoint a virtually unknown backbencher with no financial management expertise. David van Rooyen had been mayor of a small municipality in the Free State province. He had performed his civic duties so poorly that local protestors had driven him out of office. The reaction to this appointment resembled a tsunami. Cabinet and advisors all denied that they had been consulted in the matter. The rand, already in the doldrums, lost ten per cent of its value virtually overnight. Share markets in what was already a bearish market entered into a heavy slump. Threats to reduce South Africa's bonds to junk status became more real. And a spontaneous set of protests, including street demonstrations in key cities, was triggered, mostly through the use of social media.

Very quickly Zuma was besieged by delegations from the banking community and other concerned lobbies. Although it proved difficult to persuade Nene to resume his position, within two days Zuma had ditched Van Rooyen and appointed Pravin Gordhan, a former finance minister and Nene's predecessor, to his old position. Public confidence, although shattered, was somewhat assuaged. The markets gained back some of their dramatic losses.

Gordhan immediately made sure that Nene's stance with respect to the conflict at SAA was upheld, and his response to cabinet's endorsement of the nuclear procurement process was to remind the country that the deal had to conform to the constitutional preconditions of fairness, transparency and cost effectiveness. It seems that the finances of the deal may be adjudged as too risky to conform to fiscal discipline in the context of an already over-indebted economy. Aside from the R200 million that the Treasury has provided the Department of Energy to 'research' the procurement, the full extent of the deal has received no budgetary support.

The Treasury has also been sitting on reports on nuclear financial modelling and cost benchmarking submitted by consultancy firms KPMG, Deloitte and Ingerop.[10] These reports were not initially put in the public domain, generating rumours that they were too adverse to the success of the project. The excuse for not releasing them was that the information is confidential and could impact negatively on the tendering process if openly released.

It became clear that the Treasury would stand against Zuma's nuclear plans, but for a period a showdown was avoided. The Treasury also tried to stave off the possibility of the ratings agencies declaring the country to be of junk status. This raised tensions with the presidency, and culminated in a second cabinet reshuffle on the night of 31 March 2017. Amongst others, Gordhan lost his post as minister of finance, and Joemat-Pettersson as minister of energy. Joemat-Pettersson was accused of slow progress in the matter of the nuclear procurement. New appointees were drawn from Zuma loyalists. The incoming energy minister, Mmamaloko Kubayi, had no prior experience in relation to the portfolio. The reshuffle was conducted without any reference to ANC structures.

The global response included an almost immediate downgrade of South Africa to subinvestment (junk) status by the ratings agencies. At home, people flocked to a series of protest marches outside parliament and the Union Buildings, the administrative hub of government in Pretoria, as well as in a myriad of local neighbourhoods. The key call was for the dismissal of Zuma, and the links with the nuclear procurement were clearly drawn.

NARRATIVES OF RESISTANCE

Meanwhile, the balance sheet of public resistance grows more intense. Once the orbit of a dogged but small anti-nuclear movement, active since the 1980s when the Koeberg power reactors were being built, opposition has been manifested from a far greater footprint of civil society organisations.

The anti-nuclear movement in South Africa is constituted by a number of environmental organisations, of which the most effective has been Earthlife Africa. A series of local anti-nuclear campaigns has also been developed, reflecting concerns of local residents in the face of threats to build nuclear plants in their communities. This encompasses a range of coastal towns around the country, and now includes Durban, where provincial politicians keep igniting concerns that the city could host future reactors. Recent efforts to coordinate anti-nuclear work led to the establishment of The South African United National Anti-nuclear Mobilising Initiative, known as Tsunami.

There has been significant support from the trade union movement in the form of the Congress of South African Trade Unions (Cosatu) and its mining affiliate, the National Union of Mineworkers, both of which have long records of passing anti-nuclear resolutions and opposing the government's nuclear stance, despite being in a formal alliance with the ANC. Large demonstrations of workers have been mobilised against Eskom in recent years. The largest union in the country, the National Union of Metalworkers, expelled from Cosatu due to its severe critique of the alliance with the ANC, has helped to organise a united front with sympathetic civil society organisations. This in turn has led to a response to Eskom's power cuts and mismanagement in the form of a cross-union/civil society body, the Electricity Crisis Committee, which has also taken up an anti-nuclear stance.

Faith-based organisations are also in the vanguard. The multifaith South African Faith Communities' Environmental Institute has not only done considerable lobbying of energy officials and ministers, but has also, together with Earthlife, launched a fund to enable civil society to litigate against the government's nuclear plans. The Justice and Peace Commission of the Southern African Catholic Bishops' Conference has proposed a national referendum on the nuclear deal.

Even the private sector has expressed dismay about the nuclear procurement. The Electricity Intensive User Group, a lobby representing the under forty firms that utilise around half the country's electricity, has come out in opposition. So too has the Manufacturer's Circle, some chambers of commerce and other business lobbies. Their key concerns include the potential rise in electricity pricing, the further massive indebtedness and potential corruption arising from the deal. The financial media, mostly the IOL, News24 and BDFM groups, have taken up strong opposition to the nuclear path. Many business commentators now feel that the deal is too financially risky.[11]

Key research bodies funded by the government, such as the Council for Scientific and Industrial Research (CSIR), have demonstrated that the nuclear build is likely to be amongst the most expensive electricity options in future (Bischof-Niemz 2016). Already the decline in prices for most renewable energy resources has made them a preferred option for planners. Reports emanating from the highly respected Energy Research Centre at the University of Cape Town have shown unequivocally that the country can do without further nuclear build long into the future (Energy Research Centre 2015).

Other government voices have raised scepticism in relation to the need for and crippling cost of an expensive nuclear procurement process. The National Development Plan, generally held to be pro-business in orientation, stated that

> while the decision has been taken in principle, further and more in-depth investigations are needed into the implications of greater nuclear energy use, including the potential costs, financing mechanisms, institutional

arrangements, safety, environmental costs and benefits, localisation and employment opportunities, and the possibilities of uranium enrichment and fuel fabrication. (National Development Commission 2011: 176)

Another interesting surprise was the attitude towards nuclear taken in the preparatory documents for the policy conference held by the National General Council of the ANC in October 2015:

> Government must commit to a full, transparent and thorough cost benefit analysis of nuclear power as part of the procurement process, and clarify the status of the update to the Integrated Resource Plan. Government must also announce publicly that nuclear energy can only be procured in line with the legal prescripts and after a thoroughgoing affordability assessment. (ANC 2015: 75)

This statement represented some disquiet among the party's leadership on the nuclear question in the run-up to crucial local government elections in April 2016.

Given the plethora of opposition and scepticism towards the new nuclear build, who is left in favour? The short answer is the president and his immediate entourage, including some loyal ministers and key state officials. Backing them is the nuclear lobby, embodied in the Nuclear Industry Association of South Africa and sympathetic bodies like Women in Nuclear, a sprinkling of academics and former employees of or contractors to Necsa, Armscor and the Pebble Bed company.

The litigation initiated by Earthlife Africa Johannesburg in combination with the Southern African Faith Communities' Environmental Institute came to the Western Cape High Court on 22 February 2017. Proponents of the case had aimed to prevent the minister of energy from undertaking the procurement, but the court heard that the minister had passed on the responsibility for the procurement to Eskom, the electricity utility. The judge, Lee Bozalek, heard how this had been finalised at short notice, clearly in an effort to head off the proponents' case.

When it came to the judgment, which took place on 26 April, the anniversary of the Chernobyl catastrophe, the verdict was decisive. The judge ruled that the procurement was illegal because it had not followed due process. He also ruled that the effort to place the procurement under Eskom's auspices had been arranged illegally. Nersa was deemed to have rubber-stamped these arrangements instead of ensuring a public participation process in these decisions. Furthermore, the judge ruled that the nuclear memoranda of understanding with Russia, the US and South Korea had not come before parliament and were deemed illegal.

The judgment has been a vindication of the rule of law, but in practice has only set back the procurement process until such time that it can conform to the law. Government has decided not to appeal the judgment, but instead to correct its illegalities. This means that considerable time will be spent on correcting the illegalities around the procurement process, holding public hearings into the procurement and recrafting agreements with a number of the potential vendors. This is unlikely to occur within the remaining term that Zuma has in office.

Zuma, who under the constitution will leave office in 2019, can no longer see the nuclear procurement as part of his historic legacy to the country. Although he is aiming to be replaced by his ex-wife, Nkosazana Dlamini-Zuma, he will not be in as easy a position to continue to champion the procurement from the wings.

He needs to be persuaded that his legacy may be better served by cancelling the tender process. By forging ahead with this technology, he will be plunging the country into inextricable debt, raising the cost of electricity to unaffordable levels, creating new space for massive accidents and the proliferation of weapons of mass destruction, and saddling citizens with an impossible environmental legacy. Instead, the opponents of the procurement need to demonstrate effectively that Zuma's legacy would be far better served by the progressive dismantling of the nuclear industry, which has lost the confidence of vast numbers of concerned South Africans.

NUCLEAR: A FALSE SOLUTION TO CLIMATE CHANGE

Many are led to believe that nuclear is a low-carbon option because they are only told about the emissions in the reactors, which are low. However, to get to the point where nuclear fuel is burned and, later, disposed of, requires that we understand more of the steps in the nuclear fuel chain.

At the point of mining uranium, enormous amounts of rock need to be removed in order to obtain a small amount of uranium. The uranium then needs to be milled and processed into a fine power (uranium oxide, or yellowcake) for transportation. The next stage is the conversion of this powder to a gas (uranium hexafluoride), which is an essential step. The gas then goes through a process called enrichment, which enhances the amounts of the fissile isotope $_{238}U$ from under one per cent to three to four per cent for energy reactors (ninety per cent for weapons). The enriched uranium is then shaped into pellets and inserted into fuel rods, for use in the reactor. At each of these steps, use is made of masses of coal-based electricity, whose carbon emissions are significant, particularly during the mining, milling and enrichment phases.

After electricity is produced in the reactor, low and intermediate-level wastes are transported hundreds of kilometres before storage. Since we no longer enrich uranium in South Africa, the distances to the enrichment plants abroad are very far, and emissions from transport become significant.

Finally, when the reactors have to retire, the entire power station is treated as nuclear waste that must be dismantled and stored. This decommissioning process is also very carbon intensive. Over ninety per cent of South Africa's electricity is supplied by coal, and transport is based on fossil fuel consumption. Nuclear electricity in South Africa therefore cannot be seen as carbon neutral.

TOWARDS ENERGY DEMOCRACY

The pro-nuclear narrative rests on outdated conceptions of technological modernity. It makes false claims to the technology's affordability, safety, climate friendliness and employment density. The nuclear industry relies on centralised, inflexible delivery of power, creating an environmental legacy of perpetual waste. It requires levels of secrecy, opaqueness and hyper-security incompatible with democratic instincts.

The prospect of energy democracy would envision a degree of public control over our energy and electricity resources. The patrimonial powers of the current president would have to be curtailed, and the restitution of constitutional democracy would have to occur.

A new energy dispensation would need to be championed. In the first place, this would require the decorporatisation of the utility, imbuing it with a new value system aimed at serving the people as a whole. Energy policy would enter the public domain more squarely, with larger opportunities for public participation in its crafting. There would be a more hybrid system of social ownership of resources, reaching into communities, cooperatives and municipalities for the provision of power alongside existing state operations. Energy citizenship would have to be resourced to enable active participation in which the public could express its agency more effectively.

To transition out of nuclear and coal for our electricity, we need to think clearly of how a social plan would ensure a just transition. This would reassure workers in the nuclear and coal industries that there were alternative livelihood possibilities for them, and that their experience would merit relocation, retraining and rehiring. The boom in renewables would provide one avenue for employment, but a more nuanced plan would have to take many factors into consideration. Moves to lobby for new jobs in cleaner industries need to be supported.

The nuclear procurement meanwhile stands as the expression of a captured state. Its reversal will indicate a turning point in the struggle to restore constitutional power to the state.

NOTES

1   O. Mboweni, 'S&P downgrades South African credit rating to junk status', *Mail & Guardian*, 3 April 2017, http://mg.co.za/article/2017-04-03-sp-downgrades-south-african-credit-rating-to-junk-status/ (accessed 14 September 2017); Fin24, 'S & P downgrades Eskom to junk', 19 March 2015, http://www.fin24.com/Economy/SP-downgrades-Eskom-20150319 (accessed 14 September 2017); L. Donnelly, 'Junk status may scupper nuke plan', *Mail & Guardian*, 13 April 2017, http://mg.co.za/article/2017-04-13-00-junk-status-may-scupper-nuke-plan/ (accessed 14 September 2017).

2   Government Gazette 39541, 21 December 2015, https://www.greengazette.co.za/documents/national-gazette-39541-of-21-december-2015-vol-606_20151221-GGN-39541.pdf (accessed 21 August 2017), p. 4.

3   C. Paton, 'Energy department faces legal ordeal on nuclear energy deal', *Business Day*, 11 January 2016.

4   F. Wild, 'Guptas a symbol of Zuma's failing rule?' *Business Report*, 17 December 2015, http://mini.iol.co.za/business/news/guptas-a-symbol-of-zuma-s-failing-rule-1961278 (accessed 20 August 2017).

5   'Task team to investigate Necsa, NRDWI allegations', *Engineering News*, 23 February 2015, http://www.engineeringnews.co.za/article/task-team-to-investigate-necsa-nrwdi-allegations-2015-02-23 (accessed 21 August 2017).

6   'More nuclear fallout at NECSA', *Mail & Guardian*, 31 July 2015, http://mg.co.za/article/2015-07-30-more-nuclear-fallout-at-necsa (accessed 21 August 2017); 'NECSA latest state entity to be hit by boardroom and financial disarray', *Business Day*, 1 October 2015.

7   'Task team to investigate Necsa, NRDWI allegations'.
8   Brazil, Russia, India, China and South Africa.
9   Q. Hunter and L. Faull, 'Jacob Zuma's secret nuke "stitch-up"', *Mail & Guardian*, 26 September 2014, http://mg.co.za/article/2014-09-25-jzs-secrete-nuke-stich-up/; L. Faull, 'Exposed: Scary details of SA's secret Russian nuke deal', *Mail & Guardian*, 13 February 2015, http://mg.co.za/article/2015-02-12-exposed-scary-details-of-secret-russian-nuke-deal (both accessed 21 August 2017).
10 C. Paton, 'Cabinet gives green light to nuclear procurement', *Business Day*, 14 December 2015.
11 'Why South Africa's nuclear energy plan will likely fail', *News24 Wire*, 5 January 2016, http://businesstech.co.za/news/energy/108051/why-south-africas-nuclear-energy-plan-will-likely-fail/ (accessed 21 August 2017).

REFERENCES

ANC (African National Congress). 2015. *Umrabulo, special edition: Let's talk politics.* African National Congress NGC 2015 Discussion Documents. Accessed 19 August 2017, www.anc.org.za/docs/umrabulo/2015/ngc_disc_docsy.pdf.

Bhorat, H., Buthelezi, M., Chipkin, I., Duma, S., Mondi, L., Peter, C., Qobo, M., Swilling, M. and Friedenstein, H. 2017. *Betrayal of the Promise: How South Africa Is Being Stolen.* Johannesburg: Public Affairs Research Institute.

Bischof-Niemz, T. 2016. 'Can renewables supply baseload?' Presentation at the workshop Economics of Nuclear, Johannesburg, 9 March. Accessed 16 September 2017, https://africacheck.org/wp-content/uploads/2016/08/Economics-of-Nuclear-RE-baseload-CSIR-TBN-9Mar2016_PRESENTED-1.pdf.

DME (Department of Minerals and Energy, South Africa). 1998. *White Paper on the Energy Policy of the Republic of South Africa.* Pretoria: DME.

DME. 2008. *Nuclear Energy Policy for the Republic of South Africa.* Pretoria: DME.

EMG (Environmental Monitoring Group) and Western Cape ANC Science and Technology Desk. 1994. *The Nuclear Debate: Proceedings of the Conference on Nuclear Policy for a Democratic South Africa, 11–13 February.* Cape Town: EMG and ANC.

Energy Research Centre. 2015. *South Africa's proposed nuclear build plan: An analysis of the potential socioeconomic risks.* Technical Report. Cape Town: Energy Research Centre, University of Cape Town. Accessed 16 September 2017, http://www.erc.uct.ac.za/sites/default/files/image_tool/images/119/Papers-2015/15-ERC-Nuclear_build_plan_Technical_report.pdf.

Fig, D. 2010. *Nuclear energy rethink: The rise and demise of South Africa's Pebble Bed Modular Reactor.* ISS Paper 210. Pretoria: Institute for Policy Studies.

National Development Commission. 2011. *National Development Plan 2030.* Pretoria: The Presidency.

Styan, J-B. 2015. *Blackout: The Eskom Crisis.* Johannesburg: Jonathan Ball.

The Presidency. 2014. 'President Zuma works with Cabinet on nuclear matters'. 3 October. Accessed 19 August 2017, http://www.thepresidency.gov.za/content/president-zuma-works-cabinet-nuclear-matters.

13

CLIMATE JOBS AT TWO MINUTES TO MIDNIGHT

Brian Ashley

The Million Climate Jobs Campaign is an alliance of trade unions, social movements and popular organisations campaigning for a million climate jobs as part of the transition to a low-carbon and sustainable development path. The campaign is based on two fundamental points of departure. First, people want work. Globally, we are mired in an economic depression, the impact of which is aggravating already very high levels of unemployment and precariousness. Second, we have to stop the advance of climate change. To do that, we have to cut current annual greenhouse gas (GHG) emissions by seventy to eighty per cent within a ten- to thirty-year time frame (Neale 2008: 15).

Technically, that is quite feasible. We already have all the technology we need. The problem in getting action on climate change is political, not technological.[1] The governments of the world say they cannot act because it would 'cost too much'. But the cost would be the wages paid to workers to construct new renewable energy systems, public transport routes, buildings, etc.

In this instance 'cost' means jobs, yet jobs mean so much more than people just working. They mean dignity and giving expression to our creativity, and they establish the basis for our society's overall welfare. Just as there are unpaid externalities in the form of pollution from industrial processes, so there are unpaid externalities from the unemployment crisis in the form of crime, gangsterism, substance abuse, violence against women and children, and depression, which society has to bear.

Climate jobs are different to green jobs (Neale 2008). Green jobs can encompass any and all environmentally friendly jobs, such as in conservation and cleaning up oil spills. Climate jobs are those that help to reduce the emission of GHGs and build the resilience of communities to withstand the impacts of climate change. Examples of climate jobs include those in developing renewable energy plants; in energy efficiency, especially in retrofitting buildings; in public transport that reduces the pollution from cars and trucks; and, significantly, in small-scale organic agriculture, which reduces emissions of GHG in agriculture (AIDC 2011).

In this chapter I outline why climate jobs are critically important in the context of the weak outcomes of the 2015 Paris climate agreement (COP 21) and in light of South Africa's deepening economic crisis, the collapse of key industrial sectors and the mass unemployment crisis.

Albert Einstein is quoted as defining insanity as doing the same thing over and over again and expecting a different result. This is true for both South Africa's economic policies and successive agreements made during the meetings of the Conference of the Parties (COP) that are held under the auspices of the United Nations Framework Convention on Climate Change (UNFCCC). In both instances, the more things change, the more they stay the same. In the case of South Africa's economic policies, the Growth, Employment and Redistribution (GEAR) strategy, the Accelerated Shared Growth Initiative for South Africa, the New Growth Path and the National Development Plan have all codified mainstream orthodox economic policies, such as fiscal 'prudence', inflation targeting and monetarism, with disastrous consequences for employment. Similarly, each COP climate summit avoids taking the necessary steps to cut GHG emissions, agreeing to a carbon budget and funding comprehensive adaptation strategies, including technology transfers for so-called developing countries.

If we are to avoid insanity then we will need to develop a strategy that delegitimises the power of those that stand in the way of dealing with the climate crisis and build a counterpower to the capital and the states invested in the fossil fuel system. This is easier said than done, but starts with developing a coherent and realistic alternative around which people can organise and mobilise.

SOUTH AFRICA'S MASS UNEMPLOYMENT CRISIS

In South Africa the greatest determinant of poverty and income inequality is unemployment. Earnings from work are the most important source of household income and in the absence of a comprehensive welfare programme unemployment has a dramatic impact on household poverty (Adelzadeh 2003). The fact that South Africa is widely regarded as being the most unequal country in the world, as measured by the Gini coefficient, confirms the scale of the problem (Anand, Kothari & Kumar 2016).

Official figures record South Africa's rate of unemployment at about 27.7 per cent (Stats SA 2017: 1). However, the official statistics grossly underestimate the number of unemployed by excluding discouraged workers – the millions who have given up looking for work – and by including as employed anyone who has earned any nature of income, and performed any nature of work, paid or unpaid. When discouraged workers are included, the unemployment rate increases to 36.4 per cent (Stats SA 2017: 10).

Nevertheless, 27.7 per cent represents a massive social disaster. It is worth recalling that when unemployment reached twenty-five per cent in the US, it was the time of the Great Depression and the introduction of the New Deal, an extraordinary set of measures to give relief to the unemployed, stimulate the recovery of the economy and reform the financial system to prevent a reoccurrence of the depression. Under the weight of South Africa's unemployment crisis, the social fabric of society is collapsing, giving rise to a pandemic of crime, gangsterism and substance abuse.

The advent of neoliberal globalisation and the opening up of the South African economy to the world economy through trade liberalisation and the liberalisation of the current account, ultimately led to the financialisation of the economy, deindustrialisation and worsening unemployment levels (Marais 2013). The South African economy's vulnerability to shocks from the global economy was harshly exposed during the 2007/08 global financial crisis. Between October 2008 and March 2010, more than 1.2 million workers lost their jobs as the crisis took its toll, particularly in the mining and manufacturing sections of the economy (Ashman, Fine & Newman 2011: 179).

Once again, the winds of the global economy, this time the slowdown in growth in China and the decline in demand for mineral commodities, are pushing the South African economy to the point of recession. A new wave of retrenchments is destroying thousands of livelihoods. An economic growth strategy based on intensified exploitation of its natural resource wealth, combined with debt-driven consumption, offers virtually no hope for dealing with South Africa's unemployment crisis. A new sustainable development path and industrial strategy is needed. A low-carbon transition offers such a possibility, especially if it is combined with other strategies to deal with poverty, such as a mass housing programme and agrarian transformation (land redistribution, enhanced food production and seed sovereignty).

ECONOMIC CRISIS AND THE DECLINE
OF THE MINERALS–ENERGY COMPLEX

As suggested by the saying 'never let a good crisis go to waste', crises are not necessarily just about threats but can be the harbingers of opportunity. Things that seemed previously impossible suddenly appear feasible and realistic. This is perhaps no truer than with reference to the existential crisis unfolding in South Africa's industrial heartland. It is not just the mining sector that is facing a crisis – the entire minerals, minerals-beneficiation and related manufacturing sector appears to be in decline (Moyo 2015).

The South African economy has been heavily reliant on cheap and abundant supplies of electricity (McDonald 2012). The energy and carbon intensity of the South African economy is a legacy of the evolution of a relatively narrow accumulation path, which has become known as the minerals–energy complex (MEC) (Fine & Rustomjee 1996). This has been an extractivist accumulation path focused on mining and mineral beneficiation based on cheap coal for generating cheap electricity. Together with cheap labour, cheap electricity has been critical to the growth and development of the MEC and central to South Africa's industrial expansion strategies throughout its history (Fine & Rustomjee 1996).

Crucial to understanding the structural basis and dimensions of the MEC is to see just how central coal has been to South Africa's energy system. Sixty-five per cent of South Africa's primary energy supply is accounted for by coal in conversion both to electricity and to liquid fuels by Sasol (Baker et al. 2015: viii). Consequently, in the mining, concentrating, smelting and refining of various commodities, electricity, liquid fuels and even direct coal use are important inputs, accounting for a considerable proportion of their input costs.

Over eighty-five per cent of coal supply to Eskom remains concentrated in the major mining houses of Anglo American, Exxaro, BHP-Billiton, Glencore and Sasol. Coal mines, together with the mining of other minerals, especially gold and platinum, are in turn heavy consumers of electricity. Several of the big mining houses run major metal smelters that ensure that the Energy Intensive

Users Group, comprising thirty-one of Eskom's largest customers, consumes almost forty-four per cent of the electricity produced by Eskom (EIUG 2015).

However, the electricity supply and coal sectors are undergoing rapid change as both face mutually intersecting and related crises. The global economic crisis, especially its impact on commodity-producing countries like South Africa, aggravates the internal dimensions of these crises. So profound are these changes that they threaten the erosion of the MEC and its centrality to the economy, presenting both threats and opportunities.

ESKOM CRISIS

Eskom faces both a capacity and a financial crisis, the combination of which has ensured regular power outages that have inconvenienced consumers, slowed economic growth and led to investment uncertainty in the mining and related sectors. Taken as a whole, the impact of the crisis has been to undermine the legacy of cheap electricity so crucial to the mining and related industries.

While the electricity supply crisis is the result of many factors (poor planning, management, corruption, etc.), it nonetheless has its roots in GEAR, the neoliberal policy agenda adopted in 1996. GEAR curtailed state investment and promoted liberalisation and privatisation with severe consequences for Eskom.

Ever since Eskom was corporatised, its finances have been under stress. In March 2015 Eskom saw its investment rating downgraded to junk status by Standard & Poor's. This necessitated a R23 billion government bailout package to ensure the utility was able to prevent further blackouts. The financial difficulties experienced by Eskom forced the utility to take out a US$3 billion World Bank loan in 2010, the bulk of which went towards the construction of the Medupi coal-fired power plant.

With major power shortages in 2007, a decision was taken to build two new coal plants, Medupi and Kusile, to meet growing demand. Both have been subject to major delays, technical challenges and massive cost overruns. Originally, it was estimated that Medupi would cost R30 billion. It has now grown more than tenfold to R105 billion.[2]

Several other factors, such as escalating costs of coal purchases, inflated salaries, gratuitous and costly bonuses and perks for a crisis-ridden organisation, ageing infrastructure, high maintenance costs and other inefficiencies, have made it difficult for Eskom to run a cost-effective utility.

The Eskom crisis is important from the perspective of transitioning to a low-carbon development path and in the increased role of renewable energy in the overall energy mix. Under the Renewable Energy Independent Power Producers Procurement Programme (REI4P) launched in 2011, only 3725 megawatts (MW) of renewable energy were to be sourced. However, due to the scale of the electricity supply crisis, the minister of energy announced in December 2012 that a further 3200 MW were to be procured. This was followed by a further allocation of 6300 MW in August 2015, such was the pressure coming from rolling blackouts.

GREEN ECONOMY

Climate jobs are often confused with green jobs and with the green economy. Undertaking a transition to a low-carbon economy via the creation of millions of climate jobs should not be confused with green economy strategies and initiatives. The green economy is a process of marketising, commercialising and commodifying nature as a strategy to drive investment into fixing the damage capitalism, marketisation, commercialisation and commodification have done to the environment. This way of thinking was well captured by Janez Potočnik, former European Union environment commissioner, on the eve of the Rio+20 Summit: 'We need to move from protecting the environment from business to using business to protect the environment' (Potočnik 2011).

Yet, it is this approach of trying to develop a profit incentive strategy for dealing with the environmental and climate crisis that has been so detrimental to finding real solutions. A decade of potential action has been lost through false solutions such as carbon markets, the Clean Development Mechanism, reducing emissions from deforestation and forest degradation and other mechanisms for the commodification of the biosphere. That decade has seen no slowdown in the deepening of the climate crisis. It is precisely in this era of the green economy that GHG emissions have increased and that we have had the sharpest increases in temperature.

There are several problems with the whole green economy discourse. Not least is the duality it creates between the existing economy, which is dirty, polluting and unequal, and the clean green economy, which is not only good for the environment but is invested with characteristics like social inclusiveness and equity.

Yet the green economy is neither separate nor new. It is an expansion of the non-green economic system into new (and often artificially created) markets. Thus, the green economy is marked by the same imperatives of profit maximisation and competition as the non-green economy. Not surprisingly, the imperatives of addressing climate change are conditional on the same criteria shaping investment decisions in the broader economy. This means investments in green economy projects will occur at a level and pace essentially determined by the expectation of suitable levels of high profit and low risk (Rudin 2013).

The South African government has adopted the discourse of the green economy, promising to reconcile low-carbon and sustainable development with other valued outcomes, including job creation and poverty alleviation. In essence, the government's orientation and the dominant meaning it attaches to the green economy is green growth (Death 2014).

Two examples underscore how the workings of capital keep the green economy so underdeveloped. Eskom's inability to provide electricity is the first example. Contrary to widespread views, the government did not ignore the warning given in 1998 of an impending electricity supply shortage. Rather, it sought the partial privatisation of the utility. It invited business to become private power producers but the invite went disastrously unanswered. Eskom's boast of producing the cheapest electricity in the world kept capital away. The very cheapness of electricity was sufficient to deter would-be investors from coming to the government's proposed electricity party for private capital. Regardless of the profitable opportunity offered to investors and the country's need for electricity, capital stayed away. This was because capitalists invest not when simple profit can be made, but when profit can be maximised.

Renewable energy is the second example. The government is jubilant about what it claims to be the success of its current renewable energy programme. What it is less keen to make public is that this programme was delayed for several years. International capital finally became interested in South Africa's small-scale programme only when sufficiently maximised profit was guaranteed and when the renewable energy markets in other countries became saturated.[3] Moreover, the programme is limited so far to supplying nine per cent of South Africa's electricity from renewable energy.

This second example shows that the green economy is subject to the same imperatives as Eskom's carbon economy. Equally unsurprising is the failure of government's green economy initiatives – where they have been successful in attracting investment and delivering profit – to fulfil their trumpeted social benefits. Consider the government's solar water heating programme. In 2011, the government announced the start of an ambitious programme to install a million solar water heaters that would be delivered by the private sector. Funding of R4.7 billion was set aside for the programme. The government placed a local content target of seventy per cent to ensure local jobs. The results have been quite disastrous. According to the report of the Department of Environmental Affairs, only 336 391 solar water heaters had been installed as of May 2013 (Green 2015). This is some way short of the one million installations targeted by 2014/15. Targets have constantly been revised and the programme ground to a halt as a result of disputes over local content and disappearing state financing. A new target of March 2014 was set and then revised to March 2015. No solar water heaters were installed, despite stock sitting in warehouses, which has led to factories being mothballed and hundreds of workers being retrenched (Green 2015).

Of similar concern is the failure to stimulate downstream manufacturing and job creation through the programme. Only twenty per cent of the solar water heaters installed by 2013 were made in South Africa (Economic Development Department 2013) and all the available evidence to date suggests a very low rate of direct job creation through the programme.

One has to be sceptical about whether capital will invest in, never mind drive, a transition to a low-carbon economy. According to Jeff Rudin, a research associate with the Alternative Information and Development Centre,

> it is important to bear in mind that the Green Economy is neither separate nor new. Rather, it is simply an extension of the same economic system that is responsible for climate change. This system is one in which the competition for profit leads to unending and limitless compound growth. The Green Economy simply extends this competition for profit into activities associated with clearing up and containing ecological destruction. It does not challenge or supplant the fossil fuel economy. Instead it provides ideological cover for the reproduction and continuation of that economy. It does this by creating the illusion that something is being done about climate change. But the impact the green economy has on reducing and mitigating climate change is totally insignificant compared to what is needed to prevent a terrible global crisis affecting both the whole of humanity and the planet. The green economy distracts us from the radical changes that are needed to prevent this from happening. In that way, it is part of the problem, not the solution. (Rudin 2013: 6)

CLIMATE JOBS AND TRANSITIONING
TO A LOW-CARBON ECONOMY

South Africa can create many climate jobs that would contribute to reducing emissions of GHGs and other pollutants, as well as to unemployment. For this to happen, the state must take the lead and coordinate these efforts.

Climate jobs involve building renewable solar, wind, wave, tidal current and other power-generation options. Climate jobs also include work related to the building of a safe and efficient public transport network that would help reduce the number of cars and trucks on the road. Other areas include renovating and insulating buildings, transforming industrial agriculture, reforming production and consumption, and increasing energy efficiency. Additionally, water and sanitation have many climate change links, many but not all of which would create jobs. Significant jobs would be created in the related areas of research, education and training to ensure the country has the skills to undertake the transition to a low-carbon, labour absorbing and socially developed sustainable future economy.

In 2011, activists from trade unions, social movements, non-governmental organisations and academics came together to develop the platform of the Million Climate Jobs Campaign. They undertook a collaborative study, researching possibilities for creating decent work through transitioning to a low-carbon economy. Over thirty papers were commissioned from a diverse range of sectors, including the less obvious areas of tourism, health, waste management and ecosystem restoration. The Million Climate Jobs Campaign study found that, given the political will, over three million jobs of varying quality could be created in combating the emission of GHGs and building the resilience of communities to withstand climate change.

Recently, the campaign completed a research process that updated the 2011 platform, focusing on the key sectors that would have the most significant impact for emission reduction and job creation. Findings indicated that within a twenty-year period it would be completely feasible to make a significant step towards shifting to a low-carbon economy in the areas of electricity generation and distribution, transport, energy efficiency and construction, agriculture and managing waste to reduce current emissions from 547 million tons of carbon dioxide equivalent (CO_2e) to 129 million tons. This would involve creating at least one million sustainable and quality jobs (Table 13.1).

Table 13.1 Job estimates

Sector	Number of jobs
Electricity and renewable energy	250 000
Transport	390 000
Construction and repairs	150 000–200 000
Agriculture	100 000–500 000
Waste, industry and education	110 000
Total	1 000 000

With those jobs, emissions of GHG can be cut by more than three-quarters. Table 13.2 indicates how this can be accomplished. The second column shows current actual emissions in megatons of CO_2e. The third column shows estimated emissions after twenty years of climate jobs, showing a seventy-six per cent cut in total emissions.

The campaign readily acknowledges several methodological weaknesses in the study undertaken, not least in defining what is meant by a job. For example, the study draws on research undertaken by the Sustainability Institute (Spencer et al. 2010) for the Gauteng government in relation to promoting small-scale agriculture. Clearly, many of the jobs in small-scale agriculture take the form of livelihoods and are difficult to compare with, for example, jobs in manufacturing solar water heaters. Similarly, jobs created in transforming the health sector away from an institution-based curative model to a community-oriented preventative model can create a large number of part-time community health workers, which is not the same as formal jobs in low-carbon industries.

In addition, the Million Climate Jobs Campaign did not have the use of complex modelling tools to test and generalise the job creation strategies across sectors. Nevertheless, the evidence remains persuasive of the great many jobs that can be created through low-carbon economic strategies.

Embedding a shift to a low-carbon economy within a more comprehensive strategy and programme to meet the mass housing needs of poor South Africans, and stimulating small-scale production of food on a mass level through a programme of rural industrialisation, could secure the economic and social sustainability of this shift. Each of these areas has a reinforcing logic on the other in ways that ensure the whole is much greater than the sum of its parts.

Table 13.2 Total annual emissions in million tons of CO_2e

	Current* (million tons)	After (million tons)
Producing electricity	237	4
Transport	81	8
Industry	85	53
Agriculture	52	35
Heating buildings	42	17
Leaks	26	5
Waste	20	6
Other	4	1
Total**	547	129

Notes: *The figures are from 2010, the last year for which there are reliable numbers. **These figures are calculated as percentages from those given in the official government report for the UN (DEA 2014: 76, 275). The figures do not include land use. Including land use would reduce the total from 547 million tons to 521 million tons. This is because there is a net reduction in emissions due to the fact that agriculture has been declining in South Africa, which means that some farming land has changed into grazing, forestry or unused land, and some grazing land has changed into forestry or unused land. There is no reason to assume that this trend will continue. Indeed, some proposals for supporting small farmers would probably lead to an increase in land under cultivation and used as pasture. The manufacture of liquid fuel, mainly by Sasol, and the small emissions from refineries in transport are included. Aviation fuel is included in transport. Our total is three million tons higher than the official total without land use, because we have included the three million tons from international aviation bunkers in transport; in the official records they are recorded only as a note, not as part of the total.

However, moving from the current extractivist economy to a diversified low-carbon economy is easier said than done. Doing so in ways that do not lead to massive job losses is even more difficult. Nevertheless, regardless of the substantial restructuring that is required, the depth of the crisis in the mining sector and the broader economy creates the opportunity. The urgency for this transition is made more acute when taking into account the crises of resource depletion (water resources, soil, air) (Swilling & Annecke 2011), the climate crisis and the carbon intensity of the South African economy.

In fact, the mining sector could be an integral part of the transition to a low-carbon sustainable path. For example, renewable energy technologies are built from minerals, of which South Africa is a major producer. Recent research indicates that solar and wind facilities require up to fifteen times more concrete, ninety times more aluminium and fifty times more iron, copper and glass than fossil fuels or nuclear energy (Montmasson-Clair 2015: 9).

Other low-carbon technologies could also constitute major opportunities for some mining value chains in South Africa. These include fuel cells, an energy storage and conversion technology that could notably power electric transport. They require a number of metals as catalysts. Since the electricity and transport sectors are the biggest contributors to South Africa's GHG, it makes sense to focus on these sectors.

ELECTRICITY SECTOR

The biggest contributor to both jobs and emission reduction would be to decarbon the energy sector (Altieri et al. 2015). South Africa is the twelfth largest emitter of GHGs in the world (Environmental Defence Fund 2014) and has a per capita emission profile similar to large industrialised economies such as Germany and Britain. As noted, this is because of the energy intensity of the economy. South Africa's coal-dependent electricity sector is responsible for forty-five per cent of national emissions (237 megatons of CO_2e in 2010) (Baker et al. 2015: viii).

South Africa has access to some of the world's best renewable energy sources. South Africa's location, geography and size all play a role in providing the country with multiple renewable energy resources. A coastline of approximately 3 000 km provides favourable conditions for wind power throughout the country. Most areas in South Africa average more than 2 500 hours of sunshine per year, and average solar radiation levels range between 4.5 and 6.5 kilowatt hours/m^2 in one day.

A clear trend documented in international studies is that utilising diffuse renewable energy resources is more labour-intensive than utilising the highly concentrated energy in fossil fuel resources. A report in June 2015, *Global Green Growth*, found that

> per $1 million in spending in each country (converted at current exchange rates), clean energy investments generate, on average, about 37 jobs in Brazil, 10 jobs in Germany, 100 jobs in Indonesia, 70 jobs in South Africa, and 15 jobs in the Republic of Korea. Critically, ... we also find that the clean energy investments create more jobs in all five

283

countries than spending the same amount of funds within each country's fossil fuel sectors. In the cases of Brazil, Indonesia, and South Africa, the net employment gains for clean energy investments are substantial. (UNIDO & GGGI 2015: 24)

INDEPENDENT POWER PRODUCERS PROCUREMENT PROGRAMME

South Africa's renewable energy programme, the REI4P, has been underperforming in terms of job creation, while overperforming in terms of attracting investment.

The REI4P has resulted in the approval of over 6327 MW of renewable energy under four bidding rounds. Of this, fifty-three per cent is for wind, thirty-six per cent for solar PV and ten per cent for concentrated solar power. Ninety-two projects have been approved, attracting a combined investment value of R192 billion (approximately US$13 billion). Forty-two projects totalling 2142 MW were connected to the grid by October 2015. Successful projects sell to Eskom's grid under a twenty-year government-backed power purchase agreement.

The programme won several accolades, especially from the international renewable energy industry and developers who found in the South African programme a viable alternative to the constrained markets in the US and Europe. But it has not delivered on jobs, social benefits to local communities and knock-ons to downstream industries. This is due to the initiative being framed in terms of the government's green growth perspective. As opposed to locating the sourcing of renewable energy as part of a comprehensive programme of transitioning to a low-carbon economy, where industrial and trade policies could be recast to support the development of downstream renewable energy-related industries, renewable energy is promoted as simply diversifying the energy mix, alongside gas, nuclear and coal.

Hence, it is not surprising that the programme has failed to live up to its job creation potential and has not led to substantial emission reductions. Table 13.3 highlights the dearth of jobs created in this privatised, profit-maximising programme.

Table 13.3 Jobs in the REI4P

	Bid Window 1	Bid Window 2	Bid Window 3
Construction jobs	6074	5221	7813
Operational jobs	9960	7227	17749
Total	16034	12448	25562

Source: DoE (2015: 135).
Note: One job = 12 person months.

MOVING TO ONE HUNDRED PER CENT RENEWABLES

Research conducted by the Million Climate Jobs Campaign in 2016 indicates that in a twenty-year period it would be possible to generate almost all our electricity from renewable energy sources, even when this is based on a dramatic increase in the amount of electricity needed (AIDC 2017). According to the Council of Scientific and Industrial Research (CSIR), there is no longer any technical reason why renewable energy could not provide one hundred per cent of our electricity most of the time, with open-cycle turbine back-up when necessary (Bofinger et al. 2016). The campaign's research envisages a tripling of electricity so that clean electricity can replace coal, oil and gas in many parts of the economy. Extrapolating from the CSIR study, the campaign established it would be necessary to build six gigawatts of capacity of wind energy a year for twenty years and nine gigawatts of solar PV (AIDC 2017: 24). It would also involve the construction of a new smart grid to accommodate the many more 'suppliers' of electricity.

Table 13.4 shows estimates of how many jobs would be required. These estimates are based on the number of jobs that are currently required around the world to build wind and solar capacity. Also taken into account is the marked recent fall in the number of workers required to manufacture solar PV cells.

The fact that most existing coal-fired plants are reaching the end of their lifespan makes this transition both possible and realistic. It is also worth noting that the costs of generating electricity from solar and wind have come down substantially to levels on a par with or cheaper than coal-fired energy (WWF 2014). However, such levels of job creation are predicated on local production

Table 13.4 Average number of new energy jobs each year

Building and installing wind power	66 000
Building and installing solar power	122 000
Building and operating a smart grid	62 000
Maintenance and repairs	0–88 000
Total	250 000*

Note: *When 'maintenance and repairs' is taken as 0.

of the inputs into the renewable energy programme. In the REI4P, most of the inputs are imported and the jobs created are relatively short term, concentrated in construction, security and maintenance. Based on the advance in renewable energy technologies, we believe we can be even more ambitious in shifting to renewable energy as the main source of energy, especially if there is a state-driven and socially owned programme.

New research is required to take into account new modelling studies that indicate a much greater potential for job creation, as well as the current experience of the REI4P, which has shown much lower impacts on job creation.

TRANSPORT

After the electricity sector, transport accounts for approximately thirteen per cent of South Africa's total GHG emissions, most of these as a result of road transport (Table 13.5). Finding ways to cut emissions from transport would go a substantial way towards reducing the carbon intensity of our current development path.

Expanding public transport is central to transitioning to a low-carbon economy and reducing the carbon intensity of the economy. Expanding public transport in ways that reduce our GHG emissions can lead to the creation of 390 000 climate jobs. Furthermore, the expansion of public transport has several important social benefits: overcoming the still dominant racial segregation of our cities, increasing the mobility of poor people and facilitating a greater public role for women in society. To achieve these objectives, it is vital to get more people to use public transport, to shift freight from roads to rail,

Table 13.5 Contribution of different modes of transport to emissions, 2000–2010*

Mode and energy carrier	% contribution to overall emissions
Domestic aviation (kerosene and aviation gas)	7.08
Road	91.56
Rail	1.36

Source: DEA (2014: 95).
Note: *Excluding emissions from the production of fuels.

to transition the energy source of public transport from oil to electricity and to source that electricity from renewable forms of energy.

The legacy of apartheid, especially the spatial dimensions whereby workers live far from their places of work, as well as the privatisation of the transport sector, especially freight, have contributed enormously to the legacy of high GHG emissions in transport (Prozzi et al. 2002: iii). This was spelled out in a 2002 study on GHG scenarios for South Africa:

> Privatization in the freight sector has also propelled large modal shifts from rail to truck. Until 1988, trucks were not allowed to compete with the government-owned railroad. When the freight sector was deregulated in 1988, truck use rapidly expanded, resulting in lower freight tariffs, and a large drop-off in rail use. (Prozzi et al. 2002: iv)

Hence, the most important way of cutting emissions in transport and creating jobs is by expanding the public transport system for both commuters and freight, and transitioning commuters and freight into electric-driven modes of transport, especially rail. Rail expansion is particularly important in mitigating emissions in transport when taking into consideration that diesel rail locomotives use about one-sixth of the diesel used by trucks carrying the same volume of freight (Barrett 2011).

The impact on the reduction on emissions would be most significant were rail transport to be powered by renewable energy. This is something that could be considered after a decade of undertaking a planned transition to a low-carbon economy and once the most pressing uses for renewable energy have been taken care of. Table 13.6 shows current figures for modes of transport

Table 13.6 Commuter use of different modes of transport

Mode of transport	%
Trains	4.4
Buses	10.2
Minibus taxis	41.6
Cars	13.7

Source: Stats SA (2014).

used to travel to work and education each day. Over fifty per cent of people use some form of public transport, with just under fourteen per cent using a private car. In addition, one million people walk to their places of education and 2.9 million walk to work (Stats SA 2014).

By expanding the public transport system and using various incentives and regulations, it would be possible to switch half of all car journeys to public transport (twenty-five per cent rail and minibus, respectively, and fifty per cent bus). That would account for four million people in total. It can also be assumed that an additional four million people would take public transport each day: workers who now have climate jobs, people who previously walked to work and people who are attracted to a better transport system. In sum, that would be eight million more travellers on public transport: two million on light rail, four million on buses and two million on minibus taxis. That would require building new light rail and bus rapid transit lanes. It would also mean building better and safer facilities for walkers, safe cycle-only lanes and proper waiting stations and sanitary facilities at the start of minibus lines. To make bus transport attractive, it would be necessary to have bus-only lanes and roads during rush hours. This would discourage people from using private cars to commute, and massively cut transport times for people in buses and minibus taxis, who would get to work quickly, comfortably and safely. Table 13.7 shows the estimated number of new jobs that would be created if there were eight million new travellers using public transport.

In this scenario, a far better transport service could be supplied. It would be safer, much quicker due to fewer traffic jams, and less crowded. There would also be more cheap transport for people who currently walk to work and better, safer routes for cyclists and walkers. Better, cheaper and quicker transport could also be supplied to and from rural areas.

Table 13.7 Estimated number of jobs created each year by expanding the public transport system

	New travellers (million)	No. of new jobs
Rail	2	30 000
Bus	4	100 000
Minibus	2	100 000
New building/construction required		70 000
Total		300 000

CONCLUSION

South Africa faces a major crisis in the electricity supply sector that is estimated to continue until at least 2020. The mining sector is also in crisis, signalling a spiralling process of deindustrialisation and stranded assets. The major mining houses that have been central to the development of the South African economy over many decades have now reinvented themselves as global corporations. With collapsing commodity prices, these corporations have undertaken a major restructuring effort, which will see tens of thousands of jobs disappear. At the same time the coal industry is reorganising itself away from dependence on long-term supply contracts to Eskom, favouring exports into international markets. Eskom itself is in major financial difficulties, with its credit rating valued at junk status. At the same time it is expected to drive a major build programme which includes a nuclear programme that is set to cost over R1 trillion. Many of its existing coal-fired plants are coming to the end of their life cycle. In other words, the entire MEC is facing its own organic crisis, to use Gramscian terms.

To this we must add the accelerating climate crisis and the successive failures of the intergovernmental process within the UNFCCC to bring about the necessary emission reductions to stop runaway climate change. South Africa's current energy policy locks the country into a carbon-intensive future. The shift to a low-carbon equitable and sustainable development path will not be the outcome of polite lobbying of government ministers and policy makers. It is impossible to believe that the foreign transnational corporations and their junior Black Economic Empowerment partners can be relied on to drive such a transition. To achieve this, it will be necessary to put together a new political bloc drawn from organised labour; small and medium-sized enterprises with strong roots in the local economy; community-based social movements representing unemployed sectors of our society; enlightened and radical environmentalists; and the potentially new organic intellectuals of the radicalising student movement. Some steps in this direction are present and growing as people question in more fundamental ways the current political-economy trajectory in South Africa.

In this bloc of social forces, the trade union movement will play a critical role. They (at least their members) have the most to lose by ignoring climate change. It is well documented that climate change will most adversely affect the poor, workers and other vulnerable sections of the population (Stern 2007). A strategy focused on saving jobs in traditional sectors such as coal mining, road transport and the fossil fuel energy sectors is a recipe for failure. In most cases these industries are already in decline and shedding jobs. For example, there has been a progressive loss of jobs in the coal sector over several years, even though it was earmarked in the government's economic strategy for substantial growth. In addition, research has indicated that there are more jobs in shifting to low-carbon industries than in the traditional polluting industries (UNIDO & GGGI 2015).

It remains to be seen whether the response to the current electricity crisis will be confined to shoring up the existing system or whether the opportunity will be taken to embrace a sustainable energy paradigm.

The power of the Million Climate Jobs Campaign lies in taking up the two most compelling challenges of our time in a single campaign, namely climate change and mass unemployment. By demanding that governments create climate jobs and by mobilising millions of working people around these demands, it is possible to begin the necessary task of shifting the balance of forces between labour and the state and the state and the market.

NOTES

1   B. McKibben, 'Global warming's terrifying new math', *Rolling Stone*, 19 July 2012, http://www.rollingstone.com/politics/news/global-warmings-terrifying-new-math-20120719 (accessed 21 August 2017).
2   S. Tau, 'Medupi to cost R105 billion – Eskom', *Citizen*, 30 August 2015.
3   J. Rudin, 'Imprisoned in Paris: Alternatives to the green economy', *Amandla*, 43/44 (2015): 26–27, http://aidc.org.za/amandla-media/amandla-magazine/back-issues/ (accessed 19 August 2017).

REFERENCES

Adelzadeh, A. 2003. *South Africa Human Development Report 2003: The Challenge of Sustainable Development: Unlocking People's Creativity*. Cape Town: Oxford University Press.

AIDC (Alternative Information & Development Centre). 2011. 'One million climate jobs: A just transition to a low carbon economy to combat unemployment and climate change'. Million Climate Jobs Campaign South Africa.

AIDC. 2017. 'One million climate jobs: Moving South Africa forward on a low-carbon, wage-led, and sustainable economic development path'. Million Climate Jobs Campaign South Africa.

Altieri, K., Trollip, H., Caetano, T., Hughes, A., Merven, B. and Winkler, H. 2015. 'Pathways to deep decarbonization in South Africa'. Sustainable Development Solutions Network and Institute for Sustainable Development and International Relations. Accessed 19 August 2017, http://www.erc.uct.ac.za/sites/default/files/image_tool/images/119/Papers-2015/15-Altieri-etal-Pathways_to_deep_carbonisation.pdf.

Anand, R., Kothari, S. and Kumar, N. 2016. *South Africa: Labor market dynamics and inequality*. IMF Working Paper 16/137. Accessed 19 August 2017, https://www.imf.org/external/pubs/ft/wp/2016/wp16137.pdf.

Ashman, S., Fine, B. and Newman, S. 2011. 'The crisis in South Africa: Neoliberalism, financialization and uneven and combined development', *Socialist Register*, 47: 174–195.

Baker, L., Burton, J., Godinho, C. and Trollip, H. 2015. 'The political economy of decarbonisation: Exploring the dynamics of South Africa's electricity sector'. Research Report Series. Energy Research Centre, University of Cape Town. Accessed 19 August 2017, http://www.erc.uct.ac.za/sites/default/files/image_tool/images/119/Papers-2015/15-Baker-etal-Political_economy_decarbonisation.pdf.

Barrett, J. 2011. 'Transport and climate jobs – SATAWU research paper'. Accessed 19 August 2017, http://aidc.org.za/BACKUP/climatejobs/download/research/campaign_research/Transport%20and%20Climate%20Jobs%20by%20Jane%20Barrett.pdf.

Bofinger, S., Zimmermann, B., Gerlach, A.K., Bischof-Niemz, T. and Mushwana, C. 2016. 'Wind and solar PV resource aggregation study for South Africa: Public presentation of results'. Accessed 19 August 2017, http://www.wasaproject.info/docs/PVWindAggregationstudy.pdf.

DEA (Department of Environmental Affairs, South Africa). 2014. *GHG Inventory for South Africa 2000–2010*. Pretoria: DEA.

Death, C. 2014. 'The green economy in South Africa: Global discourses and local politics', *Politikon*, 41 (1): 1–22.

DoE (Department of Energy, South Africa). 2015. *State of Renewable Energy in South Africa*. Pretoria: DoE.

Economic Development Department. 2013. 'Summary report 1 on implementation of social accords'. Accessed 19 August 2017, http://www.economic.gov.za/communications/publications/report-on-social-accords.

EIUG (Energy Intensive Users Group). 2015. 'About EIUG'. Accessed 19 August 2017, http://www.eiug.org.za/about/.

Environmental Defence Fund. 2014. 'South Africa: The world's carbon markets: A case study guide to emissions trading'. Accessed 19 August 2017, https://www.edf.org/sites/default/files/South-Africa-Case-Study-March-2014.pdf.

Fine, B. and Rustomjee, Z. 1996. *The Political Economy of South Africa: From Minerals–Energy Complex to Industrialisation.* London: C. Hurst & Co.

Green, J. 2015. 'South African government solar water heating outlook for 2016 – is the DOE's latest initiative reason for optimism or further exasperation?' Sustainable Energy Society Southern Africa. Accessed 20 June 2016, http://sessa.org.za/about-sessa/chairman-s-blog/740-solar-water-heating-outlook-2016.

Marais, H. 2013. *South Africa Pushed to the Limit: The Political Economy of Change.* London: Zed Books.

McDonald, D.A. (ed.). 2012. *Electric Capitalism: Recolonising Africa on the Power Grid.* New York: Routledge.

Montmasson-Clair, G. 2015. *Mining value chains and green growth in South Africa: A conflictual but intertwined relationship.* TIPS Working Paper. Accessed 19 August 2017, http://www.tips.org.za/files/mining_value_chains_and_green_growth_in_south_africa_working_paper_may_2015.pdf.

Moyo, T. 2015. *Global Economic Crisis and South Africa's Manufacturing Industry: Case of the Automotive, Textile and Clothing, and Mining Industries.* Dakar: Codesria.

Neale, J. 2008. *Stop Global Warming: Change the World.* London: Bookmarks Publications.

Potočnik, J. 2011. 'Towards the green economy'. European Commission Press Release, 22 February. Accessed 19 August 2017, http://europa.eu/rapid/press-release_SPEECH-11-115_en.htm?locale=EN.

Prozzi, J.P., Naude, C., Sperling, D. and Delucchi, M. 2002. *Transportation in Developing Countries: Greenhouse Gas Scenarios for South Africa.* Washington, DC: Pew Center on Global Climate Change.

Rudin, J. 2013. *Green Economy: The Long Suicide – The Different Worlds of Green Jobs and Climate Jobs.* Cape Town: Alternative Information and Development Centre.

Spencer, F., Swilling, P.M., Everatt, P.D., Muller, P.M., Schulschenk, J. and Du Toit, J. 2010. 'A strategy for a developmental green economy for Gauteng'. Report prepared for the Gauteng Province Department of Economic Development. Johannesburg: Gauteng Provincial Government.

Stats SA (Statistics South Africa). 2014. *National Household Travel Survey: February to March 2013.* Statistical Release P0320. Pretoria: Stats SA.

Stats SA. 2017. *Quarterly Labour Force Survey, Quarter 1 June 2017.* Statistical Release P0211. Pretoria: Stats SA.

Stern, M. 2007. *The Economics of Climate Change: The Stern Review.* Cambridge: Cambridge University Press.

Swilling, M. and Annecke, E. 2011. *Just Transitions: Explorations of Sustainability in an Unfair World.* Cape Town: Juta.

UNIDO and GGGI (United Nations Industrial Development Organization and Global Green Growth Institute) 2015. *Global Green Growth: Clean Energy Industry Investments and Expanding Job Opportunities. Volume I: Overall Findings.* Vienna and Seoul: UNIDO and GGGI.

WWF (World Wildlife Fund, South Africa). 2014. 'Renewable Energy Vision 2030 – South Africa'. Technical Report. Accessed 20 August 2017, http://awsassets.wwf.org.za/downloads/a16369_wwf_reip_report_online.pdf.

14

DEEPENING THE JUST TRANSITION THROUGH FOOD SOVEREIGNTY AND THE SOLIDARITY ECONOMY

Andrew Bennie and Athish Satgoor

Realising a 'just transition' requires movement from below that mobilises to contest and reshape relations to overcome the structural barriers to such a transition. This brings to the fore alternatives that seek to reshape humans' relationships with the key factors that structure our lives and the planet, and which we shape, namely nature, the economy and, critically in this current conjuncture, food. The question of food is central to the climate crisis and the just transition because it 'stands squarely at the crossroads of the ecological, social and financial crises and provides a graphic example of how they reinforce each other' (George 2010: 110).

The struggle for food sovereignty is a grassroots response to these dimensions as experienced by peasant food producers and the hungry across the world, and its objectives traverse nature, society and the economy, contesting the relations between them. Food sovereignty is therefore about more than just food – it offers a path, informed by social movement struggle, out of the climate and social crises. The climate crisis and the barriers to confronting it are grounded in the capitalist logic of expansion. Within this dynamic, capitalism separates control over production from labour and nature. The solidarity economy is a response to the impacts arising out of this disarticulation, and aims to re-embed labour democratically within human creativity, production and nature (Wainwright 2014). As such, the solidarity economy and food sovereignty play crucial roles in advancing each other, and together provide important means to struggle for structural change to deepen the just transition.

We argue that the logics of food sovereignty and the solidarity economy are taking root at the grassroots in South Africa, in various, uneven and contextual ways. After exploring the food sovereignty and solidarity economy alternatives, and providing a background to the South African context, we provide a brief overview of the South African Food Sovereignty Campaign (SAFSC) to illustrate our argument. We conclude by posing a key challenge to consciously situate the solidarity economy and food sovereignty in the struggle for the commons as a means to deepen the just transition.

THE GLOBAL FOOD SYSTEM AND RESISTANCE

Despite the fact that enough food is produced globally to feed everyone on the planet, and more than enough food than they need every day, at least a billion people suffer from hunger (Hickel 2016). Key to understanding this contradiction is the structure and operations of the global corporate food regime. Globally, movements have arisen that aim to address the problem of hunger. They are explicitly political in that they situate the causes of global hunger in neoliberal capitalism broadly, and more specifically in corporate control of the food system, lack of land and agrarian reform, ongoing land and resource dispossessions, and public policies that favour the global market rather than the interests of farmers and citizens who require access to affordable and nutritious food. These movements take the form of landless movements, small farmers who appear to bear the brunt of neoliberal restructuring in agriculture, urban farmers, community gardens, and alternative forms of food distribution in the global South as well as the global North, including the United States (see Alkon 2013; Field & Bell 2013). The most prominent form of global organisation around the question of food has emerged through the radical peasant and small-scale farmers' movement La Via Campesina (meaning 'way of the peasant'), which has built a membership of over 200 million people worldwide.

Much of what unites many of these initiatives across the globe is the call for food sovereignty, a concept credited to La Via Campesina. What food sovereignty and its principle global protagonist practically represent is a radical challenge to the industrial model of agriculture that has become globalised through international commodity circuits, with corporations as its key active agents in shaping a globalised corporate food regime (McMichael 2009). There is no single definition of food sovereignty and its meaning has evolved over time, but in the People's Food Sovereignty Statement, drafted in 2001 at the World People's Summit, it was described as 'the right of nations and peoples to control their own food systems, including their own markets, production modes, food cultures and environments' (Wittman, Desmarais & Wiebe 2010: 2). This notion of control goes beyond national policies of self-sufficiency to questions of power, corporate control and democracy at the global, national and subnational levels.

Critical to the struggles of championing food sovereignty is the context of the climate crisis. The neoliberal policy shifts have intensified the climate crisis as well. Both industrialised agriculture and industrial development have increased carbon emissions exponentially in the twentieth and twenty-first centuries. Climate change is expected to increase the frequency of climate-related shocks, which in turn will put pressure on food, energy and water supplies, and the impact will be amplified through the interconnections and interdependence among these three resources (WWF 2014).

Central to food sovereignty is democracy: the right of people and communities to control and influence their food systems. The question then arises as to the specific economic and social forms through which to develop and institutionalise this democracy in the production, processing, distribution and consumption of food. The solidarity economy emerges as a counterhegemonic transformative alternative (Williams 2014) that stands in direct opposition to capitalist power formations. The solidarity economy is emerging as a grassroots response to the economic and social crises, and as a way of embedding collective ownership, control and self-management in economic and social activities (Satgar 2014). Extended to food sovereignty, the institutions of the solidarity economy, like cooperatives, can offer the institutional forms and principles that socially embed and democratise alternative food systems.

DEFENDING, RECLAIMING AND CONSTRUCTING THE COMMONS

Essentially, it can be argued that the solidarity economy and food sovereignty, as responses from below to capitalist dispossession, are attempts to reclaim and rebuild the commons – but it requires building power to do so. Central to the ecological crisis is capital's ability to appropriate nature in the form of land seizures, dispossession and commodification. This requires removing control over resources from people, communities and farmers. A critical dimension to curbing the climate crisis by challenging the relations centred around private property that this appropriation produces, is to reclaim nature, goods, labour and ideas as the commons. The commons refers to shared and decommodified resources and the social interactions and rules governing their use (HBF 2014), as well as the means and rules by which people allocate the goods that come from those resources, such as food (Linebaugh 2014; Patel 2009). The most prominent resource attributed to the commons is land, but the commons in terms of the production process and the utilisation and management of the output can include all natural resources like water and seeds, as well as digital development, labour and food. The commons is essentially about the socialisation of the essentials of life as opposed to their privatisation. To fully realise the commons in general, and particular items such as food as part of the commons, requires institutions, organisational forms and broader social relations that make the commons possible.[1] Situating the commons as a political goal and a guiding ideal challenges us to consciously build the solidarity economy and food sovereignty in ways that move us towards the commons. For example, as David Harvey (2011) argues, a key way that capitalism captures and undermines the commons is through capitalists' appropriating surplus value. The implication is that institutional forms to foster the commons should do away with the distinction between the producers of value and those who appropriate it. This is part of the essence of forms such as worker cooperatives. To advance food sovereignty and the solidarity economy therefore requires constructing institutional arrangements, from worker cooperatives, to seed banks, to knowledge commons. Their exact form will vary depending on the resource (i.e. seeds, knowledge, land or food), but commoning provides an important frame for guiding political and practical action. It is about ensuring the decommodification of the elements of life and community, and subjecting them to democratic and collective management.

THE SOUTH AFRICAN CONTEXT

Since 1994, the South African government has adopted a macro-economic policy path that largely adheres to neoliberal precepts and eschews the possibility of more progressive transformation in the economy and society (Marais 2011; Satgar 2008). Key pillars of economic power have been left intact, resulting in many social inequalities remaining firmly in place. The intensification of inequality as a result of the interaction of structures built up under apartheid with a globalising economy is starkly indicated in the case of food. Despite the fact that South Africa is one of only 23 countries in the world whose constitution guarantees all citizens the right to food, structural realities mean that about twenty-six per cent of South Africans suffer from hunger and only forty-six per cent of households are food secure (HSRC & MRC 2013). The spread of this hunger is spatially and racially uneven and the highest levels of hunger coincide with the most historically marginalised communities in the country – black urban informal settings (32.4 per cent) and rural populations (37.0 per cent) (HSRC & MRC 2013). These levels of hunger are of course a direct consequence of poverty in that such households simply do not have sufficient income to afford all their nutritional requirements. However, the historic development of South Africa's agrarian structure and agri-food system is also intertwined with the creation of poverty and hunger.

As a result of land dispossession, proletarianisation, depeasantisation and the deliberate creation of a strong, white commercial farming sector, by 1994 South Africa had a highly skewed agrarian structure, with approximately 60 000 commercial farmers controlling over eighty per cent of agricultural land, and more than two million subsistence farmers farming on about thirteen per cent of the land (Hall & Ntsebeza 2007; Hendricks, Ntsebeza & Helliker 2013; Jara 2014). The agri-food complex as a whole, including activities upstream and downstream of farming, was also highly centralised. A number of institutions, like marketing and producer cooperatives, credit bodies and marketing boards, were established during apartheid to support the white commercial farming sector, to reduce reliance for food on international trade in the context of sanctions, and to regulate food price levels, partly in the interests of reproducing a cheap labour force. Beginning in the 1980s, significant restructuring of agriculture began to take place. Most of the large cooperatives that dominated input supplies and marketing of produce were allowed to privatise and register on the stock exchange as private companies and to transnationalise their operations (Satgar 2011). This privatisation of cooperatives 'permitted white agriculture to reposition itself and privately appropriate the congealed value of decades of state support and monopoly control over entire nodes of the value chain' (Greenberg 2010: 5). Liberalisation and deregulation resulted in increased concentration throughout the agro-food system, with the balance of power shifting towards corporate retailers and brand owners and away from agricultural producers (Bernstein 2015; Greenberg 2010). This has given rise to sharp contradictions in South Africa's agro-food system across the spectrum, from patterns of land ownership and rural class relations to ownership and control in the food value chain, and the associated social effects thereof. The result is that most of the production, processing, distribution and retailing of food is controlled by a small number of corporations with inordinate power in the food system, deepening the commodification of food.

As noted, the food crisis is integrally connected to the climate and ecological crisis. South Africa is no exception. The country remains a major emitter of greenhouse gases, and its fossil fuel reliance continues to drive rising electricity costs (hitting the poor hardest) and to destroy water resources and agricultural capacity (Gore & McDaid 2013; Greenpeace 2012). At the same time, South Africa's industrial agricultural system contributes to climate change through its reliance on fossil fuels, and is vulnerable to climate change impacts (WWF 2014).

South Africa's food system is therefore unsafe, unjust and unsustainable (Cock 2015) and is failing to meet the food needs of all South Africans, in line with their constitutional right to food. South Africa's inequalities have consistently driven social instability in the form of open protest, as well as crime, violence against women and children, xenophobia and racial division. Some commentators are increasingly starting to point towards hunger as a key driver of escalating social instability (Cock 2015; WWF 2014). One activist argues that 'service delivery protests' are in fact 'food riots' (Mukaddam 2015). These forms of protest have been located as part of a 'rebellion of the poor' (Alexander 2010), and employ relatively dramatic tactics aimed at capturing government attention but usually last for only a few days. However, this frame of analysis captures only a specific dimension of resistance and mass politics in South Africa. Vishwas Satgar (2015) argues that post-1994 a number of movements and campaigns have struggled around the points of systemic crises in a concerted, sustained manner informed by a politics of transformative alternatives, in ways not captured by Peter Alexander's concept of 'rebellion of the poor'. Beyond localised sporadic outbursts, they undertake mass popular education and adopt a flexible repertoire of tactics, including organising activities aimed at meeting community needs. While such campaigns and movements are networked and operate nationally, they are grounded in communities as the site of the crisis of social reproduction. In the next section, we further analyse this form of politics by focusing on the case of food. We explore how food sovereignty and the solidarity economy represent one such form of transformative politics that, grounded in communities but nationally networked, has the potential to bridge the divide between work and community, and social struggle over these realms. Based on participant observation and a selection of interviews, we argue that the alternatives of food sovereignty and the solidarity economy exist in various forms through community-based organisations (CBOs), social movements, farmers' movements and the landless as part of a transformative response to multiple crises in South African society.

EMERGENCE OF THE SOUTH AFRICAN FOOD SOVEREIGNTY CAMPAIGN

The development of alternatives around food and land has been ongoing in post-apartheid South Africa. They are struggles that are not as openly explosive as the 'rebellion of the poor' but are an important dimension through which grassroots organisations and movements have been strategically organising, sometimes with the assistance of non-governmental organisations (NGOs). Some have specifically framed their work in terms of food sovereignty while others have not necessarily adopted it as a frame of struggle and vision, but both engage in building alternatives around the crisis, specifically in relation to food. These struggles in the food system have included farmworker campaigns, land struggles, localised seed-saving initiatives, farmers' cooperatives, and advancing agro-ecological training, knowledge and production as an alternative to industrial agriculture. Transformative politics over land and agriculture has thus been ongoing at various levels, and SAFSC[2] represents one attempt at contributing to building a politics of transformative alternatives around the question of food in South Africa.

The SAFSC emerged from discussions, strategies, education and grassroots work in the Solidarity Economy Movement (SEM).[3] The SEM attempted to advance a grassroots approach to cooperative movement building in South Africa in response to the state's failed top-down approach. A grassroots NGO, the Cooperative and Policy Alternative Centre, has been working to support cooperatives and develop educational tools for cooperatives since 1999. In 2010 it published a grassroots activist guide on the solidarity economy and made a call to grassroots movements and organisations to advance the solidarity economy from below in South Africa. In 2011 it hosted an international conference on the solidarity economy in Johannesburg, which was attended by activists, cooperators and researchers involved in the solidarity economy from various parts of the world and South Africa. The conference deliberated on developing understandings of the solidarity economy and generated a strategic approach to advancing such an economy in South Africa. An important component of this strategy was to build a food sovereignty campaign as a campaign of the SEM.

This resulted in grassroots engagements and work around developing the thrust of food sovereignty in existing local struggles and solidarity economy movement building in fifteen local sites across South Africa. This work was connected through national conversations and platforms such as the 2013 National Solidarity Economy Conference. The anti-systemic ideas of the solidarity economy and food sovereignty have also been connected to the wider project of democratic eco-socialism through debates and envisioning the future while transforming the present now (see, for example, *Solidarity Economy News* No. 5, 2013).[4]

At the annual assembly of the SEM at the end of 2014, a further strategic framework and proposed programme of action for advancing the food sovereignty campaign was deliberated on and finalised. In addition, provincial dialogues on the right to food were undertaken throughout 2014 by a coalition of organisations to explore the dimensions of hunger and food system challenges experienced by various sectors of society, including small farmers, the urban poor, trade unions and the religious sector. This culminated in a Right to Food National Conference in November 2014, where the need for convergence and joint action was highlighted. The campaign was launched at the Food Sovereignty Campaign Assembly in February 2015. Despite important work around alternatives and struggles in land, food and agriculture in post-apartheid South Africa, with some organisations and movements framing their struggles in terms of food sovereignty, it was felt by some that there could be more convergence and coordination on a national level between these struggles, which are nonetheless closely aligned in terms of objectives and ideals (Interview, SAFSC 2, Johannesburg, 23 June 2015). As such, the campaign emerging from the SEM aimed to bring organisations and movements in South Africa fighting such food sovereignty struggles into a national platform. The assembly that took place in February thus brought together over fifty movements and organisations, including CBOs, small farmers' organisations and movements, cooperatives, environmental justice organisations and land and agrarian organisations. It involved presentations on the various key problems in our food system followed by intense group engagement. Together with a proposed programme of action, the assembly decided on the strategic focus of campaigning for 2015. It thus declared:

> Our campaign seeks to unify struggles on the ground and progressive social forces to ensure food sovereignty is placed on the national agenda and is an alternative way forward for our food system. We are not simply calling for technical solutions for households to access food as encapsulated in the government's recently proposed *Food Security and Nutrition Policy* and *Implementation Plan*. We reject the latter and instead are calling for the deep transformation of our food system by breaking the control of food corporations, repositioning the state to realise the Constitutional right to food and as part of creating the conditions and space for the emergence of food sovereignty alternatives from below.[5]

Building power for transformation and commoning

The SAFSC thus represents an attempt to contest and build power to transform the food system through grassroots mobilisation, initiative and action. Understanding the potential and the means for social transformation thus rests on an understanding of power that goes beyond purely revolutionary notions of radical change. This approach rests on a relatively singular notion of power as embedded in the state and capitalist class, and hence the necessity of revolutionary uprising to seize this power on behalf of the working class. However, translated into practice, this has resulted largely in the failed socialist experiments of the twentieth century, thus necessitating a rethink of the horizons and means for radical social change, including by many radical grassroots movements across the globe. Some of the most radical anti-capitalist social movements today, like La Via Campesina, have developed a form of activism and politics through practice and engagement that seeks to build power to push back the frontiers of capitalism and actively construct an alternative – hence its clear articulation and constant deliberation on the concept of food sovereignty. These movements thus rest on a more nuanced notion of anti-capitalist power and the means of building it. Drawing on the experience of the Zapatistas,

John Holloway (2002) has called this a politics that aims to 'change the world without taking power'. Olivier de Schutter has applied this understanding to the global food sovereignty movement, arguing that 'Changing society without seizing power is what food sovereignty movements are about'.[6]

However, the SEM did not eschew power but actively articulated a transformative understanding of power that strategically guides and informs practice (COPAC 2010). Capitalism inherently undermines the commons (Harvey 2011) and hence defending and constructing the commons is a key form of building power against the forces of capitalism. This involves understanding the potential to build structural power, in which alternative structures such as worker cooperatives, community markets, seed banks and the like are built to provide alternatives to the structures of the capitalist economy. As an activist in the campaign, a small farmer from Botshabelo in the Free State province, put it:

> We want to dismantle those food regimes that are controlled by the big mighty corporations that are dominating the food prices, and also to give us platform as marginalised people to decide how our food should look like … I want to advance this issue of food in our community so that my community knows exactly what food sovereignty is and also to build the solidarity economy to advance our needs, more especially to have access to a market, to produce things ourselves and distribute to our own market. (Interview, SAFSC 1, Johannesburg, 22 June 2015)

Food sovereignty for many in the campaign is thus also about constructing a structural alternative through alternative means of food provisioning.

This aspect of mobilisation relates to movement power, which rests on organising communities around the solidarity economy and food sovereignty alternatives, bringing together into a movement all actors that are working on and contributing to building such alternatives, and thus building power. Direct power involves actions that build awareness in society and directly confront power through open activism and public education. Symbolic power is the power of the alternative, grounded in creating viable options and practising the values and principles of the solidarity economy alternative. This conception of power was taken into the SAFSC's plan of action, resulting in two courses of action. The first is to directly confront and challenge, on specific issues, the state and corporations in the food sector for their role in reproducing the hunger crisis. The second is to actively promote and build the alternative. For example, to openly challenge the use of genetically modified organisms (GMOs) in the food system through movement and direct power, but also to build structural power by, for example, promoting seed sovereignty (farmer control over seed) through seed banks.

These understandings of power therefore form a key link between food sovereignty and the solidarity economy. A third critical dimension that the campaign aims to advance is agro-ecology. Food sovereignty is thus seen as part of the solution to climate change. As the Declaration of the Food Sovereignty Campaign argues:

> Climate shocks are already impacting negatively on our food system with volatile food prices, droughts, heavy rainfall and flooding. This necessitates advancing food sovereignty, to ensure our food and water needs are not compromised and ordinary citizens have the means to meet food production and consumption needs on their terms in the midst of the climate crisis.[7]

The climate crisis poses a transformational necessity to shift our food production systems away from the ecologically unsustainable model of industrial agriculture. This has given rise to the promotion of agro-ecology as a critical dimension of transformed food systems. Those in the campaign recognise that industrial agriculture is ecologically unsustainable and that it is therefore critical to advance forms of food production without 'destroying the environment but to plant in a natural way, to look after nature because at the end of the day if the plants are destroyed, and the environment are destroyed, and the ozone layer are destroyed what will happen?' (Interview, SAFSC 2, Johannesburg, 23 June 2015). Agro-ecology is therefore a method of food production that is grounded in ecology, respects natural systems and harnesses natural processes for biological control and increased productivity (COPAC 2014). Its actual practices differ according to agro-ecological and geographical context, as well as histories and traditions of food production. However, it draws on existing and traditional farmer knowledge, as well as farmer-led science, for constantly improving techniques. Due to its low dependence on external inputs and its use of organic processes, it is not reliant on fossil fuels, as industrial agriculture is, and so is a critical response to the need to reduce emissions in the context of the climate crisis. It has also proven to be more resilient than conventional farming systems (Holt-Giménez 2006). The principles and practices of agro-ecology lend themselves to a more democratic mode of production, and localising its practice to decentralise and build social control over this form of food production is seen as a key step in mitigating and adapting to the climate crisis. A number of organisations and small farmers in the campaign have been at the forefront of promoting agro-ecology as a practice in South Africa, and so the campaign is well positioned to advance this as an alternative for the South African food system.

Building a grassroots campaign

The campaign assembly deliberated on ensuring national-level coordination of the campaign and elected a national coordinating committee. Their tasks include overseeing the national interventions of the campaign such as the website, social media, media engagements and national organising. However, in order to effectively advance an alternative in South Africa around the forms of power outlined above, it is critical that the campaign is rooted in communities and local-level struggles, where the impacts of the skewed food system are felt most keenly.

A notable feature of the campaign that emerged over the course of 2015 is its embeddedness in communities through local activism and in forms that suit the context of specific communities. Thus, while the campaign agreed at the first assembly that the key issues to focus on in 2015 would be high food prices and lack of land and agrarian transformation, local practice tended to diverge along various aspects of food sovereignty. For example, in some places the focus has been on developing agro-ecological production; in others, it has focused on education around seed issues and seed saving; and in yet others it has focused on the issue of land. For example, in the case of Botshabelo in the Free State, they are taking the issue of high food prices and lack of land and agrarian transformation forward through the struggle over commonage land and state support for farmers on such land in order to produce more affordable and nutritious food for their community. The important point is that the campaign has provided activists with a wealth of information, possibilities and networks enabling them to take forward issues in campaign building that they see as aligning with the needs and interests of their organisations and communities.

A key tactic for building the campaign at the grassroots that emerged during 2015 was exchange visits. Such visits are deliberately aimed at decentring knowledge production and sharing in the campaign. They involve campaign activists travelling to one another to share knowledge and training, as opposed to only 'experts' delivering such information. This is based on the recognition that there is a significant commons of knowledge, capacity and experience within the campaign that can be harnessed through activists learning from one another. These exchange visits have become one of the most highly regarded and sought-after practices in the campaign. This is unsurprising given the power of horizontal, farmer-to-farmer, practical demonstration and learning, as illustrated by Eric Holt-Giménez (2006) in the case of Latin America. One campaign activist, Nosintu Mcimeli, described an exchange visit in which two small farmers came to give training on agro-ecology and seed saving to farmers in her village:

> The information was too much but the excitement went on when these two ladies took turns on seed banking. We were all overwhelmed and thankful for the info. You could see the amazement when we were shown all the different seeds that are there for us to try and plant in our village in order to take care of our land, families and promote food sovereignty. (Email communication, 29 September 2015)

She went on to describe further activities undertaken and the importance of the exchange visit in contributing to the larger project of building momentum towards food sovereignty in her village. Her work has included organising the people she is working with into a forum, as a space for planning and building the campaign in a collective manner. The key methodology being evolved for localised campaign building is the establishment of food sovereignty forums as important spaces for bringing together actors in the community to be part of advancing the campaign, planning, education and problem solving. At the time of writing, processes to establish these forums were ongoing. In practice, these forums have been used as information and networking platforms, established to address particular challenges and problems faced by the supporters of the forum. The forum objectives can extend to provide educational and learning materials around issues related to the struggles, and valuable strategic planning and coordination of activities and actions.

Popular education for commoning

Food sovereignty is a global discourse and practice of struggle that arose out of particular historical and political circumstances. However, it resonates with the struggles of farmers, the hungry, the landless and the poor and is hence a grass-roots discourse and practice grounded in a transformative politics. A critical common feature of struggles such as these is that, in various forms, they defend and promote the commons as a source of sustenance, cohesion and democracy (Klein 2001). Furthermore, transformative politics is grounded in a high level of consciousness by activists themselves, and therefore rests on constant learning as a key basis for struggle. As such, a significant thrust of the campaign has been popular education through creating a knowledge commons. This has involved developing activist guides that, based on popular education principles, explore the key aspects of food sovereignty and the solidarity economy, and rounds of localised workshops based on these guides. As part of the commoning practice in the campaign, these resources are made freely and openly available in hardcopy and on an internet platform.[8] They have also been taken into a number of activist schools and used to further build an activist core in the campaign. Activist schools provide a space where knowledge is shared horizontally between activists, trainers and resources.

Popular educational resources are developed as part of the commons, and the resources deal with developing and expanding the commons itself. For example, in 2016 the SAFSC released a guide on seed saving (COPAC 2016). Seed saving is critical in dealing with the impacts of climate change as it is one way in which traditional and ecologically suitable and resilient varieties of crops can be reproduced and strengthened. The guide was developed through a workshop with seed-saving practitioners and small farmers who offered their knowledge. Developing capacity to defend and grow the seed commons is thus an act of resistance against the capitalist penetration of agriculture and food systems, and provides an important dimension to advancing alternatives to the climate crisis as well as corporate power.

Popular education is a creative and varied process. On 16 October 2015, World Food Day, the SAFSC hosted a food sovereignty festival. The aim was to 'celebrate people's alternatives to the unjust food system'.[9] The event was hosted in partnership with the Greenhouse Project, an initiative in the inner city of Johannesburg that was established in the early 2000s as a site to construct and demonstrate sustainable food, energy and construction. The festival combined celebration with education and learning – conceptual, visual and practical. The programme involved a combination of parallel panel discussions, workshops, practical demonstrations and documentary screenings on topics such as corporate power in the food system, GMOs, climate change and food sovereignty, agro-ecology, seed saving, recycling, and so on. The festival was therefore a nodal space for bringing together the many strands of practice, ideas and politics that constitute food sovereignty and disseminating them through the participants that attended the festival. The importance of this event to the popular learning process proved indispensable. As one participant said, 'Yesterday I was blind but today my eyes are open.'[10] This process, and the festival itself, was also part of advancing a knowledge and practice commons through the campaign, bringing together knowledge, experience, practice and people into the open space of the festival, where information, experience and practice (and food!) were shared openly and freely towards the goal of advancing food sovereignty politics.

Shifting the public debate

Critical to the aims of the SAFSC is to challenge the 'hunger denialism' in South Africa, which is also seen in various levels of the mainstream media and its silence on hunger and its causes. The SAFSC has thus deliberately engaged the media – through national and local radio interviews, newspaper articles and interviews on television news – to advance a critical perspective on the hunger crisis and the frame of food sovereignty as central to thinking about alternatives. A number of organisations in the campaign have also made headway in discussing the campaign and food issues on local radio stations.

Key to pushing the prevalence of hunger into the public discourse is to surface the voices of the hungry themselves. In this regard, the SAFSC has also tried to create its own platforms for airing the voices of the hungry. In May 2015, the SAFSC hosted a People's Tribunal on Hunger, Food Prices and Landlessness, the aim of which was to 'put food corporations and the state on trial for their role in perpetuating hunger in South Africa and provide a platform for grassroots voices to communicate their experiences'.[11] The tribunal consisted of twenty-one people giving their testimonies on experiences of hunger, rising food prices and landlessness, as well as ten 'expert witnesses' who helped to provide further information on the broader context in which these experiences of hunger manifest. These testimonies were listened to by an audience and a panel of 'judges', which included representatives from the South African Human Rights Commission, religious organisations and the Right2Know Campaign.[12]

The hungry told how 'hunger is the middle name of the country we are living in' (SAFSC 2015: 5). A woman from the ranks of the millions of hungry in South Africa described what it is like to try to raise children in the midst of hunger:

> After my husband was retrenched from work, then hunger came to my house. I then started to think of how to get rid of this hunger. I started

cutting aloe. We get the juice out of it and sell it. Those who buy from us also sell it. We take that juice into 5 litres. It's very difficult to fill 5 litres, especially in winter. Where there is no water we sell it for R60 per container. When it's mixed with water it goes to R45. We do this to have something to eat at home. We wake up very early at 5:30 and prepare leftover food for the children. I managed to pick some chillies sometimes so that we have something to eat now. My mother helps me take care of my kids. She also doesn't have much income because she is a domestic worker. It is painful when you get home and your kids are hungry – you can't even think. When you leave your children at home, you worry about what you will bring when you come back. Even at supper time, your children notice the others next door eating. You let them play outside to see if the neighbour will prepare something for them to eat. (SAFSC 2015: 7)

The media was invited to attend and report on the testimonies at the tribunal, but there was a large media blackout surrounding the event, confirming the necessity of occasions such as the tribunal to raise the profile of the hunger crisis in the public conversation. After the first day of the tribunal, SAFSC activists descended on the head office of a major newspaper publisher to protest the mainstream media's uncritical reproduction of industrial agriculture and the corporate food system's perspectives.

Because of the role of the media, the SAFSC has also developed its own media and information through, for example, a recently launched website and a newsletter. The website is aimed at being a key campaign-building tool that facilitates learning and information access, links movements and organisations constructing the food sovereignty alternative, and provides campaign and movement-building tools. The campaign recognises the necessity of producing information as a means of shifting public discourse and linking it to practical struggles and movement building.

CONFRONTING THE DROUGHT AND THE CLIMATE CRISIS: CONVERGENCE OF ANTI-SYSTEMIC MOVEMENTS?

As has been argued, the food, climate, energy, water and social crises are all closely connected. This was starkly illustrated by the drought that hit South Africa in 2015 and continued into 2016. A clear illustration of the impacts of the climate crisis, the drought led to drastically rising food prices that hit the poor hardest. It also put a stop to production by many small farmers throughout the country who simply ran out of water, and revealed a shamefully inadequate state response to the drought specifically, and to the climate crisis generally. The convergence of multiple crises necessitates a convergence by anti-systemic movements of ideas, practices and activism to challenge the powers driving the crisis and to articulate and advance alternatives. An important part of this is defending and reclaiming the commons.[13]

In May 2016, SAFSC, climate and environmental justice organisations, Earthlife Africa, Mining Affected Communities United in Action, the Right2Know Campaign and the National Union of Metalworkers of South Africa cooperated to coordinate three days of activism that joined up the food and climate crises and the social and environmental injustices of extractivism. A speak-out held in the coal-mining town of Emalahleni gave a platform to communities affected by coal mining to voice their suffering and connected the issues of water and coal extraction, with its massive contribution to climate change, with the impacts of climate change itself. The second day was held at the Constitutional Court, where a speak-out on the drought allowed for small farmers from South Africa and from other southern African countries to tell of the extensive hardship that the climate change-induced drought had wrought on small farmers in the region, leading to rising food prices and growing hunger. The information from this speak-out was drafted into a memorandum and handed to the supermarket chain Pick n Pay at the end of a bread march, which was aimed at highlighting the scandal of the super-profits earned by corporations in the food sector alongside massive and growing hunger, and the impacts of this on poor communities, workers and rural dwellers. A memorandum was also handed to the management of the University of the Witwatersrand (Wits) which, like most other university campuses in the country, experiences stark levels of student hunger. Through the Inala Forum for Food Sovereignty and Climate Justice, students demanded that Wits work towards 'zero hunger at Wits and an end to dangerous greenhouse gas contributions from Wits', and that it show institutional leadership in reducing its emissions and tackling the climate and hunger crisis (Inala & SAFSC 2016: 1).

These days of action highlighted the potential for uniting and building a climate justice platform in South Africa to advance transformative alternatives and the just transition from below. However, such linkages should be deepened, which requires overcoming challenges to the building of these linkages, such as territorialism in civil society and the current nature of trade unions and their ability to practically involve themselves in issues connected to, but outside of, the workplace, so that red–green alliances may be strengthened in the context of climate change and the urgent need for transformed food systems.

CONCLUSION

This chapter has argued that food sovereignty and the solidarity economy present important grassroots alternatives that can be part of deepening a just transition by challenging existing structures of production and consumption. This requires building various forms of power to advance alternatives. The case of food, which is at the centre of the climate crisis, demonstrates how food sovereignty presents an alternative vision for a just, democratic and sustainable world. In this context, transformative alternatives that challenge existing structures of power and control, and portend non-capitalist alternatives, although not sufficiently acknowledged and studied, are in the making at the grassroots level in various ways. For example, through various tactics, the SAFSC is adopting a range of approaches centred around raising awareness about the challenge of hunger and its causes; challenging existing structures of injustice in the food system; and proposing and enacting alternatives to the unjust food system that signal a shift away from the commodifying and centralising tendencies of the capitalist food system, towards collective, democratic initiatives. A just transition requires the construction of the commons, and the solidarity economy and food sovereignty can provide important means with which to do so. However, this can only be achieved through mass struggle from below in order to deepen the solidarity economy and food sovereignty logics, and to build power to advance the commons. As the SAFSC continues to build, this is its key task.

NOTES

1   McCarthy (2005) and Harvey (2011) discuss the questions of defining in practice what the commons is and the matter of the institutional arrangements to defend, secure and propagate the commons.
2   All SAFSC documents cited in this chapter are available at www.safsc.org.za (accessed 21 August 2017).

3   The SEM is a loose association of like-minded movements (such as waste pickers and unemployed people's organisations), NGOs and community organisations. Its emphasis has been on learning from practice, sharing experiences and campaigning for worker cooperatives and food sovereignty.
4   All issues of the newsletter can be found at www.sem.org.za (site in the process of being constructed as at August 2017).
5   See 'Declaration of the South African Food Sovereignty Campaign and Alliance', http://www.copac.org.za/files/Food%20Sovereignty%20Assembly%20Declaration. pdf (accessed 21 August 2017), pp. 1–2.
6   O. de Schutter, 'Don't let food be the problem', *Foreign Policy*, 2015, http:// foreignpolicy.com/2015/07/20/starving-for-answers-food-water-united-nations/ (accessed 20 July 2015).
7   'Declaration of the South African Food Sovereignty Campaign and Alliance', p. 1.
8   See www.safsc.org.za and www.copac.org.za (both accessed 21 August 2017).
9   SAFSC flyer advertising the Food Sovereignty Festival, 2015.
10 Scribe's notes from SAFSC Assembly, 17 October 2015, p.1.
11 SAFSC, 'Invitation to the media to attend people's tribunal on hunger, food prices and landlessness', https://www.facebook.com/safoodsovereignty/posts/1580464838891022 (accessed 21 August), p. 1.
12 A freedom of expression and democratic information campaign.
13 See Klein (2001) for a discussion on the importance of a convergence of movements fighting struggles over the commons at local levels.

REFERENCES

Alexander, P. 2010. 'Rebellion of the poor: South Africa's service delivery protests – A preliminary analysis', *Social Movement Studies*, 27 (123): 25–40.
Alkon, A.H. 2013. 'Food justice, food sovereignty and the challenge of neoliberalism'. Paper presented at Food Sovereignty: A Critical Dialogue, International Conference, 14–15 September, Yale University.
Bernstein, H. 2015. 'Commercial farming and agribusiness in South Africa since 1994'. In *Land Divided, Land Restored: Land Reform in South Africa for the 21st Century*, edited by B. Cousins and C. Walker. Johannesburg: Jacana Media, pp. 104–119.
Cock, J. 2015. 'The food crisis in contemporary South Africa'. Presentation at workshop The Future of Food 2015–2030, March, Johannesburg.
COPAC (Cooperative and Policy Alternative Centre). 2010. *Building a Solidarity Economy Movement: A Guide for Grassroots Activism*. Johannesburg: COPAC.
COPAC. 2014. *Food Sovereignty for the Right to Food: A Guide for Grassroots Activism*. Johannesburg: COPAC.
COPAC. 2016. *Advancing Food Sovereignty through Seed Saving: An Activist Guide*. Johannesburg: COPAC.
Field, T. and Bell, B. 2013. *Harvesting Justice: Transforming Food, Land and Agricultural Systems in the Americas*. New Orleans, LA: Other Worlds.
George, S. 2010. *Whose Crisis, Whose Future? Towards a Greener, Fairer, Richer World*. Cambridge: Polity Press.
Gore, T. and McDaid, L. 2013. *'You can't eat electricity': Why tackling inequality and hunger should be at the heart of low carbon development in South Africa*. Oxfam

Discussion Paper, Oxfam International. Accessed 20 August 2017, http://www20. iadb.org/intal/catalogo/PE/2013/12301.pdf.

Greenberg, S. 2010. 'Contesting the food system in South Africa: Issues and opportunities'. PLAAS Research Report No. 42. Bellville: Institute for Poverty, Land and Agrarian Studies.

Greenpeace. 2012. *Water Hungry Coal: Burning South Africa's Water to Produce Electricity.* Johannesburg: Greenpeace Africa.

Hall, R. and Ntsebeza, L. 2007. 'Introduction'. In *The Land Question in South Africa: The Challenge of Transformation and Redistribution*, edited by L. Ntsebeza and R. Hall. Cape Town: HSRC Press, pp. 1–24.

Harvey, D. 2011. 'The future of the commons', *Radical History Review*, 109: 101–107.

HBF (Heinrich Böll Foundation). 2014. *Resource Politics for a Fair Future: A Memorandum of the Heinrich Böll Foundation.* Volume 38 of the Publication Series on Ecology. Berlin: HBF.

Hendricks, F., Ntsebeza, L. and Helliker, K. 2013. 'Land questions in South Africa'. In *The Promise of Land: Undoing a Century of Dispossession in South Africa*, edited by F. Hendricks, L. Ntsebeza and K. Helliker. Johannesburg: Jacana Media, pp. 1–23.

Hickel, J. 2016. 'The true extent of global poverty and hunger: Questioning the good news narrative of the Millennium Development Goals', *Third World Quarterly*, 37 (5): 749–767.

Holloway, J. 2002. *Change the World without Taking Power: The Meaning of Revolution Today.* London: Pluto Press.

Holt-Giménez, E. 2006. *Campesino A Campesino: Voices from Latin America's Farmer to Farmer Movement for Sustainable Agriculture.* Oakland, CA: Food First Books.

HSRC and MRC (Human Sciences Research Council and Medical Research Council). 2013. *The South African National Health and Nutrition Examination Survey SANHANES-1.* Cape Town: HSRC Press. Accessed 19 August 2017, http://www. hsrc.ac.za/uploads/pageNews/72/SANHANES-launch%20edition%20(online%20 version).pdf.

Inala and SAFSC (South African Food Sovereignty Campaign). 2016. 'Joint SAFSC and Inala memorandum to Wits University: Towards zero hunger and zero carbon emissions'. 13 May. Accessed 19 August 2017, http://www.safsc.org.za/wp-content/ uploads/2016/05/SAFSC-INALA-memorandum.pdf.

Jara, M. 2014. 'The solidarity economy response to the agrarian crisis in South Africa'. In *The Solidarity Economy Alternative: Emerging Theory and Practice*, edited by V. Satgar. Pietermaritzburg: University of KwaZulu-Natal Press, pp. 227–248.

Klein, N. 2001. 'Reclaiming the commons', *New Left Review*, 9: 81–89.

Linebaugh, P. 2014. *Stop, Thief! The Commons, Enclosures, and Resistance.* Oakland, CA: PM Press.

Marais, H. 2011. *South Africa Pushed to the Limit: The Political Economy of Change.* London: Zed Books.

McCarthy, J. 2005. 'Commons as counterhegemonic projects', *Capitalism Nature Socialism*, 16 (1): 9–24.

McMichael, P. 2009. 'A food regime genealogy', *Journal of Peasant Studies*, 36 (1): 139–169.

Mukaddam, I. 2015. 'Presentation on rising food prices in South Africa'. South African Food Sovereignty Campaign Assembly, 28 February–1 March.

Patel, R. 2009. *The Value of Nothing: How to Reshape Market Society and Redefine Democracy*. London: Portobello Books.

Satgar, V. 2008. 'Neoliberalised South Africa: Labour and the roots of passive revolution', *Labour, Capital and Society*, 41 (2): 38–69.

Satgar, V. 2011. 'Challenging the globalized agro-food complex: Farming cooperatives and the emerging solidarity economy in South Africa', *WorkingUSA: The Journal of Labour and Society*, 14: 177–190.

Satgar, V. 2014. *The Solidarity Economy Alternative: Emerging Theory and Practice*. Scottsville: University of KwaZulu-Natal Press.

Satgar, V. 2015. 'Radical agendas #6: Where to for South Africa's Left?' Accessed 19 August 2017, http://roape.net/2016/01/27/radical-agendas-6-where-to-for-south-africas-left/.

SAFSC (South African Food Sovereignty Campaign). 2015. 'People's Tribunal on Hunger, Food Prices and Landlessness: Report'. Accessed 19 August 2017, http://safsc.org.za/wp-content/uploads/2015/09/Tribunal-Report.pdf.

Wainwright, H. 2014. 'Notes on the political economy of creativity and solidarity'. In *The Solidarity Economy Alternative: Emerging Theory and Practice*, edited by V. Satgar. Scottsville: University of KwaZulu-Natal Press, pp. 64–100.

Williams, M. 2014. 'The solidarity economy and social transformation'. In *The Solidarity Economy Alternative: Emerging Theory and Practice*, edited by V. Satgar. Scottsville: University of KwaZulu-Natal Press, pp. 37–63.

Wittman, H., Desmarais, A. and Wiebe, N. 2010. 'The origins and potential of food sovereignty'. In *Food Sovereignty: Reconnecting Food, Nature and Community*, edited by H. Wittman, A. Desmarais and N. Wiebe. Halifax and Winnipeg: Fernwood Publishing, pp. 1–14.

WWF (World Wildlife Fund-SA). 2014. *The Food Energy Water Nexus: Understanding South Africa's Most Urgent Sustainability Challenge*. Cape Town: WWF-SA.

INTERVIEWS

SAFSC 1, Stay City, Johannesburg, 22 June 2015.
SAFSC 2, Stay City, Johannesburg, 23 June 2015.

15

ECO-CAPITALIST CRISES IN THE 'BLUE ECONOMY': OPERATION PHAKISA'S SMALL, SLOW FAILURES

Desné Masie and Patrick Bond

The mid-2014 South African introduction of the 'big fast results' methodology behind Operation Phakisa ('hurry up' in Sesotho) – applied in the first instance to the ocean's 'blue economy' – followed President Jacob Zuma's 2013 visit to Malaysia, whose leaders applied the strategy to economic policy. The nomenclature, process and strategy reflected the increasing desperation and quickening of what might be considered an 'extractivist' metabolism (Martinez-Alier 2002) between global capital, local ruling classes, society and nature (Terreblanche 2017).

Though Zuma's (2014) stated objectives of 'growing' ocean-related economic activities – especially shipping, boat construction and offshore oil and gas exploration – are running afoul of global economics, the conversion of nature into capital and attempts at 'deriving value' – as Zuma (2014) put it – from ecosystem services are increasingly common internationally. But the Phakisa rush follows a period of upsurging fusions between what Jacklyn Cock (2004) calls 'red, brown and green' resistance movements, including mineworkers, fisherfolk, farmers, feminists and climate activists, to name a few of the more prominent, some of which aim to introduce strategies associated with 'just transition' philosophy.

Regardless of the capacity of bottom-up resistance, Phakisa soon appeared to be on the verge of failing due to the trajectory of crashing commodity prices *from above*, as China's growth slows and as the global North's financial speculators moved from one bubble to the next. Shipping, mining, smelting and petroleum industry firms were demolished in the world's main stock markets during 2015. Either this stage of world capitalist crisis would require from South Africa's elites a more intense extraction of the country's resource base, or an entirely new trajectory, aimed at accumulation via routes other than what Ben Fine and Zavareh Rustomjee (1996) termed the 'minerals–energy complex' (MEC).

Recall the exhortation from leading business publisher Peter Bruce to 'please, mine more and faster and ship what we mine cheaper and faster'.[1] Economic policy makers soon moved to the very depths of their terrain: the 3.5 kilometre deep trenches below the treacherous Agulhas Current offshore of Durban. Rumoured to be full of oil and gas, along with the rest of the nearly 3 000 kilometre long coastline, the new opportunities for capital accumulation are setting climate activists against the world's biggest oil companies, at a time when the former are also slowly coming to grips with the durability of the South African ruling class's coal addiction, including exports through the Richards Bay and Durban ports.

In this chapter, we consider the oceans, specifically, and argue that the Phakisa concept of 'big fast results' has been characterised, in reality, by *small, slow failures* in planning and implementation, with miserable overall outcomes for the economy, polity, society and ecology. As political–economic constraints became acute, the Phakisa team reacted by downplaying the numerous environmental and democratic costs of the blue economy. The project's overhyped GDP-led evaluation of the oceans' potential did not sufficiently balance short-term economic and political gains – which are mainly grabbed by multinational corporations (in oil and shipping), political oligarchs and well-connected tenderpreneurs – against Phakisa's massive eco-social destruction.

To make this case, we first map out how Phakisa fits within the current political economy. Second, we explain the problems caused by shoreline expansion for ocean pollution and multilateral arrangements. Third, we show that notwithstanding environmental and economic risks that should have been vividly evident to planners in 2014, Phakisa has been overhyped to an extraordinary degree. Fourth, we explain the deeper-rooted crises of capital accumulation that threaten the viability of Phakisa. Fifth, we argue that Phakisa's top-down economic development strategy – in a setting characterised by insufficient democratic and diplomatic consultation, along with uncritical GDP evangelism – is already failing.

Finally, we contend that Phakisa's recklessness in relation to social justice, the environmental commons and meaningful economic empowerment will cost South Africa dearly. A just transition approach to *decarbonising* the ocean and coastline is needed. Otherwise, billions of rands are being thrown at the project not only under highly unfavourable global macro-economic conditions, but also at a time when climate change throws world trade into question (because of a future maritime carbon tax imposition). In addition, Phakisa will lead to economic losses being socialised and gains privatised, as is the case in so many state–market–society–nature relations.

SITUATING THE OCEANS ACCELERATOR IN AN EXTRACTIVE POLITICAL ECONOMY

A great many state subsidies are already dedicated to exploiting the ocean, in part by promoting minerals exports at all costs. Phakisa will accelerate this process not only by intensifying shipping, but by adding offshore oil and gas to the MEC. (Other elements such as micro-aquaculture entrepreneurialism are trivial in comparison, so we leave them to other critics.) Then finance minister Pravin Gordhan promised in his 2016 budget speech:

> Building on the Phakisa oceans economy initiative, a R9 billion investment in rig repair and maintenance facilities at Saldanha Bay is planned, and work has begun on a new gas terminal and oil and ship repair facilities at Durban. Transport and logistics infrastructure accounts for nearly R292 billion over the next three years ... Transnet is acquiring 232 diesel locomotives for its general freight business and 100 locomotives for its coal lines. (Gordhan 2016)

The profitability of those lines – from north-eastern South Africa to Richards Bay and Durban – depends upon coal's export potential. The first Presidential Infrastructure Coordinating Commission project (National Planning Commission 2012) anticipates eighteen billion tons becoming available for digging, transport and then shipping. Local ecological destruction and climate change were not considered worthy of mention. In mid-2011, export coal prices were US$120/ton and the rand was R6.3/US$. Although international coal prices fell to as low as US$50/ton, they recovered to US$75/ton by 2017 while the currency crashed in half to R13/US$, so in rand terms the R800 billion project appeared viable, although it has been delayed due to financing constraints. The US$5 billion loan, made by the Chinese state bank to Transnet at the 2013 Durban BRICS[2] summit for purchasing 1 064 coal-bearing locomotives capable of hauling three-kilometre-long trains, became a matter of intense controversy in 2017. It was revealed that the parastatal systematically overpaid (by US$1.3 billion) thanks to an apparently brazen backhander (of US$400 million) to the corruption-riddled Gupta network (one repeated in a Chinese sale of seven container cranes to Transnet for the Durban port, worth $92 million, of which $12 million was a kickback). In addition, many of the Chinese-made locomotives did not comply with localisation construction requirements (amaBhungane and Scorpio 2017a, 2017b).

Moreover, announced Gordhan (2016), the parastatal agency Transnet aimed to 'accelerate private sector participation in the ports and freight rail sector ... In taking this forward, we are able to draw on our experience in road-funding concessions'. The unfortunate reference was to the public–private partnership initiative known as 'e-tolling' in Gauteng province (especially the Johannesburg ring road and Pretoria highway). That project earned over R1 billion in 2011 alone for the Austrian company Kapsch TrafficCom that won the contract,[3] about the same amount Gauteng taxpayers paid in additional annual unbudgeted subsidies. Popular rejection of e-tolling continued through 2017, with less than a forty per cent payment rate.

Notwithstanding growing concerns around South Africa's fossil fuel addictions, Zuma (2014) announced more extraction opportunities through Phakisa: within six years, US$7 billion would be sunk in investments in thirty offshore oil and gas rigs by Total, ExxonMobil, Shell, Anadarko and other drillers, in search of nine billion barrels of oil and sixty trillion cubic feet of gas. A plethora of oil and gas platforms would accompany the refinery boom signalled in the 2012 National Development Plan (NDP), including a US$25 billion South Durban port-petrochemical complex expansion (the Presidential Infrastructure Coordinating Commission's second priority) featuring the doubling of refining and pumping capacity from Durban to the Gauteng market and an (imagined) eightfold rise in container traffic (National Planning Commission 2012).

As Phakisa emerged, Roger Southall (2015) documented how Zuma's patronage networks were placed under further stress because of South Africa's 'fiscal cliff'. The networks required the 'oil and gas bonanza' promised in what Jedrzej Frynas and George Paulo (2007) described as the 'new scramble for African oil'. In addition to polluting South African politics, these activities are threatening the very viability of the proximate seas – the Indian and Atlantic, and indeed the world's entire ocean body.

SHORELINE EXPANSION, OCEAN POLLUTION AND PHAKISA'S FOSSIL-EXTRACTION ACCELERATOR

In October 2014, Zuma offered a commitment to protect the environment by lowering the national economy's extreme carbon intensity:

> If all sectors implement the measures to fight climate change at the same time, together we can build the biggest mitigation buffer against climate change. We can save our country and the world for future generations. Our economy will become resilient to the possible effects of climate change only when we take bold steps like the reduction of emission of carbon dioxide and other gases that lead to increasing global temperatures. (Zuma 2014)

By then it was clear that pollution of the world's oceans – nature's main form of sequestering carbon dioxide – had reached dangerous levels of saturation, resulting in higher levels of acidification, rising temperatures (hence more intense hurricanes and typhoons), coral reef blanching and loss of marine micro species. The dumping of plastics and other pollutants in the ocean's gigantic 'sink' became so prolific by the early twenty-first century as to threaten the marine food chain, while secondary plastics – such as water bottles – fragment (due to ultraviolet rays) into microbial pieces of less than five millimetres, and are then ingested by zooplankton and fish. Phakisa is also reckless about the dangers of ocean phosphate mining. Prohibited in every other country in the world, three prospecting permits have been granted by the Department of Mineral Resources to allow prospectors to cut up the ocean floor with cylindrical drums studded with metal teeth, endangering fish stocks and increasing pollution.[4]

To address ocean pollution at this ecosystem-threatening scale, collaboration between national states is vital. The main multilateral ocean initiative was the 1982 United Nations Convention on the Law of the Sea, with its focus on capital's geopolitical and property-right imperatives. Dating to the seventeenth century's 'freedom of the seas', agreements on the extension of sovereign territorial coastline crept up from three nautical miles (4.8 km, a cannon shot's distance) to today's twelve nautical miles (22.2 km). Nearly all emerging national states made attempts to colonise ocean areas for the sake of protecting fish stocks and engaging in minerals exploitation. The United States led the extension of such claims out to the continental shelf in 1945, which in turn generated the argument that 200 nautical miles (370 km) would be the appropriate border for national sovereignty in the form of exclusive economic zones.

Here, a country can claim control over all marine resources, oil and gas, and minerals. South Africa's reaches out not only beyond its immediate mainland borders into an area of 1 069 million square kilometres, but since 2006 Pretoria has also claimed another 0.467 million square km around the Prince Edward and Marion islands. This grab was made, according to Petroleum Agency of South Africa chief executive Jack Holliday, because 'We hope, of course, to find oil and more exploitable gas. But much of the extended claim is in very deep water, more than 2.5 km, where hydrocarbon, gas hydrates, minerals and placer deposits are thought to exist' (SA Info 2006). Phakisa contemplates the extension of South Africa's continental shelf claim by around five per cent and this could lead to as yet untested diplomatic constraints (Van Wyk 2015).

Transnational agreements are vital to address border overlaps, especially with regard to pollution, systemic overfishing, shipping lane access, piracy and other aspects of ocean regulation. As the chair of the Global Ocean Commission, former South African finance and planning minister Trevor Manuel confessed,

> the inability of African countries to work together on this issue is what continues to hinder meaningful development and allows others to benefit from Africa's resources. The benefits of co-operation are not limited to coastal countries; the benefits are spread to neighbouring landlocked countries that rely on these ports for export and trade. (Philip 2014)

South Africa's 2002 New Partnership for Africa's Development reduced the scope for collaboration projects such as the 1980 Lagos Plan of Action and the 1989 African Alternative Framework to Structural Adjustment Programmes, which Pretoria's continental policy architects explicitly ignored (Bond 2005). The 2012 African Union 2050 Integrated Maritime Strategy sets as its main premise that Africa's maritime domain 'has vast potential for wealth creation', although also expresses concern about oceans in relation to

> virtually all major issues that Africa is confronted with, namely diverse illegal activities which include toxic waste dumping and discharge of oil, dealing in illicit crude oil, arms and drug trafficking, human trafficking and smuggling, piracy and armed robbery at sea, energy exploitation, climate change, environmental protection and conservation and safety of life and property at sea. (AU 2012: 9)

Less well articulated are costs associated with capital's impacts on coastal climate change. In addition to more powerful storms, ice melts caused by higher levels of atmospheric carbon dioxide are destroying glaciers and large parts of Antarctica, the Arctic and Greenland. As the ocean warms, water's physical mass expands and the sea level rises, in recent years by five millimetres per annum, the fastest rate ever recorded. Ecological crises caused by capital's externalisation of costs are exceptionally difficult to resolve, unlike other obvious maritime problems such as geographically specific piracy or border disputes. And it is here, too, that the Phakisa rhetoric of economic gain most explicitly runs up against the limits of ocean exploitation in a context of capital's global overaccumulation (i.e. over-capacity in relation to consumer buying power), especially in shipping and oil.

PHAKISA'S PROCESS

The glaring contradiction between South Africa's attempt to amplify capital accumulation through shipping, coal, oil and gas on the one hand, and the promise to 'build the biggest mitigation buffer' on the other, can in part be explained by the Phakisa oceans process that unfolded in July–August 2014 at Durban's Riverside Hotel. It was a helter-skelter, non-consultative, elite navel-gazing and ultimately unrealistic exercise, devoid of awareness of the capitalist crisis bearing down on South Africa's two oceans. At the time, mid-2014, the oil price, the world's demand for minerals and the main global shipping indices were already crashing, and the climate crisis was evident in worsening droughts and floods.

Yet at the Durban hotel, more than 650 experts and officials – with predictable race/class/gender biases – brainstormed an ocean commodification drive in which these crises were reduced to 'policy conflict' and hence the state's 'capacity to manage and mitigate the environmental impact' of Phakisa. For these techno-crats, South Africa's existing negative 'general public perception' about oil and gas exploration could be explained away – as was done in early Phakisa pres-entations (The Presidency of South Africa 2014) – mainly by the public's alleged 'general lack of knowledge' and 'lack of understanding' regarding the country's supposedly admirable governance systems, especially in regulating fossil fuels.

The main Phakisa activities Zuma expressed a desire to pursue – shipping (especially coal, platinum and iron ore), boat building and refurbishment, and offshore oil and gas exploration – were at that very moment in the process of plummeting to unprecedented low levels of profitability. Yet simultaneously, reflecting a predictable myopia in the business press, a flurry of excitement prevailed about the blue economy rising from two to four per cent of GDP from 2010 to the near future, once Phakisa delivers 'big fast results'. A journalist reported in the main newspaper chain:

> Phakisa is about tapping into our off-shore oil and gas reserves, which international oil giants say are enormously significant, as well as some other areas of our oceans' economy. The headline results are stagger-ing and suggest that if the resources tied up in our oceans are unlocked without any further delay, they have the potential to contribute approx-imately R177 billion to GDP in 20 years from now, compared to the current contribution of R54 billion.[5]

The country's most powerful corporate publisher, *Business Day*'s Peter Bruce, was effusive in mid-2015:

> Phakisa is a terrific idea. A little like tourism, it's a potential forex earner, an export, that doesn't even have to move. You just have to invest in it where it is. What could be more simple? … Phakisa holds open an opportunity to create new industrial and service industry value on a grand scale.[6]

CAPITALIST CRISES VISIT THE SEASHORES

Like most hopes for ocean riches, the contradictions of micro capitalism are on view in many of the cities Phakisa hopes will stitch down the broader investment fabric. These include Indian Ocean ports – Richards Bay, Durban, East London and Port Elizabeth – but it is at the global scale that the capitalist crisis is most debilitating. Those tendencies include a dramatic 2014/15 slow-down in global trade (UNCTAD 2016), declines in foreign direct investment (FDI) and cross-border financial asset holdings, and the associated overaccumulation of shipping capital, speculative currency crises and commodity price rises and falls.

Although unmentioned in Phakisa documentation, the mid-2008 peak for pricing the transport of a typical container across the world's main routes reflected the intense metabolism of commodity trading at the time. But measured as the Baltic Dry Index (the most reliable measure of container shipping capacity and pricing), the collapse exceeded ninety per cent within six months. The Baltic Dry Index level of around 12 000 in 2008 fell to below 300 by early 2016, as vast overcapacity came online. The Index subsequently rose back to the 1 000 level but new capacity continued to threaten industry upheaval, especially involuntary mergers and acquisitions. So-called 'post-Panamax' ships – carrying more than 5 000 containers (until 2015, the limits of the size that fit through the Panama Canal) – came to dominate world shipping, to the point that vessels with more than 10 000 containers were flooding the market. Such robotised ships carried only thirteen crew. But shallow berths characterise Durban, East London, Port Elizabeth and Cape Town (the four main port cities). There are only three deep-water ports in South Africa that can potentially handle the newer Supramax and Capesize ships (some now carrying 21 000 containers): Richards Bay, Coega and Saldanha (all far from the major markets) (Pieterse et al. 2016).

The shake-out of excess capacity that followed was uneven, and created havoc for massive port construction projects that Chinese state capital had promoted along its Maritime Silk Road. Fifty ports have annual container throughput of more than a million twenty-foot equivalent units, of which a large proportion are on the Chinese coast. Durban's 2.5 million containers a year represent the largest such facility in Africa. The NDP projected an increase in Durban's container processing to twenty million annually by 2040 (from 2.5 million in 2012), an estimate far out of line (by 150 per cent) with even the most optimistic growth figure generated by the shipping industry (National Planning Commission 2012).

One reason for sluggish container growth is the extreme expense associated with processing freight in the two main South African ports, Durban and

Cape Town: US$1 080 per container, making them the two most costly ports in the world (Pieterse et al. 2016). It is inconceivable that an additional US$25 billion in Durban port refurbishment and dig-out port investment (no doubt much greater sums, what with recent mega-project trends doubling or tripling original estimates) will cut operating and maintenance costs to competitive levels. Repaying the principle, interest on the capital and all the additional operating costs will force much higher container handling charges, leaving the likely prospect of another Durban white elephant (joining similar projects that were anticipated to earn profits – such as the airport, stadium, convention centre and marine entertainment complex – but which have needed multimillion dollar annual taxpayer bailouts). For these reasons, it was myopic for Zuma (2014) to declare:

> Compatriots, we were concerned that South Africa did not own vessels while we are surrounded by about three thousand kilometres of a coastline … Through the oceans economy segment of Operation Phakisa, we are trying to solve this challenge … I am pleased that two bulk carrier vessels have been registered in Port Elizabeth, and a third tanker in Cape Town under the South African flag.

Ship building in South Africa is impossible under conditions of world merchant-capital overaccumulation, in part because more than 1 400 dry bulk ships (fifteen per cent of the world fleet) were scrapped in 2016 (Ship & Bunker 2016),[7] and in part because of limited economies of scale within the local construction industry. This point was also recognised by Peter Bruce:

> One of the problems with any industrial effort in SA – and one the shipbuilders return to time and again – is the prices of marine plate, both aluminium or steel. All the shipbuilders complain that import parity pricing by local steel and aluminium producers hurts them … when your domestic market is only capable of ordering in small batches, those customers are never going to attract the discounts that really big orders do. Shipbuilders complain they cannot buy plate at a competitive price in SA. On finding the plate at a better price in Asia, it has more than once arrived in SA only to bear the name of a South African mill on it.[8]

Indeed, at that time, not only were the three main ship builders on the verge of trying desperately to consolidate so as to survive the downturn, but

South Africa's steel industry was being flattened by Chinese imports, with the second largest producer, Evraz Highveld (owned by a Russian), moving quickly to formal bankruptcy in 2015, while the largest, ArcelorMittal (owned by an Indian), shut a half-dozen of its foundries. Likewise in Brazil, the iron-ore operations of what was South Africa's largest corporation over the prior century – Anglo American – resulted in a US$8 billion loss, leading to the main executive's humiliating resignation and contributing to the firm's ninety-four per cent decline in London Stock Exchange share value.[9] Notwithstanding intra-BRICS solidarity rhetoric, in the face of a global capitalist crisis the desperate emerging economies' corporations engaged in ruinous competition in steel, mining and commerce (Timmons 2015).

Given the slowing Chinese import and export growth, in addition to vast overcapacity in shipping and steel (including iron ore), nearly all minerals and other commodity prices began crashing in 2011. The process intensified in mid-2014, though this somehow went unnoticed at the Phakisa think tank held in the Durban luxury hotel. In the following year alone, prices of oil fell by fifty per cent, iron ore by forty per cent, coal by twenty per cent and copper, gold and platinum by ten per cent. Mining houses as large as BHP Billiton, Anglo American and Lonmin lost, respectively, eighty-seven, ninety-three and ninety-nine per cent of their share value in 2015. Yet a scenario of deflated demand was not worthy of Phakisa strategists' consideration – even though a commodity price collapse on the same scale was experienced from July to December 2008.

By early 2016, the oil glut was partly catalysed by Saudi Arabia refusing to hold back supply, so as to maintain its market position in the face of American shale oil production and new African oil finds (Masie 2015). The oil price collapse not only caused spectacular devaluation of capital and job losses for oil majors such as BP, Tullow and Royal Dutch Shell, it also placed oil-dependent economies under immense stress, resulting in austerity. Nigeria and Angola were soon unable to deliver on government planning commitments, and hence lowered their own demands for products and services in the offshore oil industry – contracts that Cape Town firms had anticipated supplying under the Phakisa rubric.

BIG, FAST RESULTS REDUCED TO SMALL, SLOW FAILURES

The words 'Operation Phakisa' were applied to several aspects of state policy after 2014, including the oceans economy, mining, education, technology and health care. These Phakisa strategies are meant to support the government's NDP, specifically to ameliorate poverty, inequality and unemployment by accelerating policy implementation, setting clear targets and emphasising monitoring and evaluation. On paper, the scale and potential of the projects are impressive, but as is the case with so many of South Africa's hastily assembled mega projects, the underlying imperatives are bedevilled by capital's overaccumulation crisis and accelerating climate change. These are becoming increasingly debilitating, with centrifugal, deglobalising forces bedevilling the world economy and especially BRICS (Bond 2017), leaving Phakisa vulnerable to a series of slow, small failures.

As it became evident that Phakisa would not deliver any real results in a big or fast way, environmental affairs minister Edna Molewa became defensive: 'Contrary to recent media reports questioning our progress, we continue to register notable successes.'[10] Yet the first-year investment flows she referenced are woefully insufficient to meet the R180 billion target by 2030 or projected production of 370 000 barrels of oil per day (Zuma 2015). At the time of writing, the oil price was trading around US$50 for a barrel of Brent crude, just over half of the US$70 considered economic for existing projects by Goldman Sachs (Masie 2015).

As for assessment of the impact on climate change and the environment, Zuma bragged in his 2015 report on Phakisa, 'With regard to legislative reform, the Environmental Impact Assessment (EIA) and Biodiversity Regulations have been amended. A Basic assessment is now required instead of a full environmental impact assessment. This will certainly reduce the timeframes tremendously and ensure faster implementation' (Zuma 2015). The kinds of EIA delays witnessed by Transnet in expanding its Durban harbour operations when the South Durban Community Environmental Alliance (SDCEA) complained of various ecological attacks, from sandbank destruction to climate change,[11] would no longer merit official state attention (Bond 2014). Moreover, probable diplomatic conflicts – such as South Africa's desire for an expanded continental shelf (by five per cent) – have been neglected (van Wyk 2015). Instead, the higher priority appears to be facilitating incentives for international investors.

GDP EVANGELISM AND COMMODIFICATION

Finally, South Africa's economic slowdown coupled with capital flight and pressures from the country's neopatrimonial, rent-seeking patronage networks are contributing factors to Phakisa's haphazard, frenetic planning. The merits of a GDP growth-driven, mega-project promotion are dubious. GDP attempts to compress the immensity of the national economy into a single data point of surpassing density. As Jon Gertner remarks, GDP 'has skewed global political objectives towards the single-minded pursuit of economic growth'.[12] In Africa, Morten Jerven (2015: 56) points out that comparative GDP estimates 'tell us nothing about the relative distribution of wealth within each economy. The pitfalls of using these variables alone, without any information to contextualise the data, become clear' (see also Fioramonti 2013; Sen 2007; Stiglitz, Sen & Fitoussi 2010).

GDP-led economic incentives thus perpetuate the drive to bluntly quantify and commodify everything. But what will foil Phakisa as a GDP generator using FDI, is that short-term inflows of billions for oil-rig construction are vastly outweighed by natural capital depletion, as well as multinational corporate profits and dividends – a problem already profoundly unsettling to South Africa's current account balance. That balance turned decisively negative once the largest Johannesburg Stock Exchange firms shifted financial headquarters to London in the early 2000s.

Phakisa's ocean valuation methodology within the oft-quoted report by Nelson Mandela Metropolitan University (NMMU) marine economists calculates *only the positive contribution* of the oceans economy to 'ecosystem services' generated through 'competitive markets' (Tate et al. 2012: 19). The NMMU study calculates natural capital extraction as having a substantial positive impact upon GDP: 'value added of natural gas for 2010 was 1,222 kilotons ... (R2.012 billion) [and] total production of crude petroleum for 2010 was 1.358 million barrels ... (R1.018 billion)' (Tate et al. 2012: 19).

But the researchers neglected to observe that when non-renewable petroleum, gas and mineral resources are removed (forever), then South Africa's natural capital shrinks. This wasting away of net natural capital (as part of a measure of overall societal wealth) is a major problem for African economies, eighty-eight per cent of which the World Bank (2014: vii) found suffered a net negative impact from resource extraction. The resulting reinvestment of profits (by multinational corporate extractors) fell far short of the value of the non-renewable resources that left the continent. In contrast, three wealthy resource-intense countries – Australia, Canada and Norway – had positive net wealth effects because the corporations doing the extraction recirculated profits back within the home economies (World Bank 2011).

In South Africa's case, there was a positive contribution of mineral extraction to GDP, to be sure, but in the last year that the World Bank (2011) broke down the detailed impact on 'genuine savings' (wealth that includes natural capital), the impact of coal combustion and export was a *negative* 6.4 per cent of GDP. This was the single largest debit in their methodology for adjusting GDP so as to find a genuine savings rate, dragging down wealth generation per capita to a negative US$245/person/year. In short, the more that is extracted, *the poorer South Africa becomes* once full ecological costs are accounted for. It is logical to expect the same results once the ocean economy is rigorously understood, since fossil fuel extraction is largely done by foreign-based firms such as ExxonMobil, Shell and Anadarko.

Phakisa does concede that marine protection and governance should be a component of the plan and that degraded marine resources are both socially and economically costly to replace. But it does so by describing such stakeholder frictions as 'issues that may undermine or subvert lab aspirations' (The Presidency of South Africa 2014). One methodology does exist (and is ignored by NMMU and the Phakisa planners): the Gaborone Declaration for Sustainability in Africa (2012: 1), whose nine African signatories (including Molewa) committed in May 2012 to 'integrate the value of natural capital into national accounting and corporate planning and reporting processes, policies, and programmes'. A government report on subsequent Gaborone Declaration implementation progress reaffirmed: 'A true understanding of the value of using those resources, including all externalities, is needed. Methods for recognising the value of natural capital need to be more widely adopted and integrated into national reporting to reduce the reliance on solely GDP figures' (DEA 2013: 5).

The opposite trend is more obvious: ignoring natural capital accounting and downplaying EIAs. Perhaps most dangerous is the 2014 Infrastructure Development Act which fast-tracks mega projects – including the critical energy, port, rail and road projects associated with Phakisa – by setting artificial time limits on environmental considerations. As GDP critic Lorenzo Fioramonti (Interview, Pretoria, 1 March 2016) told us, 'Operation Phakisa is potentially very dangerous. There may be some small entry points and windows of opportunity to bend it towards radical change, but otherwise it is a powerful move towards broad-based commercialisation through GDP-based industrial expansion policies.'

Phakisa fails to balance social, environmental and democratic values with narrowly calculated economic objectives. The top-down approach places more emphasis upon investment promotion and implementation, leaving public and environmental concerns as perfunctory box-ticking exercises. One problem of balancing the marine-protected areas is their competition with sites of offshore oil and gas exploration. The twenty-one proposed marine-protected areas are under continuous pressure not to overlap the prospecting areas (Miza, Malebu & Sink 2015).

Earthlife Africa (2014) was particularly alarmed about Phakisa's promotion of oil and gas exploration, as this would surely 'break SA's carbon budget' at a time when the country's emissions rate per person was already forty-three per cent higher than the global average. Earthlife advised that corporations 'should definitely not be exploring for any new reserves'. Moreover, in the event of an oil spill, hazardous materials are nearly impossible to remove from contaminated water. The South African National Biodiversity Institute revealed the mood of hostility to such concerns in a 2015 Phakisa presentation (Miza, Malebu & Sink 2015): potential conflicts between 'stakeholders' (i.e. the citizenry) and offshore leaseholders were detailed as one of the 'obstacles'.

FROM GDP EVANGELISM TO FDI EVANGELISM

Phakisa's official outreach to international investors took place initially at South Africa House in London in July 2015. At the time, Jo-Ansie van Wyk (2015) expressed concern that mimicking Malaysia's approach would entrench the increasingly undemocratic nature of development practice in South Africa. Malaysia's strategy was led by an executive and implemented at breakneck speed. Phakisa's delivery laboratories were described by Zuma (2014) as intensive work sessions where 'multiple stakeholders work full-time in one location for about five weeks'. They 'create transparency and help to remove bottlenecks and resolve the most critical challenges facing a sector'. The delivery lab teams were comprised of '180 delegates from national Government departments, provincial Government departments, civil society, private sector, labour and academia' (Zuma 2014).

This strategy fits within two South African government traditions dating to the mid-1990s: dependency upon elite focus groups and consultants, and the imperative to uncritically attract FDI as a means to its ends. FDI incentives have been skewed, as Zuma (2014) made clear by amending the Mineral and Petroleum Resources Development Act (MPRDA), the Royalties Act and the

Income Tax Act for the purpose of 'increasing South Africa's attractiveness as an investment destination for international oil and gas companies'. The involvement of PetroSA in Operation Phakisa is also a worrying element. PetroSA was involved in several large-scale fraud and corruption scandals, and has a US$8 billion strategy for expanding oil refining at the port of Coega.

FDI can be useful for expanding a country's productive forces but is often economically disadvantageous when corporations (and their northern governments) engage in trade and investment negotiations over taxes, incentives, capital flows, employment conditions and protection of the environment (Jones 2013, 2014). The repeated danger arises of FDI serving as a vehicle to externalise hot money and internalise patronage networks in vulnerable communities, societies and ecologies. As Earthlife Africa (2014) warned,

> the national government wants to fast track service delivery and reduce unemployment and poverty through Operation Phakisa. It won't work. Phakisa has very little to do with poverty alleviation and everything to do with profits for corporates, most likely with the familiar kickbacks for well-connected tenderpreneurs and their political allies.

If profits and dividends are then repatriated to foreign corporate headquarters, the balance of payments falls further into deficit, driving the current account into crisis. That, in turn, requires that state elites attract yet more new FDI or borrow abroad, so as to have hard currency on hand to pay returns on old FDI. And since FDI flows have stagnated (UNCTAD 2016), that puts rising pressure on foreign debt (which exceeded US$150 billion by 2017), and also renews the need for ever more frenetic extraction. All of this generates a desperate sense by policy makers that they should pump even more public subsidies into corporate-friendly infrastructure, which was the objective of the 2017 G20 Compact with Africa.

Ashwin Desai (2015: 24) worries that Phakisa is resonant of similar 'Faustian pacts' with multinational capital: 'government, as the pronouncements of President Zuma and Minister Malusi Gigaba indicate, remains obsessed with driving an economy that always requires one more mega-project [or] mega event to facilitate the Rostowian take-off into the flight path of the Northern economies'. New York consultancy McKinsey was chosen by the Zuma government to manage Phakisa, but within three years came under attack because of its alleged links to the Guptas, ostensibly by entering a Black Economic

Empowerment arrangement with Gupta-linked company Trillian. While McKinsey asserts that the deal with Trillian failed its own due diligence tests six months into the arrangement, the firm has been criticised for exorbitant fees taken for advising electricity parastatal Eskom on potential restructuring. The opposition centre-right Democratic Alliance filed a lawsuit against the consultancy in mid-2017 for fraud, racketeering and collusion as a result of further Eskom kickback allegations drawn from leaks within a damning Gupta-related email cache.[13]

Nevertheless, minister in the presidency, Jeff Radebe, exhibited blind faith in McKinsey's stewardship of the 'big fast results' methodology, hoping to 'create a conducive enabling environment' for attracting blue economy FDI: 'We have a new kind of leadership now and when we, as a government, talk about radical economic transformation, this is what we are talking about. We are not about to watch our wealth be exported.'[14] However, exemptions were offered to multinational oil and gas corporations from MPRDA provisions promoting state ownership and beneficiation. Thanks to such small, slow failures, it is logical for progressive social forces across South Africa to mobilise in coming years, demanding that Phakisa be replaced – but by what?

CONCLUSION: JUST TRANSITION STRATEGIES AGAINST BLUE ECONOMY EXPLOITATION

The uncritical market-based philosophy that has resulted in ineffective macro-economic policies and Phakisa-style accumulation could instead be replaced by the logic of the just transition: a decisive move away from carbon-intensive 'development', but in a manner that takes seriously the need to protect capital's victims in poor and working-class, female and black, and differently-abled populations from further upheaval. To do so, the prevailing mega-project strategies must have their technological and rhetorical assumptions disrupted, their underlying economic assumptions questioned, environmental risks recalibrated, and leadership displaced by progressive, democratic forces.

However, the task of facilitating a just transition quickly runs up against an even more powerful logic: clientelist politics in the African National Congress's factional patronage networks. Zuma's 2016 State of the Nation Address confirmed the South African government's ongoing desire for 'big fast results', no matter the cost. Mounting evidence of small, slow failures confirms that

Phakisa suffered excessive hype, a top-down non-consultative process and an extraordinary belief in the wisdom of multinational extractive-industry corporations, despite the vulnerability of the polity and environment to extraction, and despite the dangers to small open economies such as South Africa's in a turbulent global economy (Zuma 2016).

In short, there is no point in assuming that ideas alone will be persuasive, especially given the Zuma government's 2014 downgrading of EIAs and fast-tracking of mega projects in the Infrastructure Development Act. Aside from the top-down capitalist and climate crises discussed above, the greatest risk to Operation Phakisa's proposed port and petrochemical expansions is a still-to-be entrenched form of progressive activism that unites a variety of critics in a coherent, ideologically clear political project: the just transition.

Mark Swilling and colleagues (2016: 12) argue that 'Although a just transition in South Africa is currently unlikely, the rapid emergence of the renewable energy niche signals what may be possible'. That 'niche' is far too limited, mainly because of Pretoria's tacit approval of Eskom's fossil fuel addictions, its failure to subsidise solar and wind properly and its failure to deliver a democratised renewables project, ultimately leaving it to wealthier households to go off-grid and insulate themselves from load shedding. This means that merely minor augmentations – not transformations – of South Africa's unsustainable economic and social ecosystems are under way, not mainly because of pressure from below but through market-based processes. Describing this phenomenon, Jacklyn Cock (2013: 8) observes that a minimalist just transition 'emphasises shallow, reformist change with green jobs, social protection, retraining and consultation. The emphasis is defensive and shows a preoccupation with protecting the interest of vulnerable workers'.

In contrast, Cock (2013: 9) argues (and we agree) that a deeper, necessary just transition entails 'an alternative growth path and new ways of producing and consuming'. The richer sense of the term 'just transition' is also being explored by those with a post-Phakisa perspective on oceans: progressive environmentalists and affected communities (including fisherfolk) who become militant once the opportunities of standard 'stakeholder participation' are exhausted. Although they mostly operate in separate silos, the defence of South Africa's oceans and coastal land will necessarily bring together a wide variety of these forces as logical allies in coming decades.

Meaningful job creation has not yet been scoped out by South Africa's Million Climate Jobs researchers (Alternative Information and Development

Centre 2014), but parallel British campaigners believe that 270 000 annual jobs can be created merely on the electricity-generation work associated with wind, tidal and wave energy (representing more than half of Britain's post-carbon grid within two decades):

> About half of the jobs in offshore wind will be the same as onshore wind – at first mainly in factory jobs. The other half, though, will be in assembling the turbines, taking them out to sea, and putting them in place. There are also more maintenance jobs offshore. Turbines break down more often at sea … a new technology called 'floating wind' now makes it possible to go out to depths of 1,000 metres – a turbine rises from a broader platform that is anchored to the ocean floor by cables … (Campaign against Climate Change 2014: 19, 20)

As for communities, consider cases representing alternatives to Phakisa-logic on the Eastern Cape's Wild Coast and in South Durban. In the former, a campaign has been waged since 2008 by the peasant-dominated Amadiba Crisis Committee (ACC) and allies in the green network Sustaining the Wild Coast, against coastal mineral extraction in Xolobeni (Bennie 2010). In the latter, untrammelled South Durban port and petrochemical expansion has, since 2010, threatened intensified displacement and amplified pollution (Bond 2016). The two communities' successes to date in stalling these coastline projects were in part due to the just transition framing adopted by advanced activists as they withstood extractive and expansion attacks.

Space constraints do not permit a full exploration of how defensive manoeuvres against commodification of the coastline contain within them the seeds of just transition strategies. But the ACC's desired just transition is articulated in these terms:

> Development strategies in keeping with these principles will include the utilisation of the natural beauty of our environment, fertile land and good rainfall, integrating tourism, enhanced agricultural production and the necessary infrastructure including health, education, road access and services. (Amadiba Crisis Committee 2016: 13)

Higher levels of social grants would help, as would decommodified access to clean water, electricity, a clinic, better roads and expanded conservation zoning, including a marine-protected area (Bennie 2010). The MPRDA is one of the terrains of struggle, with the Constitutional Court likely to be asked to rule that the law is unconstitutional due to the inability of a community (with collective tenure rights) to turn down mining licence applications. A victory there would confirm sufficient security to expand alternative strategies consistent with a just transition to local autonomy, preservation of indigenous values and expansion of ubuntu society–nature values.

A more expansive project is required in the second case, where the SDCEA has made various post-carbon development demands for the South Durban Basin, in opposition to the massive port-petrochemical expansion (Bond 2016; SDCEA 2008, 2011). Defensively, the SDCEA would reverse the liberalised zoning that currently allows freight transport to creep into historic Clairwood, displacing thousands of black households. It would also defend and generate more green space in the toxic-saturated industrial and petrochemical areas. As an antidote to Operation Phakisa, the SDCEA's (2008: 1) thirty-page *Spatial and Development Vision* includes demands such as 'a halt to the privatisation of ocean, Bay and shore resources that belong to all the people of this country'. A lengthy follow-up statement just prior to the SDCEA's co-hosting of the climate counter-summit to the 2011 UN Conference of the Parties 17 included this language appropriately critical of the state's pro-shipping agenda: 'localisation is essential to any serious programme of mitigation and requires that national resources should be focused on supporting people's capacities to direct local development … We call for people's energy sovereignty founded on democratic and local control' (SDCEA 2011: 73).

The struggle against projects such as Oceans Phakisa will not be won by default thanks to conditions of capitalist crisis, or in technicist argumentation or because of activists' defensive critiques alone. A just transition will occur only with visionary ambition and ideological clarity about what is at stake, forged in ever more intense eco-social struggle, as it becomes clear that carbon-intensive, tinkering-type reforms like Phakisa simply fall flat, and progressive openings necessarily emerge.

NOTES

1   P. Bruce, 'Thick end of the wedge', *Business Day*, 13 February 2012.
2   Brazil, Russia, India, China, South Africa.

3   A. Serrao, 'E-tolls' billions flow to Austria', *Independent Online*, 20 March 2012.
4   S. Kings, 'SA gung ho about mining oceans', *Mail & Guardian*, 3 July 2015, http://mg.co.za/article/2015-07-02-sa-gung-ho-about-mining-oceans (accessed 17 June 2017).
5   F. Forde, 'The treasure beneath our oceans', *Sunday Independent*, 19 October 2014.
6   P. Bruce, 'Phakisa floats hope for shipyards', *Business Day*, 24 August 2015.
7   Dry Bulk Market, International Shipping News, 'Will the Baltic Dry Index (BDI) rebound or further decline?' Accessed 28 August 2017, http://www.hellenicshippingnews.com/will-the-baltic-dry-index-bdi-rebound-or-further-decline/.
8   Bruce, 'Phakisa floats hope for shipyards'.
9   J. Wilson, 'What end of the resources boom means for Anglo', *Business Day*, 16 February 2016, http://www.bdlive.co.za/opinion/2016/02/16/what-end-of-the-resources-boom-means-for-anglo (accessed 17 June 2017).
10 E. Molewa, 'We have the means to solve problems in the oceans economy', *Business Day*, 27 November 2015.
11 C. Paton, 'Transnet's Durban Port plan earns "climate-change denialist" gibe', *Business Day*, 20 January 2014.
12 J. Gertner, 'The rise and fall of GDP', *New York Times*, 13 May 2010.
13 J. Gapper, 'McKinsey has closed its eyes in South Africa', *Financial Times*, 20 September 2017; Y. Groenewald, 'McKinsey faces legal action over Gupta-linked Eskom saga', *Fin24*, 18 September 2017, http://www.fin24.com/Economy/Eskom/mckinsey-faces-legal-action-over-gupta-linked-eskom-saga-20170918 (accessed 21 September 2017).
14 Forde, 'The treasure beneath our oceans'.

REFERENCES

Alternative Information and Development Centre. 2014. 'Million climate jobs'. Accessed 17 June 2017, http://aidc.org.za/programmes/million-climate-jobs-campaign/about/.
amaBhungane and Scorpio. 2017a. 'Guptas and associates score R5.3 billion in locomotive kickbacks'. Accessed 21 September 2017, http://amabhungane.co.za/article/2017-06-01-guptaleaks-guptas-and-associates-score-r53bn-in-locomotives-kickbacks.
amaBhungane and Scorpio. 2017b. 'A third Gupta-Transnet "kickback" contract unearthed'. Accessed 21 September 2017, http://amabhungane.co.za/article/2017-09-18-guptaleaks-a-third-gupta-transnet-kickback-contract-unearthed.
Amadiba Crisis Committee. 2016. 'Objection in terms of Section 10(1)(b) of the MPRDA against the mining right application filed by Transworld Energy and Mineral Resources (SA) (Pty) Ltd'. Pretoria, 4 March. Accessed 20 August 2017, http://lrc.org.za/lrcarchive/images/pdf_downloads/Law_Policy_Reform/2016_03_04_S10_Objection_TEM_mining_right.pdf.
AU (African Union). 2012. '2050 AIM strategy'. Accessed 20 August 2017, https://www.au.int/web/en/documents/30928/2050-aim-strategy.
Bennie, A. 2010. 'The relation between environmental protection and "development": A case study of the social dynamics involved in the proposed mining at

Xolobeni, Wild Coast', MA Research Report, University of the Witwatersrand, Johannesburg. Accessed 17 June 2017, http://wiredspace.wits.ac.za/xmlui/bitstream/handle/10539/8875/A%20Bennie%20Research%20Report.pdf?sequence=1&isAllowed=y.

Bond, P. (ed.). 2005. *Fanon's Warning: A Civil Society Reader on the New Partnership for Africa's Development*. Trenton, NJ: Africa World Press.

Bond, P. 2014. *Elite Transition: From Apartheid to Neoliberalism in South Africa*. London: Pluto Press.

Bond, P. 2016. 'Red–green alliance-building against Durban's port-petrochemical complex expansion'. In *Grassroots Environmental Governance: Community Engagements with Industrial Development*, edited by L. Horowitz and M. Watts. Oxford: Oxford University Press, pp. 59–79.

Bond, P. 2017. 'BRICS Xiamen summit doomed by centrifugal economics'. *Pambazuka*, 31 August. Accessed 21 September 2017, https://www.pambazuka.org/global-south/brics-xiamen-summit-doomed-centrifugal-economics.

Campaign against Climate Change. 2014. 'One million climate jobs: Tackling the environmental and economic crises'. Accessed 20 August 2017, https://www.campaigncc.org/sites/data/files/Docs/one_million_climate_jobs_2014.pdf.

Cock, J. 2004. 'Connecting the red, brown and green: The environmental justice movement in South Africa' (research report for the Globalisation Marginalisation and New Social Movements Project). Durban: University of KwaZulu-Natal.

Cock, J. 2013. '"Green economy": A sustainable development path or "wolf in sheep's clothing"?' Paper presented at Conference on Land Divided: Land and South African Society in 2013 in Comparative Perspective, 24–27 March, University of Cape Town.

DEA (Department of Environmental Affairs, South Africa). 2013. 'Report on South Africa's implementation of the key areas of the Gaborone Declaration for presentation at the follow-up meeting on the Sustainability in Africa Summit'. Accessed 13 September 2017, http://static1.squarespace.com/static/52026c1ee4b0ee324ff265f3/t/52582ec8e4b0d6c3d3429090/1381510856823/REPORT+ON+SOUTH+AFRIC AS_+IMPLEMENTATION+OF+THE+GABORONE+DECL+-+Sept+2013.pdf.

Desai, A. 2015. 'Of Faustian pacts and mega projects: The politics and economics of the port expansion in the south basin of Durban South Africa', *Capitalism Nature Socialism*, 26 (1): 18–34.

Earthlife Africa. 2014. 'Environmentalists protest against Zuma's plans for our coasts'. Press Release, Johannesburg, 15 October. Accessed 17 June 2017, http://earthlife.org.za/2014/10/press-release-environmentalists-protest-against-zumas-plans-for-our-coast/.

Fine, B. and Rustomjee, Z. 1996. *The Political Economy of South Africa: From Minerals–Energy Complex to Industrialisation*. London: Christopher Hurst.

Fioramonti, L. 2013. *Gross Domestic Problem: The Politics behind the World's Most Powerful Number*. London: Zed Books.

Frynas, J.G. and Paulo, M. 2007. 'A new scramble for African oil? Historical, political and business perspectives', *African Affairs*, 106 (423): 229–251.

Gaborone Declaration for Sustainability in Africa. 2012. 'Declaration'. Gaborone, Botswana, 12 May 2012. Accessed 20 August 2017, http://www.gaboronedeclaration.com/.

Gordhan, P. 2016. '2016 Budget speech'. Pretoria: National Treasury. Accessed 20 August 2017, http://www.treasury.gov.za/documents/national%20budget/2016/speech/speech.pdf.

Jerven, M. 2015. *Africa: Why Economists Get It Wrong*. London: Zed Books.

Jones, E. 2013. *Negotiating against the Odds: A Guide for Trade Negotiators from Developing Countries*. New York: Palgrave Macmillan.

Jones, E. 2014. *When do "weak" states win?* Global Economic Governance Working Paper 2014/95, University of Oxford.

Martinez-Alier, J. 2002. *The Environmentalism of the Poor*. Cheltenham: Edward Elgar.

Masie, D. 2015. 'How will the oil price collapse affect the Africa Rising story?' *African Arguments*, 27 January. Accessed 17 June 2017, http://africanarguments. org/2015/01/27/how-will-the-oil-price-collapse-affect-the-africa-rising-story-by-desne-masie/.

Miza, S., Malebu, T. and Sink, K. 2015. 'Unlocking obstacles in the Phakisa expansion of South Africa's marine protected areas'. South African National Biodiversity Institute, 2015 Biodiversity Planning Forum, 23–26 June, Salt Rock Hotel and Beach Resort, KwaZulu-Natal.

National Planning Commission. 2012. *National Development Plan: Vision for 2030*. Pretoria: National Planning Commission.

Philip, S. 2014. 'South Africa could be swimming in opportunity'. *Brand South Africa*, 16 October. Accessed 17 June 2017, https://www.brandsouthafrica. com/investments-immigration/economynews/south-africa-could-be-swimming-in-opportunity.

Pieterse, D., Farole, T., Odendaal, M. and Steenkamp, A. 2016. *Supporting export competitiveness through port and rail network reforms: A case study of South Africa*. Policy Research Working Paper 7532, World Bank Trade and Competitiveness Global Practice Group, Washington, DC.

SA Info. 2006. 'SA claims vast tracts of sea floor'. *Brand South Africa*, 20 June. Accessed 17 June 2017, https://www.brandsouthafrica.com/south-africa-fast-facts/news-facts/maritime-claims-200605.

SDCEA (South Durban Community Environmental Alliances). 2008. *Spatial and Development Vision for the People of South Durban*. Durban: SDCEA.

SDCEA. 2011. 'Feeling the heat in Durban', *Capitalism Nature Socialism*, 22 (4): 50–73.

Sen, A. 2007. 'From income inequality to economic inequality', *Southern Economic Journal*, 64 (2): 384–401.

Ship & Bunker. 2016. 'Baltic Dry Index falls to 325, 1,430 vessels need to be laid up to restore balance, says analyst'. 28 January. Accessed 17 June 2017, http:// shipandbunker.com/news/world/703305-baltic-dry-index-falls-to-325-1430-vessels-need-to-be-laid-up-to-restore-balance-says-analyst.

Southall, R. 2015. 'The coming crisis of Zuma's ANC: The party state confronts fiscal crisis', *Review of African Political Economy*, 43 (147): 73–88.

Stiglitz, J., Sen, A. and Fitoussi, J. 2010. *Mismeasuring Our Lives: Why GDP Doesn't Add Up*. New York: The New Press.

Swilling, M., Musango, J. and Wakeford, J. (eds). 2016. *Greening the South African Economy: Scoping the Issues, Challenges and Opportunities*. Cape Town: University of Cape Town Press.

Tate, D., Haines, R., Hosking, S., Kaczynski, W., Thou, G., Du Preez, D., Du Preez, M., Phiri S., Saunders, E. and Tembo, D. 2012. 'Development of the Methodology for Identifying and Assessing the Economic Contribution to the South African Economy of the Goods and Services [Ecosystems and Biodiversity] Yielded by the Oceans and Coasts Environment'. School of Economics, Development Studies and Tourism, Faculty of Economics and Business Sciences. Nelson Mandela Metropolitan University, report prepared for the Department of Environmental Affairs.

Terreblanche, C. 2017. 'Dissonances and convergences in south-north narratives of ecological justice', PhD thesis, University of KwaZulu-Natal, School of Built Environment and Development Studies, Durban.

The Presidency of South Africa. 2014. 'Unlocking the Economic Potential of South Africa's Oceans: Marine Protection Services and Governance Executive Summary'. Operation Phakisa, 15 August. Accessed 20 August 2017, http://tinyurl.com/y8vpfkpj.

Timmons, H. 2015. 'The BRICS era is over, even at Goldman Sachs'. *Quartz*, 9 November. Accessed 20 August 2017, https://qz.com/544410/the-brics-era-is-over-even-at-goldman-sachs/.

United Nations. 1982. 'United Nations Convention on the Law of the Sea of 10 December 1982'. United Nations Treaty Series. Accessed 17 June 2017, http://www.un.org/depts/los/convention_agreements/convention_overview_convention.htm.

UNCTAD (United Nations Conference on Trade and Development). 2016. *World Investment Report*. Geneva: UNCTAD.

Van Wyk, J. 2015. 'Crouching tigers, leaping lions? Developmental leadership lessons for southern Africa and Malaysia'. Conference paper on Building Democratic Developmental States for Economic Transformation in Southern Africa, 20–22 July, Pretoria, South Africa.

World Bank. 2011. *The Changing Wealth of Nations*. Washington, DC: World Bank.

World Bank. 2014. *Little Green Data Book*. Washington, DC: World Bank.

Zuma, J. 2014. 'Address by President Jacob Zuma at the launch of Operation Phakisa Big Fast Results Implementation Methodology, Inkosi Albert Luthuli International Convention Centre, Durban'. Accessed 20 August 2017, http://www.gov.za/address-president-jacob-zuma-launch-operation-phakisa-big-fast-results-implementation-methodology.

Zuma, J. 2015. 'Report on Operation Phakisa implementation'. Report by President Jacob Zuma to media and stakeholders on Operation Phakisa implementation, Sefako Makgatho Presidential Guest House, Pretoria, 13 August.

Zuma, J. 2016. State of the Nation Address, 11 February, National Assembly, Cape Town.

INTERVIEW

Lorenzo Fioramonti, Pretoria, 1 March 2016.

CONCLUSION

Vishwas Satgar

D onald Trump, his administration and the finance–fossil fuel forces supporting him (such as the billionaire Koch brothers), have openly challenged a
global scientific consensus that climate change is real, is human induced and will
have disastrous consequences for many societies. Hurricanes (such as Harvey and
Irma) and raging wildfires in the US have not pushed back the Trump administration's denialist positions and pro-fossil capitalism politics. While the UN-led Paris
climate agreement has brought too little, too late, for systemic transformation,
Trump's withdrawal from the agreement marks not only the further decline of US
hegemony in the world but places the US on a collision course with humanity and
all life forms. The ecocidal logic of this imperial politics threatens all of humanity
but will increasingly become fascist to ensure zones of privileged existence are
protected for the few, while policing and imposing regimes of dispossessing life at
the frontiers of complex hydrocarbon extraction, land grabs for export-led food
production, collapsing societies due to climate shocks and flexible accumulation
premised on wageless majorities. Has the time come for climate justice sanctions
against the US carbon criminal state? Should the world isolate the US? We believe
this is very necessary and mass power has to be built to achieve this.

Transnational ruling classes and elites have failed humanity. This volume
emphasises this through rigorous political economy analysis. Moreover, the
corporate- and imperial-induced climate-driven world we inhabit is new and
holds out serious challenges for present and future generations. In this regard,
climate justice politics is also a new politics, seeking to provide an alternative

way forward for humanity in its interconnectedness with ecosystems. Climate justice politics connects the dots of fossil fuel extractivism, hunger, inequality, imperial domination and corporate-induced climate change. It stands in opposition to a failing capitalist system, recognising that such a system is racist, patriarchal, exploitative and driven by a logic of imperial ecocide. Through this recognition, climate justice asserts that the victims of capitalism's oppressions are not going to pay the cost for more of the same.

At the same time, this volume emphasises the need for climate justice politics derived from a dialogue between Marxism and contemporary anti-capitalism to be transformative, through advancing systemic reforms and deep just transitions at different scales. This means climate justice politics can no longer be a symbolic politics or just a street politics or just radical intellectual critique. Climate justice politics has to be counterhegemonic, about a new class project for society and civilisation, in which socialism is renewed as democratic eco-socialism. Such a renewal will not only come from an ecologically aware Marxism, but also from other bodies of thought resisting the capitalist destruction of life. Indigenous thought, currents of radical spirituality, emancipatory religious perspectives, African humanist conceptions and everyday popular resistance are all yearning for a post-capitalist world. We profiled some of these ideological orientations in this volume. At the convergence of resistance and through dialogue, climate justice as democratic eco-socialism could become counterhegemonic.

The articulation of climate justice as democratic eco-socialism is laying the basis for an alternative to techno-fixes such as nuclear, market-centred solutions – such as carbon trading, electric cars and desalination - green neoliberal capitalism and even arguments made by extractivist classes that more extraction of fossil fuels is necessary to pay for the transition. The latter message is heard in Canada, in Bolivia and all the way to South Africa (in the National Development Plan). In South Africa it's not just more coal extraction but also fracking and deep-water fossil fuel extraction. The world is running out of time and we have to turn our backs on carbon criminality and fossil fuel-driven societies. This volume makes such a case.

BEYOND CLIMATE CATASTROPHISM

With a climate-driven world already hotter by 1°C since before the Industrial Revolution, we are experiencing extreme weather shifts such as droughts, floods, hurricanes, heat waves and wildfires. This threatens rich and poor countries and

subordinate classes disproportionately. The awakening of human consciousness to this new reality is just beginning and therefore explains the lack of mass
urgency across the planet. In time, climate determinism through climate shocks
will awaken a new planetary awareness and a desire for societies to sustain life.
Ruling in the old way, with outdated ideas merely serving monopoly and transnational capital and reproducing an ecocidal capitalist system, will be discarded.
But we are not there yet and merely expecting climate determinism to bring about
change will be too late; climate determinism will take us into a world where life
might be impossible. Moreover, where there is awareness of the challenges climate change presents to life, the instinct and impulse to survive is driving mass
consciousness into despair, resignation to catastrophism, or millenarian 'ends of
time' discourses. Those who occlude systemic understandings and individualise
the climate challenge tend to end up with this orientation. The worst expression
of this is an outright rejection of humanity: we are a species that deserves to be
destroyed. The logic of such an eco-fascist position is that we need a culling of
the human race. While the catastrophism of climate shock determinism and the
impulse of human survival are powerful forces that will increasingly play a role in
our world, this volume calls for a global climate emergency to be recognised. We
argue for deep just transitions, at different scales, to take forward systemic alternatives to transform energy systems, production, consumption and everyday life.
These are alternatives and perspectives emanating from solidarity struggles at
the frontlines of climate shocks, against extractivism and movements resisting
the oppressions and exploitations of contemporary capitalism.

Many of these theoretical analyses, conceptual ideas and concrete systemic
reforms for deep just transitions are about a new paradigm, a new framework
to sustain life. In this volume we refer to this as democratic eco-socialism. As
a bridge to the future these perspectives are seeking to renew a civilisational
vision, bottom-up transformative practices as part of building elements of the
future now, engendering convergences, debates and rethinking programmatic
politics. The propositions in this volume are not in themselves solutions to
the climate crisis. But through constructing new political alliances and grass-
roots-driven historical blocs of social forces, such ideas could mature and find
expression in programmatic but mass-based transformative politics. Many
more systemic alternatives need to be invented, learned from and translated
from local, national, continental and global levels. The water commons, zero
waste, democratic public utilities, democratic planning, participatory budgeting and various other systemic reforms necessary for deep just transitions have

not been engaged with in this volume, or have merely been alluded to. That is because this volume is intended to lay the basis for deeper conversation and debate about such systemic alternatives as part of class and popular struggles. Ultimately, such struggles must seek to crystallise a democratic eco-socialist project and programme for societies to sustain life.

DEMOCRATIC ECO-SOCIALISM AND TRANSFORMATIVE POLITICS

The material conditions of a conjuncture of systemic crises and transformation are upon us. For workers working in coal mining or fossil extractivism, standing against climate justice activism is understandable given that their jobs make the difference between survival and unemployment. However, systemic alternatives such as the universal basic income grant, set at a substantially high level, could enable a transition out of coal jobs and ensure workers' families are not condemned to suffering. Add to this climate jobs, worker cooperatives, food sovereignty, socially owned renewables, mass public transport systems and other systemic reforms, and there are feasible pathways for workers and for society beyond ecocidal capitalism. These are argued for in this volume. But while these are possible futures and options, the challenge remains: what is the politics to achieve such systemic alternatives?

While unions are beginning to appreciate the importance of taking climate change and the deep just transition seriously, this has not gone far enough. Neither has the climate justice movement been able to overcome its weaknesses to ensure various social forces converge around a new class project for society, particularly given the failings of the multilateral climate negotiations. This volume argues that red and green alliances are possible in the context of a post-vanguardist world. However, three obstacles have to be overcome to lay the basis for a renewed transformative politics on the Left. First, the Left has to appreciate that we need a new theory of crisis. Classical Marxist accounts of overaccumulation, even contemporary versions of financialised overaccumulation, are not sufficient to comprehend the systemic contradictions of contemporary capitalism. The systemic crises of contemporary capitalist accumulation imperil planetary life. Climate change is one of these systemic crises and we need to build a politics that solves this problem, in its interconnections with inequality, hunger, resource peak and the hollowing out of democracy. An ecological awareness has to be central to a left identity, politics and strategic programme. Climate justice politics is one step in this direction.

Second, transformative politics to advance systemic alternatives requires capacities from below to be developed, to champion and build such alternatives. This requires a new praxis of deepening democracy, institutionalising values-centred institutions like solidarity economies, worker cooperatives and food and water sovereign spaces, and mass popular education through a knowledge commons and through digital platforms for replicating such alternatives. Central to this is a new conception of power as decentred and constituted from below. This means electoral politics is not central to left politics but rather building powerful movements that open up pathways, prefigure futures beyond capitalism, concretise radical non-racial solidarities and give momentum to just transitions from below (in villages, towns, cities, provinces and beyond) that are crucial. It is this critical mass, rooted in building systemic alternatives in the now, that has to be prioritised. All of this has to contribute to ensuring climate justice politics constitutes powerful social alliances and historical blocs to articulate democratic eco-socialist alternatives for society and the world.

Third, without the former conditions being realised, the Left will not be able to transform the state to realise just transitions to sustain life. If the former conditions are realised then the state does become a crucial site and terrain of struggle. In this context, the electoral fixation of green parties, mainly in the global North, is a crucial guide of what not to do. Neither is the co-option of mass power into the state, like through the African National Congress-led Alliance, a way forward. Instead, a new left instrument has to be considered that is not party centred or party-movement oriented (such as the Workers Party in Brazil, which had a loose articulation with movements). Rather, there is a need to think in terms of 'movement–citizen-driven parties'. Fanon's notion of the 'people-driven party' comes closest to this idea. Such a configuration requires the independence of popular movements within a historic bloc, a movement-driven common programme for democratic eco-socialist alternatives to take forward the just transition from below (and in which the role of the state is specified to deepen democracy), and a party form that gets its programmatic mandate, its orientation and its role defined by mass movements and citizens. Such a political instrument still has to be invented in reality but the conditions are emerging for such a movement–citizen-driven party form. It is only this kind of transformative politics that can realise democratic eco-socialism and ensure human and non-human life survives the disasters of a climate change world.

CONTRIBUTORS

Mateo Martínez Abarca is a philosopher, activist and writer from Ecuador. He is a PhD candidate in Philosophy at the National Autonomous University of Mexico and a junior researcher at the Center for Social Studies, Universidade de Coimbra, Portugal.

Alberto Acosta is an Ecuadorian economist, a professor and researcher in FLACSO-Ecuador and honorary professor at Ricardo Palma University in Lima. He is the former minister of energy and mines, the former president of the Constitutional Assembly and former candidate to the presidency of the republic of Ecuador. He is the author of several books and, above all, a comrade of popular struggles.

Brian Ashley is the director of the Alternative Information and Development Centre in Cape Town, South Africa, and the editor of *Amandla*, a current affairs and new politics project.

Nnimmo Bassey is director of the ecological think tank Health of Mother Earth Foundation based in Nigeria. His books include *To Cook a Continent: Destructive Extraction and the Climate Crisis in Africa* (Pambazuka Press, 2012) and *Oil Politics: Echoes of Ecological War* (Daraja Press, 2016).

Andrew Bennie has been a Co-operative and Policy Alternative Centre organiser for the solidarity economy and the South African Food Sovereignty Campaign. He is currently a PhD fellow at the International Centre for

Development and Decent Work in the Sociology department at the University of the Witwatersrand, Johannesburg.

Patrick Bond is professor of Political Economy in the School of Governance at the University of the Witwatersrand. His latest book (co-edited) is *BRICS: An Anticapitalist Critique* (Pluto Press, 2015).

Jacklyn Cock is a professor emeritus in the Department of Sociology at the University of the Witwatersrand. She has published widely on gender, militarisation and environmental issues. Her last book was *The War against Ourselves: Nature, Power and Justice* (Wits University Press, 2007).

David Fig is an environmental sociologist and political economist freelancing out of Johannesburg, mostly working with the environmental justice movements of southern Africa. He has written extensively on energy and environmental problems, corporate behaviour and extractivism. He is a fellow of the Transnational Institute in Amsterdam, and a research associate of the University of Cape Town's Chair in Bio-Economy and the University of the Witwatersrand's SWOP Institute.

Dorothy Grace Guerrero is head of policy and advocacy at Global Justice Now (UK). She works on and writes about climate change and energy issues, impacts of globalised trade and investments on people's livelihoods, China's new role in the global political economy, gender justice and other related economic justice concerns from a radical pluralist left perspective.

Hein Marais is an independent writer and journalist, and the author of *South Africa: Pushed to the Limit: The Political Economy of Change* (Zed Books, 2011), *Limits to Change: The Political Economy of Transition* (Zed Books, 1998, 2001), and *Buckling: The Impact of AIDS in South Africa* (Centre for the Study of AIDS, 2005).

Desné Masie is an expert in international economics and financial markets. She is currently a visiting scholar in international political economy at the School of Governance at the University of the Witwatersrand. She is a Chevening Scholar, HSBC fellow and an associate of the Democracy Works Foundation. Most recently, she has been published in the *Guardian*, *New African* and *The Times*.

Devan Pillay is a professor in Sociology at the University of the Witwatersrand. He is active in the Global Labour University and International Centre for Development and Decent Work networks. He currently co-edits the *New South African Review* (Wits University Press).

Vishwas Satgar is a democratic eco-socialist and has been an activist for over three decades. He is an associate professor of International Relations at the University of the Witwatersrand and edits the Democratic Marxism series, for which he received the distinguished contribution award from the World Association of Political Economy. He recently co-edited *COSATU in Crisis: The Fragmentation of an African Trade Union Federation* (KMM, 2015).

Athish Satgoor was a Co-operative and Policy Alternative Centre organiser for the solidarity economy movement and the South African Food Sovereignty Campaign.

Pablo Sólon is a social activist, an analyst and a researcher on the issues of climate change, water, the rights of Mother Earth, trade agreements and integration processes. He served as ambassador of the Plurinational State of Bolivia to the United Nations from January 2009 to June 2011.

Christelle Terreblanche is a PhD candidate in Development Studies, Centre for Civil Society at the University of KwaZulu-Natal. Her publications include 'Ecofeminism' (forthcoming in *The Post-Development Dictionary: From False Solutions to Radical Alternatives to Development*).

Michelle Williams is associate professor in Sociology and chairperson of the Global Labour University programme at the University of the Witwatersrand. Her publications include *The Roots of Participatory Democracy: Democratic Communists in South Africa and Kerala, India* (Springer, 2008).

INDEX

A

Ackerman, Diane 51, 58, 61–62
African agriculture 62, 175, 192, 197–201
  impact of SAPs on 202–204
  see also small-scale/smallholder
    farmers
African Centre for Biodiversity (ACB) 197,
  202
African National Congress (ANC) 23, 84,
  153, 242, 259, 267
  Cosatu alliance with 265–266
  patronage networks 260, 263, 325,
    329–330
  stance on nuclear energy 254–255, 267
  Women's League 213
  Youth League 153
African Regional Intellectual Property
  Organisation (ARIPO) 201–202,
  206n16
African socialism 15, 169–171, 173–174,
  178
  ecological principles of 172, 177–178,
    181
  Marxist roots of 170–173, 178–179
African Union 199, 205
agrarian transformation/revolution 144,
  185n8, 275, 304
agri-business 190
  and G8 food security strategies
    198–199
  industrial agricultural model 191,
    294–295, 297–298, 303
  seed colonialism 191, 201–202
agro-ecology 14, 21, 216, 225, 303–306
Amin, Samir 150, 164n7, 171
Andean-Amazonian region 18–19, 42,
  108–109, 124, 132–134, 174

  see also indigenous peoples of
    Abya Yala
Anglo American 240–241, 253, 275, 324
Angola 171, 196, 324
Angus, Ian 8, 53, 65, 226
animal rights 114–117
Anthropocene discourse on climate change
  1, 3, 7, 17, 35, 47–48, 50, 57,
  59–62, 64, 110–111, 191
  Marxist ecology critique of 17, 48,
    51–56, 58–59, 61
  see also imperial ecocide, US-led
Anthropocentrism 12, 18, 107–108, 113,
  117, 126–128, 133–135
anti-capitalism 2, 10–11, 13, 19, 43, 162,
  171, 181, 211, 220, 301, 339
anti-fossil fuel networks 180
  Oilwatch 174
  see also post-extractivism
apartheid 156, 174, 213, 297
  legacy 153, 212, 254, 287
  narrow democracy of 243, 248
  nuclear programme 23
Arab Spring 162, 234, 239
Arctic 3–4
Armstrong, K 158–159, 163n1
authoritarianism 2, 22, 43, 135, 156, 210,
  218, 220–221, 226
Axial Age 149, 157, 163

B

Bahro, Rudolf 11, 26n10
Barchiesi, Franco 83, 85, 89, 92, 95
Barlow, Maude 125, 225
Bello, Walden 41, 203, 225
Bentham, Jeremy 114–115
Berry, Thomas 19, 107, 113–119, 127–128

BHP Billiton 241, 275, 324
biodiversity
    agricultural 201, 204–205
    conservation 124–126
    destruction 13, 56, 151
    offsetting 125
biotechnology industry 191, 197–198, 204
    GMO debate 195–198, 201, 204–205,
        303, 306
Bolivia, Plurinational State of 8, 41, 123–124,
        127, 159–160, 173, 205, 339
    Bolivian Alternative for the Americas
        (ALBA) 160, 163
    Cochabamba summit 18, 122
    constitution of 121–122, 131
    see also buen vivir; Rights of Mother
        Earth movement
Boron, Atilio 160, 163
Brazil 132, 238, 253, 262, 283–284, 324, 342
    Bolsa Escola 93
    Bolsa Família 86
Breman, Jan 71, 73
BRICS 262–263, 317, 324–325
Bruce, Peter 315, 321, 323
Buddhism 20, 112, 157–159, 161, 163
buen vivir 19–20, 42, 157, 169, 180, 185n4
    alternative economy to support
        136–145
    as societal construct 131–134,
        160–161, 174, 177–178
    violation of 173
Burdon, Peter 113, 118, 126–127
Burkina Faso 194, 197, 199–200
    Sahel region 193, 201, 206n8

C
Cabral, Amilcar 169, 172, 178
Camus, Albert 88, 100n29
Canada 82–83, 326, 339
Cape Town 254, 322–324
capital accumulation
    class as constituent of 214
    through dispossession/ appropriation
        14, 56, 150, 154, 226, 253,
        296–297
    industrial 12, 55, 150, 275
    overproduction crisis 1–2, 6, 18–19,
        24–25, 54, 137–138, 169, 315–
        316, 323, 325, 341
    see also growth economics, fixation on;
        industrialisation; Marxist/socialist

productivism; neoliberal capitalist
        crisis; social reproduction
capitalism 75
    carbon/fossil fuel 7, 10, 20, 30, 152,
        216, 227
    financialised 1, 59–60, 63–64, 70, 77,
        274
    as geological force 17, 47, 57, 60
    globalised/transnational 6, 8, 11, 13,
        32, 36, 55–57, 71, 77, 139
    origins/history of 52, 55–56
    as process of primitive accumulation
        55–56
    see also carbon corporations;
        neoliberal capitalist crisis; social
        reproduction
capitalist logic of expansion see growth
        economics, fixation on
Capitalocene, notion of 17, 52–53, 65n4
carbon corporations 9, 125, 203, 223
    fracking 7, 13–14, 39, 124, 244–245,
        339
    and state-corporative alliances
        173–174, 183, 199, 234, 237–238
    see also capitalism: carbon/fossil fuel
carbon emissions 3, 7, 16, 34, 59, 148, 282
    industrial food systems and 14
    inequalities around see environmental
        inequality
    link with climate change 35, 151
    see also greenhouse gas emissions
carbon emissions, reduction of 17, 23–24,
        32, 42, 57, 148–149
    carbon tax proposals 81, 161, 316
    climate smart agriculture 21, 34, 125,
        194, 197, 200–201, 204
    intended nationally determined
        contributions (INDCs) 33, 35–36
    low-carbon technologies 282–283
    offset mechanisms 7, 32, 60, 63, 125, 195
    reducing emissions from deforestation
        and forest degradation (REDD) 7,
        34, 36, 60, 125, 194–195, 277
carbon trading 7, 32, 34, 39, 60, 176,
        194–195, 339
    Clean Development Mechanisms
        (CDMs) 34, 36, 39, 41, 277
China 5, 11–12, 38, 152, 156, 258, 262–263,
        317, 322, 324
    emerging economy of 71, 75, 238
    slowdown in growth 73, 75, 274, 315

Chuwa, LT 169–172, 177–178, 181, 183, 185n6
class 1, 13, 298
  as constituent of capital accumulation 214
  ruling/capitalist 6–8, 63, 150, 259, 301, 314–315, 338
  see also inequality: class; working class
class analysis
  interaction with race, gender and ecology 13, 22, 30–31, 43, 58, 180, 184, 214, 218, 320
  Marxist perspective 59, 61, 164n5&6, 212, 214
class struggles 20, 49, 144, 149–150, 154–155, 162, 234
  women's 215, 224
Climate Action Network 8
climate change 16
  'changes everything' 9, 40, 53, 63, 175, 222, 231
  denialism 6, 31–32, 57, 338
  impact on peasantry 6, 10, 42, 49, 62
  impact on V20 countries 4–5, 40–41
  inequalities around *see* environmental inequality
  as systemic crisis 1–3, 7, 9, 18, 190, 341
  see also Anthropocene discourse on climate change; global warming
climate change, impact on Africa 21, 63
  false solutions to 194–201, 204–205, 252, 268–269
  nutrition/food security 192, 195–200, 203–204, 211, 253
climate debt 5, 40–41, 177
  reparations 5, 136, 177
climate justice activism 16, 18, 21, 24, 37, 43, 219, 309–310
  feminist 22, 37, 217–219
  proposals for systemic change 32
  transnational 18, 21, 41
  see also grassroots/localised activism
climate justice politics 2, 13, 338–339, 342
  corporate capture of 16–17, 33–34, 36, 38–39, 42–43
  and labour movement 221–223, 227
  see also just transition; restorative justice ethics
Climate Vulnerable Forum 38

coal industry 7, 22–23, 25, 30, 35, 39, 60, 148, 175
  labour demands of 232–233, 235–236
  and shift to oil 231–232, 235–237, 240
  see also fossil fuel extractivism; minerals–energy complex
colonialism 52, 172
  carbon 195
  modern day/neocolonialism 134, 173–174
commodification of nature 25, 52, 59, 169, 218, 277, 296, 320, 332
  coastline/oceans 320, 332
  payments for ecosystem services (PES) 125, 314
commons 56, 65
  environmental 316
  knowledge 306
  reclaiming/rebuilding the 24, 30, 294–296, 302, 304
  separation of peasantry from the 51, 55
  see also proletarianisation
communism 15, 85, 94, 154, 220
  primitive 158
communitarianism 23, 137, 169, 171, 182
Conference of the Parties *see* UN-COP summits
Congress of South African Trade Unions (Cosatu) 83, 221–223, 265–266
Co-operative and Policy Alternative Centre (COPAC) 302–303, 306
Copenhagen 33–34, 36, 63
  Accord 37
Cornell, D 168–169, 172, 177, 180–181, 183
Crutzen, Paul 49–50
Cullinan, Cormac 117, 128

D

Dalai Lama 112, 159
Death, C 219, 278
decarbonisation 7, 316
decentralisation 144, 169, 179, 182, 215, 225, 246, 248, 304
decolonisation 19, 21, 133, 168–170, 173, 177, 184, 205
decommodification 44, 87, 92–93, 144, 296, 332
Deep Ecology 19, 26n12, 115–116
degrowth movement 149, 157, 160–161, 164n9
deindustrialisation 223, 274, 289

democracy 14–15, 233–235
    corporate 234
    securitisation of 60, 64
    see also energy–democracy nexus;
        participatory democracy
democratic eco-socialism 9–10, 13–17,
    20–22, 65, 162, 178, 220–221,
    248–249, 339, 342
    greening of Marxism 2, 10–12
    see also ecological Marxism; eco-
        feminism; ubuntu: dialogue with
        eco-socialism
displacement 4–5, 194–195, 200, 226,
    332–333
    of workers 80, 91, 95, 98, 193
droughts 3, 5, 8, 24, 37, 192–193, 211, 253,
    261, 303, 308–309, 320, 339
Duchrow, U 158–159, 163n1
DuPont 191, 199
Durban 38, 265, 320, 323–324, 332
    Durban Declaration 176
    port 315–317, 322
    South Durban Community
        Environmental Alliance (SDCEA)
        219, 221, 325, 333

E
Earth Charter 112–113
Earth Jurisprudence 19, 113–119, 127
    see also rights of nature; Wild Law
Earthlife Africa 217, 219, 309, 328–329
    anti-nuclear campaign 256, 258, 262,
        265–267
    Sustainable Energy and Livelihoods
        Project 217
    Women, Energy and Climate Change
        Forum 217
ecocentrism 21, 115, 168, 178–182
eco-feminism 14, 37, 116, 166, 144, 179,
    182
    see also social reproduction: Marxist-
        feminist approach to
eco-feminism, South African context 22,
    210, 212–214, 217, 227
    core values 22, 224–226
    Rural Women's Assembly 215–216
    WAMUA 215
    women of Xolobeni 216–217, 332
    WoMin (Women in Mining) 215,
        219
ecological catastrophism 2–4, 8, 35, 37,
    54–55, 225, 227, 340

ecological Marxism 149, 154, 157, 161, 172,
    179, 339
    see also Marxist ecology
economic growth see growth economics,
    fixation on
economic sufficiency, concept of 136–137,
    139–141
eco-socialism see democratic eco-socialism;
    eco-feminism
ecosystems 15, 41–42, 182, 339
    destruction of 37, 48, 50, 55–56, 59,
        125, 191, 225, 231
    protection/restoration of 117, 120–121,
        176–177, 185n14
    UN Millenium Ecosystem Assessment
        111
    see also commodification of nature
Ecuador 19
    Acción Ecológica 174
    constitutionalisation of nature rights
        42, 108, 121–125, 131, 135–136
    see also indigenous peoples of Abya
        Yala
employment
    informalisation of 72–73, 95, 148, 151
    vulnerable 72–73, 98n2, 222, 331
energy–democracy nexus 22–23, 231–23,
    234–236, 239, 248, 253
    implications for 'just transition' 225,
        232, 244–249, 269–270
    and labour control mechanisms
        232–233, 235–237, 243
    see also minerals–energy complex
environmental degradation 7, 56, 59, 62,
    112, 136, 138, 150, 193
environmental ethics 15, 112, 171, 174,
    176–177, 181
Environmental Impact Assessments (EIAs)
    256–257, 325, 327, 331
environmental inequality 5–6, 17, 21,
    31, 34, 36, 38–40, 50, 62–63, 190,
    224, 226
    racialised 184, 213–214, 218–219, 231
environmental justice see climate justice
    politics
environmentalism 15, 21–22, 58, 61, 181,
    210–211, 216, 218–219, 226–227,
    231
    market-based 21, 34, 195
    see also Deep Ecology
equal rights 126, 172
Eskom 23, 217, 240, 267–268, 275, 284

electricity crisis 253–254, 266, 276–278, 289–290
  Koeberg power station 255–257, 265
  Medupi project 260
  pebble bed project 255–256
Ethiopia 171, 193–194, 199
Exxaro 241, 275
ExxonMobil 237, 317, 327

F

Fanon, Frantz 168–169, 172, 184, 342
feminism *see* eco-feminism
Ferguson, James 86, 97, 101n39
financialisation *see* capitalism: financialised
financialisation of nature 125–126
Fine, Ben 240–241, 274–275, 315
Fioramonti, Lorenzo 150, 159–160, 163n2, 326–327
floods 3, 5, 37, 193–194, 211, 303, 320, 339
food sovereignty 13–14, 21, 24, 41, 64, 144, 172, 176, 204
  in context of climate change 194, 293, 295, 303
  democracy as central to 295–296
  People's Food Sovereignty Statement 205
food sovereignty movement/struggle 180, 204, 224, 275, 293–294, 302, 305, 342
  Alliance for Food Sovereignty in Africa (AFSA) 202, 205
  South African Food Sovereignty Campaign (SAFSC) 24, 205, 294, 299–310
  see also La Via Campesina
fossil fuel extractivism 30, 41, 59, 139, 141, 148, 173–174, 231, 339
  just transition from *see* just transition
  neo-extractivism 160
  struggles against/resistance to *see* post-extractivism
fossil fuels 1, 5–7, 16, 30, 41
  continued expansion/growth paradigm 9, 17, 20, 39, 148, 151
  see also coal industry; oil extractivism
Foster, John Bellamy 12–13, 25n8, 56, 59, 158
France 33, 71–72, 123, 258, 262–263 *tab*
Frase, Peter 88–90, 94–95

G

GDP paradigm
  critique of 20, 22, 38, 40, 43, 64, 78, 133–138, 141, 143, 148–150
  maintenance of 151–155, 162

gender equality/justice 32, 113, 179, 205, 213, 215
geo-engineering 47, 50, 60, 194, 206n8
geopolitics 6, 23, 56, 77, 150, 263
  of oil 235, 237, 319
Germany 90, 115, 283
  Energiewende 246–247
  greens 11
Glaser, Daryl 170–173
Glencore Xstrata 241, 275
global ecological-economic-social crisis
  counterhegemonic alternatives 20, 49, 61, 63, 149, 154, 157, 159–163, 169, 339
  role of hegemonic power elite in 40, 42–43, 148, 150–153, 161, 164n5,6&10, 234, 243, 245, 338
  social crises 151–152
  see also neoliberal capitalist crisis; solidarity economy
global South 17, 19, 31, 37, 40–42, 64, 73, 125, 145, 170, 173, 176, 178, 182
global warming 2–4, 17, 32–38, 80–81, 152, 277, 339
  in Africa 191–193
Gordhan, Pravin 264–265, 326–327
Gorz, Andre 71, 90, 95–98, 101n38, 161
Gramsci, Antonio 150, 156, 164n5, 180, 289
Graness, A 180, 183–184
grassroots/localised activism 2, 9–10, 14, 16, 25, 64
  South Africa 22, 161, 175
  see also Niger Delta activism; peasant agency/activism
Greece 44, 72, 76, 89, 93, 154
  Ancient 126
'green economy' 8, 34, 38, 58, 148, 225, 277–279
green economy, South Africa 152–218, 226, 278
  failure of 278–279, 284–285
  green jobs 153, 225, 273, 277, 279
greenhouse gas (GHG) emissions 2, 4, 31, 34–35, 57, 252, 277, 283
  measurement of 3, 14, 33
  reduction of 5, 15, 24, 35–36, 191, 272–273, 280–281, 286
  in transportation 5, 286–287
  see also carbon emissions

growth economics, fixation on 1–2, 22,
24–25, 42, 225, 293
see also GDP paradigm

H
Hansen, James 2, 33, 37
Happiness Index 20, 137
Harvey, David 56, 151, 165n13, 183, 211,
219, 225, 227, 296, 302
Hinkelammert, FJ 158–159, 163n1
Holocene 3, 47, 49, 53
human-nature dualism 18–19, 114, 169,
172, 175, 178, 180, 227
humanism 58, 163, 221, 339
African 172–173
see also under Marx/Marxist theory
hurricanes 3, 8, 318, 338–339

I
imperial ecocide, US-led 7, 14, 17, 21,
54–55, 60–61, 64–65, 168–169,
203, 338
industrial characteristics of 56–57
racialised dominance as part of 17, 49,
56, 61–63
India 38, 55, 72–73, 75, 132, 158–159,
186n18, 238, 260
Indian Ocean 318, 322
indigenous peoples of *Abya Yala*
belief systems of 19, 108–109, 131–133,
135
indigenous people's movements 18–19, 125,
173–174
indigenous systems of knowledge 19, 21,
131, 133, 139–140, 144–145,
179–180, 182
individualism 145, 172, 210, 224
industrial development *see* industrialisation
Industrial Revolution 3, 5, 7, 37, 52, 54, 339
industrialisation 5, 50, 57, 64, 75, 160, 171,
195, 198
'catch-up' 1–2, 22
rural/agricultural 233, 281, 295
see also deindustrialisation
inequality 18, 78, 84, 87, 134–135, 137–138,
148, 150–151, 153, 157, 161–162,
169, 172
agrarian 297–298
class 17, 62–63, 157
deglobalisation strategy 41–42
income 71, 74, 79, 81, 143, 241–242,
273–274

structural 137–138, 170, 172, 297
see also environmental inequality;
power relations, asymmetries of
Intergovernmental Panel on Climate
Change (IPCC) 3, 33–35, 37, 47,
51, 54, 57–58, 60–61, 191–192
International Energy Agency 37, 239
International Labour Organisation (ILO)
72–74, 99n13, 222
International Union for the Protection of
New Varieties of Plants (UPOV)
convention 201–202

J
job creation 70, 72–73, 79, 82, 89, 91, 94,
97–98, 141, 143, 223
climate jobs 9, 64, 223, 283–284
Joemat-Pettersson, Tina 262, 265
just transition 6, 8, 19, 32, 48, 149, 190, 339
deep 8, 25n6, 64–65, 170, 340–341
emerging theory of 178–180, 314,
340–342
food sovereignty and 293–294, 310
intergenerational ethics and 182
redistributive interventions 70, 135,
144
transformative 7, 9, 10, 16–18, 21–22,
32, 41, 61, 63, 70, 81, 97, 169, 222
see also red–green alliances; restorative
justice ethics; solidarity economy
just transition, South Africa 25, 216, 221,
223–225, 252, 274–275, 277, 282
deep 22–24, 249, 294, 301, 310, 331
expansion of public transport 286–288
food sovereignty and 24, 299, 301, 310
Million Climate Jobs Campaign 23–24,
222, 248, 270, 272–275, 280–281,
285, 289–290, 331–332
role of trade union movement in 222,
290
strategies against blue economy
exploitation 330–333
transformative 20, 210, 222, 226–227,
309
see also energy–democracy nexus;
renewable energy, South Africa;
solidarity economy, South African
context

K
Kenya 175, 194–195
Kernot, C 232, 240, 242

King, Martin Luther 113, 127
Klein, Naomi 9, 13–14, 40, 60, 63, 174–175, 218, 222, 231, 246–247, 249, 306,
Kolbert, Elizabeth 51, 54, 58–59, 61–62
Kovel, Joel 21, 60, 168, 170, 176, 178–180, 182
Kunkel, Benjamin 78–79, 94
Kyoto Protocol 5, 35, 57, 176
  US withdrawal from 2, 36

L
La Via Campesina 13, 24, 41, 180, 204, 294, 301
labour 12, 52
  gendered division of 62, 80, 213, 217, 226
  racialised division of 242–243
labour-democracy nexus 231–232
labour markets 60, 73, 75–76, 80, 85, 90–94
  see also employment; wage labour
labour movement
  diminishing power of 22–23, 60, 71, 74–77, 232–233, 236
labour movement, South Africa 156, 161, 221–222, 227, 239
  Marikana strike 175, 239
  role in struggle for democracy 231, 239–240, 242
  see also under minerals–energy complex
labour productivity 72–74, 76, 78, 83
land grabs 21, 195, 200, 203, 319, 338
Leopold, Aldo 112–114
Li, Minqi 11–12
Löwy, Michael 219–220, 248
Lynas, Mark 51, 58–60, 62

M
Malawi 194, 197, 199
Mali 193–194, 205
Mandela, Nelson 84, 263
Manuel, Trevor 84, 255, 319
Marx/Marxist theory 2, 10, 15, 19–20, 77, 85, 137, 145, 150, 341
  humanist-atheist vision 20, 158–159, 163
  see also African socialism; New Left; socialism
Marxist ecology 13, 138, 182
  critique of socialist productivism 2, 11–12, 14, 19, 22, 55, 17, 48, 51–55, 58–59, 61, 150, 210, 220, 222

  see also Anthropocene discourse on climate change: Marxist ecology critique of; ecological Marxism
Marxist-Leninist perspective 2, 10, 20, 149, 156, 170–173
Mbeki, Thabo 153, 242, 259–260
McMichael, P 233, 295
methane gas 3, 14, 49–50
Metz, T 169, 173, 177, 181–183
Mexico 37, 74, 132
  Opportunidades 86
Miliband, Ralph 150, 164n6
Mill, John Stuart 81–82
Mineral and Petroleum Resources Development Act (MPRDA) 328, 330, 333
minerals–energy complex (MEC) 22, 25, 148, 153, 220, 244–245, 248
  coal-based 215, 217–218, 221–223, 240–241, 252, 275, 315
  decline of 253, 275–276, 289–290
  Department of Minerals and Energy (DME) 245, 257–259, 263–264
  organised labour and 23, 240–243
  see also energy–democracy nexus; nuclear energy procurement, South Africa; Operation Phakisa
Mitchell, T 231–233, 235–237
modernity 157, 169, 171, 177, 183–184, 269
  capitalist 19, 131, 155, 160, 163n1
Molewa, Edna 325, 327
Monsanto 191, 197, 199
Moore, Jason 52, 65n4, 227
Motlanthe, Kgalema 242, 259

N
Næss, Arne 115–116
Naicker, I 172, 181
National Aeronautics and Space Administration (NASA) 2, 33, 110
National Development Plan (NDP) 20, 148, 153, 244–245, 266–267, 317, 322, 325
  see also Operation Phakisa
National Union of Metalworkers of South Africa (Numsa) 161, 222–223, 242, 247, 266, 309
National Union of Mineworkers (NUM) 221–222, 242, 265
Neale, J 272–273
Negritude 21, 170, 172, 177–179, 185n6
  see also Senghor, Leopold

Nene, Nhlanhla 258, 263–264
Neocosmos, M 154–155, 159
neoliberal capitalist crisis 1–2, 5, 10–11, 64,
	75, 155, 274, 324
	in 'blue economy' 315, 320–324
	foreign direct investment (FDI)
		declines 322, 326, 328–330
	link to climate crisis 13, 16, 30, 34, 36,
		38–40, 43, 48, 54, 57, 60–63, 134,
		138, 151, 219, 221, 293
	see also GDP paradigm; global
		ecological-economic-social crisis;
		imperial ecocide, US-led
neoliberalism 6, 20, 30, 36, 39–41, 63, 85
New Alliance for Food Security and
		Nutrition (NAFN) 190, 199–200
New Alliance for a Green Revolution in
		Africa 190
New Left 149, 155–156, 342
Niger Delta activism 9, 174–176, 183
	Environmental Rights Action
		movement 174
	Eti uwem worldview 176
Nigeria 194, 197–199, 324
	Niger Delta 193
	see also Niger Delta activism
non-renewable resources
	depletion of 62, 148, 151, 177, 282
	see also fossil fuels
nuclear energy 23, 124, 152, 247
nuclear energy procurement, South Africa
		23, 148, 217, 226, 244–245,
		254–255, 258–261
	anti-nuclear movement 265–268
	cost of 253, 256–257, 260, 266–268
	Energy White Paper on 255, 257
	illegality of process 267–268
	National Energy Regulator of South
		Africa (Nersa) 261, 268
	National Radioactive Waste Disposal
		Institute (NRWDI) 261
	opposition of private sector to 266
	opposition of Treasury to 264–265
	Rosatom (Russia) agreement 262–263,
		268
	South African Nuclear Energy
		Corporation (Necsa) 255, 261, 267
Nyerere, Julius 169, 181
	ujamaa programme 170–172,
		185n6&8

O
Obama, Barack
	Clean Power Plan 6, 25n5
Occupy movements 162, 234, 239
oil extractivism 12, 14, 22, 25, 30, 35, 60, 92,
		151, 177
	declining 238–239
	deep-water drilling 7, 13, 59, 339
	ITT oil field, Ecuador 124
	Marshall Plan 237
	Middle East 72, 76, 235–236, 238
	Niger Delta 174–176, 193
	rights 126
	tar sands 7, 13, 59
	US 83, 237–238
	Venezuelan 160
	see also coal industry: and shift to oil;
		Operation Phakisa
Operation Phakisa 24–25, 314, 317
	environmental impact of 315–316,
		318–321, 324–325, 327–328
	failures of 315–316, 325, 327, 329–330
	McKinsey management of 329–330

P
Pacha Mama 19, 109, 121, 135–136, 139
	see also Rights of Mother Earth
		movement
Paris Agreement 3–7, 33, 38, 63, 273, 338
	US withdrawal from 31
participatory democracy 65, 137, 141, 144,
		149–150, 152, 156, 159, 171,
		224–225, 234
patriarchy/patriarchal oppression 2, 43,
		133, 144, 156–159, 181, 213–214,
		227, 339
peasant agency/activism 13–14, 18, 172
	women 175–176
	see also grassroots/localised activism;
		Niger Delta activism
Peck, Jamie 85–86
People's Climate March 33
people's power 14–15, 19, 159, 163
Peru 33, 123
	Lima 35
Philippines 8, 99n9, 123
Picketty, Thomas 74, 78
Polanyi, Karl 151, 234–235
pollution 1, 59, 112, 150–151, 191, 195, 218, 272
	air 38–39, 215–216

by global North 5, 21, 31, 36
of oceans/water 13, 120, 212, 216, 244, 315, 318–319, 332
see also carbon emissions; imperial ecocide, US-led
Port Elizabeth 256, 322–323
Coega port 322, 329
Portugal 44, 72
post-extractivism 13, 20–21, 169, 173–174, 176–178, 215, 219, 227
see also anti-fossil fuel networks
power relations 58, 163, 214
asymmetries/imbalances of 6, 8, 31, 36–37, 39–40, 48, 63, 163, 183, 298
gender 179, 212, 223–224
proletarianisation 75, 154, 171, 297

R
racism 2, 22, 43, 133, 183, 214, 219, 339
environmental *see* environmental inequality: racialised
neo-Malthusian 48–49, 61–62, 116
rain forests, destruction of 3, 151
red–green alliances 8, 10, 24–25n6, 173, 341
redistribution
of wealth/income 70, 85, 87
of work 141–142
renewable energy 23–24, 41, 284
democratising role of 232
socially owned 9, 64–65, 152, 160, 225, 247
see also energy–democracy nexus
renewable energy, South Africa 148, 152, 161, 216–217, 226, 244, 254, 278, 283, 285
Integrated Resource Plans (IRPs) 245, 257–258, 267
private–public partnerships 245–246
Renewable Energy Independent Power Producers Procurement Programme (REI4P) 277, 284
socially owned 23, 161, 223–225, 241, 247–249, 269–270
solar/wind electricity 216–217, 244, 246–247, 279–286
restorative justice ethics 169, 174, 176–177, 181–183
Richards Bay 240, 249n2, 315–316, 322
Right2Know Campaign 307, 309

Rights of Mother Earth movement 18–19, 42, 107–108, 123, 131–133
ethical stream 111–113
implementation challenges 123–125
indigenous stream 108–109, 113
juridical stream 113–115
proposals/aims 114–115, 122, 127–128
scientific stream 109–111, 113
Universal Declaration on 122
rights of nature 9, 13, 18–19, 107–109, 114, 116–118, 120–121, 127, 135
contradiction between property rights and 119, 123, 126–127, 172, 183
Ethics Tribunal 123
Global Alliance for 123
see also animal rights; Earth Jurisprudence
Rudin, Jeff 153, 278–279
Russell, Bertrand 88, 95
Russia 238, 245, 258, 262–263, 268, 324
Rustomjee, Zavareh 240–241, 274, 315

S
Saro-Wiwa, Ken 174, 176
Sasol Mining 241, 275, 282
Saul, John 170–173
sea levels, rising 3–5, 38, 194
Second World War *see* World War Two
Senegal 170, 177–178, 199, 205
Senghor, Leopold 21, 169–172, 177–182
Shell petrochemical company 175, 317, 327
Royal Dutch 237, 260, 324
Shiva, Vandana 13–14, 127
Shutte, A 169, 171, 179, 181
small-scale/smallholder farmers 24, 41, 62, 200, 202, 205, 302
Bt/GM cotton production 196–197
impact of climate change on 21, 34, 190
organic agriculture 273, 281
use of local technology 200–201, 204
see also La Via Campesina
social reproduction 18, 62, 179, 211–212
Marxist-feminist approach to 210–212, 214, 217, 224
women's role in 212, 215–216, 224
socialism 10–12, 14–16, 22, 158, 162, 210–211
Nehruvian 15
notion of radical egalitarianism 169

socialism (*cont.*)
  reclaiming 219–221, 226–227
  statist 22, 152, 155–156, 159, 164n11,
    171, 220
socialist modernisation 12, 22, 154, 170, 178
solidarity economy 19, 24, 136–137–139,
  142, 144–146n4, 171, 293, 295–296
  see also buen vivir: alternative economy
    to support
solidarity economy, South African context 24,
  294, 297, 300, 302–303, 306, 310
  Solidarity Economy Movement (SEM)
    299–300, 302, 311n3
South Africa 89
  corruption/state patrimony in 23, 161,
    253–254, 259, 263–264, 266, 276,
    317, 325, 329
  economic crisis/indebtedness 253, 258,
    264–266, 273–275, 315, 325–327
  food insecurity/crisis 253, 297–298,
    307–309
  Free State province 264, 302, 304
  Gauteng province 218, 242, 281, 317
  Growth, Employment and
    Redistribution (GEAR) strategy
    273, 276
  Infrastructure Development Act 327, 331
  KwaZulu-Natal province 175, 242
  New Growth Path 153, 220, 244–245,
    273
  'rebellion of the poor' in 298–299
  small-scale farming in 196–197
  social grants system in 86–87, 226, 274
  state-owned enterprises 253, 255, 259,
    261
  trade union movement in *see* labour
    movement, South Africa
  UBIG campaign in 83–84
  unemployment crisis in 72, 76, 84, 93,
    153, 222, 253, 272–274
  see also National Development Plan
South African Airways (SAA) 263–264
South African Communist Party (SACP)
  153, 210, 220, 259
South African Transport and Allied
  Workers Union 223, 242
Southern African Faith Communities'
  Environmental Institute 258,
  266–267
Soviet Union/Bloc 11–12, 152, 155, 164n11,
  210, 220
  Russian revolution 15

Spain 44, 72, 76, 93, 162
Stockholm Conference of the Human
  Environment 36, 39
Switzerland 81, 99n12
Sudan 193, 196–197
sumak kawsay see buen vivir
Swilling, Mark 282, 331
Syngenta 191, 199

T
Tanzania 170–171, 194, 199
  Arusha Declaration 185n6
Terkel, Studs 85, 87, 91
Thatcher, Margaret 84–85
Trans-Atlantic Trade and Investment
  Partnership (TTIP) 39
Trans-Pacific Partnership 39
Trapp, K 73–74, 99n3
Trump, Donald 6–7, 31–32, 43–44, 57,
  338
Turner, Rick 20, 149, 156–157, 162, 165n14

U
ubuntu 9, 132, 161
  dialogue with eco-socialism 20–21,
    157, 168, 170, 173–175, 181–183,
    185n14, 333
  ethics of 169–172, 174–180, 182–183
  nation-building experiments 169–170
  respect for diversity 171
  revolutionary 183
  see also restorative justice ethics
UN conference on the Environment and
  Development (UNCED) 35–36
UN Convention on the Law of the Sea 319
UN-COP summits 3, 8, 13, 16, 31, 33–34–
    38, 48, 63
  ineffectiveness/failed leadership of 1, 7,
    21, 33–37, 63–64, 273, 289
  see also Paris Agreement
UN Environment Programme (UNEP)
  34–36, 38, 249
UN Framework Convention on Climate
  Change (UNFCCC) 3, 7, 31, 39,
    41, 273, 289
UN Global Compact 38
unemployment 18, 23, 59, 142, 274
  global increase in 71–72, 76
  impact of labour-replacing
    technologies on 76
  psychological impact of 90, 101n32
  youth 72, 93

see also South Africa: unemployment
        crisis in
universal basic income grant (UBIG) 82,
        84–85, 96
    advantages of 70, 79, 81–83, 86–88,
        91–95, 97–98
    arguments against 70, 82, 84–85, 88,
        93–94, 97
    in context of 'just transition' 18, 70, 80,
        87, 92, 97–98, 101n33
    funding of 80–81
Uruguay 203, 247
US 155, 274
    anti-capitalist activism in 162
    basic income grant 82–83
    food aid 195–196
    military repression 175
    resistance to Trump's policies 44
    rights of nature initiatives in 118–120,
        123
    wage labour/workers' movements in
        74–76, 232–233
    see also imperial ecocide, US-led

V
Van Marle, K 168–169, 172, 177, 180, 183
Venezuela 160, 173, 205, 235, 239
vivir bien see buen vivir
Vulnerable 20 (V20) *see under* climate
        change

W
wage labour 18, 55–56, 212
    declining share of income 73–74,
        77–78, 99n3&4, 151
    perceived importance of 90, 92, 94, 98
Wild Law 19, 115–117
    see also Earth Jurisprudence

Williams, Raymond 14–15
work
    meanings of 88–89, 91, 101n38
    post-work vision 94–95, 98
    socially determined 96–97
workers' organisations/movements 18, 71,
        74–75, 77, 92
World Bank 34, 72, 86, 153, 203, 225, 253,
        276, 326–327
World Food Programme (WFP) 192, 196
World Meteorological Organisation
        (WMO) 3, 35
World People's Conference on Climate
        Change and the Rights of Mother
        Earth 42
World Trade Organisation (WTO) 36, 39
World War Two 74, 76, 151, 155
working class 9, 49, 61, 150, 243, 330
    as 'gravedigger' of capitalism 152, 154
    impact of climate change on 9, 63,
        211–212, 226–227, 340
    women 212–216, 226–227, 330

Y
'Yes to life, no to mining' campaign
        176–177, 185n14

Z
Zambia 72, 195–196
Zimmerman, Michael 115–116
Zuma, Jacob 153, 213, 242, 254, 265, 268
    blue economy initiative 314, 317–318,
        321, 323, 325, 328, 330–331
    corruption/patrimonial politics of
        259–260, 262–265, 317–318
    relationship with Guptas 260–261,
        317–318, 329–330

Printed and bound by CPI Group (UK) Ltd, Croydon, CR0 4YY

16/04/2025

14658440-0001